Venice

Damien Simonis

W9-AFG-191

LONELY PLANET PUBLICATIONS
Melbourne • Oakland • London • Paris

MAP 1 – VENICE AREA

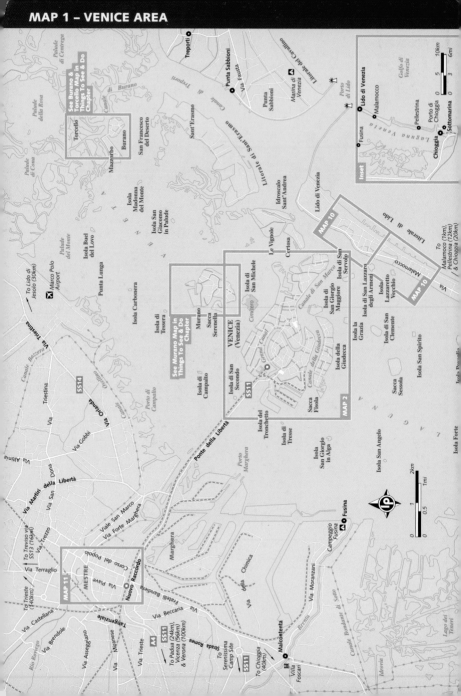

MAP 2 – VENICE

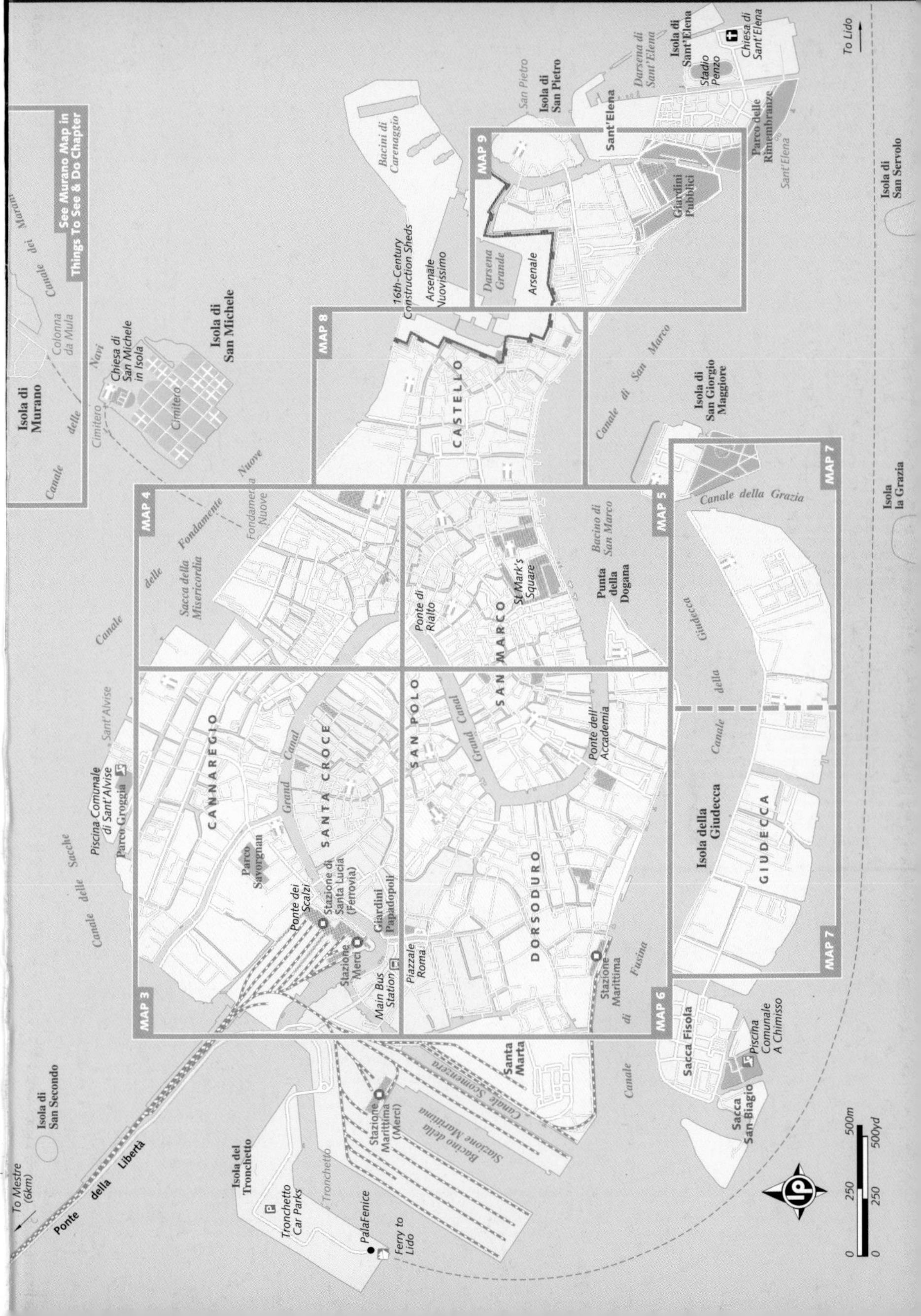

See Murano Map in Things To See & Do Chapter
Isola di Murano
Isola di San Michele
Chiesa di San Michele in Isola
Cimitero
Canale delle Navi
Fondamenta Nuove
Isola di San Pietro
Isola di Sant'Elena
Chiesa di Sant'Elena
Stadio Penzo
Sant'Elena
Parco delle Rimembranze
Giardini Pubblici
Bacini di Carenaggio
16th-Century Construction Sheds
Arsenale Nuovissimo
Darsena Grande
Arsenale
CASTELLO
Canale di San Marco
Isola di San Giorgio Maggiore
Isola di San Servolo
Isola la Grazia
Canale della Grazia
Bacino di San Marco
Punta della Dogana
St Mark's Square
SAN MARCO
Ponte di Rialto
Sacca della Misericordia
CANNAREGIO
SANTA CROCE
SAN POLO
Grand Canal
Ponte dell'Accademia
Giudecca
Canale della Giudecca
Isola della Giudecca
GIUDECCA
DORSODURO
Parco Savorgnan
Piscina Comunale di Sant'Alvise
Parco Groggia
Canale delle Sacche
Ponte dei Scalzi
Stazione di Santa Lucia (Ferrovia)
Giardini Papadopoli
Stazione Merci
Main Bus Station
Piazzale Roma
Stazione Marittima
Canale di Fusina
Santa Marta
Sacca Fisola
Piscina Comunale A Chimisso
Sacca San Biagio
Canale Scomenzera
Bacino della Stazione Marittima
Stazione Marittima (Merci)
Isola del Tronchetto
Tronchetto Car Parks
PalaFenice
Ferry to Lido
Isola di San Secondo
Ponte della Libertà
To Mestre (6km)
To Lido
MAP 3
MAP 4
MAP 5
MAP 6
MAP 7
MAP 8
MAP 9
0 250 500m
0 250 500yd

Venice
2nd edition – March 2002
First published – April 2000

Published by
Lonely Planet Publications Pty Ltd ABN 36 005 607 983
90 Maribyrnong St, Footscray, Victoria 3011, Australia

Lonely Planet Offices
Australia Locked Bag 1, Footscray, Victoria 3011
USA 150 Linden St, Oakland, CA 94607
UK 10a Spring Place, London NW5 3BH
France 1 rue du Dahomey, 75011 Paris

Photographs
All of the images in this guide are available for licensing from
Lonely Planet Images.
email: lpi@lonelyplanet.com.au
Web site: www.lonelyplanetimages.com

Front cover photograph
Gondolas moored along the Bacino di San Marco (Jon Davison)

ISBN 1 86450 321 1

text & maps © Lonely Planet Publications Pty Ltd 2002
photos © photographers as indicated 2002

Printed by The Bookmaker International Ltd
Printed in China

Although the authors
and Lonely Planet try
to make the informa-
tion as accurate as
possible, we accept
no responsibility for
any loss, injury or
inconvenience sus-
tained by anyone
using this book.

Contents – Text

Contents – Maps

The Author

Damien Simonis

With a degree in languages and several years' reporting and sub-editing on Australian newspapers (including the *Australian* and the *Age*), Sydney-born Damien left the country in 1989. He has since lived, worked and travelled extensively throughout Europe, the Middle East and North Africa. Since 1992, Lonely Planet has kept him busy with *Jordan & Syria*, *Egypt & the Sudan*, *Morocco*, *North Africa*, *Italy*, *Tuscany*, *Florence*, *Spain*, *The Canary Islands*, *Barcelona*, *Madrid* and *Catalunya*. He has also written and snapped for other publications in Australia, the UK and North America. When not on the road, Damien resides in splendid Stoke Newington, deep in the heart of north London.

FROM THE AUTHOR

Dr Alberto Stassi, longtime food and wine taster and now permanent resident of Padua, gave me a temporary home in the Veneto while I skittled around the countryside. Should there be a next time, I hope we have more *free* time to tool about and shoot the breeze. In the meantime, I can only heap loads of humble thanks on the good Doc for putting up with yours truly for so long!

In Venice itself, several people welcomed me back into their lagoon city. They include: Irina Fraguia (who helped out on several fronts), Michela Scibilia, Roberta Guarnieri, Bernhard Klein, Federica Centulani, Caterina De Cesero, Susanne Sagner and Bridget Smyth.

Thanks also to Signora Rodati, who provided me with a pleasant flat in the Cannaregio district during my research time.

The staff of the Venice tourist offices, particularly in the Venice Pavilion near St Mark's Square, were always obliging when dealing with oddball queries. Alessandra Smith of the Italian Tourist Board (ENIT) in London also helped me out with some statistical queries.

As always, the crew in Milan had the welcome mat out when the road became too much and thoughts turned to a one-time home. Daniela Antongiovanni, Sergio Bosio, Anna Cerutti, Paola Brussa, Lucia Spadaro, Maurizio Gallotti and Sara Bigatti helped to make my time in Italy as pleasurable as it was profitable (indeed more so!).

LP authors in the same country help each other by trading and pooling information. I owe a particular debt of thanks on this score to Sally Webb, my colleague on LP's *Italy* book. Thanks also to Rachel Suddart (UK), Leonie Mugavin (Aus) and Pelin Thornhill (USA) for help with travel information.

Last but not least. Following the school of thought that it is better late than never, I owe many thanks (and a thousand apologies) to Carolyn Bain, backdated to the 1st edition of this book. May the ink in your travelling pen never run dry!

This Book

This is the 2nd edition of Lonely Planet's *Venice* city guide. It was written and updated by Damien Simonis, who also wrote the 1st edition.

From the Publisher

This edition of *Venice* was edited in Lonely Planet's London office. Fran Parnell coordinated the editing and proofing, with assistance from Charlotte Beech, Arabella Shepherd and Sam Trafford. David Wenk coordinated the mapping, design and layout and was assisted by Liam Molloy, Fiona Christie and James Timmins. James Ellis drew the climate chart, Annika Roojun designed the cover and Lachlan Ross drew the back-cover map. Lonely Planet Images provided the photographs, and chapter ends and decorative borders were designed and drawn by Liam. Amanda Canning, Michala Green and Paul Piaia gave much-appreciated help and advice. Thanks to Quentin Frayne for his expertly produced Language chapter, and to Tom Hall, Emma Sangster and Rachel Suddart for their useful comments on the Sport, Health and Getting There & Away sections respectively. Thanks also to Sally Schafer and Damien Simonis for all their help. Grateful acknowledgement is made to ACTV for granting us permission to reproduce the ACTV Network Map, copyright 2001.

Thanks

Many thanks to the travellers who used the last edition and contacted us with helpful hints, advice and interesting anecdotes:

Salim Akbar, Mike Appleyard, Lorraine Bick, Jeanne Bollendorf, Robin Bush, Frauke Chambers, Julie Collins, Phil Davies, Carmen Luisa Forsberg, Roelof Hans, Ciaragh Hubert, Per Iko, Pablo Iveli, Francesca Jaggs, J Kamea, Timo Knaebe, Irene Kontje, Eleni Koutrigaros, Dr P A Lekhi, Bethan Lewis, Li-Chin Lin, Quentin Martin, Katy McClure, James Parkhurst, Sacha Pearson, Laurence Pinturault, Charity Pitton, Louisa Prest, Gavin Russell, Emily Sachs, Ed Sawyer, Adam Schreck, Paolo Simeone, Krystina Stermole, Deborah Sterpin, Michael Sykes, Ian M Taylor, Helen Wilms, Fiona Wilson

Foreword

ABOUT LONELY PLANET GUIDEBOOKS

The story begins with a classic travel adventure: Tony and Maureen Wheeler's 1972 journey across Europe and Asia to Australia. There was no useful information about the overland trail then, so Tony and Maureen published the first Lonely Planet guidebook to meet a growing need.

From a kitchen table, Lonely Planet has grown to become the largest independent travel publisher in the world, with offices in Melbourne (Australia), Oakland (USA), London (UK) and Paris (France).

Today Lonely Planet guidebooks cover the globe. There is an ever-growing list of books and information in a variety of media. Some things haven't changed. The main aim is still to make it possible for adventurous travellers to get out there – to explore and better understand the world.

At Lonely Planet we believe travellers can make a positive contribution to the countries they visit – if they respect their host communities and spend their money wisely. Since 1986 a percentage of the income from each book has been donated to aid projects and human rights campaigns, and, more recently, to wildlife conservation.

Although inclusion in a guidebook usually implies a recommendation, we cannot list every good place. Exclusion does not necessarily imply criticism. In fact there are a number of reasons why we might exclude a place – sometimes it is simply inappropriate to encourage an influx of travellers.

UPDATES & READER FEEDBACK

Things change – prices go up, schedules change, good places go bad and bad places go bankrupt. Nothing stays the same. So, if you find things better or worse, recently opened or long-since closed, please tell us and help make the next edition even more accurate and useful.

Lonely Planet thoroughly updates each guidebook as often as possible – usually every two years, although for some destinations the gap can be longer. Between editions, up-to-date information is available in our free, quarterly *Planet Talk* newsletter and monthly email bulletin *Comet*. The *Upgrades* section of our website (w www.lonelyplanet.com) is also regularly updated by Lonely Planet authors, and the site's *Scoop* section covers news and current affairs relevant to travellers. Lastly, the *Thorn Tree* bulletin board and *Postcards* section carry unverified, but fascinating, reports from travellers.

Tell us about it! We genuinely value your feedback. A well-travelled team at Lonely Planet reads and acknowledges every email and letter we receive and ensures that every morsel of information finds its way to the relevant authors, editors and cartographers.

Everyone who writes to us will find their name listed in the next edition of the appropriate guidebook, and will receive the latest issue of *Comet* or *Planet Talk*. The very best contributions will be rewarded with a free guidebook.

We may edit, reproduce and incorporate your comments in Lonely Planet products such as guidebooks, websites and digital products, so let us know if you don't want your comments reproduced or your name acknowledged.

How to contact Lonely Planet:
Online: e talk2us@lonelyplanet.com.au, w www.lonelyplanet.com
Australia: Locked Bag 1, Footscray, Victoria 3011
UK: 10a Spring Place, London NW5 3BH
USA: 150 Linden St, Oakland, CA 94607

Introduction

For 1000 years the Repubblica Serenissima (Most Serene Republic) – or La Serenissima – as Venice is known to its own, led a proud and independent existence. Woven together like a fine piece of Burano lace from a myriad of malaria-infested islets, the city came to be one of the canniest and longest-lived mercantile sea powers in history. Until Napoleon's arrival in 1797, the Venetian Republic had probably come closer than any other European polity to the modern concept of democracy. Its doges were elected (admittedly not by universal suffrage), religious and racial tolerance (at least more than elsewhere) were considered common sense and few of its dominions ever felt the need to rebel, even when the city clearly did not have the means to resist.

Venice was and remains a sore point with the rest of Italy (and beyond), a source of envy and irritation. Throughout its history, rivals as varied as the popes, Milan, Genoa, Padua, Imperial Spain and the Turks sought to break the haughty masters of the Adriatic. Often they came close. Nowadays, other Italians consider the city to be as stuck-up as ever.

Whether anyone likes it or not, Venice is unique, and not only for its watery home. Here East met West, witnessed time and again in the city's art and architecture. The city's builders seem to have delighted in variety as they draped it in an ever-thickening patchwork mantle of monumental splendour. From the great mosaics of St Mark's Basilica (Basilica di San Marco) and Torcello to the sober Gothic majesty of the Frari, from the simplicity of Romanesque to the discipline of Palladio, from the sensuality of Veneto-Byzantine to the extremes of Baroque, the concentration of architectural gems is astonishing.

The same is true of its art. From the time Venetian painting took off with the Bellini family in the 15th century, the march past of greats from the Venetian school seems infinite. Some of their works are scattered in galleries far from home, but the number of masterpieces by Tiepolo, Tintoretto, Veronese, Titian and others still to be seen in the city is the equivalent of death by chocolate for art lovers.

There is more to Venice than history, art and architecture. Exploring the lagoon's islands, each vastly different from the main spectacle, is essential to a broader understanding of the whole.

Look, too, behind the facade. Were he still alive today, Thomas Mann, author of the best-known novel about the city, *Death in Venice* (1912), might well pen Death *of* Venice. The proud city of the winged lion is slowly expiring.

International organisations fight to preserve its monuments and engineers debate how to stem Adriatic floods. Press coverage of the battle to clean the lagoon of toxic waste excreted by the mainland petrochemical industry alternates with alarmed reports on building subsidence and rotting foundations. Everyone, from the mayor of Venice to ministers in Rome, from art historians in Britain to architecture buffs in the USA, expounds unendingly about the need to do *something*.

Perhaps they have missed the point. The lifeblood of a city is not its palaces and churches. It is its people. And the people of Venice are voting with their feet. Since the 1950s, the population has more than halved. Housing is too expensive, transport too complicated, jobs too scarce. Talk to Venetians and you get the uncanny feeling you are on a sinking ship. One day it may truly be just a theme park open daily from eight till late.

For the moment you can still feel the pulse, and Venice has returned from the brink of extinction before – who knows what rabbit it may pull out of the hat? This city defies its admirers and detractors alike. It is, above all, elusive. The tides rise and fall every six hours, pushing the water first this way then that along the canals. More than a 'sight', Venice seems to be time and motion itself.

Facts about Venice

HISTORY

To transport yourself back to the origins of La Serenissima – damp early days of refugees who chose the dubious swampy safety of the Venetian lagoon over the hazards of the lawless Italian mainland – get out of Venice (Venezia). The grand *palazzi* (palaces), the busy canals, the splendid squares – none of this existed in the beginning. Strike out for the distant scrub-covered flats of Torcello, in the north of the lagoon, where the first mainlanders sought haven as the edifice of empire and the rule of law on the mainland crumbled before the barbarian invasions at the beginning of the Dark Ages. That's how it began.

Origins

For some, history begins only with the Roman Empire, but of course Caesar and co were preceded by several thousand years of comings and goings. In the Veneto, the region of which Venice is today the capital, all sorts of theories abound as to the origins of its inhabitants prior to Roman conquest.

Increasingly, historians seem convinced that the **Veneti** were of Celtic origin. Educated guesstimations have eastern tribes moving west into north-eastern Turkey from the Caspian and Aral Seas around 1500 BC. From there, some tribes are then said to have moved on, settling on the mainland of what is today the Veneto, while others went on to Brittany, in France. The next stage supposedly came after the fall of Troy in 1183 BC. Another wave of migrants left Turkey and joined their confreres in the Veneto. It was the Veneti who founded towns such as Padua (Padova), Vicenza, Treviso and Belluno.

As Rome's grip on the north tightened in the wake of the **Punic Wars**, Padua took on the role of capital of the Veneti in their dealings with the emerging superpower. By the time Caesar was off invading Gaul, in 50 BC, the Veneto territory had been incorporated (as the province of Venetia) into what was soon to consider itself the **Roman Empire**. And thus it remained for more than four centuries.

Twilight of the Gods

When Emperor **Theodosius** died in AD 395, the lumbering wreck of the Roman Empire was already on the skids. From now on, it was effectively divided in two. Rome (Roma) remained the capital of the western half, while Constantinople (present-day Istanbul) assumed a parallel role in the east.

Already the 4th century had been marked by increasing disorder, plagues, poverty and growing pressure from 'barbarian' tribes beyond the frontiers of the Empire. The 5th century opened in a particularly ominous fashion for the Italian peninsula with the **Visigothic invasion** led by Alaric in 402. He entered Italy through Venetia, sacking the bishopric of Aquileia and pillaging at leisure along the way. The first waves of refugees from the coastal towns and even farther inland opted to seek haven on the islands of the Venetian lagoon. When Alaric was tossed out of Italy, they mostly returned to rebuild their homes.

After Alaric more Visigoths, Goths, Suevi, Germans, and, perhaps the most fearsome of all, Attila's Huns descended on various parts of the Empire. Attila's incursion into Venetia in 452 in particular had the refugees swarming back to the islands. By now the writing was on the wall. The good old days of the Pax Romana were over and no-one could guarantee safety on the mainland. Increasingly, the refugees opted to stay on the islands. The nascent island communities elected tribunes and in 466 met in Grado, on a lagoon south of Aquileia. There they formed a loose federation and established a degree of self-rule. Little evidence supports the traditional 'foundation' date of 25 March 421.

In the meantime, the Western Roman Empire crumbled. Britain, Spain, Gaul and North Africa, the latter long the granary of Imperial Rome, had all fallen or were about to fall into barbarian hands by 476, when the last, ineffectual emperor, Romulus, capitulated to the German Odoacer. Odoacer in turn was replaced by the Ostrogoth **Theodoric**, who proclaimed himself king in 493 and installed

8

himself in Ravenna – previously the preferred bolt hole of fearful Roman emperors.

Early Days, the Eastern Empire & the Lombards

Theodoric seems to have kept on good terms with the small island population of the lagoons north of Ravenna. Their maritime skills came in handy for transporting supplies to Ravenna and it appears the islanders were already becoming enterprising local traders.

Theodoric no doubt had more pressing concerns anyway. In 535, the eastern emperor Justinian, as leader of the successor to the Roman Empire, decided it was time to turn the tide and recovering Italy became his top priority. Venetia (very roughly equivalent to the modern Veneto region), the islands and Ravenna were all thus bound loosely into the Eastern, or Byzantine, Empire by 540.

Meanwhile, **Constantinople** pursued the conquest of Italy. All was proceeding much as had been hoped until HQ decided to relieve the key commander in the field, Narses, of his duties. The ensuing squabble opened the way for the last great barbarian invasion. This time it was the Lombards, invited by Narses, and when they entered northern Italy in 568 they meant to stay. As they swept across the Po plains, refugees made for the islands in unprecedented numbers. Aquileia was again sacked.

The new migrants settled primarily on Torcello, which would for some time remain the commercial centre of the islands, as well as Malamocco (the southern end of what today is known as the Lido), Chioggia and Rivoalto. The latter, subsequently known as Rialto (high bank), was no more than the highest of a small huddle of islets in the middle of the Venetian lagoon. In 639 the last mainland town in Venetia, Oderzo, fell to the Lombards.

A Doge Is Born

Anti-Byzantine uprisings began to shake the Empire's Italian possessions in the early 700s and the Venetian lagoon communities were not immune to the spirit of rebellion. They named a certain **Orso Ipato** as their dux, or leader, in 726. Dux in Venetian dialect comes

out as *doge* – and in this figure (another 117 followed) would reside the office of head of the Venetian state for the ensuing millennium. Various tales and legends surround the story of the creation of the first doge. It is equally possible that the dux was simply a military nomination by Constantinople. Some hold that Orso was preceded by two other doges, beginning with Pauluccio Anafesto in 697.

At any rate, the lagoon communities of Venetia continued to belong to the Byzantine sphere of influence, even after the Lombards took Ravenna in 751. No sooner had they achieved this than the Franks, on the invitation of the pope, descended into northern Italy and quickly replaced them as the area's overlords. The fact that none of these interlopers reached the islands led the Venetian islanders to claim, however spuriously, direct descent of their people and institutions from those of the Roman Empire.

The islands remained unmolested, but internal intrigues kept them busy. Doge Orso and many of his successors found it hard to resist the temptation of turning an elected office into a hereditary one. It became common for a doge to associate his sons with himself in the exercise of power. One of those sons was then often elected as doge. Theoretically, the doge was kept in check by two counsellors and the Arengo, a general assembly of the people. In practice, most of the doges in the first centuries of what came to be known as the **Repubblica Serenissima** (Most Serene Republic) behaved as autocrats. Some paid for such arrogance with deposition and occasionally their lives, for political murder (Orso himself was assassinated) and coups were a common trait of early Venetian politics.

In 800 the Frankish king **Charlemagne** elevated himself to Holy Roman Emperor. By this time the Venetian communities were deeply divided into at least three factions: pro-Byzantine, republican and now pro-Frankish. When the latter called upon Pepin (Charlemagne's son) to occupy Venetia and the lagoons, the remaining islanders united to stop the assault. The outcome was a peace treaty signed by Charlemagne and the Eastern Empire in 810. In return for Constantinople's recognition of him as Holy Roman

Emperor, Charlemagne abandoned claims to the **Duchy of Venetia** (as the Venetian Republic was also known), which remained anchored in the Byzantine sphere of influence. The papacy had come up with the idea of the Holy Roman Empire as the symbolic successor to the Roman Empire, only now with its spiritual base in Rome but its politico-military weight in Germany. Recognition of such an empire must have been hard to swallow for Constantinople, to all intents and purposes the true rump successors to ancient Rome.

The Duchy of Venetia was the only part of Italy to be officially allotted to the East (although parts of southern Italy remained in Byzantine hands for several centuries to come) and the decision effectively sealed off the emerging republic from the events that would take mainland Italy down a very different road.

Emergence of the Republic

The hero of the battle against Pepin was **Agnello Partecipazio**, from the tranquil island of Rivoalto. He was elected as doge in 809 and the cluster of islets around Rivoalto became the focus of community development. They were virtually impregnable to all who did not know how to navigate the deep-water channels that crisscross the lagoon, and were an obvious improvement on the previous administrative capital, Malamocco (on the Lido), which Pepin had come too close to destroying.

It was in this, the 9th century, that the Venetian lagoon settlements began to come into their own. Their commercial and naval fleets were already the most powerful in the Adriatic, and Venetian ships were trading as far away as Egypt.

At home, Partecipazio had a fortress built on what would later be the site of the Palazzo Ducale. To the east, a church to San Zaccaria was going up at Byzantine expense. As the islands of Rivoalto were too small, too few and often too waterlogged for sustained settlement, land was drained and canals cleared. Most impressive of all, the land mass was extended by driving great clusters of wooden piles into the muddy depths as foundations – a system still in use in the 20th century.

Body Snatchers

As Byzantine power gradually waned, the nascent republic assumed greater autonomy, all the while paying homage to Constantinople, at least in name.

What the republic needed was a symbol to distinguish it from its official patrons. Legend had it (or was now cooked up) that the evangelist **St Mark** (San Marco) had once visited the lagoon islands and been told by an angel that his body would rest there. A band of Venetian merchants apparently decided to make true the prophecy and in 828 spirited the saint's corpse out of Alexandria, Egypt. To house the holy relics, the doge ordered the construction of a new basilica, which would rise next to the Palazzo Ducale. Thus was the lagoon community's Byzantine-imposed patron saint, St Theodore (San Teodoro), unceremoniously replaced by St Mark.

By the end of the century, local administration had been centred in Rivoalto (at the core of what, by the 12th century, would be known instead as Venezia). A new series of bishoprics, independent but loyal to the Republic, was established to counteract any leverage from Rome (ie, the papacy) through the see of Aquileia. A board of *giudici* (judges) was also set up to curb abuses of power by the doge. The office was, after all, supposed to be electoral and the political system in some way democratic.

Phoenix from the Flames

The 10th century was, however, characterised by the growing tendency of the doges to rule as monarchs. Never was this clearer than in the case of the fiery Pietro Candiano IV. By 976 he had so incensed the people by his self-aggrandisement that the mob burned most of Venice down as they cornered Candiano in the flaming wreckage of the Palazzo Ducale and, with a stroke of the sword, sent him to his maker.

Things began to look up when **Pietro Orseolo** was elected as doge in 991. Orseolo was one of the most gifted leaders the Republic ever had. By careful diplomacy, he won the medieval equivalent of most-favoured-nation status in Constantinople and in much of the Holy Roman Empire. Constantinople went

With This Ring I Thee Wet

Pietro Orseolo's successful campaigns to subdue the Dalmatian coast and hamstring piracy from that corner earned him the title of Dux Dalmatiae. So chuffed were he and the nobles of Venice by their success that in 998 they ordained that the events should be celebrated every year on Ascension Day.

The doge, accompanied by bishops, nobles and other important citizens, would sail out to the Lido on the ducal galley, the *bucintoro*, and carry out a brief ceremony. 'Oh Lord, keep safe your faithful mariners from storms, sudden shipwreck and the perfidious machinations of wily enemies.'

The ceremony developed in pomp and circumstance over the years and came to be known as the *Sposalizio del Mar*, the Wedding with the Sea. It became customary for the doge to cast a ring into the waves just in front of the Chiesa di San Nicolò (at the northern end of the Lido) as part of this ritual, although few now believe the story that the pope himself donated a gold ring for the occasion in 1177. The ceremony at sea was followed by a solemn Mass in the Chiesa di San Nicolò.

further before the century was out, virtually opening up all of the Orient (the lands east of the Mediterranean) exclusively to Venetian merchants. Placing the importance of trade before all other considerations, Orseolo also courted Muslim capitals from Damascus to Cordova (Córdoba).

The last years of the 11th century brought two momentous events. In 1094, the third and (to this day) final **St Mark's Basilica** was consecrated. This gaudy display of Byzantine-inspired construction was a declaration to the world that Venice had arrived.

The following year, Pope Urban II called the **First Crusade**. Ostensibly aimed at liberating the Holy Lands from the Muslims, the exercise seems to have been more an early European version of employment creation for frustrated knights and bounty-hunting adventurers of all classes. While they raped and ransacked their way across a horror-struck Byzantine Empire, before moving on to sack

Jerusalem and exterminate its Muslim and Jewish inhabitants, Venice looked on. The city's rulers were unwilling to get too involved in an exercise that could easily have damaged its highly developed trade relations with the Near East.

Between Byzantium & Barbarossa

In the first years of the 12th century, Venice did send fleets to Palestine to shore up the efforts of the mainly Frankish Crusaders on land, but only in return for trade concessions.

The Republic could not fail to notice the emergence of rival sea powers such as Pisa and Genoa (Genova), and perhaps this is what spurred it on to establish the **Arsenale**, a fortified zone on the eastern Castello end of the lagoon city. The Arsenale was the kernel of what would later emerge as Europe's first great shipyard, where commercial and fighting ships could be constructed more efficiently than hitherto imaginable. Venice was going to need every last one of them.

Venetian participation in the First Crusade, though limited, spoilt relations with Constantinople. In 1171 the Byzantine emperor John Comnenus staged an assault on the newly formed Genoese colony in Constantinople, blaming it on the long-established, wealthy Venetian community, who were promptly clapped into irons. The Venetian response was swift and disastrous. A fleet set sail bent on war, but Doge Vitale Michiel II made the mistake of accepting a proposal of talks. They dragged on for so long that his inactive fleet collapsed as the crews were ravaged by plague, a disease they carried back home.

Things sometimes have to get worse before they can get better. And they did. The Holy Roman Emperor **Frederick Barbarossa** had come to the throne in 1152 determined to re-create a single Roman empire, grinding under his heel the northern Italian cities, Rome and the pope, Norman-controlled southern Italy, and the Eastern Empire. It was an ambitious programme that by the late 1160s had produced mixed results, among them the creation of the Greater Lombard League to oppose him. Venice had seen itself with little choice but to join the league.

So, in 1172 Venice was technically at war with the two biggest powers in Europe and deeply divided internally. Doge Michiel had been lynched on his return with his plague-decimated fleet, most of which had been wiped out (much of it burned to contain the plague). The coffers were empty and the citizenry were fighting the disease brought home by the surviving seamen.

Checks & Balances

The failure of Doge Michiel was in part attributed to his refusal to listen to counsel. Refusing to listen was going to be harder from now on. A constitution and a series of bodies to protect it were now put into place.

From the beginning, the base of the pyramid of power had been the **Arengo**, or Assamblea General – an assembly of all the people (albeit always dominated by the wealthier families). If only because of the growing population, such assemblies were hardly ever called by the 12th century, except to rubber-stamp the choice of doge. (By the mid-15th century, the Arengo had been abolished altogether.)

Now the Venetian equivalent of a parliament was formalised: at the base was the **Maggior Consiglio** (Great Council), made up of members of Venice's powerful and moneyed families. Technically at least, the approval of its 480 elected members was needed for any decision of moment. By 1340 it would have more than 1200 members (although in earlier years the number sank as low as 210). The Maggior Consiglio elected the doge (see the Election of a Doge boxed text later).

The **Quarantia** (Forty) was responsible for elaborating economic policy, while the 60-member **Senato** (Senate) dealt with lesser affairs. The decisions of either (which on occasion worked jointly) were ultimately supposed to be ratified by the Maggior Consiglio. With time, the Quarantia would evolve into the supreme judicial organ of the state.

The Quarantia elected three heads *(capi)* who were equivalent in status to the *consiglieri ducali*, the doge's counsellors. Six of the latter were elected, one for each of central Venice's six *sestieri* (municipal divisions created in 1171 for the raising of taxes for a disastrous rescue effort of Venice's jailed citizens in Constantinople). Terms lasted for a maximum of one year and consiglieri could not stand again for a minimum of two years.

The consiglieri and the three capi della Quarantia convened under the auspices of the doge to elaborate the bulk of policy, distributing tasks to the Quarantia and Senato. These 10 men together were known as the **Signoria** (Signory). With the passing of time, more and more subcommittees evolved to deal with particular issues, often made up of *savii*, or sages.

Elsewhere in the lagoon, each island or settlement (such as Chioggia) had its own statute but was subordinate to the central government.

In spite of the complexities of this system of accountability, the doge was the one official elected for life. Within the Signoria, a long-lived doge would see his counsellors come and go, but he remained in the chair.

Supreme Referee

In 1177 Venice was agreed upon as the stage for one of history's great acts of reconciliation. Emperor Frederick Barbarossa and Pope Alexander III met here to conclude a peace treaty that meant considerable humiliation for the emperor but great publicity for Venice. Naturally, the Venetians managed to win trade concessions from the Holy Roman Empire in return for having provided its good offices.

And so it was, under the watchful eye of Doge Sebastiano Zaini, that Barbarossa knelt before the pope and kissed his ring in a sign of submission. The spot where this occurred is marked in the floor of the narthex before the central entrance into St Mark's Basilica. With this kiss, peace was restored in Italy and the German-based Holy Roman Empire again fell into line with the papacy.

Revenge of the Venetian Blind

A couple of decades later, the pope was again calling for a holy crusade to strike at the Muslims in the Holy Land. When Doge **Enrico Dandolo** agreed to head up the greatest armada yet put to sea in the service of God, few

Election of a Doge

In an attempt to blunt the fierce family rivalries and corruption that the ducal elections inevitably awakened, the Venetians came up with an extraordinary system of indirect voting.

The people did not vote, although technically the Assamblea General, or Arengo, had to approve the choice of doge made by the Maggior Consiglio. This body elected a commission that would then elect a candidate for doge. To reduce to a minimum the influence of leading factions, the members of the commission were in part elected by lottery. It worked a little like shuffling a deck of cards, picking some, and then repeating the process several times over before arriving at the final choice of electoral commission. Records of the 1268 election (when the rules were tightened still further) show that the vote went like this:

The Maggior Consiglio chose 30 members by lot, who in turn were reduced to nine by lot. These nine then elected 40 members, who in turn were reduced to 12 by drawing of lots. The 12 elected 25, who again were reduced to nine. These nine elected 45, in turn reduced to 11 by lot. These 11 voted for 41 members who then voted for a candidate as doge.

Well, actually the 41 were locked away and proceeded with their work. They each scribbled down the name of a candidate. The names of all the proposed candidates were put in an urn. As each one was pulled out, the candidate's suitability was discussed (if he or anyone from his family were among the 41, they had to leave while the deliberations continued). Then the candidate would be interviewed and voted on – if he got 25 votes, he became doge. If not, they went on to the next candidate. Lorenzo Tiepolo emerged as doge from the 1268 ballot – the process took 16 days from the death of his predecessor. In earlier times, the choice of the Maggior Consiglio then went before the Assamblea General, in other words the people assembled in St Mark's Square (Piazza San Marco). This was rarely more than a rubber-stamp exercise.

Once elected, the doge had to sign a *promissione*, a contract defining the limits of his power. Initially a formality, the document had become a serious check on the doge's freedom of action by the mid-13th century. Its content changed from one election to the next, but in effect ruled out profiting financially from office, acceptance of gifts, communication with other heads of state without the knowledge of the Maggior Consiglio, and other activities potentially at variance with the welfare of the state.

of the participants in this, the **Fourth Crusade**, could have known what he had in mind.

In fact, everyone involved in the negotiations of 1201 seems to have had something to hide. At any rate, Dandolo, who had lost his sight many years before, drove an extraordinary bargain: Venice would provide a fleet to carry 30,000 men (an unheard of number for such an undertaking) at a cost of 84,000 silver marks – approximately double the yearly income of the king of England at the time.

In the end, only one-third of the proposed forces turned up in Venice the following year and their leaders couldn't pay. Venice had kept its side of the bargain. Did the wily 80-year-old Dandolo predict this situation? To compensate for non-payment, he suggested the Crusaders help Venice out with a few tasks of its own on the way to Palestine. The most important of these involved a detour to Constantinople.

The events of 1171 and 1172 had not been forgotten, and when the Christian fleet sailed up before Constantinople's mighty sea walls, its intentions as yet undeclared, the city's inhabitants must have had an uneasy sensation. The Venetian plan involved putting a pretender, Alexius the Younger, on the Byzantine throne. He in turn promised to join the Crusade and restore Church unity (breached in the schism of 1054) by submitting the Orthodox Church to Roman control. It appears other Western leaders promised themselves rich spoils from an attack on Constantinople, too.

After the first assault, in July 1203, Alexius was put on the throne, but reneged on his promises. And so the Venetians led a second seaborne attack from the Golden Horn the following April, this time sacking the city completely. The booty, including the four bronze horses that adorned the Hippodrome and would end up gracing St Mark's Basilica, seemed boundless. A puppet Frankish emperor was installed on the Byzantine throne and the doge of Venice became 'Lord of a Quarter and a Half-Quarter of the Roman (ie, Byzantine) Empire' – Venice's three-eighths of the spoils.

Enrico Dandolo, for some the greatest doge to have lived, had managed to extract from this so-called Crusade more benefits for his city than anyone could have imagined. He died in a subsequent campaign in Constantinople and was buried in the city in whose capture and sack he had been instrumental. The Eastern Empire later recovered its independence, but remained a cripple among the world's powers. It is hardly surprising that it would later cave in to the green banner of Islam under the Ottoman Turks. What *is* remarkable is that Constantinople would hold out against them until 1453.

Merchant Empire

By the early years of the 13th century, Venice was at the head of a thriving commercial empire. The city's direct control of the Adriatic was undisputed. All trading vessels had to pass through La Serenissima and pay customs. With subject cities and bases up and down the eastern coast of the Adriatic, dotted about the Greek mainland and on Crete, Rhodes and Cyprus, as well as Constantinople and along the Black Sea coast, the banner of St Mark flew all over the eastern Mediterranean.

Ever a city of shrewd businessmen, Venice had always been careful to maintain good trade relations with Egypt as well as the Christian-controlled coastal cities of Palestine. The market places around the Rialto teemed with produce from as far away as China – spices, silk, cotton and grain were all unloaded there for transport farther on into the Italian hinterland and beyond the Alps to Germany and France.

Venice was not a feudal city. Its most noble families were generally also wealthy traders.

In these early days of empire, the men who captained Venice's trading ships usually came from those trading families. Nearly all the members of the various councils that ruled the Republic had done their time abroad.

Wars with Genoa

Venice's rapid expansion in the wake of the Fourth Crusade had not gone unnoticed by the city's competitors, among whom Genoa was by far the prime rival. In the course of the 13th century, Genoa's presence in Palestine, the Black Sea and elsewhere in the eastern Mediterranean was a constant source of concern to Venice. The first scuffle between them came in the wake of riots between the Genoese and Venetian quarters in the Christian enclave of Acre, in Palestine. This ended in a rather ignominious naval defeat for Genoa off the coast of Acre in 1258.

Three years later, Venice's luck began to look distinctly pear-shaped. In Constantinople, the Byzantines, with Genoese connivance, overthrew the Latin emperor. Now suddenly Venice's possessions and trade routes were threatened. From then until a peace treaty was signed in 1299, Venetian and Genoese navies pursued each other around the Mediterranean with growing fury but little definitive success. Venice came off worst in several encounters, especially at the battle of Curzola (Korc) on the Dalmatian coast, where the Republic lost 65 out of 95 vessels and the Genoese took 5000 prisoners (among them Marco Polo). The peace treaty was little more than a pause in what would be a long, tiring and bitter conflict.

A Brave New Order

A series of reforms around the end of the 13th century and early into the next fixed the course of Venice's internal political life until the demise of the Republic in 1797.

In 1297, franchise laws known as the **Serrata del Maggior Consiglio** (Closing of the Great Council) effectively restricted access to the Maggior Consiglio or higher office to a caste of established and noble families. Money alone did not constitute nobility. By 1323 membership of the Maggior Consiglio had become permanent and hereditary.

Polos Apart

For Venice, 1261 was a disastrous year. Not only had it lost control of a trade nerve centre in Constantinople, but Venetian merchants suddenly found themselves debarred from the trading entrepots of the Black Sea. The new regime in Constantinople declared open season on Venetian traders, labelling them pirates. When captured, they routinely had their eyes put out and noses lopped off.

During the preceding years, the Mongols had consolidated an empire stretching from China to the Black Sea, incorporating Persia and Iraq. On the Black Sea, western traders dealt with the khan's local representatives, the Golden Horde. Among these traders were the Polo brothers, Nicolò and Matteo. By 1261 they were operating deep inside the Crimea and decided to venture farther. Whether or not they knew what had happened in Constantinople is unclear, but they couldn't have timed their departure better.

Local warring between various Mongol khans had blocked the roads south, so the Polo brothers went to Bukhara, in Turkestan, where they stayed for three years – time enough to learn Mongol and Persian. Getting into Persia continued to appear impossible, so they went deeper into the unknown and ended up at the court of Kublai Khan. According to some accounts, they were in Beijing (the winter residence); others talk of the Khan's summer residence, Shang-tu (better known to westerners as Xanadu). The Polos were sent back to Italy in 1269 with a request to the pope for a hundred learned men to teach the Mongols the ins and outs of Christianity and the 'seven arts' – whatever they were.

In 1271 the Polos set off again, this time with two missionaries who quickly high-tailed it back to Italy. Nicolò also brought along his 20-year-old son, Marco.

For the next few years, the Polos trundled around the Orient making a stash in the jewellery business. It took several years of overland travel from the Gulf of Iskenderun (in what is now Turkey) to China, but eventually they made it to Shang-tu. Once there, Marco entered the service of the khan and travelled extensively in China for the following 17 years.

When the Polos finally decided to return home, not everything went terribly well, for they were robbed of much of their fortune in Trebizond (Trabzon in modern Turkey). According to the Polo legend, no-one even recognised them when they finally made it back to Venice.

Marco's tales of adventure were the talk of the town, but sceptics began to consider them rather tall and they came to be known as *il milione* (the million).

In 1299 Marco ended up in a prison in Genoa. Here he met a scribbler by the name of Rustichello, to whom he dictated memoirs of his years in the East. Perhaps anticipating the disbelief of some of his readers, he called it *Il Milione*. Freed in 1300, Marco returned to Venice and settled down to a quiet life. His book, known as *The Travels of Marco Polo* in English, has been the subject of constant speculation ever since his death in 1324.

Some crumbs were left to the rising middle class of *cittadini* (citizens). The biggest of them was the office of Gran Cancelliere, or Lord High Chancellor, effectively the head of the civil service and superior in rank to the Senators. The Gran Cancelliere could only be appointed from among the ranks of cittadini, never from the aristocracy.

More important developments were afoot, however. In 1308 Venice found itself embroiled in a hopeless war against the pope and a host of allies over possession of the Po city of Ferrara. A papal interdict and blockade did considerable damage to Venetian interests – all over the Mediterranean the city's citizens were arrested, goods seized and vessels attacked by anyone who cared to take a swipe at the Republic.

Ultimately, Venice was compelled to back down, but in the meantime discontent had led several old aristocratic families to plot the overthrow of the doge, Pietro Gradenigo, in 1310. The plot failed (see the boxed text 'Knocking Rebellion on the Head' in the Sestiere di San Marco section of the Things to See & Do chapter), and in its aftermath the

Consiglio dei Dieci was set up to monitor the security situation. At first meant to last a few months, it ultimately became a kind of CIA-cum-cabinet. From then on, the Consiglio, whose members were elected in rotation from the Maggior Consiglio, wove an intelligence network in the city and throughout Europe unequalled by any of the Republic's rivals. In the Palazzo Ducale, you can still see a couple of *bocche di denunce*, a kind of letter box where informants could leave anonymous tip-offs for the Consiglio to pursue.

Years of Plenty

The first half of the 14th century was marked by comparative calm, except for a brief war against the **Scaliger** family, who from Verona had come to control Vicenza, Padua, Treviso, Parma and Lucca. Venice found plenty of allies willing to put an end to this dangerous expansion, and by the end of it all, Venice had acquired its first mainland territories – land up to and including Treviso.

The implications were important. For the first time, Venice could secure its own supplies of basic staples for a population that now numbered around 200,000 (three times the population of the *centro storico*, or historical centre, today). On the other hand, the maritime republic would never again be able to remain aloof from the intrigues of mainland politics.

Trade was improving all the time. The invention of the compass and the introduction of the rudder on boats had greatly improved seamanship. Commercial vessels were becoming larger and voyages more frequent. The dismantling of a Moroccan blockade of the Straits of Gibraltar had opened the way to more regular trading with Flanders and England.

Black Death

In the hurly-burly of medieval Europe, you could be sure peace was a fragile business. Rivalry between Venice and Genoa had persisted, but before they could even begin to grapple with one another in a satisfactory fashion, their merchant vessels had brought back from the Black Sea one of the most miserable imports imaginable.

The nasty little rats on board the vessels of 1348 were carrying the Black Death. The effect on Venice was as horrific as anywhere, with as many as 600 people dying every day. Up and down the canals, barges plied their sorry trade: 'Corpi morti! Corpi morti!' (the local equivalent of 'Bring out your dead!') the steersmen cried. Three-fifths of the city's population perished. Genoa met the same fate and the disease spread across all of Europe.

The two powers barely paused to absorb this horrible blow. Skirmishes took place regularly and in late 1354 the Venetian fleet was virtually wiped out in a surprise raid in the Greek islands.

In the following years, Venice found itself fighting numerous unpleasant wars with Padua, the Hungarians and the Austrians. The upshot of all this was the loss of all its Dalmatian possessions. Great as these setbacks were, however, they would seem minor compared with the threat that now overshadowed the city's very existence.

The War to End All Wars with Genoa

In 1372 an incident in Cyprus sparked the last and most devastating of La Serenissima's duels with Genoa. It took a while to wind up to its climax, but in August 1379, a Genoese invasion fleet appeared off the Lido. On Genoa's side were ranged Padua and Hungary, busy devastating the Venetian mainland territories, while Visconti-ruled Milan sided with Venice.

Admiral Pietro Doria's first objective was Chioggia, which fell to his combined sea and land assault, with Hungarian troops marched across from Padua. In Venice, a popular hero, **Vettor Pisani**, took overall command. The city worked day and night to build new ships and defences on and around the islands, especially on the Lido, San Giorgio Maggiore and Giudecca. Incredibly, Doria opted to starve out Venice – a decision that served only to grant the city precious time. Pisani, in fact, turned the tables by laying siege to Chioggia, but his forces were inadequate and all of Venice prayed for the return of Carlo Zeno's war fleet, which had been sent out long before the siege to patrol the Mediterranean. His appearance on the horizon at the beginning of 1380 spelled the end for the Genoese.

Venice had averted disaster, but victory only became apparent in the next century, as the Republic returned to prosperity while Genoa slumped into a century of decline.

The Fall of Constantinople

By the time the Turks marched into Constantinople on 29 May 1453 and snuffed out what remained of the Byzantine Empire, Venice had in most respects reached the apogee of its power.

Since the Battle of Chioggia, the Republic had largely managed to keep out of major naval conflicts. From 1424, with things relatively quiet elsewhere, Venice threw itself headlong into a campaign of land conquest that brought decades of sporadic warfare with Milan. In the end, La Serenissima was left master of a land empire stretching from Gorizia in the east to Bergamo in the west, but the state coffers were dangerously empty.

Overall, however, things looked good. The Republic had regained sovereignty over the many Dalmatian coastal bases that it had earlier lost to Hungary, while in the Mediterranean it maintained control over a number of Greek islands and mainland bases – not least among them Crete (direct control of Cyprus was still some years off). Despite some nasty clashes, relations with the rapidly expanding Ottoman Turkish Empire remained cordial.

Trade flourished. Spices, sugar, silks, cotton and slaves came from the East. From northern Europe, Venice sent wood and iron to the Orient, while with England and Flanders it carried on a lucrative three-way trade in wines, wool and finished textiles. At home, the great buildings of St Mark's Square (Piazza San Marco) as we now know them neared completion.

In the years immediately after the capture of Constantinople, Venice still found cause to hope the event would make no difference to it. As Greek refugees poured into Venice and confirmed its reputation not only as the most Eastern of Western cities, but also as one of the most tolerant (the Orthodox population was given its own church), La Serenissima's ambassadors hammered out new commercial treaties with the victorious Sultan Mehmet II.

For a while, Venice managed to kid itself about the Turks' intentions, but the scales fell from its eyes in 1470. By then, most of mainland Greece was in Turkish hands – only the various Venetian outposts had been spared. One of the most important was **Negroponte**, or Khalkis as it is now called (the ancient Chalcis on the island of Euboea). Its fall after a three-week siege and the inexplicable inaction of a Venetian fleet sent to relieve it came as a heavy blow. The next 10 years brought more bad news, with the loss of several more Greek-island outposts and the Turks advancing savagely in the Balkans. They even raided the Friuli area. They say the fires raging in destroyed villages could be seen from the Campanile in St Mark's Square.

The biggest problem through all this period was Western disunity. Venice, exhausted by continual warfare against an infinitely more powerful foe, gratefully signed a peace treaty in 1479 with Sultan Mehmet. This counted for little. In 1499 Venice lost its two remaining key ports in mainland Greece – Modone (Methoni) and Corone (Koroni) in the Peloponnese peninsula (also known then as the Morea).

A Lousy Start to a Century

The last days of the 15th century brought still more bad news. The Portuguese navigator **Vasco da Gama** had returned to Lisbon, having reached India by sailing around the Cape of Good Hope in Africa. Suddenly, the Mediterranean seemed irrelevant. All the riches of the East could now be brought directly to Lisbon and from there sold on to northern Europe – avoiding the uncertainties of desert caravans and the certainty of expensive taxes added to the prices of goods by Middle Eastern potentates and the Venetians.

News of da Gama's important discovery reached Venice in 1501, and the first reaction was one of panic, with many Rialto banks going bankrupt. Pessimists were already predicting the end for Venice when things took yet another turn for the worse.

League of Cambrai

The lead-up to the formation of the League of Cambrai is a typically convoluted example of European politics. Suffice to say that Pope Julius II had decided that Venice was too powerful a state in Italy and drummed up support from France, the Holy Roman Empire (in the person of the Habsburg ruler of Austria, Maximilian), Spain and several Italian city-states. In return for cutting Venice to pieces, all were promised rich territorial rewards. In April 1509, French forces marched on Venetian territory.

The initial campaigns boded ill for Venice – within less than a year, most of its mainland empire was in enemy hands. Only the Friuli area and Treviso still flew the banner of St Mark. Not since the Battle of Chioggia had Venice stood so close to the precipice.

No-one would have made bets on Venice's recovery at that point, but the shifting sands of Italian politics changed matters repeatedly. All the participants in the League of Cambrai changed sides with monotonous regularity, so that by 1516, when the war finally sputtered to an end, Venice was left with almost all the territory it had begun with, including the cities of Padua, Vicenza, Verona, Brescia and Bergamo.

But something fundamental had changed. In 1519 **Charles V** ascended the Habsburg throne and would later be the last sovereign to be crowned Holy Roman Emperor by the pope. His domains spread from Austria to Spain, into which latter country was pouring the newly found wealth of the Americas. Francis I was king of France and Henry VIII of an increasingly self-confident England. The Turks had taken Cairo and were moving rapidly across North Africa. In the emerging world order of nation states and global empires, Venice, whose coffers had been bled dry by all the warring, was distinctly small fry.

Battle of Lepanto

More than ever, Venice knew it had to tread a subtle and, at times, almost impossible line to ensure survival against the unquestionably greater powers around it. So, as Charles V took his empire into repeated conflicts with France and the pope, Venice kept a polite distance from all concerned.

For some years the Republic was able to avoid trouble from Turkey too, which was otherwise engaged in Eastern Europe (Vienna came within an ace of falling to **Suleiman the Magnificent** in 1529). But it was only a matter of time. In 1537 Suleiman tried and failed to take the stoutly defended Corfu. Frustrated, he quickly swallowed up a series of small Venetian-run Greek islands and two remaining bases in the Peloponnese. Venice was not strong enough to take on the Ottoman Empire alone and its repeated calls for united Christian action came to little.

The subsequent lull was followed by another hammer blow. Suleiman invaded **Cyprus**, an island governed rather unhappily by Venice. La Serenissima appealed again for Western help, to little avail. A large fleet of Venetian ships was joined by other ships under the standards of the Vatican and Spain, but the latter's distrust of Venice was stronger than its desire to stem the Ottoman tide.

In the end, the island's defenders held out heroically against overwhelming odds while the relief fleet dallied and finally, deciding there was no hope, simply turned around to head home. The slaughter and violence carried out by the Turks after the fall of Famagusta in the island's east was unusually barbarous, even by the standards of the day (see the boxed text 'The Infamy of Famagusta' in the Sestiere di Cannaregio section of the Things to See & Do chapter).

Revenge was not long in coming. This time, even Spain saw that something had to be done and formed a solemn league with Venice and the Vatican. They vowed to assemble a fleet every year and return to the fight until 'the Turk' was destroyed. In 1571 a huge allied fleet led by Don John of Austria (much of it provided by Venice) appeared off Lepanto, in Greece, and in the last great encounter between rowed galleys inflicted a resounding defeat on the Turks. Venice urged its allies to press the victory home but they refused and so let the Turks off the hook. Seeing the allied resolve so brittle, Venice had little choice but to sue for a separate peace with the Ottomans.

The watchword in the remaining years of the century was caution. Venice had by now embarked on the most illustrious period of its diplomatic career. In other words, from here on its single greatest weapon would be lots of fast talking.

Decline

As the 17th century dawned, Venice was launched into a slow decline. Although not as immediately disastrous as initially thought, the rounding of the Cape of Good Hope a century earlier had changed much. A great deal of the spice trade now went through Lisbon, and northern European cartels buying in bulk were undercutting Venetian prices. Now the Dutch and English were becoming bolder too, and before long the Dutch would assume control of the Atlantic trade with the East.

Mediterranean trade had not, for all this, been truncated. Atlantic piracy, especially towards the end of the 16th century, often made supplies through the eastern Mediterranean more reliable. Increasingly, however, Venice's position had been eroded. Not only had it lost most of its Mediterranean bases, but under the Ottomans its trading privileges were gradually rolled back.

At home, quite simply, the core was going soft. **Corruption** was on the rise and the Consiglio dei Dieci increasingly overstepped its constitutional brief. The city's well-heeled nobs wallowed in luxury. Meanwhile, in the face of the great nations and empires around it, Venice had neither the will nor the manpower to equip great enough fleets, let alone armies, to match those of their competitors.

This was not to say that the Republic couldn't carry off the occasional victory. In 1606 Pope Paul V faced down La Serenissima with an interdict on the city in an argument over temporal and spiritual authority. Led by the greatest thinker Venice ever produced, **Paolo Sarpi**, the Republic serenely repudiated the arguments of the Vatican and won support from around Europe – much of it by now Protestant. It was a silly argument in one sense, but the pope was compelled to back down. Never again would the papacy be able to impose its will on nations through

fear of spiritual castigation. What was a minor victory for Venice represented a lasting blow to the papacy's temporal power.

Venice's policy of maintaining neutrality wherever possible helped turn it into a den of espionage. A rather absurd Spanish conspiracy of 1618 to seize the city from the inside was merely one example among many of the plotting that characterised life in the city.

The Consiglio dei Dieci, in its role as the state's security service, had plenty to do in these years of intrigue. Its **spy network** within and beyond the Republic was one of the most effective in the world. Given Venice's delicate position in the balance of world affairs, it needed to be. In the case of the 1618 plot, the Consiglio, once it had been informed and had gathered evidence, quietly dispatched about 300 conspirators. The Consiglio worked fast and without ceremony. Trials, torture and executions were all generally carried out in secret. That said, compared with its neighbours to the east and west, Venice remained a haven of tolerance.

Venice did what it could to avoid costly conflict but in 1645 the Turks landed a huge invasion force on the island of **Crete** and launched what turned out to be a 25-year campaign to conquer the island. Defence of the main town, Candia, was dogged and the Venetians won a surprising number of engagements at sea. However, unaided by any of the other Christian powers, the island was lost from the beginning. With the town's surrender, Venice's presence beyond the Adriatic expired.

One Last Hurrah

In 1683 the Turks were again at the gates of Vienna, but this time they were cut to pieces. Euphoric at the victory, the Habsburg forces and their Hungarian, Polish and German allies set off in swift pursuit across Hungary. Other Christian forces poured into the Balkans. Venice was asked to join in the fray and the following year a fleet under Francesco Morosini set out with a mercenary army under a Swedish general.

By the end of 1687, after a series of summer campaigns, Venice seemed to have returned to the days of the Fourth Crusade.

Almost all of the Morea (the Peloponnese peninsula) was back in Venetian hands. Athens, too, fell in a siege, during which the invaders managed to blow up most of the Parthenon, which the Turks had converted into a munitions dump. By the **Treaty of Karlowitz**, Venice ended up with the Morea and various other conquests, but Athens and everything north of the city in Greece was handed back to the Turks.

Administering the Morea turned out to be more trouble than it was worth, and in any case, the Turks were soon back. They broke the treaty in 1715 and within a few months had recaptured most of the peninsula. The following year they tried again to invade Corfu and failed. The Austrians were by then on the march in the Balkans. The ensuing **Treaty of Passarowitz**, signed in 1718, was La Serenissima's last. Venice was left in control of its mainland empire, which included Brescia, Bergamo, Cremona, Verona, Vicenza, Padua, Treviso and the Friuli area. In addition, it had Istria, Dalmatia, parts of coastal Albania, Corfu and a spattering of other Ionian islands.

The Finest Drawing Room in Europe

Venice had become irrelevant. If La Serenissima lasted until the arrival of Napoleon at the gates in 1797, it was as much due to luck and the simple fact that the big players in Europe had other fish to fry.

Venice reverted to its by now increasingly familiar policy of determined neutrality. The War of the Austrian Succession, the Seven Years War and numerous other European conflicts passed, if not unnoticed, at least unheeded in the Republic. As the years floated by, the Republic's navy shrank to a shadow of its former self. In any case, the shipbuilders of the Arsenale and their techniques had long since been eclipsed by their counterparts in England, France and the Netherlands.

No longer master of the Adriatic, the Republic had also come to realise it could not oblige foreign shipping to unload in Venice and pay customs duties. What's more, the Habsburg-held port of Trieste and the papacy's Ancona had been made free ports.

The only way to respond was to abandon protectionism and open Venice up to free trade – mostly in local goods from around the Adriatic and as far south as Greece. Business was pretty brisk until the end of the Republic but for many years now, trade had been seen as beneath the nobility. The great commercial families that had made Venice's wealth and provided many of its most illustrious characters had long ago lost interest in the sea. They neither traded nor had any desire to endure the rigours of naval life. These tasks they left mostly to the minority communities resident in Venice, such as the Greeks and Armenians. The nobles, or at least those who had not become impoverished, looked instead to their estates on the mainland.

Impoverishment of many inactive noble families was causing its own problems. Numbers in the Maggior Consiglio were in constant decline, and to stem the tide, it had become habitual to sell membership of the nobility. The new rich members weren't always welcome, but there was little choice. In any event, by the 18th century rule of Venice was effectively in the hands of a narrow oligarchy of 42 families.

News of the **French Revolution** hit Venice with much the same force as it did the rest of Europe. But while the monarchical powers of Europe talked of alliance and left France friendless and isolated, nothing could persuade the Venetian Republic to shift from its policy of neutrality.

Events moved swiftly and by 1795 **Napoleon** was in Italy giving chase to the Austrians. Both the Austrians and French violated Venice's neutrality. Back in the lagoon, the leaders of La Serenissima debated back and forth how to deal with this menace. In the end, they followed a course tantamount to suicide. Napoleon's campaign took him through Lombardy to Verona and then north in pursuit of the Austrians. Just when he decided to crush Venice is unclear, but as the doge and his counsellors bowed and scraped in an attempt to keep the dashing French general sweet, Napoleon offered up the Republic to Austria as the price of a temporary peace.

On 12 May 1797, with Napoleon's guns ranged along the lagoon ready, if necessary, to pound Venice into submission, the panicking Maggior Consiglio, which could not manage a quorum, voted the Republic out of existence. Napoleon was charmed by Venice, describing St Mark's Square as the 'finest drawing room in Europe', and now it was his.

The Aftermath

For around six months, the Republic lived as a puppet 'democracy' under the French. In January 1798 Venice and most of the Veneto, along with Istria and Dalmatia, passed into Austrian hands. As Napoleon swept across Europe, Venice became just another playing piece to be shunted around among the great powers.

In 1805 Napoleon incorporated Venice into his **Kingdom of Italy**. It would be too simplistic to write off what followed as 10 years of oppression. The city's administration was tidied up in line with French precepts. Plans were laid for urban renewal, the setting out of public gardens, the building of a road connection to the mainland and the rehabilitation of the port. On the down side, the expropriation, and in many cases downright looting, of churches, convents and religious schools deprived the city of many of its artistic treasures.

It all came to an end in 1815, when Austria was awarded Venice (along with much of the rest of northern Italy) by the **Congress of Vienna**.

Trieste was the Austrians' gateway to the sea, so Venice was largely neglected in the early years of Austrian hegemony. Nevertheless, the city was made a free port in 1829. In the 1830s bulwarks were built to protect the three entrances to the lagoon from high tides. The resulting narrower entrances were dredged and deepened for shipping. By 1846 Venice was linked to Milan by rail (although the train station was not inaugurated until 1865). Dredging work near the station meant that merchant ships could unload right by the trains destined to transport goods into Italy.

The Austrians never managed to endear themselves to the Venetians, who in 1848 joined the long list of rebels who rose up against the established order across Europe.

The Republic was again proclaimed and the city held out until August of the next year.

Italy United

The movement for Italian unification spread quickly through the Veneto and, after several rebellions, Venice was finally united with the Kingdom of Italy in 1866.

During the last decades of the 19th century the city was a hive of activity. Increased port traffic was coupled with growing industry. Canals were widened and deepened and pedestrian zones laid out in the city centre. Tourism began to take off around the turn of the century, as the fine hotels along the Grand Canal came into their own. And by 1922, **La Biennale**, or the Esposizione Internazionale d'Arte (International Art Expo), was firmly in place as an added attraction.

Under Mussolini, the road bridge linking Venice with the mainland was built parallel to the railway bridge, and this event in essence marked the shift of business and industry to what is now 'greater' Venice: Mestre and Porto Marghera. Years later they would bear the brunt of Allied bombing campaigns during **WWII**, while the Arsenale continued to be used as a naval dockyard. It still is, although its importance is negligible. Venice came out of WWII pretty much unscathed.

Venice since WWII

Porto Marghera, industrialised since 1920, was extended southwards into reclaimed land in the course of the 1960s and 1970s. The creation and expansion of petrol refineries and metallurgy, chemical and plastics industries brought thousands of jobs to Venice – and plenty of problems too. For more on these see Ecology & Environment later in this chapter.

The threat to Venice from the sea became abundantly clear to anyone who had not already seen it when **floods** crashed into the city in 1966. To date, they were the most disastrous demonstration of what could be the city's fate if steps are not taken to protect it. International organisations were set up in the wake of the flooding to collect funds intended to be spent on projects to protect the city and also to save and restore its monuments (see the boxed texts 'Acque Alte', later in this chapter and 'Saving Venice' in the Sestiere di San Marco section of the Things to See & Do chapter). But the years since the 1966 floods have been a lamentable time of prevarication and corruption in Venice. No-one can be sure just how much money intended for projects to save Venice from sinking has instead ended up lining the pockets of politicians, bureaucrats and lobbyists.

In late 1998, the charismatic left-wing mayor **Massimo Cacciari** threw in his lot with the Greens, who insisted on further environmental impact studies before approving the floating barriers to stem tidal damage in the city. Exasperation with the lack of action after more than 20 years led even the European Parliament to intervene in 1999, urging the authorities to decide in favour of the barriers as soon as possible. Cacciari left the mayor's office in 2000 to run for president of the Veneto region in 2001 (he failed) and was replaced by a pro-barrier former public works minister, **Paolo Costa**, at the head of a centre-left coalition. Recently, the barriers got the go-ahead, but sceptics note that the legalese that would define a start date is missing.

In August 2001, a few hours before Italy's recently elected right-wing prime minister and tycoon **Silvio Berlusconi** visited the city, a bomb ripped through the court buildings of Rialto. At the time of writing, it was unclear who had planted the device. Coming in the wake of bloody **anti-globalisation** (and many feel anti-government) riots in Genoa in July, the attack was seen as a sign of growing tension in Italian politics.

GEOGRAPHY

The role of geography has been critical in the development of Venice. For hundreds of years, the city's greatest defence was its unique position in the middle of a lagoon. Now, the one-time guarantor of Venice's survival seems bent on the inexorable eradication of the city.

The territory of the Comune di Venezia extends over 457.5 sq km, of which 267.6 sq km are lagoon waters, canals and so on. On the mainland, the city's boundaries take in 132.4 sq km. The *centro storico* (old city) is just 7.6 sq km of land, while the remaining islands together total 49.9 sq km.

It is tempting when gazing across the lagoon to think of it as a simple extension of the sea. No impression could be more mistaken. The Adriatic forces its way into the lagoon through three *bocche* (mouths) that interrupt the bulwark of narrow sandbanks strung north to south in a 50km arc between the mainland points of Jesolo and Chioggia.

The **lagoon** was formed by the meeting of the sea with freshwater streams running off from several Alpine rivers. It is like a great shallow dish, crisscrossed by a series of navigable channels. These were either the extension of river flows or ditches created by the inflow of sea water. One of the deepest is the Grand Canal (Canal Grande), which runs through the heart of the city. It is thought to have been an extension of the Brenta (which has since been diverted south) or another river – human intervention has been so constant that by now it is all but impossible to say with any certainty. Other channels have been dredged and deepened since WWII to allow huge oil tankers to pass through to Porto Marghera.

No-one knew the lagoon better than the Venetians – whenever invaders threatened (such as in 1379–80, during the Battle of Chioggia), the Venetians would pull up buoys marking the course of navigable channels and so pretty much close access to the city. The channels are marked today by lines of wooden pylons *(bricole)*.

Over 40 islands and islets dot the lagoon. The better-known ones include the Lido, Pellestrina, Murano, Burano and Torcello. The tinier ones have served as convents, quarantine stations, hospitals and cemeteries. Today, some belong to the city of Venice, while others are privately owned. Some, such as San Michele, are easily accessible, while others have been abandoned to decay.

The 7.6 sq km of Venice today weren't always there. The islands that together formed Rivoalto were a fraction of the area now covered. The very shallowness of the lagoon allowed the next step. Along the edge of the deeper channels, the inhabitants began to expand their tiny islands. They did this by creating platforms on which to build new structures. Pine pylons were rammed into the muddy lagoon floor, then topped by layers of Istrian stone. The action of the sea water on the wood caused a process of mineralisation that hardened the structure, while the upper stone layers were impervious to the tides. It was an ingenious solution and the method has remained pretty much the same to the present day.

CLIMATE
Summer is probably the worst time of year to be in Venice – average daytime temperatures hover around 27°C but can go considerably higher. High humidity also makes for rather sticky weather, and the combination of heat haze with air pollution makes it highly unlikely you'll be able to espy the Alps from any point in the city. Prevailing winds (the sirocco) are from the south and hot.

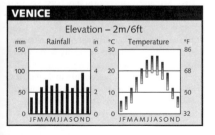

In spring the weather is often crisp and clear and the temperatures pleasant. That said, quite a lot of rain falls in May and into June. In July and August the humidity can bring cracking storms in the evening.

The first half of winter sees heavy rainfall, with flooding (see the boxed text 'Acque Alte' in the following Ecology & Environment section) most likely in November and December. On bad days, the city and lagoon are enveloped in mist (which some find enchanting), but every now and then you get lucky and the sky clears.

January and February are the coldest months, with average temperatures hovering between 0°C and 7°C. Because of its position on the lagoon, snow is a rarity.

ECOLOGY & ENVIRONMENT
Venice is under siege. For the most part, public attention on the city's ailments has focused on **flooding** and the chilling cry: 'Venezia sprofonda!' ('Venice is sinking!')

While the growing threat from Adriatic tides washing up against the city was dramatically brought home by the disastrous floods of 1966, the hue and cry over this issue has tended to obscure other, more complex problems that ultimately are just as dangerous to the city's future.

The narrow issue of tidal flooding and the wrangling over a project designed to put a brake on it are dealt with in this section in the boxed text 'Acque Alte', along with the related issue of **subsidence** (sinking).

Pollution
Heavy industry has brought other problems. The establishment and expansion of the petroleum and chemical plants in Porto Marghera was designed to breathe life into the Venetian economy. This it did – but at a price.

Human, agricultural and industrial waste is all cheerfully dumped into the lagoon off Venice, the islands and the mainland, the biggest offender by far being the Petrolchimico industrial complex at Porto Marghera: about half of all the cyanide, heavy metals and other toxic waste that winds up in the lagoon comes from the plants. By the late 1990s, the cost of the damage done to the lagoon by the company's dumping of toxic waste stood at around €36 billion.

In court hearings that began in 1998, 28 top managers of Petrolchimico were accused of knowingly dumping dangerous chemicals into the lagoon and endangering the health of the complex's employees from the 1960s on. A total of 157 deaths were associated with the company's activities, and 103 further cases of sickness.

The waste and air pollution from the petrochemical complex are also corroding Venice's buildings. Although funds have been allocated for the reduction of lagoon pollution, city officials admit that little progress has been made so far.

The passage of supertankers across the lagoon to Porto Marghera presents another disaster waiting to happen. Cleaning up an oil spill in the lagoon would be fraught with difficulty. The shallow waters would impede access for emergency vessels and the chemical techniques usually used could not be applied here because of the threat they would pose to vegetation and fish life in the lagoon. In 1999, a ruling set a limit on the size of tankers allowed into the lagoon but this has hardly removed the potential hazard.

In the summer of 2001, an initial regional plan to continue cleaning up the lagoon was proposed. More than €200 million were to be set aside for projects ranging from renewal of the sewerage system to the creation of aqueducts on the mainland to bring an end to the use of lagoon water for irrigation. It was estimated that continuing clean-up operations in the next decade would cost at least €720 million.

A Delicate Balance

Sea water itself is causing damage, and herein lies a particular rub. Ever since the foundation of the Republic, Venetians have continually intervened to keep a degree of

---

Acque Alte

Venice can be flooded by high tides during winter. Known as *acque alte*, these mainly occur between November and April, flooding low-lying areas of the city such as St Mark's Square (Piazza San Marco). Serious floods are announced several hours before they reach their high point by 16 sirens throughout the city and islands. In some areas, you can see the water rising up over the edge of the canal, although most of it actually bubbles up through drains.

Although the floods rarely last more than a few hours, the rise can happen with surprising speed and so leave you stranded. The best thing to do is arm yourself with a pair of gumboots *(stivali di gomma)*. Raised walkways *(passerelli)* are set up in St Mark's Square and other major tourist areas of the city (you can pick up a brochure with a map of the walkways at the tourist office).

Floods are measured against average sea level. Officially, *acqua alta* (a high tide) begins at 0.8m above average level. The sirens go off if it is expected to hit 1.1m. At this level, about 11.5% of the city is under shallow water. If the flood level exceeds 1.2m you can be in trouble, as even the walkways are no use then. At this level, about 35% of the city's pavements are covered. Add 10cm and 70% of the town is under. At 1.4m, a state of emergency would be declared, with most of the city under water. The November 1966 flood level was 1.94m. Floods above 1.2m are pretty rare. On average, flooding at 1.4m happens once every five years. The 1.3m mark has been reached twice every three years since 1966. Floods of the catastrophic 1966 kind are considered unlikely more than once in 180 years.

Venice's flooding problems are caused and compounded by numerous factors. The ebb and flow of the Adriatic tides is actually essential to the survival of the lagoon (see A Delicate Balance later in the Ecology & Environment section), but their effect on the city can be exacerbated by other factors. To the normal daily rhythm of two high tides is added the lunar push and pull at the new moon and full moon. Winds from the south (sirocco) can sometimes whip up waves, while the north wind (bora) causes problems for Chioggia. High and low pressure systems also affect tides.

The very shape of the Adriatic Sea, a little like a washtub, can see northbound waves bouncing at the top end of the sea and then spilling back southwards, washing into the lagoon. Extra fresh water draining off the mainland can add to the problem. And, of course, in the long term, the greenhouse effect can only be expected to worsen matters, by increasing the overall average sea level of the Adriatic.

Sinking

To make things worse, as has often been observed, Venice is, or at least was, sinking. It has been estimated that the city 'sank' 23cm in the 20th century. Of that total, 9cm are due to the rising sea level, so actual subsidence has probably been in the order of 14cm. That was in part due to natural long-term

stability in the lagoon (maintaining and dredging canals and so on), which is around 6000 years old.

The very survival of the lagoon relies on a delicate and rarely stable ebb and flow of sea and fresh water. River water brings sediment into the lagoon, some of which accumulates along canals and elsewhere to form sandbanks *(velme)*. Some of these sandbanks are then consolidated by hardy vegetation able to survive whether submerged or not. These *barene* serve as extra internal bulwarks against the potential rage of tides.

The main islands of the lagoon were probably formed this way.

On the other hand, too much sediment would fill the lagoon. The regular sea tide is essential to take away the surplus.

Until the 16th century, human intervention in the lagoon was minimal, aiming to do little more than maintain channels and stability. Then, however, interference became more drastic. The flow of fresh river water was diverted away from the lagoon to reduce the build up of sediment and the course of many channels was altered. In the 20th century, a

Acque Alte

giving way of the lagoon floor, but more importantly to the excessive pumping of subterranean water – mostly for industrial purposes – in Porto Marghera. That practice has now been largely stopped and, as ground water again builds up, subsidence may well give way to heave, the opposite phenomenon.

Searching for Solutions

Ever since the disaster of 1966, experts, committees and politicians have scratched around for a solution. The single most popular approach to dealing with Venice's problems has been to attack the tides.

Of the many plans put forward, the one that first won Italian government approval in the 1980s was based on an experimental moveable dike. The idea is to build mechanical walls into the sea bed at the three entrances into the lagoon, known as the *bocche di porto* ('port's mouths'; from north to south Lido, Malamocco and Chioggia). The walls, weighed down with water, would lie flush with the seabed until threatening high tides were on the way. At the flick of a switch, the watery ballast would be expelled from the walls, which would then rise up and keep the Adriatic out of the lagoon until the tide subsided. The plan has come to be known, incorrectly, as Mose (from the Modulo Sperimentale Elettromeccanico, a prototype in the lagoon).

Since the 1980s, arguments have raged over the long-term effectiveness of the plan and its impact on the fragile lagoon. After various commissions approved it in 1998, it was stopped in December that year when left-wing and Green politicians said the US$2.5 billion plan needed further study and that funds for the project (which would need up to US$10 million worth of maintenance annually) would be better spent on cleaning up pollution and dredging silted-up canals (see A Delicate Balance above).

The authorities finally gave the go-ahead to the Mose project at the end of 2001, and the barriers should be completed in eight years. Another decision was made to build a petroleum delivery platform off the Lido shore and to lay a petroduct to deliver crude oil to Marghera. This would keep tankers out of the lagoon and avoid the ever-present risk of oil spills. Both are big decisions, although sceptics note that a piece of legalese is missing that would define start dates. However, relevant ministries in Rome, the region and the city government all seem to be in agreement. Maybe this really is the green light.

Other alternative palliatives are also on the table. A programme to raise the level of pedestrian areas is already under way. This is not a novelty – the extreme lowness of some doorways is testimony to earlier municipal projects. Work to raise St Mark's Square to a point where it would be protected against flooding of up to one metre was supposed to begin in early 2001 but at the time of writing, the plan still had not left the drawing board. Well might Lord Byron have sighed: 'Oh Venice, Venice, when thy marble walls are level with the waters there shall be a cry of nations o'er thy sunken halls.'

concerted campaign of land reclamation wiped out vast areas of the lagoon.

That is nothing, however, compared with what has happened since the end of WWII. The digging of the Canale dei Petroli (Petrol Canal) in the 1960s to allow **oil tankers** into Porto Marghera created a new problem. It is deeper than the natural channels and allows too much sea water into the lagoon. Tidal movements are therefore faster and more violent.

People are busy making things worse in other respects too. The use of dragnets to harvest clams is ripping up great swathes of rich vegetation from the lagoon floor. That vegetation holds in a reasonable amount of sediment, which in turn holds up the influx of sea water. The barene are also under threat: fun-lovers zipping around in motorboats at weekends help erode the sandbanks.

All these elements constitute an incursion into the lagoon's natural defences against the sea, leading to what the Italians call the *marinizzazione* of the lagoon – its 'seafication'. With less to hold up outward flows, far more sediment is leaving the lagoon than coming in – it is estimated that the lagoon is losing a million cubic metres of sediment every year.

Another charming side effect of the clam harvesting is the replacement of the lagoon-bed vegetation with rootless algae. The lagoon and its coast have suffered repeatedly from such algae plagues in recent years – they're not pleasant on the nose.

On the subject of the nose, the digging of the Canale dei Petroli had another unexpected result. As the even ebb and flow of the tide has been altered by human activity, it no longer acts as efficiently in one of its traditionally vital tasks – flushing out the lagoon. While at deeper levels sediment is being carried out to sea, at the surface all the waste dumped into the lagoon tends increasingly to remain there.

All the fuss over the **Mose dike project** to stem the Adriatic flood-tide threat is seen by its opponents as a costly diversion from other real problems that, they say, could ultimately have an equally, if not more, devastating effect on the city. Merely blocking high tides, they say, is not the answer. The lagoon itself has to be helped to rebuild its own defences.

GOVERNMENT & POLITICS

Venice is the capital of the region known as the Veneto (one of 20 in Italy), which extends west to Verona and the Lago di Garda and north into the Alps.

The Veneto is then subdivided into seven provinces, of which the area around Venice – Venezia – is one (provinces are named after the main town in each). The other provinces are: Belluno, Padova (Padua), Rovigo, Treviso, Verona and Vicenza.

Since 1927, the *comune*, or municipality, of Venice has comprised the islands of the lagoon (including Murano, Burano, Torcello, the Lido and Pellestrina), as well as Mestre, Porto Marghera and Chioggia on the mainland. Locals often divide the lot into three general areas: *terraferma* (mainland), centro storico (Venice proper, including Giudecca) and the *estuario* (all the remaining islands).

Traditionally, Venice itself is divided into six *sestieri*: San Marco, Castello, Cannaregio, Dorsoduro, Santa Croce and San Polo. Nowadays, the territory of the comune is divided up into 13 *quartieri*. The sestieri and the island of Giudecca (which is part of the Sestiere di Dorsoduro for administrative purposes) are grouped into the first two of these 'quarters'. The remaining 11 cover the islands and mainland parts of the comune.

The present *sindaco* (mayor), Paolo Costa, has been in power at the head of a left-centre coalition since his predecessor, the charismatic left-winger Massimo Cacciari, vacated the position in May 2000. Costa is a stout defender of the Mose project to stem tidal flooding and has recently managed to overcome opposition to the plan.

ECONOMY

The ignominious fall of Venice in 1797 had its economic fallout. Although the port was not completely neglected under Austrian rule and a rail link was established with Milan, the city sank into something of a morass. While the north-western triangle of Italy embarked on a programme of industrialisation in the

1880s, the north-east remained fundamentally rural. Well after the end of WWI, more than 60% of the workforce was agricultural. The Veneto remained largely neglected until after WWII.

Industrialisation came mainly with the creation and expansion of Porto Marghera. In the following decades, the port and the metallurgy, chemical and petrol industries became major employers, not just in Venice, but for the whole region. By the late 1980s, only 7% of the population worked in agriculture, while 40% was in manufacturing and 53% in services. At 4.54 million, the whole Veneto region contains around 7.5% of the country's population, but contributes 12% of exports. Since the early 1980s, the Veneto region has experienced steady growth, outstripping much of the rest of the country – a pattern destined to continue in the foreseeable future.

Tourism plays a pivotal role in the life of the Veneto, and above all in Venice. The Veneto as a whole contributes 13% of all Italy's tourist revenue. In 1998 it was estimated that 1.5 million tourists visited Venice each year, staying an average of 2½ days. In 2000 the city's tourist board claimed some 3.5 million visitors stayed at least one night in the lagoon city! In addition, it is guessed that as many as 15 million day-trippers (people who don't stay overnight and leave no statistical trace) pour in. The majority are Americans, followed by Italians and Japanese. Everything was pointing to 2001 being another bumper year for Venice.

Of the lagoon's remaining traditional industries, **glass-making**, is perhaps the one with the highest profile. Although clearly directed at the tourist trade, some of the work coming out of Murano's glass factories remains of the highest quality.

Venice's once-proud shipbuilding industry had already wilted to virtually nothing by the time the Republic fell in 1797.

POPULATION & PEOPLE

The population of the Veneto region is 4.54 million. The region's largest centres are Venice (including the mainland), Padua and Verona, each with over 200,000 inhabitants.

The rest of the populace is spread out across a sea of smaller towns and countryside.

Some 274,580 people live in the Comune di Venezia. Only 65,909 are still resident in the centro storico. The **exodus** has been slow but constant. It began in part as the mainland areas of Mestre and Porto Marghera expanded and offered greater chances of employment. Constant talk (and little action) of Venice's sinking feeling must have had an effect too. Back in the 1950s, more than 170,000 lived in the lagoon city, and at various points in its long history the total nudged 200,000.

Demographically, the place seems condemned. Talk to the average Venetian about his or her city and it is hard not to detect a note of despair. Said one: 'Venetians have the feeling that nothing is done for them. Those who have made lots of money just buy up houses and keep them empty or rent them out to tourists. And the little people find they have to go.'

And as people leave, so shops and businesses collapse for want of local custom. All that remain are pizzerias and *gelaterie* (ice-cream shops) for day-trippers. 'Here there used to be 50 little shops – fruit sellers, bakers, butchers, delicatessens.' Our friend sweeps his hand across his neighbourhood. 'Now there is nothing. All those families have had to leave.'

The remaining islands are home to 45,200 people, leaving almost two-thirds of the people within the city boundaries on the mainland.

As elsewhere in Italy, the population is tending to shrink, kept afloat largely by immigration. In 2000, for the first time since 1983, the Veneto region recorded population growth (a grand total of 1255 extra souls).

EDUCATION

The Università Ca' Foscari officially came into being in 1968, although it had already been turning out graduates for 100 years. It began as Italy's first school of commerce. For more details, see Universities in the Facts for the Visitor chapter.

Illiteracy is barely an issue in the Veneto. The national Italian average of 97% literacy can be accepted as a standard reading for this part of the country.

ARTS

Venice was by tradition a city of practical people – merchants interested above all in the business of trade. This is not to say that the city and its people were indifferent to more aesthetic pursuits – periods of uncontested greatness in fields such as painting are proof enough of a substantial creative streak in the Venetians. Other arts, such as literature, seem to have excited them considerably less, however.

Architecture

Of the early centuries in the life of Venice, no visible sign remains today. The earliest surviving architectural testimony to the Republic's long history dates from the 11th century.

Veneto-Byzantine East was West, and for that matter vice versa. That Venice stood apart from the rest of the Italian peninsula is never clearer than in the city's monuments and art. The obvious starting point is not in Venice proper at all, but rather on the island of Torcello. Here, the Cattedrale di Santa Maria Assunta is a singular lesson in a cross-cultural experiment. Essentially following the Byzantine style we can see in the basilicas of Ravenna, its builders were also influenced by the Romanesque developments to the west, in Padua, and beyond in the Lombard plains.

The term '**basilica**' dates back to pre-Christian Roman times, when many major public buildings, from markets to courts, were constructed in this style. The basic plan is of a covered hall flanked by two columned aisles. When Emperor Constantine (AD 280–337) founded his new capital at Constantinople, he initiated an extensive church-building programme. Two basic types emerged: the long, rectangular, hall-and-two-aisles style already described and used mainly for public worship, and so-called 'centralised' churches. These latter were circular, square or octagonal and had a more commemorative role.

The cathedral is typical of the original standard basilica plan. There is no transept, although even in Constantine's time they had been employed in some churches. Perhaps the main giveaway feature is the iconostasis separating the central nave from the presbytery – a prime feature of Eastern Orthodox churches, in this case made up of six thin columns.

Although what we see today is largely the rebuilt church of 1008, a few parts date back to the 7th (main apse) and 9th centuries (side apses). Other than the apses, little remains of the original church founded in 639.

The real treasures are inside. Craftsmen from Ravenna came here to create some of the finest mosaics ever. The 12th- to 13th-century mosaic of the *Madonna col Bambino* (Madonna and Child) in the semi-dome of the central apse is one of the most exquisite examples of Byzantine handiwork. Some art historians rate it more highly than anything done in Constantinople itself.

The use of mosaics dates from Roman times, when the well-to-do covered the floors and walls of public and private buildings with geometric designs or images of people, beasts and events. Remnants of them can be seen in places like Pompeii and as far away as ancient Roman sites in Syria and Tunisia.

Under the Byzantine Empire, the custom was continued but tastes changed. In Venice, the use of a gold background became the norm. Nowhere is that clearer than in the dazzling decor of the city's star attraction, **St Mark's Basilica**.

This also started off as a three-nave basilica when founded in the 9th century to house the remains of the city's newly promoted patron saint. Later, two wings were added to create a Greek-cross form, again a Byzantine idea (and based on the Church of the Holy Apostles in Constantinople). To the casual observer, the clearest sign of its Eastern form are the five domes – add a couple of minarets and change the surrounding scenery and you could almost think yourself in Istanbul.

Less visible from the outside, but still another characteristic that separates St Mark's from Western churches, is the narthex (or atrium) wrapped around the front and side of the church up to the arms of the cross.

The kaleidoscope of mosaics inside the basilica is described in more detail under St

Mark's Basilica in the Sestiere di San Marco section of the Things to See & Do chapter. Suffice to say that, once again, the tradition is evidently Byzantine – the entire place is seemingly covered with these glittering tapestries of tiny tiles. The creation of mosaics requires glass, and the glass-makers who established themselves in Venice at the same time as the mosaicists soon set up an important local industry on the island of Murano. Their handiwork came to be among the most sought after in the world, ranging from the practical to the most exquisitely decorative.

Medieval Venice was largely a city of wood. Apart from the grand churches, only a handful of buildings were constructed of brick and/or stone. The Byzantine touch can still be made out in a few buildings, mostly trading houses, from the 12th century. The Ca' Farsetti and Palazzo Loredan are good examples, retaining features such as the two-storey loggias (open galleries), with their graceful rounded arches. To a lesser extent, you can make out the same style in the lower floor of the Ca' da Mosto. Even the Fondaco dei Turchi, much altered in the 19th century, clearly cries out its Veneto-Byzantine origins.

Romanesque The architectural expression of Europe's reawakening, this style that swept across Western Europe made less of an impact on Venice. Much of what was built in Romanesque style was later demolished and replaced.

A reasonable example of it is the **Chiesa di San Giacomo dell'Orio**, in Santa Croce. Here, you can see all the classic elements of the style. The Romanesque church tended to be squat and simple, with up to three apses. Decoration was minimal and the semi-circle dominant. Doorways and windows, in the church as well as in the square-based and equally squat bell towers, were capped by semi-circular arches. Architectural or sculptural ornament was otherwise virtually absent from most Romanesque buildings.

The pretty cloisters at the Museo Diocesano d'Arte Sacra, just behind (east of) the Palazzo Ducale, are a perfect specimen of Romanesque simplicity.

Several Romanesque bell towers, such as that of the Chiesa di San Geremia (near the train station), are scattered about the city. Time and again they were left intact even as the churches of which they were part were replaced or heavily restructured.

Closer inspection of several monuments also reveals that the influence of Romanesque, while subtle, was perhaps more pervasive than often thought. Churches such as Murano's Chiesa dei SS Maria e Donato and Torcello's Santa Maria Assunta, readily identified as Veneto-Byzantine, contain Romanesque elements. The same goes for St Mark's Basilica itself.

Gothic In the 13th century, Gothic winds began to prevail in Venice, although the Byzantine aesthetic continued to inform artistic and architectural thinking for a good time to come. One way of identifying Venetian Gothic is by looking at the windows. Where you see them in clusters, with their tops tapering to a point, you can be reasonably sure the building you are looking at is Gothic (or perhaps a remake!). Bobbing along the Grand Canal, in particular, you will hardly fail to notice the many **mansions** built in this style. It is, however, a very Venetian twist on the theme – the shape of the windows is a hallmark of Venetian design.

Of the city's great Gothic monuments, the **Palazzo Ducale** stands out. It is a remarkable creation and representative of the unique turn the style took in Venice (known as 'florid Gothic'). What you see is a mixed result of building started in the early 15th century, with several extensions and then reconstruction after fires in the late 16th century. Palladio wanted to demolish it then and start from scratch. Luckily for us, the Republic's conservative rulers wanted to replicate what had stood before the blaze. The graceful porticoed facades facing the Bacino di San Marco and the square are given a translucent quality by the use of white Istrian stone and pink Verona marble. Otherwise, the decoration is restrained. This is less the case on the side facing St Mark's Basilica. The carving on the Porta della Carta and Arco Foscari are fine examples of the intricacy reached in Gothic sculpture.

The two greatest Gothic churches in Venice were, however, built earlier than this, at the height of the style's sway. Santa Maria Gloriosa dei Frari (or the Frari for short) was built over a century, from 1338 to 1443, while the Chiesa dei SS Giovanni e Paolo (aka Zanipolo) was completed in 1368. Both are magnificent edifices on a Latin-cross plan. Work on the decoration of both lasted long after the construction was completed and reflects changing tastes. The Frari, a tower of elegance in brick, eschews almost completely the twisting lace-like external decoration typical of French and German Gothic. SS Giovanni e Paolo is partly decorated in marble and shows signs of the transition to the Renaissance.

Many architects at work in Venice were Lombards. **Mauro Codussi** (aka Coducci; c.1440–1504), from Bergamo, was responsible for the imposing facade on the Chiesa di San Zaccaria (1483), although much of the florid Gothic flavour (see the apse) is the work of another architect, Antonio Gambello. Codussi also designed the Palazzo Vendramin-Calergi and Palazzo Corner-Spinelli on the Grand Canal. In all of his buildings, the transition away from Gothic to a more classical approach is a clear harbinger of the arrival of the Renaissance in architectural thinking.

Renaissance The Renaissance cracked over Italian and then European society like a dam burst. Revelling in the rediscovery of the greats of classical literature, philosophy, science and art, writers, thinkers and artists embarked on a frenzied study of the ancient and an impatient search for the new. This was also reflected in architecture. Rejecting the clerical haughtiness of the Gothic and the Eastern rigidity of the Greek and Byzantine, architects of this new age put classical models to their service in a quest for harmony and rationality.

If Gothic churches soared high into the heavens, reminding people of their smallness compared with the Almighty, Renaissance grandeur spread laterally, luxuriating in the powers of the human mind and the pleasure of the human eye. While tall Gothic spires might be topped by the cross, a building such as the Libreria Nazionale Marciana (aka Biblioteca di San Marco, or Libreria Sansoviniana in memory of its creator) is low, flat-roofed and topped by statues. It is a house of learning.

Of course, it is not as simple as that. Among the identifying signs in Venetian Renaissance building is a proclivity for spacious rounded arches on all levels (usually two, sometimes three storeys). Fluted half-columns often feature on the upper storey, but otherwise ornamentation is generally restrained. The classical triangular pediment borne up by columns is another common touch, never seen more clearly than at the front of Andrea Palladio's Chiesa di San Giorgio Maggiore.

Three of the city's master architects were from out of town. **Jacopo Sansovino** (1486–1570), whose real name was Tatti, was born in Florence and lived and worked there and in Rome. **Michele Sanmicheli** (1484–1559) came from a little closer to home, Verona, but he, too, was drawn to Rome. The sack of that city in 1527 spurred them both to pack their bags. Sansovino moved to Venice and Sanmicheli back home. Both remained from then on in the service of the Republic. **Palladio** (1508–80) was from Padua – more about him later.

Sanmicheli's most important contribution to La Serenissima was the Palazzo Grimani (built 1557–59). The Republic's leaders kept him busy engineering defence works for the city and Venice's scattered possessions.

It was, however, Sansovino who dominated the scene in Venice. To him was entrusted the task of revamping the city's look and he had a hand in 15 buildings, among them the Zecca (the Mint), the Loggetta (on St Mark's Square), the Palazzo Dolfin-Manin on the Grand Canal, the Ca' Grande and the Chiesa di San Francesco della Vigna. Perhaps the most prominent testimony to Sansovino's work in Venice is his Libreria Nazionale Marciana (Biblioteca di San Marco), opposite the Palazzo Ducale (see the Gothic section earlier).

Quite a deal older than the others, Pietro Lombardo (1435–1515) was another out-of-towner. While he was chiefly a sculptor (see Sculpture later in this section), his latter years were occupied principally with building. One pleasing result was the Chiesa di Santa Maria dei Miracoli (1489). A few years earlier, he was also involved in the building of the Palazzo Dario, a cheerfully imaginative edifice topped by characteristically Venetian funnel chimneys. His Scuola di San Marco (built 1487–90) is a monumental but playful affair. In its fine marble facade, rounded arches, striking statuary and trompe l'oeil trickery compete for the eye's attention.

A unique Renaissance item is the Palazzo Contarini del Bovolo, built in 1499 by Giovanni Candi (died 1506). The gracious arches of the time are much in evidence, but the draw here is the inspired external spiral staircase.

Palladio Although Palladio (1508–80) was active in Venice, the greater concentration of his work is in and around Vicenza. Palladio's name has a far greater resonance for a wide audience than any of his contemporaries, such as Sansovino, largely because his classicism was later taken as a model by British and American neoclassicists. The White House in Washington DC owes much to Palladio.

It is for his **villas** in the Venetian hinterland that Palladio is best known. Of them, La Villa Rotonda (just outside Vicenza) is among the most famous. These villas were built for those well-to-do Venetians who had turned their backs on the sea and sought to consolidate their position on the mainland. They were conceived with a double role in mind – pleasure dome and control centre over agricultural estates.

Steeped in the classicism of Rome that had inspired a great deal of Renaissance architecture, Palladio produced buildings rich with columns and triangular pediments and occasionally with a central dome (La Rotonda). Palladio's version of Renaissance architecture is often described as 'archaeological' due to his unswerving recourse to antiquity for inspiration. For more on the villas, see the Excursions chapter later.

Palladio was made Venice's official architect on the death of Sansovino in 1570. His single greatest mark on the city was the Chiesa di San Giorgio Maggiore, on the island of the same name. Even in the distance, seen from St Mark's Square, its majesty cannot fail to impress the observer. It was preceded by its equally significant Chiesa del Redentore, on Giudecca, built as an offering to God in the hope of the city's deliverance from the plague.

It is probably no accident that Palladio received commissions to work his particular magic in these two relatively isolated corners of the city. Bereft of surroundings of any significance, these grand churches, with their weighty columns, high domes and strong classical facades, command respect – and are best contemplated at a distance. Part of their majesty lies in the rigorous eschewing of superfluous ornament. Inside San Giorgio Maggiore, the eye rests on an interplay of rounded arches buttressed by columns and pilasters – there is virtually no decoration.

The grandness of his churches does not by any means imply that Palladio's was a sluggish, ponderous style. His playfulness within the classical traditions that informed his thinking is perhaps best observed in Vicenza. The Palazzo della Ragione, in the heart of that city, is laced with great open porticoes that create an altogether different sensation, one of lightness within the dignity of a grand structure.

Palladio died before finishing many of his projects, including San Giorgio Maggiore. For their completion, we are largely indebted to Vincenzo Scamozzi (1552–1616), who faithfully carried out their designer's plans. Scamozzi did his own thing too. He designed the Procuratie Nuove in St Mark's Square (completed by Baldassare Longhena).

Baroque The 17th century in the Venetian building industry was dominated by **Baldassare Longhena** (1598–1682). A master of Baroque, which took to florid ornament in seeming reaction to what some plainly considered the austerity of the Renaissance,

Longhena cannot be said to have fallen for the most extreme of its decorative excesses.

His masterpiece is the Chiesa di Santa Maria della Salute, the great dome of which dominates the south-eastern end of the Grand Canal. An octagonal church, its classical lines are a reminder of Palladio, but the sumptuous external decoration, with phalanxes of statues and rich sculpture over the main entrance, shows where Longhena is headed. To see where he ended up, you only need to look at the facade of the Chiesa dell'Ospedaletto, north-east of St Mark's Square. You will see his imprint all over the city, even in the Ghetto, where he had a hand in the design of the two larger synagogues (the Schole Levantina and Spagnola).

Antonio Gaspari (c.1670–1730) was one of several less-outstanding architects to follow in Longhena's footsteps, albeit at a distance. He had a hand in the Ca' Pesaro.

18th Century Venice's last century of independence was something of a twilight period, although architectural activity, leaning by now towards neoclassicism, bubbled along. The style, to some minds a bit of a poor relation to the more inventive Renaissance investigation of the classical genre, was popular throughout Europe. One of the senior names of the period was **Giorgio Massari** (1686–1766). Inspired by Palladio, his more lasting works include the Chiesa dei Gesuati, the Palazzo Grassi and the completion of Ca' Rezzonico on the Grand Canal.

Giannantonio Selva (1753–1819) carried the neoclassical torch into the next century and the days of Napoleon. He is best remembered for the Teatro della Fenice (completed in 1792), damaged by fire in 1936 and then destroyed the same way in 1996.

To the Present Day Palladio frequently found himself up against the conservative habits of the town fathers. His plans for the Palazzo Ducale and for a new Rialto bridge were overruled. The attitude persists to this day, but not necessarily with the same happy results. A design for a magnificent building on the Grand Canal by Frank Lloyd Wright,

and Le Corbusier's plans for a hospital in the area of the ex-Macello Comunale in Cannaregio, are among many to have received the thumbs down.

This is not to say that absolutely nothing has been done. Probably the best known of Venice's modern architects was **Carlo Scarpa** (1906–78). He designed the entrance to the Istituto Universitario di Architettura di Venezia (IUAV) in Santa Croce and redesigned the inside of several museums, including the Gallerie dell'Accademia, the Museo Correr and Palazzo Querini-Stampalia. He also worked on pavilions for the Biennale in Castello from 1948 to 1978. Others to contribute to the Biennale include Studio BBPR, Francesco Cellini and James Stirling. Stirling's book pavilion is said to be the only example of British architecture in Italy.

Painting

Artists tend to be a peripatetic lot. A wealth of paintings by Venice's most gifted can be found in the city. But a great deal of their work was either produced in other cities or has found its way to distant collectors' homes and galleries.

Medieval In addition to the treasure chest of mosaics (see Veneto-Byzantine in the preceding Architecture section), some fairly pedestrian fresco painting was also used in Venetian churches – fragments remain in churches such as San Giovanni Decollato, San Nicolò dei Mendicoli, SS Apostoli and even St Mark's.

Il Trecento Painting's first real name in Venice was **Paolo Veneziano** (c.1300–62). In his earlier days it appears he was open to some exciting innovations in painting (Giotto was at work in nearby Padua in the first years of the 14th century). One example of this is his *Incoronazione della Vergine* (Coronation of the Virgin), now in the National Gallery of Art in Washington. Later on, however, he reverted to Byzantine type. Gold backgrounds predominated and his figures were bloodless and didactic. The *Madonna col Bambino* (Madonna and Child) is a perfect example. The almost expressionless face of the Virgin

Living in geometric bliss – a house in Burano

ROBERTO SONCIN GEROMETTA

Carving detail, Palazzo Ducale

JULIET COOMBE

Cock-a-hoop – a glittering glass mosaic from Murano

BETHUNE CARMICHAEL

Even Venetian lights have style.

OLIVIER CIRENDINI

Can you tell what it is yet? Painter on the Ponte dell'Accademia

Venice's Jewish Nuovo Ghetto

Take a break from the cultural stuff and join the beach bums at the Lido.

Chipping away at a wood relief

Only 20 more boats to go... cleaning the hull of a traditional gondola

Mary and the Christ child inside the almond are typical Eastern touches. This and several more of his works can be seen in the Gallerie dell'Accademia. He also painted the cover of the Pala d'Oro (a jewel-encrusted altarpiece) in St Mark's Basilica.

Others to toe the Byzantine line were Lorenzo Veneziano and Nicoletto Semitecolo. You can see some of Lorenzo's work, which shows a little more life than that of Paolo, in the Gallerie dell'Accademia. Semitecolo worked a good deal of the time in Padua, where he left behind works in the Duomo and the Chiesa degli Eremitani.

Gothic With **Gentile da Fabriano** (c.1370–1427) came a turning point in Venetian art. He had the travel bug and worked in many Italian cities, but if anyone can be said to have brought the so-called International (or Late) Gothic style to the lagoon city, it was probably da Fabriano. He worked on several frescoes in the Palazzo Ducale (itself a remarkably eclectic Gothic celebration – see the preceding Architecture section) that were subsequently lost. Without him, the work of people like Pisa's Pisanello (c.1380–1455) would have been unthinkable. Venetian painters directly inspired by da Fabriano include Jacobello del Fiore (died c.1439) and Michele Giambono (died c.1462), both of whom are represented in the Gallerie dell'Accademia. Some Giambono works can also be seen in the Museo Correr.

Early Renaissance You might have already guessed that, one way or another, Venice tended not to be in the artistic vanguard. Rather, influences from the outside (at first from the East, later from the West in the form of Gothic) served to stimulate local artists to contemplate the next step. It was little different in the transition from Gothic to the Renaissance (Il Rinascimento to the Italians).

Getting Noticed With the Renaissance came great change in the artist's station. In earlier periods (such as the Romanesque period in Western Europe and the contemporary period of Byzantine art in Venice and the East), artists generally remained anonymous. This

began slowly to change in the Gothic period, but it was really only with the arrival of the Renaissance that artists began to claim, and receive, individual recognition and even acclaim for their work.

In practice, the distinction we might make today between 'art' and 'craft' only now began to make itself felt, although painters continued to operate workshops in much the same way as the glass-blowers of **Murano**, or other craftsmen. But while glass-blowers remained largely anonymous (at least to later generations), the illustrious names of the Renaissance would remain forever branded in history's long memory.

Rising Tide The starburst of creativity that flowed forth from Renaissance Florence sooner or later had to wash over the lagoon defences to Venice. Padua, just 37km distant, served as a conduit for this artistic tide. If Paolo Uccello (who did a stint in Venice), Donatello and Filippo Lippi (both of whom worked long in Padua) and others formed the Florentine vanguard, Padua's **Andrea Mantegna** (1431–1506) was the connection between them and Venice. He never worked in Venice, but Venetian artists came to know him and his work.

Two Venetians straddling the abyss between Gothic and the Renaissance were **Jacopo Bellini** (c.1396–c.1470) and **Antonio Vivarini** (c.1415–c.1480). Both headed what would prove to be potent artistic families and presided over prolific workshops. (The business of painting was, in many respects, similar to any other artisanal craft. People ordered paintings and frescoes and workshops produced them – paintings attributed to masters were in fact often carried out by apprentices under the master's supervision.) You can see works by both artists in the Gallerie dell'Accademia. Vivarini left behind some works in the Frari too.

Bellini and Vivarini both clearly injected a growing sense of movement, emotion and depth into their work, but it was Mantegna who took the great steps and arrived with both palette and brush firmly entrenched in the latest fashion. He embraced use of perspective to create a sense of three dimensions and the depiction of the full array of human feelings.

All three artists knew each other and Vivarini worked for a while in Padua. It was his younger brother, Bartolomeo (c.1432–99), who picked up the baton from Mantegna and ran with it. Altarpieces by him can be seen in the churches of the Frari, San Giovanni in Bragora and SS Giovanni e Paolo, as well as the Gallerie dell'Accademia.

Carlo Crivelli (c.1430–c.1494) was born in Venice and attended both the Bellini and Vivarini workshops. He too ended up under the spell of Mantegna's work in Padua, but in 1457 was exiled and ended up in Le Marche. His work is at times a curious blend of the new Renaissance ethos and vestiges of a more Gothic rigidity. His *Madonna della Passione* (in Castelvecchio, Verona) is a good example.

The Bellini Boys A switch came with Jacopo Bellini's sons Giovanni (1432–1516) and Gentile (1429–1507). The latter had a crystal-clear eye for detail, evident in works such as *Processione a Piazza San Marco* (Procession to St Mark's Square), one of three paintings by him in the True Cross cycle, which can be viewed in Room *(Sala)* 20 of the Gallerie dell'Accademia. He was something of a specialist portraitist in his early career, too – the Turks even requested he visit Constantinople in 1479 to do Sultan Mehmet II's profile (now in London's National Gallery).

It was his little brother, however, who shone out above all his contemporaries. Giovanni went beyond what he had learned from Mantegna, and his entire career was marked by a constantly renewed search for innovation. The central figures in his more mature works betray the link with Mantegna by their great clarity, standing out from their landscape backdrops, however sweeping. But Bellini extracts greater variety in tone and colour, creating a softness and meditative quality largely missing in the harsher works of Mantegna. He moves further away from the allegorical stamp that still greatly dominated art at this stage. Later on in his career, he began to experiment more with oil paint in place of tempera (powdered pigments mixed with egg yolk and water), which would eventually be displaced by the new medium.

A great number of Giovanni Bellini's works are scattered around Italy, Europe and the USA, but you can see some in the Gallerie dell'Accademia, the Museo Correr and elsewhere. His *Pala di San Zaccaria* (1505), in the church of the same name, is a monumental work that shows he was not lost for answers to his younger rivals.

A New Generation Among these latter were Vittore Carpaccio (1460–1526), Cima da Conegliano (c.1459–c.1517), Giorgione (1477–1510), from Castelfranco, and Lorenzo Lotto (c.1480–1556).

Carpaccio was fascinated by Venetian court life and the pageantry of the city in his times, but his best-known works are narrative cycles (of the lives of Sant'Orsola, San Giorgio degli Schiavoni, Albanesi, Santo Stefano) painted for the Venetian schools. Check out his *Storie di Sant'Orsola* (History of St Ursula), nine works in all, in the Gallerie dell'Accademia. Perhaps more interesting for the observer today is the fantastical depiction of the Venetian-style background against which the story of the saint unfolds.

Cima da Conegliano was active in Venice from the 1480s. His work is a little more rigidly classical and less innovative than that of some of his contemporaries. Some is on view in the Gallerie dell'Accademia.

Giorgione, on the other hand, was quite another character. Although he is thought to have been a student of Bellini and may have met Leonardo da Vinci during the latter's stay in 1500, he did not follow the usual route of joining one of the art workshops to make his living. He wrote poetry and music. In his paintings, which cover a wide range of subjects, he breaks new ground in his manipulation of light and colour. *La Tempesta* (The Storm), in the Gallerie dell'Accademia, shows him painting without having first drawn his subject – a striking step into new territory at the time. Titian would later become his student and partner.

Lorenzo Lotto spent a good deal of his life moving around between Venice, Treviso, Bergamo and Le Marche. His was a vast palette, ranging from religious works through to portraits, but he never quite got the recognition that was perhaps his due and he died in poverty. In Venice he left a few pieces behind, such as the *Elemosina di Sant'Antonio* (St Anthony's Alms) in the Chiesa dei SS Giovanni e Paolo. The *Ritratto del Giovane Gentiluomo nel Suo Studio* (Portrait of a Young Gentleman in His Studio) is a striking painting now on view in the Gallerie dell'Accademia.

Other lesser artists worth looking out for are Marco Basaiti (c.1470–c.1530), Giovanni Mansueti and Antonio da Negroponte, who came to Venice from one of its colonies (Negroponte, Greece) in the second half of the 15th century. Some of their works are on display in the Gallerie dell'Accademia.

Late Renaissance Venice might have been a little slow to catch on to the flowering of artistic innovation that came with the Renaissance, but the age of the Bellini brothers was but a launch pad for still greater achievement in the lagoon city.

Titian the Titan One reading of Lotto's departure from Venice in 1542 was that the town wasn't big enough for him and his closest rival, Titian (c.1490–1576), known in Italian as Tiziano Vecellio.

Titian is an all-time great, a 'sun amidst the stars', as one admirer put it. Born at Pieve di Cadore into a family of artists, he was a pupil of Giovanni Bellini. In his early years he worked with Giorgione, and experts have had great difficulty in working out which of the two did what in the early years of the 16th century. They first collaborated on frescoes at the Fondaco dei Tedeschi, all since lost except for some fragments that are now on display in the Ca' d'Oro. Even after Giorgione's death in 1510, Titian continued for a while to work under the spell of his former master.

Titian's was a poetic approach to painting, full of verve and high drama. By 1514, when he completed his allegorical *Amor Sacro e Profano* (Sacred and Profane Love; now in Rome's Galleria Borghese), Titian had established himself as one of the leading artists of his time. Confirmation came in 1518 with the unveiling of his monumental *Assunta* (Assumption) in the Chiesa di Santa Maria Gloriosa dei Frari. Hanging in a place of honour above the high altar, it was quickly seen as a work of genius.

It was barely the beginning. Titian's fame spread across the peninsula and Europe. Commissions came from left and right, keeping him busy until his final days. His oeuvre falls broadly into three categories: portraiture, religious paintings and mythological subjects. His images of the great and the good are legion. The Habsburg emperor Charles V was so enamoured of his likeness that he knighted the artist – a rare honour. He also made sure his son and successor, Philip II, was immortalised by the genius' brush. Pope Paul III, the dukes of Urbino and Francis I of France were also among his many subjects.

Considering his output, not an awful lot of Titian's works can be seen in Venice. Apart from the Frari, they can be found in the churches of Santa Maria della Salute, the Gesuiti and San Salvatore. Those works alone are demonstration of the movement, humanity and often startling colour that distinguish his works. In the Gallerie dell' Accademia are his last strokes on *Pietà*, intended for his burial chapel but actually finished after his death by Palma il Giovane.

Tintoretto It seems churlish to speak of the likes Jacopo Robusti, better known as Tintoretto (1518–94), and Veronese (1528–88; aka Paolo Caliari) as though they were in any way 'lesser' painters. Masters of the late Renaissance Venetian school, they had the 'misfortune' to be at work at much the same time as Titian, who would have been a hard act to follow anywhere or any time.

Tintoretto was, however, a proud and successful painter who established a singular reputation. His children carried on the business of his workshop after his death. He is now regarded as the greatest of all Mannerists in Italy, going beyond Michelangelo's lead in this respect and is considered to be right up there with El Greco in Spain. Mannerism is one of those twilight phases in the history of art, falling between the splendours of the late Renaissance and the excesses that would come with Baroque in the 17th century. It is characterised in painting by a yearning to break with convention and a certain wilful capriciousness in the use of light and colour and the depiction of human figures.

In El Greco's work, the move away from the Renaissance could not be clearer. In the case of Tintoretto, it is more subtle and restrained. He was heavily influenced by Michelangelo and may have visited Rome. In his earlier stages at least, Tintoretto makes some remarkably similar choices to those of El Greco in terms of colour (a predominance of muted blues and crimsons). El Greco studied in Venice in 1560, so the two may well have had some shared experience.

Tintoretto was fascinated by architecture and sculpture, reflected in his love for creating three-dimensional panoramas much in the style of a stage set. A telling example is his *Crocifissione* (Crucifixion), in the Sala dell'Albergo of the Scuola Grande di San Rocco. Another is the *Trafugamento del Corpo di San Marco* (Stealing of St Mark's Body) in the Gallerie dell'Accademia.

The latter painting shows as clearly as any his mastery of the swift brushstroke, which lent an effervescence to his figures that further removes him from earlier Renaissance standards. In contrast, he is decisive in his use of light, or rather the lack of it. A great many of his later paintings seem buried in darkness, with shafts of light used to illuminate only the key characters and scenes.

The place to gorge yourself on the best of late Tintoretto is the **Scuola Grande di San Rocco**. He dedicated the last 23 years of his life to bedecking it with more than 50 paintings. He is also well represented in the Palazzo Ducale. His *Paradiso* (Paradise), in the Sala del Maggior Consiglio, is a work of extraordinary complexity. We have to assume, given the amount he had on his plate with the San Rocco project, that much of the material in the Palazzo Ducale was overseen by Tintoretto but executed by his workshop. Some fine pieces by him are also housed in the Gallerie dell'Accademia.

Veronese Paolo Veronese was also busy in the Palazzo Ducale. Born in Verona (hence the sobriquet), he spent the last 30 years of his life in Venice, which likes to claim him as one of its own. His first jobs there were decoration in the Palazzo Ducale and painting the ceiling of the Libreria Nazionale Marciana across the square. He is, above all, remembered for the grandeur and sheer colourful spectacle of many of his frescoes and paintings. Initially influenced by the trend towards Mannerism, he was later increasingly attracted by certain aspects of architecture; he decorated Palladio's Villa Maser, and was pushed towards a more serene harmony in the composition of scenes by the latter's interpretations of classical building.

He also liked to have all sorts of characters in his paintings, something that brought him uncomfortably close to the Holy Inquisition. His *Ultima Cena* (Last Supper), done for the Dominicans in the Chiesa dei SS Giovanni e Paolo, included some figures the Inquisitors found rather impious, including a dog and a jester. It is unlikely Veronese's defence of freedom of artistic expression won the day. The Inquisition was not viewed in a kindly way by the leaders of La Serenissima and so it decided on the face-saving solution of proposing another title for the painting, *Convito in Casa di Levi* (Feast in the House of Levi). It can be seen in the Gallerie dell'Accademia.

Among the masterpieces of Veronese's later years are *Virtù* (Virtue) and *Allegorie di Venezia* (Venetian Allegories), on the ceiling of the Sala del Collegio (Palazzo Ducale), and the *Trionfo di Venezia* (Venice's Triumph), in the Sala del Maggior Consiglio. They are riots of festive colour. Interestingly, in the last works of his life, he tended to tone down the colour, slipping back into softer hues more in line with Venetian tradition (itself surely influenced by the natural light prevailing in the lagoon city).

In his lifetime, Veronese was assisted by his brother Benedetto and later his two sons, Gabriele and Carletto, who maintained the family business after his death.

Bringing up the Rear Other artists of this epoch worth bearing in mind include **Palma il Vecchio** (1480–1528), originally from

Cremona, and his grandson **Palma il Giovane** (1544–1628). Various works have been attributed to the former, but the young Palma was more prolific. He finished Titian's final work, the *Pietà*.

Another busy family were the Da Pontes, also known as the **Bassano** because they were born in Bassano del Grappa (of liquor fame). Francesco Bassano il Vecchio worked in the first half of the 16th century. Four of his descendants stayed in the family trade: Jacopo (1517–92), Francesco Bassano il Giovane (c.1549–92), Leandro (1557–1622) and Gerolamo (1566–1621). Of the lot, Jacopo stands out. Although fully a part of the Venetian school, he actually lived most of his life in Bassano. A handful of his works is on display at the Gallerie dell'Accademia.

A Sorry Century The 17th century brought the age of Baroque in European art. It has been getting bad press from one quarter or another ever since. A celebration of curvaceous and gaudy over-embellishment, it is not so simple to judge whether works produced in this century and the first half of the next fall into the category of Baroque or of rococo (see the following section).

Compared with earlier, more illustrious days, the directory of important artists in Venice at this time makes brief reading. **Sebastiano Ricci** (1659–1734), from Belluno, and his nephew **Marco** (1676–1730) were both successful, winning commissions from all over Europe. They travelled and worked extensively in England, where many of their paintings remain.

Last Flash of Glory The 18th century was marked by the steady decline of the once-proud Venetian Republic. In the sphere of the arts, a handful of greats kept the flag flying before the end finally came.

Rococo & the Tiepolos Gian Battista Piazzetta (1683–1754) paved the way into the new century – the Republic's last. This rococo painter had a particular eye for the manipulation of light and chiaroscuro effects. In his later career, he dedicated more effort to the depiction of secular scenes and figures.

In 1750 he founded the art school that would later become the Accademia di Venezia.

Venice's greatest artist of the century and one of the uncontested kings of rococo was **Giambattista Tiepolo** (1696–1770). He lived most of his life in the lagoon city and preferred to send works which had been commissioned abroad to their purchasers by coach rather than execute them *in situ*. Two exceptions were his stay in Würzburg, Germany, in the 1750s, and his move to Madrid in 1762, where he remained until his death in spite of the stuffy nobility's ambivalent reaction to his work there, above all in Madrid's Palacio Nacional.

Tiepolo initially followed Piazzetta's lead and indulged in furious chiaroscuro games, relying on them to convey the passions of his subjects. He soon abandoned the method, preferring to infuse his work with vigorous colour. Among his early masterpieces are the cycle of biblical stories and the *Caduta degli Angeli Ribelli* (Fall of the Rebel Angels) painted in the Palazzo Arcivescovile (Archbishop's Palace) in Udine in 1726.

Commissions poured in, from Milan, Bergamo (he decorated the Cappella Colleoni there), Germany, Sweden and Russia. You can see some of his work in the Chiesa dei Scalzi, the Gesuati and Ca' Rezzonico. The Gallerie dell'Accademia has a fair smattering of paintings, too.

His son **Giandomenico Tiepolo** (1727–1804) worked with him to the end, returning to Venice after his father's death. Some caricatures of his, now housed in the Ca' Rezzonico, presage the Spaniard Goya and the Frenchman Daumier.

The Big Picture Antonio Canal, better known as **Canaletto** (1697–1768), became the leading figure of the so-called *vedutisti* (landscape artists), quite a different genre from his rococo contemporaries. It is hardly surprising that he went down that road, given his background as a set painter for opera and theatre.

His almost painfully detailed *vedute* (views) of Venice, filled with light, were a kind of rich-man's postcard. Many of the well-to-do visitors to 18th-century Venice took home with them such a souvenir. Canaletto was backed by the English collector John Smith, who lived most of his life in Venice, bringing Canaletto a steady English clientele. This led to a 10-year stint in London, where Canaletto was also busy with the brush. His success with foreigners was such that few of his paintings can be seen in Venice today.

As Canaletto approached his twilight years and his output dwindled, **Francesco Guardi** (1712–93) stepped in to fill the gap in the market. He had earlier worked with his elder brother, the Vienna-born Giovanni Antonio Guardi (1699–1760), on religious and other paintings. As Francesco's success in the veduta field grew, the Republic increasingly turned to him to paint official records of important events, such as the visit of Pope Pius VI.

Although in his early landscapes his reliance on Canaletto's example is all too clear, he soon developed a dreamier, hazier style. Instead of a painstaking documentation of the city's many faces, which in any case was no longer in vogue either in Venice or abroad, Guardi opted for a more interpretative approach, his buildings almost shimmering in the reflected light of the lagoon. Popular with foreign art-buyers, Guardi's paintings are to be found scattered in galleries and private collections around the world. One of the few of his major works in Venice is the *Incendio di San Marcuola* (Fire at San Marcuola), in the Gallerie dell'Accademia.

Quite a different story is that of **Rosalba Carriera** (1675–1757), one of the few Venetian women to succeed as a painter. As a portraitist she was much in demand not only in her home city but, thanks in part to the efforts of John Smith, across Europe.

19th & 20th Centuries Even before the fall of La Repubblica Serenissima in 1797, the art scene had decayed, much as everything else had. It may seem a little brutal, but the end of the 18th century essentially also meant the end of Venetian art.

A handful of dim lights flickered in the artistic void. Ippolito Caffi (1809–66) was a landscape artist of talent, while Francesco Hayez (1791–1882) embarked on his career in Venice but ended up spending most of his working life in Milan. He began in a strict neoclassical vein, but as the century wore on succumbed to the more sentimental feelings of the times and their artistic reflection, Romanticism.

Federico Zandomeneghi (1841–1917) received his formal education at the Accademia di Venezia, but he didn't exactly set the art world on fire. In any case, he ended up in Paris, where socialising with Impressionists did little to alter substantially the realist nature of his work, such as it is.

Gino Rossi (1884–1947), whose career took him from Symbolism to a growing interest in Cubism, was one of Venice's biggest names in the first half of the 20th century. He frequently exhibited at the city's pre-WWI art expos in the Ca' Pesaro.

One of the few noteworthy names to emerge since WWII is **Emilio Vedova** (born 1919). Setting out as an Expressionist, he joined the Corrente movement of artists, who opposed the trends in square-jawed Fascist art. Their magazine was shut down in 1940. In postwar years, Vedova veered more towards the abstract. Some of his works can be seen in Rome's Galleria Nazionale d'Arte Moderna.

Among young artists hard at work today is Udine-born Mauro Eraldo, whose work has had some success in Italy and abroad (mainly the USA). Mestre-based Tiziana Piccioni has a highly personal style, proudly declaring she has stayed clear of all art schools. Rossella Girardini also lives on the mainland, in Marghera. A lot of her work has Venice as its subject. She has followed the Croatian naive school, inspired by painters such as Zacero and Generalic.

Sculpture

For some reason, sculpture and its creators did not achieve such prominence in Venice as in other Italian cities. That's not to say sculptors were not active here, though. It's just that their work, usually in the form of adornment of the city's great houses and public buildings, has remained mostly anonymous.

Romanesque to Renaissance While the mosaic was the dominant Byzantine element in decoration from the 11th to the 13th centuries, sculptors were not idle. The interior of St Mark's Basilica was fully laden with sculpture and the main entrance represents one of the finest of the few displays of Romanesque sculpture in the city.

Some of Venice's best Gothic sculpture is represented in the tombs of the doges Michele Morosini and Marco Corner in the Chiesa dei SS Giovanni e Paolo. The latter was done by a Pisan, Nino Pisano (c.1300–68).

As the Renaissance blossomed in Venice, sculpture remained something of a poor cousin next to the outpourings on walls, ceilings and canvas. Again, the funerary statues of doges are among the most important single pieces. The Lombard **Pietro Lombardo** (1435–1515) spent most of his working life in Venice. Among his more notable efforts are the monuments to three of Venice's leaders: Pasquale Malipiero, Nicolò Marcello and Pietro Mocenigo, all in the Chiesa dei SS Giovanni e Paolo. Pietro's sons Antonio and Tullio carried on the family business. Antonio tended to follow in papa's footsteps, but Tullio was a little more independent. His more interesting sculptures are no longer in Venice.

To the Present Day A handful of notable sculptors were at work in the 17th century, including Orazio Marinali (1643–1720) and Andrea Brustolon (1660–1732), the latter in particular known for his wood and furniture carving.

Born in Possagno near Treviso, **Antonio Canova** (1757–1822) was the most prominent sculptor to emerge in late-18th-century Italy. He debuted in Venice, but by 1780 he had shifted to Rome, where he ended up doing most of his work. A few of his early forays, such as *Dedalo e Icaro* (Daedalus and Icarus), remain in Venice, in the Museo Correr. If you really want to get an idea of his work, head for Possagno itself (see the Excursions chapter).

Literature
The Early Days As has already been hinted, Venice's literary heritage is not among the most brilliant in Italy. Relatively few Venetians have received more than passing recognition in the pantheon of national greats.

One of the first writers to cast an eye over the affairs of the Venetians was Cassiodorus (AD 490–583). In the employ of Theodoric, he was for a while active at the highest levels of the imperial administration and based in Ravenna. It is from him that our earliest descriptions of the lagoon city come – to him, the Venetians' houses seemed 'like seabirds' nests, half on sea and half on land'.

Middle Ages to the Renaissance In the Middle Ages, education was limited largely to private classes, among them philosophy sessions given in Rialto and financed by wealthy families.

Francesco Petrarca (Petrarch; 1304–74), one of the 'big three' behind the birth of literary Italian in Florence, came to live in Venice in the latter part of his life. He had already gained considerable fame for his sonnets in Italian, although he continued to write much in Latin as well. He encouraged instruction in Latin, but his humanistic ideals and belief in the need to spread and deepen education were not universally welcome in a still comparatively austere city. Only in the century following his death, as the city grew richer, did the noble classes begin to take a closer interest in learning.

One of the earliest Venetian writers of any importance was **Leonardo Giustinian** (1388–1446). A member of the Consiglio dei Dieci and author of various tracts in Latin, he is remembered for his *Canzonette* and *Strambotti*. They are a mix of popular verses wrought in an elegant Venetian-influenced Italian. Although he used Italian, Giustinian resisted the Tuscan hegemony established a generation before by the likes of Dante, Petrarch and Boccaccio.

By the time he died, humanist education had caught on. Professors of Greek were being invited to Venice to instruct students, more and more of whom were now able to study the seminal Greek philosophers in the original. This growing interest in what might be called a 'liberal education' encouraged another hobby among the well read – history.

Of the several figures who embarked on this kind of project, Marin Sanudo (1466–1536) left behind probably the most detailed account of early Renaissance Venice in his 58-volume *Diarii* (Diaries), written in Venetian dialect. Sanudo was not, to his lasting disappointment, appointed official historian of the Republic.

Era of the Printing Press That role fell to **Pietro Bembo** (1470–1547). His *Historia Veneta*, written in Latin and translated into Italian, was not, however, his most lasting work. In his *Rime* (Rhymes) and other works he defined the concept of platonic love and, above all, gave lasting form to Italian grammar.

Bembo also worked with Aldo Manuzio on a project that would help revolutionise the spread of learning and literature. Manuzio arrived in Venice, where he would remain, in 1490 and set up his Aldine Press. During the following years, he and his family became the most important publishing dynasty in all Europe. He produced the first printed editions of many Latin and Greek classics, along with a series of relatively cheap volumes of literature, including Bembo's *Cose Volgari* (Ordinary Things). In all, the Manuzio family are thought to have printed 1000 editions.

Domenico Venier (1517–82), virtually paralysed by illness and confined to his home, is viewed by many as a faithful follower of Bembo, although his poetic style was quite a deal more experimental. Although barely known now, he was considered one of the best poets of his time. The southern Italian Torquato Tasso, one of the great names of Italian poetry, humbly submitted his works to Venier for his appraisal before publishing.

In **Paolo Sarpi** (1552–1623), Venice found a powerful defender of the Republic and its only philosopher of note. A Servite friar, he had a distinguished career as a diplomat and theologian, travelling extensively throughout Italy before returning to Venice in 1588. He was one of the earliest proponents of the separation of Church and State, something that only came to pass in Italy in 1985. In 1606 he became the voice of Venice after Pope Paul V placed the city under an interdict (see the earlier History section) and Sarpi launched a campaign calling for numerous reforms of the Church. His ideas found their ultimate expression in the *Istoria del Concilio Tridentino* (History of the Council of Trent), considered a masterpiece of clear, unadorned Italian prose and translated into Latin, English, German and French in his lifetime.

A Ray of Gold Venice cannot be said to have enjoyed a golden age of literature, but a flash of glory came with the playwright **Carlo Goldoni** (1707–93). His stormy life saw him moving around from one city to another, at times practising law but dedicating most of his energies to the theatre. From 1748 in particular, the prolific playwright produced dramas and comedies at an extraordinary rate.

He single-handedly changed the face of Italian theatre, abandoning the commedia dell'arte, with its use of masks, a certain rigidity in storytelling and concentration on standard characters. This form of theatre had dominated the stages and public squares of Italy, and to a large extent France, for the previous couple of centuries, but Goldoni would have none of it. Instead, he advocated more realistic characters and more complex plots. *Pamela* (1750) was the first play to dispense with masks altogether.

Some of his most enduring works came during the 1750s and 60s. Among the best known are *La Locandiera* (The Housekeeper), *I Rusteghi* (The Tyrants, written in Venetian dialect) and *I Malcontenti* (The Malcontents). Not everyone agreed with his ideas on theatre and, feeling the heat from some of his adversaries in Venice, he decided to shift to Paris in 1762. It was not an entirely happy move. With the exception of *Il Ventaglio* (The Fan), little of great note came out of his Paris years, which were mostly spent on writing memoirs. Overtaken by the French Revolution, he lost his pension and died in penury.

Goldoni by far overshadowed the competition. **Giorgio Baffo** (1694–1768) is known above all for his rather risqué dialect verse (he was a pal of Casanova and particularly enamoured of the female behind), while **Francesco Gritti** (1740–1811) satirised the decadent Venetian aristocracy. The bulk of the latter's work is collected in *Poesie in Dialetto Veneziano* (Poetry in the Venetian Dialect).

19th Century to the Present Day A pale successor to Goldoni on the boards was **Giacinto Gallina** (1852–97), who wrote mostly in dialect. One of his last works, *La Famegia del Santolo*, was considered a masterpiece of realist theatre.

In 1963 a Venetian business association inaugurated the **Campiello** prize (won that year by Turin's Primo Levi for his *La Tregua*), which has become one of the country's most prestigious literary awards.

Among several scribblers at work today, **Paolo Barbaro** (a self-confessed Venetian by adoption) has taken the Campiello prize three times. His books tend to have Venice as their theme or character and make interesting reading. In *Venezia – La Città Ritrovata* (Venice – the City Rediscovered) he struggles to come to terms with the wintry lagoon city again after several years' absence. Emerging on the literary scene is the Venetian teacher and writer, **Claudia Vio**, whose short stories, *La Vocazione delle Donne*, explore the inner lives of women alone.

Music

A handful of Italy's great musicians hailed from Venice, which was also the first European city to throw opera open to a wide public by establishing public opera houses in the first half of the 17th century.

Renaissance, Baroque & Classical A native of Cannaregio, **Andrea Gabrieli** (1510–86) was a student of the great Flemish composer Adriaan Willaert at St Mark's Basilica. Some attribute the invention of the madrigal to Willaert. On his return to Venice in 1564 after considerable travel abroad, Gabrieli became an organist at the basilica and dedicated himself to writing both gracious madrigals and large-scale choral and instrumental works for affairs of Church and State. The work for which he is principally remembered is his *Magnificat* for three choirs and orchestra.

Andrea's nephew Giovanni (1556–1612) joined him as an organist in 1584 and specialised in the composition of liturgical music, some of it choral and some of it instrumental. The bulk of his work was published in two books known as the *Sacrae Symphoniae*.

The greatest musical name to come out of Venice was **Antonio Vivaldi** (1678–1741). A gifted violinist from an early age, he completed his first important compositions in 1711. By the time he died, he had left a vast repertory behind him. Some 500 concertos have come down to us today. He was not simply prolific, but innovative, perfecting the three-movement concerto form and introducing other novelties that allowed greater room for virtuoso displays. Surely his best-known concerto is *Le Quattro Stagioni* (The Four Seasons). Although instrumental works were his forte, he also wrote operas and, in his earlier days, sacred vocal music. For all the fame he enjoys today, Vivaldi struggled to make a decent living. Much of his music might have been lost to us if collections had not been maintained in Turin and Dresden (Germany).

A near contemporary much overshadowed by the genius of Vivaldi was **Tomaso Albinoni** (1671–1750). Albinoni was something of a dilettante who nevertheless produced a small body of exquisite music. Notable is the *Sinfonie e Concerti a 5*.

Marcello Benedetto (1686–1739) was a comparatively minor figure in the world of Venetian music. A member of the Quarantia and at one time governor of Pola in Istria (Croatia), he dabbled in music as a sideline. His only significant work was *Estro Poeticoarmonico*, a vocal and instrumental interpretation of the first 50 psalms.

Opera The combination of music and drama is as old as classical Greek theatre, but opera in the sense we understand it today was born in Italy in the latter half of the 16th century. Giulio Caccini (1550–1618) and Jacopo Peri (1561–1633) were among the first composers to try out and develop this form of entertainment in Florence. These composers, together with other intellectuals, frequented salons in Florence to discuss and perform their work. An occasional visitor was **Claudio Monteverdi** (1567–1643). Born in Cremona, he cut his teeth as a composer at the court of the Gonzaga family in Mantova. His opera *Orfeo* (Orpheus; 1607) has been commonly acclaimed as the first great opera ever presented. Monteverdi's relationship with the Gonzagas was not a happy one, so it is hardly surprising that he snapped up Venice's offer to make him music director at St Mark's Basilica in 1613.

Here he sank himself into composing church music, not only for the basilica but for elsewhere in the city. There was little interest in opera in Venice at this point, so he intermittently returned to Mantova to stage new operas, developing his musical theories. In opera, Monteverdi increasingly sought to portray real characters and reflect human emotion in the music he composed. As he grew older, his work acquired a poise and majesty missing in his more passionate earlier works.

Up until 1637, opera and most chamber music had been the preserve of the noble classes, performed in private session for a privileged audience. This now changed in Venice. The city Monteverdi had adopted, and where he would die six years later, threw open the doors of the first public opera houses. As the only composer with any real experience in the genre, the elderly Monteverdi set himself to the task of producing material for the new houses. Perhaps his two greatest surviving works emerged at this time: *Il Ritorno di Ulisse al suo Paese* (The Return of Ulysses to his Country) and *L'Incoronazione di Poppea* (The Coronation of Poppea). Some have labelled these the first two works of modern opera. In each, Monteverdi created an astonishing range of plot and subplot, with strong characterisation and powerful music. Although he was not Venetian, the city liked to consider him one of its own – he was buried with honours in the Frari.

A singer at St Mark's under Monteverdi's direction, **Pier Francesco Cavalli** (1602–76),

went on to become the outstanding Italian composer of opera of the 17th century. He wrote 42 operas, which in his day were acclaimed as much for the splendour of the costumes and sets used as for the brilliance of his music and librettos.

Baldassare Galuppi (1706–84) opted for the lighter touch and in so doing gave birth to a new genre, the *opera buffa* – comic opera. Although he composed more serious material and instrumental works, it was for pieces like *Il Filosofo di Campagna* (The Country Philosopher) that he achieved widespread popularity.

Venice also likes to lay some claim to **Domenico Cimarosa** (1749–1801), despite the fact that he spent most of his life in Naples and travelled widely. Cimarosa continued the Italian tradition of opera buffa, producing his masterpiece, *Il Matrimonio Segreto* (The Secret Marriage), in Vienna in 1792. He did some work in Venice, too, but the city's main boast on this score is that he died there (in a building on Campo Sant' Angelo, in the Sestiere di San Marco – you can read the plaque there).

SOCIETY & CONDUCT
Dos & Don'ts

In Venice, as elsewhere in Italy, the locals take a good deal more care about their dress and appearance than many outsiders consider absolutely necessary. In some cases, however, those outsiders seem to abandon any norms they might usually adhere to at home as soon as they hit the holiday trail. Leaving aside the sartorial spectacle of the loud-shirts-and-shorts brigade, there are those who seem to think walking around with precious little on is the only way to fly. In the streets, locals will hardly bat an eyelid (*ah, questi turisti* – ah, these tourists – you may hear them sigh), but you should try to pick up your act a little in restaurants or when going out.

Most churches (including St Mark's Basilica) will not allow you entry if you are deemed to be inadequately clothed. No-one's suggesting you bring your Sunday best along, but a little common sense and sensitivity go a long way.

The standard form of greeting is the handshake. Kissing on both cheeks is generally reserved for people who already know one another. There will always be exceptions to these rules, so the best thing on being introduced to locals is probably not to launch your lips in anyone's general direction unless you are pretty sure they are expected. If this is the case, a light brushing of cheeks will do.

RELIGION

As elsewhere in Italy, **Roman Catholicism** is the dominant religion, but Venice and its people have traditionally viewed the Church with some nonchalance. Venice clashed with the Vatican on several occasions during the life of the Republic, brushing aside papal bans and interdicts with supreme indifference.

For a long time, La Serenissima was also a rare haven of religious tolerance. Although its Jews were squashed into what was known as the Ghetto (for more on this, see Itinerary I under the Sestiere di Cannaregio section in the Things to See & Do chapter), they had a reasonable degree of autonomy in business and were free to practise their faith. After the fall of Constantinople, a wave of Greek Orthodox refugees arrived in Venice and were also accommodated (their parish church was San Giorgio dei Greci, in Castello). The Armenians, too, were made welcome here.

Only when the '1929 Lateran Treaty between the Vatican and the Italian state was modified in 1985 was Catholicism dropped as the state religion. Still, up to 85% of Italians profess to be Catholic, and this proportion probably holds for Venice too.

LANGUAGE

There are 58 million speakers of Italian in Italy; half a million in Switzerland, where Italian is one of the official languages; and 1.5 million speakers in France, Slovenia and Croatia. As a result of migration, Italian is also spoken in the USA, Argentina, Brazil and Australia. In addition, Venice has its own dialect – Venessian (see the boxed text 'Venice's Other Tongue' in the Language chapter).

Although many Italians speak some English because they study it at school, any effort to speak Italian is generally appreciated. Staff at most hotels, *pensioni* (small hotels) and restaurants in Venice usually speak a little English.

For more information on Italian, a list of useful words and phrases and a food glossary, see the Language chapter at the back of this book.

Facts for the Visitor

WHEN TO GO

Venice, like any other of the great tourist centres in Italy, is at its worst in high summer. The whole world seems to think this a good time to be crawling around here, but it is cramped, hot and sticky. Mosquitoes can be a problem, too. Venetians mostly head for the hills at this time (which from Venice means quite a deal of running) and everything seems even more expensive than usual.

Other peak periods include Christmas, Easter, Carnevale time (around the end of February) and during the Mostra del Cinema (late August to September). Despite the difficulties of finding lodging and the usual problems associated with saturation tourism, the splendour of Carnevale (see Public Holidays & Special Events later in this chapter) warrants an effort.

The most pleasant time of year in Venice is from late March into May. The clear spring days are delightful and the hordes have yet to reach tsunami proportions (maybe Venice is sinking because of the combined weight of all its visitors), although May weekends tend to be busy with Italian tourists. Next choice is in the wake of summer. September is the best bet in terms of weather, but October is quieter.

Winter can be unpleasantly cold and this is when flooding is at its most regular (November and December are particularly bad, as rainfall is often heavy). That said, if you get lucky with the weather, it can be an enchanting time to be here. When the sky is clear, that pale winter blue helps bring out the softest tones and colour in the city's buildings. And it doesn't happen often, but seeing Venice under snow is the stuff of fairy tales! Mid-January to early March is the window of opportunity. Most Europeans are exhausted and broke after Christmas/New Year silliness and unwilling to use up holiday time in a wintry city. Consequently, hotel and restaurant proprietors are on their best price behaviour and some extraordinary deals on air fares can be had.

ORIENTATION

What one might think of as the Greater Venice Area is an odd beast. As you approach from other points in Italy, you reach Mestre, the rather humdrum industrial town that spreads inland from Venice's protective lagoon, the Laguna Veneta. Its southern half is occupied by Porto Marghera, where the petro-chemical plants and heavy shipping docks are. Increasingly the 'life' of the city is here. The SS11 highway and the train line pass through Mestre and cross a 5km bridge, Ponte della Libertà (Liberty Bridge), south-east to Venice proper, which is known to the locals as the *centro storico* (historic centre).

Venice is built on 117 small islands and has some 150 canals and 409 bridges. Only three bridges cross the Grand Canal (Canal Grande): the Ponte di Rialto, the Ponte dell'Accademia and the Ponte degli Scalzi.

Stretching away to the north and south are the shallow waters of the Laguna Veneta, dotted by what seems a crumbling mosaic of islands, islets and rocks. Among them, Murano, Burano and Torcello are all of interest and lie to the north-east. Acting as a breakwater to the east, the long and slender Lido di Venezia stretches some 10km south-west, followed by another similarly narrow island, Pellestrina, which reaches down to the sleepy town of Chioggia. The latter marks where the mainland closes off the lagoon to the south.

The city is divided into six *sestieri* (quarters): San Marco, Dorsoduro, San Polo, Santa Croce, Cannaregio and Castello. These town divisions date back to 1171. In the east, the islands of San Pietro and Sant' Elena, largely ignored by visitors, are attached to Castello by two and three bridges respectively.

Main Transport Terminals

Marco Polo Airport (Map 1) lies just east of Mestre, about 12km by road from Venice. Some flights land at a small airport just outside Treviso, about 50km north of Venice.

The Stazione di Santa Lucia train station (Map 3) is located in the north-west of town, virtually at the end of the Ponte della Libertà. The mainland Mestre station (Map 11) is a 10-minute ride north-west.

The bus station (Map 3) is on the opposite (south) side of the Grand Canal in Piazzale Roma. All local, regional and international buses leave from here. This is also one of the places where you have to leave your vehicle (the other is Tronchetto, just to the west) if you drive in.

You can get around the city by *vaporetto* (ferry) and *traghetto* (commuter gondola) or on foot. You'll find yourself doing a lot of the latter. For transport information, see the Getting Around chapter.

To walk from the train station to St Mark's Square (Piazza San Marco; Map 5) along the main thoroughfare (the first part is called the Rio Terrà Lista di Spagna) will take a good 30 minutes – follow the signs to San Marco. From San Marco, as the square and surrounding area are generally referred to, routes to other main areas, such as the Rialto and the Ponte dell'Accademia, are signposted but can be confusing, particularly in the Dorsoduro and San Polo areas.

A Street by Any Other Name

If you have travelled elsewhere in Italy and got to grips with common street terminology, abandon all hope ye who enter here. Why? Well, Venice always thought of itself as something quite apart from the rest of the peninsula and seemingly this applied even to street naming. Present-day terms for the different sorts of highways and byways go back to the 11th century.

Of course, the waterways are not streets at all. The main ones are called *canale*, while the bulk of them are called *rio*. Where a rio has been filled in, it becomes a *rio terrà* or *rio terà*.

What would be called a *via* (street) anywhere else in Italy is, in Venice, a *calle*. A street beside a canal is called a *fondamenta*. A *ruga* or *rughetta* is a smaller street flanked by houses and shops, while those called *salizzada* (sometimes spelled with one 'z') were among the first streets to be paved. A *ramo* is a tiny side lane, often connecting two bigger streets. A *corte* is a small dead-end street or courtyard. A quay is a *riva*, and where a street passes under a building (something like an extended archway), it is called a *sotoportego*. A *piscina* is not a swimming pool, but a one-time little lake of motionless water later filled in.

The only square in Venice called a *piazza* is San Marco – all the others are called *campo* (except for the bus station area, called Piazzale Roma). The small version is a *campiello*. Occasionally you come across a *campazzo*. On maps you may see the following abbreviations:

Calle – C, Cl	Fondamenta – F, Fond, Fondam
Campo – Cpo	Palazzo – Pal
Corte – Cte	Salizzada – Sal, Salizz

Street Numbering

Confused? You will be. Venice also has its own style of street numbering. Instead of a system based on individual streets, each *sestiere* (district) has a long series of numbers. For instance, a hotel might give its address as San Marco 4687, which doesn't seem to help much. This system of numbering was actually introduced by the Austrians in 1841.

Because the sestieri are fairly small, wandering around and searching out the number is technically feasible and sometimes doesn't take that long. But there is precious little apparent logic to the run of numbers, so frustration is never far away. Most streets are named, so where possible we provide street names as well as the sestiere number throughout the guide. Even where this is not the case, using the maps at the back of this book in conjunction with the sestiere numbers should clear up any mysteries. See Maps on the next page.

The most entertaining signs are those point-ing to the left and the right.

MAPS

You should be able to get by with the maps in this book, but some of those on sale are also worthwhile investments. The free one handed out by the tourist office is next to useless.

Whichever map you buy, you will find inconsistencies. The *Venezianizzazione* (Venetianisation) of street names has cre-ated more problems than it could ever have solved. Pretty much all maps seem to take a haphazard approach to using Italian, Venet-ian or mongrel versions. Usually it's no great hassle to work out – but you need to use a little lateral thinking at times. We have tried to follow common usage, but you may notice differences between spellings on the maps in this book and on the ground or on other maps. Where such discrepancies (most of them minor) occur, it is usually easy to work out what's what.

One of the best maps is the wine-red-covered *Venezia*, produced by the Touring Club Italiano. It costs €5.15 and displays the city on a scale of 1:5000. They also produce a cheap paper map of the *Centro Storico* (Historic Centre) for just €2.30. Another reasonable one is the yellow FMB map, also simply entitled *Venezia* (€5.15), which lists all street names with map references.

If you plan to stay for the long haul, *Calli, Campielli e Canali* (Edizioni Helvetica; €17.55) is for you. This is the definitive street guide and will allow you to locate to within 100m any Venetian-style address you need – saves a *lot* of shoe leather. Posties must do a course in it before being sent out to deliver the mail!

TOURIST OFFICES
Local Tourist Offices

Azienda di Promozione Turistica (APT) of-fices have information on the town and the province. There is one central information line to call in Venice (☎ 041 529 87 11, fax 041 523 03 99). The main APT office (Map 5) is at Piazza San Marco 71/f. Staff will as-sist with information on hotels, transport and things to see and do in the city. The of-fice opens 9.45am to 3.15pm Monday to Saturday. Another office, or Infopoint, oper-ates from the so-called Venice Pavilion (ex-Palazzina dei Santi; Map 5), next to the Giardini ex Reali, a quick walk from St Mark's Square. It opens 9am to 6pm daily.

The smaller APT office at the train station (Map 3) opens 8am to 8pm daily. Next door to the Garage Comunale in Piazzale Roma is another APT office (Map 3), which opens 9am to 6pm daily. There are also offices on the Lido (Map 10), at Gran Viale Santa Maria Elisabetta 6/a (summer only), and at the airport. In Mestre, there's an office (Map 11; ☎ 041 97 53 57) at Corso del Popolo 65.

In summer (ie, from Easter until at least the end of September), *punti informativi* (in-formation booths) used to set up at Campo San Rocco (Map 6), Campo San Felice (Map 4), Campo Santo Stefano (Map 6), Campo SS Giovanni e Paolo (Map 4) and Riva Ca' di Dio (Map 8). They opened 10am to 5pm (give or take) but at the time of writing were closed. No-one knew if they would reopen, so we have left them on the map just in case.

The useful monthly booklet *Un Ospite di Venezia* (A Guest in Venice), published by a group of Venetian hoteliers, is sometimes available from tourist offices. If not, you can find it in most of the larger hotels. Similar, but a little less informative, is *Pocket Venice*, sometimes available from tourist offices.

In the Veneto, you may come across the in-creasingly common Informazioni e Assis-tenza ai Turisti (IAT) offices. These are the places to go if you want specific information about bus routes, museum opening times and so on.

Tourist Helpline The APT operates a free 24-hour tourist helpline in case you have a complaint to make about services poorly rendered (from hotels, restaurants, water taxis and the like). Call ☎ 800 35 59 20 and follow the instructions.

Youth Information InformaGiovani can provide information ranging from assis-tance for the disabled to courses offered in the city. It has a branch in the Assessorato alla Gioventù (see Rolling Venice Concession Pass in the Documents section later in this chapter).

Tourist Offices Abroad

Information on Venice is available from the following branches of the Ente Nazionale Italiano per il Turismo (ENIT; **w** www.enit .it), the Italian State Tourism Board:

Australia (☎ 02-9262 1666, **e** enitour@ihug .com.au) Level 26, 44 Market St, Sydney 2000
Austria (☎ 0900-970 228, **e** enit-wien@aon.at) Kaerntnerring 4, A-1010 Wien
Canada (☎ 416-925 4882, **e** enit.canada@on .aibn.com) Suite 907, South Tower, 17 Bloor St East, Toronto, Ontario M4W3R8
France (☎ 01-42 66 03 96, **e** enit.parigi@wana doo.fr) 23 rue de la Paix, 75002 Paris
Germany *Berlin* (☎ 030-247 83 97, **e** Enit-berlin@t-online.de) Karl Liebknecht Strasse 34, D-10178 Berlin
  Munich (☎ 089-531 317, **e** enit-muenchen@ t-online.de) Goethestrasse 20, 80336 München
  Frankfurt (☎ 069-259 126, **e** enit.ffm@ t-online.de) Kaiserstrasse 65, 60329 Frankfurt
Netherlands (☎ 020-616 82 44, **e** enitams@ wirehub.nl) Stadhouderskade 2, Amsterdam 1054 ES
Spain (☎ 091-559 97 50, **e** italiaturismo@ retemail.es) Gran Via 84, Edificio Espagna 1-1, Madrid 28013
Switzerland (☎ 01-2117917, **e** enit@bluewin .ch) Uraniastrasse 32, 8001 Zürich
UK (☎ 020-7355 1557, **e** enitlond@globalnet .co.uk) 1 Princess St, London W1R 9AY
USA *Chicago* (☎ 312-644 0996, **e** enitch@ italiantourism.com) 500 North Michigan Ave, Suite 2240, Chicago, IL 60611
  Los Angeles (☎ 310-820 1898, **e** enitla@ earthlink.net) 12400 Wilshire Blvd, Suite 550, Los Angeles, CA 90025
  New York (☎ 212-245 4822, **e** enitny@italian tourism.com) 630 Fifth Ave, Suite 1565, New York, NY 10111

Italian cultural institutes in major cities throughout the world have extensive information on study opportunities in Italy. See Cultural Centres later in the chapter for more details.

TRAVEL AGENCIES

Venice is not a major centre for discount air tickets. You could start with the following agencies, but there is no substitute for shopping around.

For budget student travel, contact the Centro Turistico Studentesco e Giovanile (CTS; Map 6; ☎ 041 520 56 60, **w** www.cts.it), Calle Foscari 3252, Dorsoduro, the main Italian student and youth travel organisation. There are other branches in Mestre (Map 11; ☎ 041 96 11 25), at Via Ca' Savorgnan 8, and in Chioggia (☎ 041 550 02 80), at Via San Domenico 1124. Around the Veneto region you will also find CTS reps in Bassano del Grapa, Cittadella, Padua, Treviso, Verona and Vicenza. Before you buy tickets here you must become a member, which costs €25.80.

DOCUMENTS
Passports

Citizens of the 15 European Union (EU) member states can travel to Italy with their national identity cards alone. People from countries that do not issue ID cards, such as the UK, must have a valid passport. All non-EU nationals must have a full valid passport.

If your passport is stolen or lost while in Italy, notify the police and obtain a statement, and then contact your embassy or consulate as soon as possible.

Visas

Italy is one of 15 countries that have signed the Schengen Convention, an agreement whereby all EU member countries (except the UK and Ireland) plus Iceland and Norway have agreed to abolish checks at common borders. The other EU countries are Austria, Belgium, Denmark, Finland, France, Germany, Greece, Luxembourg, the Netherlands, Portugal, Spain and Sweden. Legal residents of one Schengen country do not require a visa for another Schengen country. Citizens of the UK and Ireland are also exempt and nationals of some other countries, including Canada, Japan, New Zealand and Switzerland, do not require visas for tourist visits of up to 90 days to any Schengen country.

Various other nationals not covered by the Schengen exemption can also spend up to 90 days in Italy without a visa. These include Australian, Israeli and US citizens.

FACTS FOR THE VISITOR

All non-EU nationals entering Italy for any reason other than tourism (such as study or work) should contact an Italian consulate, as they may need a specific visa. They should also insist on having their passport stamped on entry as, without a stamp, they could encounter problems when trying to obtain a residence permit, or *permesso di soggiorno* (see the following Permits section). If you are a citizen of a country not mentioned in this section, you should check with an Italian consulate whether you need a visa.

The standard tourist visa issued by Italian consulates is the Schengen visa, valid for up to 90 days. A Schengen visa issued by one Schengen country is generally valid for travel in all other Schengen countries. However, individual Schengen countries may impose additional restrictions on certain nationalities. It is, therefore, worth checking visa regulations with the consulate of each Schengen country you plan to visit.

You must apply in your country of residence and you can have no more than two Schengen visas in any 12-month period. They are not renewable inside Italy.

Permits

EU citizens do not need permits to live, work or start a business in Italy. They are, however, advised to register with a *questura* (police station) if they take up residence and apply for a permesso di soggiorno (residence permit). That is the first step to acquiring an *carta d'identità* (ID card). While you're at it, you'll need a *codice fiscale* (tax-file number) if you wish to be paid for most work in Italy. Go to the questura (Map 8; ☎ 041 271 55 11) at Fondamenta di San Lorenzo 5053, in Castello, to obtain precise information on what is required. Study and work visas (all non-EU citizens require them) must be applied for in your country of residence.

Travel Insurance

Medical costs might already be covered through reciprocal healthcare agreements (see Health later in this chapter), but you'll still need cover for theft or loss and for unexpected changes in travel plans (such as ticket cancellation).

You may prefer a policy that pays doctors or hospitals directly rather than you having to pay on the spot and claim later. If you have to claim for anything later, make sure you keep all documentation. Some policies ask you to call back (reverse charges) to a centre in your home country where an immediate assessment of your problem is made.

Check that the policy covers ambulances or an emergency flight home.

Driving Licences & Permits

The pink-and-green driving licences issued in all EU member states are fully recognised throughout Europe. Those with a non-EU licence are supposed to obtain an International Driving Permit (IDP) to accompany their national licence. These are available from national automobile associations.

For information on paperwork and insurance, see Car & Motorcycle in the Getting There & Away chapter.

Hostel Cards

A valid Hostelling International (HI) card is required if you want to stay in any of the Italian *ostelli per la gioventù* (youth hostels) run by the Associazione Italiana Alberghi per la Gioventù (AIG; W www.hostels-aig.org). You can get this by becoming a member of the national Youth Hostel Association (YHA) in your home country or at youth hostels in Italy. In the latter case, you must collect six stamps in the card at €2.60 each. You pay for a stamp on each of the first six nights you spend in a hostel, on top of the hostel fee. With six stamps, you are considered a full international member. HI has a Web site at W www.iyhf.org.

Student, Teacher & Youth Cards

The International Student Identity Card (ISIC), for full-time students, and the International Teacher Identity Card (ITIC), for full-time teachers and professors, are issued by more than 5000 organisations around the world. The cards entitle you to a range of discounts, from reduced museum admission charges to cheap air fares. Be aware, however, that few attractions in Venice offer discounts for holders of any international student cards (unless, in some cases, they are also EU citizens).

Student travel organisations such as Usit (worldwide), STA (Australia, the UK and the USA), Council Travel (the UK and USA) and Travel CUTS/Voyages Campus (Canada) issue these cards. See Air in the Getting There & Away chapter for some addresses, phone numbers and Web sites.

Anyone aged under 26 can get a Euro<26 card. This gives similar discounts to the ISIC and is issued by most of the same organisations. The Euro<26 has a variety of names, including the Under 26 Card in England and Wales and the CartaGiovani in Italy. The International Service and Travel Center (ISTC) has introduced a similar card, the International Youth Travel Card (IYTC), which gives people aged 25 and under benefits and access to special travel deals. The card can be obtained from Usit (who call it an IYC) or similar outlets.

Rolling Venice Concession Pass

If you are aged between 14 and 29, take your passport and a colour photograph to the Assessorato alla Gioventù (Map 5; ☎ 041 274 76 50, fax 041 274 76 42), Corte Contarina 1529, and pick up the Rolling Venice card. It costs €2.60 and offers significant discounts on food, accommodation, entertainment, public transport, museums and galleries. The office opens 9.30am to 1pm Monday to Friday and 3pm to 5pm on Tuesday and Thursday. You can also pick up the pass at the AIG (Map 6; ☎ 041 520 44 14), Calle del Castelforte 3101, San Polo, and Agenzia Arte e Storia (Map 3; ☎ 041 524 02 32), Corte Canal 659, Santa Croce. It is also available from the ACTV transport office (see Public Transport in the Getting Around chapter) and outlets of the ACTV subsidiary, Vela. Two of these are located in front of the train station (Map 3). Pick up the Rolling Venice map, which lists all the hotels, restaurants, shops, museums, cinemas and theatres where the pass entitles you to reductions.

Copies

Make photocopies of important documents, especially your passport. This will help speed replacement if they are lost or stolen. Other documents to photocopy might include your airline ticket and credit cards. Also record the serial numbers of your travellers cheques (cross them off as you cash them). All this material should be kept separate from the documents concerned, along with a small amount of emergency cash. Leave extra copies with someone reliable at home.

You can also store this information at Lonely Planet's online Travel Vault, which is safer than carrying photocopies. It's the best option if you are going to a country with easy Internet access. Your password-protected travel vault is accessible online at any time and can be created for free at ⓦ www.ekno.lonelyplanet.com.

EMBASSIES & CONSULATES

Your embassy won't be much help in emergencies if the trouble you're in is remotely your own fault. You are bound by the laws of the country you are in. Your embassy will generally replace lost passports, but loans for onward travel or free tickets home in an emergency are out of the question.

Italian Embassies & Consulates

The following is a limited selection of Italian diplomatic missions abroad. As a rule, you should approach the consulate rather than the embassy (where both are present) on visa matters.

Australia
Embassy: (☎ 02-6273 3333, fax 6273 4223, ⓔ embassy@ambitalia.org.au, ⓦ www.amb italia.org.au) 12 Grey St, Deakin, ACT 2600
Consulate in Sydney: (☎ 02-9392 7900, fax 9252 4830, ⓔ itconsydn@itconsyd.org) Level 43, The Gateway, 1 Macquarie Place, Sydney, NSW 2000
Consulate in Melbourne: (☎ 03-9867 5744, fax 9866 3932, ⓔ itconmel@netlink.com.au) 509 St Kilda Rd, Melbourne, VIC 3004
Austria
Embassy: (☎ 01-712 5121, fax 713 9719, ⓔ ambitalviepress@via.at) Metternichgasse 13, Vienna 1030
Canada
Embassy: (☎ 613-232 2401, fax 233 1484, ⓦ www.italyincanada.com) 21st floor, 275 Slater St, Ottawa, Ontario KIP 5H9

Consulate in Vancouver: (☎ 604 684 7288, fax 685 4263, ⒠ consolato@italianconsulate.bc.ca) Standard Building 1100, 510 West Hastings St, Vancouver, BC V6B 1L8

France
Embassy: (☎ 01 49 54 03 00, fax 01 45 49 35 81, ⒠ ambasciata@amb-italie.fr) 47 rue de Varenne, Paris 75007

Ireland
Embassy: (☎ 01-660 1744, fax 668 2759, ⒠ italianembassy@tinet.ie, ⓦ homepage.eir com.net/~italianembassy) 63–65 Northumberland Rd, Dublin

Netherlands
Embassy: (☎ 070-302 1030, fax 361 4932, ⒠ italemb@worldonline.nl, ⓦ www.italy.nl) Alexanderstraat 12, The Hague 2514 JL

New Zealand
Embassy: (☎ 04-473 53 39, fax 472 72 55, ⒠ ambwell@xtra.co.nz) 34 Grant Rd, Thorndon, Wellington

Switzerland
Embassy: (☎ 031-352 41 51, fax 351 10 26, ⒠ ambital.berna@spectraweb.ch, ⓦ www3.itu .int/embassy/italy) Elfenstrasse 14, Bern 3006

UK
Embassy: (☎ 020-7312 2200, fax 7312 2230, ⒠ emblondon@embitaly.org.uk, ⓦ www.emb italy.org.uk) 14 Three Kings Yard, London W1Y 2EH
Consulate in Edinburgh: (☎ 0131-226 3631, fax 226 6260, ⒠ consedimb@consedimb.demon .co.uk) 32 Melville St, Edinburgh EH3 7H

USA
Embassy: (☎ 202-612 4400, fax 518 2154, ⒠ stampa@itwash.org, ⓦ www.italyemb.org) 1601 Fuller St, NW Washington DC 20009
Consulate in New York: (☎ 212-7737 9100, fax 249 4945, ⒠ italconsulnyc@italconsulnyc .org, ⓦ www.italconsulnyc.org) 690 Park Ave, New York 10021
Consulate in Los Angeles: (☎ 213-826 6207, fax 820 0727, ⒠ cglos@conlang.com, ⓦ www.con lang.com) Suite 300, 12400 Wilshire Blvd, West Los Angeles 90025

Consulates in Venice

A limited number of countries maintain consulates in Venice. They include:

Austria (Map 6; ☎ 041 524 05 56)
Santa Croce 251
France (Map 5; ☎ 041 522 43 19) Ramo del Pestrin, Castello 6140
Germany (Map 6; ☎ 041 523 76 75) Campo Sant'Angelo 3816, San Marco

Netherlands (Map 6; ☎ 041 528 34 16)
San Marco 2888
Switzerland (Map 6; ☎ 041 522 59 96)
Dorsoduro 810
UK (Map 6; ☎ 041 522 72 07) Palazzo Querini, Dorsoduro 1051

The nearest Australian consulate (☎ 02 77 70 41) is in Milan, at Via Borgogna 2. The nearest US consulate (☎ 02 29 03 51) is also in Milan, at Largo Donegani 1. Canada is represented in Padua (☎ 049 878 11 47), at Riviera Ruzzante 25.

Embassies in Rome

Most countries have an embassy in Rome. Look them up under 'Ambasciate' in the *Pagine Gialle* (Yellow Pages). They include:

Australia (☎ 06 85 27 21) Via Alessandria 215, 00198 Rome
Austria (☎ 06 844 01 41) Via Pergolesi 3, 00198 Rome
Canada (☎ 06 44 59 81) Via G B de Rossi 27, 00161 Rome
France (☎ 06 68 60 11) Piazza Farnese, 00186 Rome
Germany (☎ 06 49 21 31) Via San Martino della Battaglia 4, 00185 Rome
Ireland (☎ 06 697 91 21) Piazza Campitelli 3, 00186 Rome
Netherlands (☎ 06 322 11 41) Via Michele Mercati 8, 00197 Rome
New Zealand (☎ 06 441 71 71) Via Zara 28, 00198 Rome
Slovenia (☎ 06 808 12 75) Via Leonardo Pisano 10, Rome
Switzerland (☎ 06 80 95 71) Via Barnarba Oriani 61, 00197 Rome
UK (☎ 06 482 54 41) Via XX Settembre 80/a, 00187 Rome
USA (☎ 06 467 41; ⓦ www.usis.it) Via Vittorio Veneto 119/a-121, 00187 Rome

CUSTOMS

There is no limit on the amount of euros brought into the country. Goods bought in and exported within the EU incur no additional taxes, provided duty has been paid and the goods are for personal consumption. 'Guidance levels' on quantities are set by the EU. They include 10L of spirits, 90L of wine and 800 cigarettes.

Duty-free sales within the EU no longer exist. Travellers coming into Italy from non-EU countries can import, duty free, 200 cigarettes, 1L of spirits, 2L of wine, 60mL of perfume, 250mL of eau de toilette and other goods up to a total of €175.50; anything over this limit must be declared on arrival and the appropriate duty paid. People travelling within the EU can import VAT-free goods (on sale at European airports) – whether you will find any truly good deals is open to question.

MONEY

A combination of travellers cheques and credit or cash cards is the best way to take your money.

Currency

On 1 January 2002, the euro became the currency of cash transactions in all of Italy, where it replaced the *lira* (plural: *lire*), and throughout the EU. After a two-month transaction period (when euros and lire circulated side by side and lire could be exchanged for euros free of charge at banks), euros became Italy's sole currency. Banks still accept lire and will continue to do so until 28 February 2012, but will only issue euros.

There are seven euro notes. In different colours and sizes, they come in denominations of €500, €200, €100, €50, €20, €10 and €5. The eight euro coins are in denominations of €2 and €1, then 50, 20, 10, five, two and one cents. Each participating state decorates the reverse side of the coins with their own designs, but all euro coins can be used anywhere that accepts euros.

Prices Quoted

This book was researched during the transition period, when not all prices were available in euros. Prices quoted (for example, by hotels, restaurants and entertainment venues) in the national currency have been converted to euros at the fixed conversion rate (€1 is equal to L1936.27). These may undergo further change as the euro comes fully into use.

Like other continental Europeans, Italians indicate decimals with commas and thousands with points.

country	unit		euro
Australia	A$1	=	€0.56
Canada	C$1	=	€0.69
Japan	¥100	=	€0.91
New Zealand	NZ$1	=	€0.46
UK	£1	=	€1.61
USA	US$1	=	€1.10

Exchanging Money

You can exchange money in banks, at post offices or in currency exchange booths (bureaux de change). Banks are generally the most reliable option and tend to offer the best rates. However, you should look around and ask about commissions. These can fluctuate considerably and a lot depends on whether you are exchanging cash or cheques. While post offices charge a flat rate of €0.50 per cash transaction, banks charge €1.30, or even more. Travellers cheques attract higher fees. Some banks charge €0.50 per cheque (minimum €1.55), while post offices charge a maximum €2.60 per transaction.

Keep a sharp eye open for commissions at bureaux de change. By way of example, Change (branches all over town) charges up to a staggering 11.9% on foreign-currency travellers cheques. Others charge still more! Thomas Cook charges 4.5% (minimum €2.85) for cash or travellers cheques (except Thomas Cook travellers cheques, which are commission free).

Where to Exchange You'll find most of the main banks in the area around the Ponte di Rialto and San Marco. Banks tend to open 8.30am to 1.30pm and 3.30pm to 4.30pm Monday to Friday, although hours can vary. Most close at weekends, but you might get lucky and find one open on Saturday morning.

Numerous change shops abound across the city and at the train station. Compare rates and commissions before parting with your hard-earned.

The American Express (AmEx) office (Map 5; ☎ 041 520 08 44) is on Salizzada

San Moisè. The postal address is San Marco 1471. For AmEx cardholders, there's an Automated Teller Machine (ATM or *bancomat*). The office is open 9am to 5.30pm Monday to Friday, and 9am to 12.30pm on Saturday.

Thomas Cook has two offices, one at Piazza San Marco 142 (Map 5; ☎ 041 522 47 51) and the other at Riva del Ferro 5126, near Ponte di Rialto (Map 5; ☎ 041 528 73 58). They open 8.45am to 8pm Monday to Saturday, and 9am to 6pm on Sunday.

When you first arrive, there are a couple of bureaux de change in the arrivals hall of the airport. A comparatively handy bank for both the train and bus stations is the Monte dei Paschi (Map 3), on Fondamenta di San Simeon Piccolo.

Cash Don't bring wads of cash from home (travellers cheques and plastic are much safer). It is, however, an idea to keep an emergency stash separate from other valuables in case you should lose your travellers cheques and/or credit cards.

You will need cash for some day-to-day transactions (many small hotels, eateries and shops do not take credit cards).

Travellers Cheques These are a safe way of carrying your money because they can be replaced if lost or stolen. Most banks and exchange offices will cash them. Thomas Cook, AmEx and Visa are widely accepted brands. If you lose your AmEx cheques, call a 24-hour freephone number (☎ 800 87 20 00). For Visa cheques call ☎ 800 87 41 55; for MasterCard or Thomas Cook cheques call ☎ 800 87 20 50.

Get most of your cheques in fairly large denominations (the equivalent of €51.65 or more) to save on any per-cheque commission charges. AmEx exchange offices do not charge commission to exchange travellers cheques (even other brands) or cash equivalent to US$500 or above.

It's vital to keep your initial receipt, along with a record of your cheque numbers and the ones you have used, separate from the cheques themselves.

Take your passport when you go to cash travellers cheques.

Credit/Debit Cards Carrying plastic is the simplest way to organise your holiday funds. You don't have large amounts of cash or cheques to lose, you can get money after hours and at weekends, and the exchange rate is better than that offered for travellers cheques or cash exchanges.

Major cards, such as Visa, MasterCard, Eurocard and Cirrus cards, are accepted throughout Italy. They can be used in many hotels, restaurants and shops. Credit cards can also be used in ATMs displaying the appropriate sign, or (if you have no PIN) you can obtain cash advances over the counter in many banks – MasterCard and Visa cards are among the most widely recognised for such transactions. Check charges with your bank but, as a rule, there is no charge for purchases on major cards and a 1.5% charge on cash advances and ATM transactions in foreign currencies.

It is not uncommon for ATMs in Italy to reject foreign cards. Don't despair or start wasting money on international calls to your bank. Try a few more ATMs displaying your credit card's logo before assuming the problem lies with your card rather than with the local system.

If your card is lost, stolen or swallowed by an ATM, you can telephone toll-free to have an immediate stop put on its use. For MasterCard the number in Italy is ☎ 800 87 08 66; for Visa it's ☎ 800 87 72 32; and for Diners Club ☎ 800 86 40 64. If you have a credit card issued in Italy, there is a plethora of numbers so you need to find out which one matches your card.

AmEx is also widely accepted (although not as commonly as Visa or MasterCard). The office in Venice (see Where to Exchange earlier in the Money section) also has an express cash machine for cardholders. If you lose your AmEx card, you can call ☎ 800 87 43 33.

International Transfers It is inadvisable to send cheques by mail to Italy because of the unreliability of the country's postal service. One reliable way to send money is by 'urgent telex' through the foreign office of a large Italian bank, or through major banks in your own country, to a nominated bank in Italy. The money will always be held at the head office of the bank in the town to which it has been sent. Urgent telex transfers should take only a few days, while other means, such as telegraphic transfer, or draft, can take weeks. It is important to keep an exact record of all details associated with the money transfer, particularly the exact address of the bank to where the money has been sent.

It is also possible to transfer money through AmEx and Thomas Cook. You will be required to produce identification, usually a passport, to collect the money.

Another option is Western Union (☎ 800 22 00 55). The sender and receiver have to turn up at a Western Union outlet with a passport or other form of ID. Fees charged for the virtually immediate transfer depend on the amount sent. In theory, the money can reach the recipient within 10 minutes of being sent. This service functions through several outlets in Italy. In Venice try the Change booths (several marked on the maps).

Another service along the same lines is MoneyGram (☎ 800 29 28 05), which operates mainly through Thomas Cook (for their addresses in Venice, see Where to Exchange earlier in the Money section).

Security

Keep only a limited amount of your money as cash, with the bulk in more easily replaceable forms, such as travellers cheques or plastic. If your accommodation has a safe, use it. If you have to leave money in your room, divide it into several stashes and hide them in different places.

For carrying money on the street, the safest thing is a shoulder wallet or under-the-clothes moneybelt. External moneybelts tend to attract attention to your valuables rather than deflect it. Watch out for people who touch you or seem to be getting unnecessarily close, in any situation. See Theft & Loss under Dangers & Annoyances later in this chapter for more advice.

Costs

As the cost of public transport (for tourists), accommodation, eating out, parking a car

and doing just about anything else spirals ever upwards, the Venetians' long history of commercial canniness comes back to mind.

Venetians point out that the city is expensive for everyone. City authorities also say, quite rightly, that the city has to foot an enormous bill cleaning the place up each day after the tourists (many of them day-trippers who do their best to leave as little money behind them as they can) have gone. Somebody has to pay for this – why not the visitors themselves? Whatever way you look at it, Venice is, with little doubt, the most expensive city in Italy.

Accommodation charges (especially in the high season) and entrance fees for many sights keep daily expenditure high. A *very* prudent backpacker might scrape by on around €46.50 per day, but only by staying in the youth hostel, eating one simple meal a day (at the youth hostel), making sandwiches for lunch, walking (*vaporetti*, or ferry, fares alone can make quite a dent in a tight budget) and keeping the daily museum and gallery intake low.

One rung higher up, you can get by on €77.50 per day if you stay in the cheapest *pensioni* (small hotels), and keep sit-down meals and museums to one a day. Lone travellers may find even this budget hard to maintain, since single rooms tend to be pricey.

If money is no object, you'll find a plethora of ways to burn it in Venice. There's no shortage of luxury hotels, expensive restaurants and shops. Realistically, a traveller wanting to stay in a comfortable lower- to mid-range hotel, eat two square meals every day, not feel restricted to one museum a day and be able to enjoy the odd drink and other minor indulgences should reckon on a minimum daily average of €130 to €180.

A basic breakdown of costs per person during an average day for the budget to mid-range traveller could be: accommodation €15.50 (youth hostel) to €41.30 (single in a *pensione* or per person in a comfortable double), breakfast €2.05 (coffee and brioche), lunch €2.60 (sandwich and mineral water), bottle of mineral water €0.75, public transport up to €9.30, entrance fee for one museum up to €6.20 and sit-down dinner €10.30 to €25.80.

Ways to Save In bars, prices can double (sometimes even triple) if you sit down and are served at the table. Stand at the bar to drink your coffee or eat a sandwich – or buy a sandwich or slice of pizza and head for the nearest *campo* (square).

Read the fine print on menus (usually posted outside eating establishments) to check the *coperto* (cover charge) and *servizio* (service fee). These can make a big difference to the bill.

Tipping & Bargaining

You are not expected to tip on top of restaurant service charges, but it is common to leave a small amount. If there is no service charge, the customer might consider leaving a 10% tip, but this is by no means obligatory. In bars, Italians often leave any small change as a tip, often only €0.05 or €0.10. Tipping taxi drivers is not common practice, but you should tip the porter at higher-class hotels.

Bargaining is common in flea markets but not in shops, although you might find that the proprietor is disposed to give a discount if you are spending a reasonable amount of money. It is quite acceptable to ask if there is a special price for a room in a pensione if you plan to stay for more than a few days.

Taxes & Refunds

A value-added tax (known as Imposta di Valore Aggiunto or IVA) of around 19% is slapped on to just about everything in Italy.

Tourists who are resident outside the EU may claim a refund on this tax if they spend more than a certain amount (€156 in 2001) in the same shop on the same day. The refund applies only to items purchased at retail outlets affiliated to the system – these shops display a 'Tax-free for tourists' sign. If you don't see a sign, ask the shopkeeper. You must fill out a form at the point of purchase and have it stamped and checked by Italian customs when you leave the country (you will need to show the receipt and possibly your purchases). At major airports and some border crossings, you can then get an immediate cash refund at specially marked booths; alternatively, return the form by mail to the vendor, who will make the refund, either by cheque or to your credit card.

For information consult the rules brochure available in affiliated stores.

Receipts

Laws aimed at tightening controls on the payment of taxes in Italy mean that the onus is on the buyer to ask for and retain receipts for all goods and services. This applies to everything from a litre of milk to a haircut. Although it rarely happens, you could be asked by an officer of the *guardia di finanza* (fiscal police) to produce the receipt immediately after you leave a shop. If you don't have it, the officer may levy a fine of up to €156.

POST & COMMUNICATIONS
Post

Italy's postal service is notoriously slow, unreliable and expensive. Don't expect to receive every letter sent to you, or that every letter you send will reach its destination. Information (in Italian) on postal rates and services can be had on ☎ 160 or online at Ⓦ www.poste.it.

Stamps *(francobolli)* are available from post offices and authorised tobacconists (look for the official *tabacchi* sign: a big 'T', often white on black). For letters that need to be weighed, what you get at the tobacconist's for international airmail will often be an approximation of the proper rate.

The main post office is on Salizzada del Fondaco dei Tedeschi, just near the Ponte di Rialto (Map 5). It opens 8.10am to 7pm Monday to Saturday. Stamps are available at windows No 1 to No 4 in the central courtyard. There is something quite special about doing your postal business in this former trading house. Stand by the well in the middle and try to imagine the bustle as German traders and brokers shuffled their goods around on the ground floor or struck deals in their quarters on the upper levels back in the republic's trading heyday.

Postal Rates The cost of sending a letter *via aerea* (airmail) depends on its weight and where it is being sent. Postcards and letters up to 20g cost €0.52 to the Americas, Australia and New Zealand and €0.42 within Italy and to Europe and Mediterranean countries. Aerograms are a cheap alternative, costing only €0.47 to send anywhere. They can be purchased at post offices.

A new priority post service, *posta prioritaria* (a little like the UK's 1st-class post), began in 1999 and is quicker. Postcards and letters up to 20g cost €0.77 to the Americas, Australia and New Zealand and €0.62 within Italy and to Europe and Mediterranean countries.

Espresso (express) costs a standard extra €2.25, but may help speed a letter on its way.

If you want to post more important items by *raccomandato* (registered mail) or by *assicurato* (insured mail), remember that they will take as long as normal mail. Raccomandato costs €2.60 on top of the normal cost of a 20g letter within Europe and the Mediterranean, and €2.70 elsewhere. The cost of assicurato depends on the weight and value of the object being sent (€5.15 for letters/packs up to 20g and up to €51.65 value within Europe and the Mediterranean; €5.25 elsewhere).

Sending Mail If you choose not to use priority post (see Postal Rates in the previous section), an airmail letter can take up to two weeks to reach the UK or the USA, while a letter to Australia will take between two and three weeks. Postcards can take even longer because they are low-priority mail.

The service within Italy is not much better: local letters take at least three days and up to a week to arrive in another city.

If you use priority post, the target is that letters within Italy should arrive the following working day, those posted to destinations in Europe and the Mediterranean basin within three days, and those to the rest of the world in four to eight days. The post office claims an 85% success rate in meeting these targets.

Parcels *(pacchetti)* can be sent from any post office. You can purchase posting boxes or padded envelopes from most post offices. Padded envelopes are also available from stationery shops *(cartolerie)* and some tobacconists. Parcels usually take longer to be delivered than letters. A different set of postal rates applies.

Express Mail Urgent mail can be sent by *postacelere* (also known as CAI Post), the Italian post office's courier service. Letters up to 500g cost €15.50 within Europe, €23.75 to the USA and €35.10 to Australia. A parcel weighing 1kg will cost €17.55 in Europe, €27.90 to the USA and Canada, and €41.30 to Australia and New Zealand. CAI post is not necessarily as fast as private courier services. It takes three to five days for a parcel to reach the USA, Canada or Australia and one to three days to European destinations. Ask at post offices for addresses of CAI post outlets, or check out W www.poste.it.

Couriers Several international couriers operate in Italy, but none have offices in Venice. DHL (☎ 800 34 53 45), Federal Express (☎ 800 12 38 00) and UPS (☎ 800 87 78 77) all operate freephone numbers. Note that if you are having articles sent to you by courier in Italy, you might be obliged to pay IVA of up to 20% to retrieve the goods.

Brusato Trasporti (☎ 041 528 98 82 or 336 59 27 17), Calle Larga G Gallina 6142, Cannaregio (Map 4), is an agent for UPS.

Receiving Mail Poste restante is known as *fermo posta* in Italy. Letters marked thus will be held at the Fermo Posta counter in the main post office in the relevant town. Poste restante mail should be addressed as follows:

John SMITH,
Fermo Posta,
Posta Centrale,
30100 Venice,
Italy

You will need to pick up your letters in person and present your passport as ID. Go to window 40.

AmEx card or travellers cheque holders can use the free client mail-holding service at the main Venice office (see Where to Exchange in the earlier Money section).

Telephone

The orange public pay phones liberally scattered about come in at least four types. The most common accept only *carte/schede telefoniche* (telephone cards), although you will still find some that accept both cards and coins. Some card phones also accept special credit cards produced by Telecom – the formerly state-owned telecommunications company – and even commercial credit cards. A few send faxes. If you call from a bar or shop, you may still encounter old-style metered phones, which count *scatti*, the units used to measure the length of a call.

There is an unstaffed Telecom office next to the post office and a bank of telephones nearby on Calle Galeazza (Map 5). Other unstaffed offices can be found on Strada Nuova, on the corner of Corte dei Pali, in Cannaregio (Map 4); Ruga Vecchia San Giovanni 480, in San Polo (Map 4); and Calle San Luca 4585, in San Marco (Map 5). You will also find phones at the train station.

You can buy phonecards at post offices, tobacconists, newspaper stands and from vending machines in Telecom offices. To avoid the frustration of trying to find fast-disappearing coin telephones, always keep a phonecard on hand. Remember to snap off the perforated corner before using them.

Public phones operated by the private telecommunications companies, Infostrada and Albacom, can be found in airports and stations. These phones accept Infostrada or Albacom phonecards (available from post offices, tobacconists and newspaper stands). The rates are slightly cheaper than Telecom's for long-distance and international calls.

Costs Rates, particularly for long-distance calls, are among the highest in Europe (although they are slowly falling).

A *comunicazione urbana* (local call) from a public phone will cost €0.20 (€0.10 when the other part answers and €0.10 for the call) for three to six minutes, depending on the time of day. Peak call times are 8am to 6.30pm Monday to Friday and 8am to 1pm on Saturday.

Rates for *comunicazione interurbana* (long-distance calls) within Italy depend on

the time of day (peak call times are the same as for local calls) and the distance involved. One minute at peak time costs at most €0.20.

Off peak for international calls is 10pm to 8am Monday to Saturday and all day Sunday. If you need to call overseas, beware of the cost. The connection charge is about €0.25. A call to the UK, France, Germany, Canada or the USA will cost around €0.30 per minute thereafter (a little less off peak). To Australia, New Zealand or Japan, the cost will be €0.60 per minute. The cost from a pay phone is considerably higher.

Domestic Calls Area codes have become an integral part of the telephone number. The codes all began with 0 and consisted of up to four digits. You must dial this whole number, even if calling from next door. Thus, any number you call in the Venice area will begin with 041.

Freephone numbers begin with 800. Nationwide standard-rate numbers start with 848 or 199. Mobile numbers begin with 3.

For directory enquiries, call ☎ 12.

International Calls Direct international calls can easily be made from public telephones by using a phonecard. Dial 00 to get out of Italy, then the relevant country and city codes, followed by the telephone number.

Useful country codes are: Australia 61, Canada and the USA 1, New Zealand 64, and the UK 44. Codes for other countries in Europe include: Belgium 32, France 33, Germany 49, Greece 30, Ireland 353 and Spain 34. Other codes are listed in Italian telephone books.

To make a reverse-charge (collect) international call from a public telephone, dial ☎ 170.

Emergency Numbers	
Military Police (Carabinieri)	☎ 112
Police (Polizia)	☎ 113
Fire Brigade (Vigili del Fuoco)	☎ 115
Highway Rescue (Soccorso Stradale)	☎ 116
Ambulance (Ambulanza)	☎ 118

It is easier and often cheaper to use the Country Direct service. You dial the number and request a reverse-charge call through the operator in your country. Numbers for this service include:

Australia – Optus	☎ 172 11 61
Australia – Telstra	☎ 172 10 61
Canada – AT&T	☎ 172 10 02
Canada – Teleglobe	☎ 172 10 01
France	☎ 172 00 33
Germany	☎ 172 00 49
Ireland	☎ 172 03 53
Japan – IDC	☎ 172 10 80
Netherlands	☎ 172 00 31
New Zealand	☎ 172 10 64
UK – BT	☎ 172 00 44
UK – BT Automatic Chargecard Operator	☎ 172 01 44
USA – AT&T	☎ 172 10 11
USA – IDB	☎ 172 17 77
USA – MCI	☎ 172 10 22
USA – Sprint	☎ 172 18 77

For international directory inquiries, call ☎ 176.

eKno Communication Service Lonely Planet's eKno global communication service provides low-cost international calls – for local calls you're better off with a local phonecard. eKno also offers free messaging services, email, travel information and an online travel vault, where you can securely store all your important documents. You can join online at Ⓦ www.ekno.lonelyplanet.com, where you will find the local-access numbers for the 24-hour customer-service centre. Once you've joined, always check the eKno Web site for the latest access numbers for each country and updates on new features.

International Phonecards & Call Centres Several private companies distribute international phonecards offering cheaper rates on long-distance calls. Some are better than others but few are available in Venice. Keep an eye out at newspaper kiosks, tobacconists and the like.

Companies like the CTS youth travel organisation are also bringing out their own cards. You need to compare values carefully.

A couple of internet centres also offer cheap-rate international calls. Net House (see Cybercafes under Email & Internet Access later) is one.

Mobile Phones Italy is one of the most mobile-phone-friendly countries on earth. In the early 1990s, when a *cellulare* was seen as a costly extravagance in most of the rest of Europe, in Italy it had already become an indispensable fashion accessory. Italy uses GSM 900/1800, compatible with the rest of Europe and Australia but not with the North American GSM 1900 or the totally different system in Japan (though some North Americans have GSM 1900/900 phones that do work here). If you have a GSM phone, check with your service provider about using it in Italy, and be aware that the costs of 'roaming' (taking your mobile abroad) can be astonishingly high.

If you're staying in Italy for more than a couple of weeks and cannot live without a phone, you might consider buying one, which can cost under €100 for the cheaper models.

Calling Venice from Abroad Dial the international access code (00 in most countries), followed by the code for Italy (39) and the full number, including the initial 0.

Telegram

These dinosaurs can be sent from post offices or dictated by phone (☎ 186) and are an expensive, but sure, way of having important messages delivered by the same or next day.

Fax

You can send faxes from post offices and private operators in Venice but Italy's high phone charges make them an expensive mode of communication. To send a fax within Italy, expect to pay €1.55 for the first page and €1 for each page thereafter, plus €0.05 per second for the call. International faxes can cost €3.10 for the first page and €2.05 per page thereafter, and €0.05 per second for the call. You can imagine what this could mean with a slow fax machine at peak rates!

The main post office operates a fax poste restante service. You can have faxes sent to you at Fax Fermo Posta. To retrieve the fax you will need a passport or some other photo ID. You pay €1.05 for the first page received and €0.25 for each page thereafter. Ask at window 40. Faxes should be sent to ☎ 041 522 68 20.

Email & Internet Access

Travelling with a portable computer is a great way to stay in touch with life back home, but unless you know what you're doing it's fraught with potential problems. Make sure you have a universal AC adapter, a two-pin plug adapter for Europe and a reputable 'global' modem. Increasingly, Italian telephone sockets are being standardised to the US RJ-11 type. If you find yourself confronted with the old-style Italian three-prong socket, most electrical stores can sell you an adapter. For more information on travelling with a portable computer, see the Web sites at **W** www.teleadapt.com or **W** www.igoproducts.com.

Major Internet service providers (ISPs), such as CompuServe at **W** www.compuserve.com, and IBM Net at **W** www.ibm.net, have dial-in nodes throughout Europe; download a list of the dial-in numbers before you leave home.

Some Italian servers can provide short-term accounts for local Internet access. Agora (☎ 06 699 17 42, **W** www.agoratelematica.it) is one of them. Several Italian ISPs offer free Internet connections: check out Tiscalinet (**W** www.tiscalinet.it), kataweb (**W** www.kataweb.it) and Libero (**W** www.libero.it).

If you intend to rely on cybercafes, you'll need to carry three pieces of information: your incoming (POP or IMAP) mail server name, your account name and your password. A final option for collecting mail through cybercafes is to open a free eKno Web-based email account online. You can then access your mail from anywhere in the world from any net-connected machine running a standard Web browser.

Cybercafes Expect to pay from €5.15 to €8.25 an hour at the following:

Chips & Colors (Map 9; ☎ 041 277 05 83) Via Giuseppe Garibaldi 1592, Castello. Open 10am-2pm & 3.30pm-10pm Mon-Sat, 3.30pm-10pm Sun. This oddly named place is part Internet cafe, part shop selling all manner of odd bits and pieces. An hour online costs €7.25.

EasyContact (Map 3; ☎ 041 71 10 97, **W** www.easy-contact.it) Campo Nazario Sauro 1005/a, Santa Croce. Open 9am-7pm daily. An hour online costs up to €7.25. Students with ISIC cards pay less.

Internet Café (Map 3; ☎ 041 524 12 00, fax 041 275 69 34) Ramo Chioverette 664/c, Santa Croce. Open 8.30am-1pm & 3pm-7.30pm Mon-Fri, 8.30am-1pm Sat. In spite of the name, there is no coffee. An hour online costs €7.25.

Internet Point (Map 3; ☎ 041 71 04 70) Ramo de la Donzela 888, San Polo. Open 8.30am-12.30pm & 3.30pm-7pm Mon-Fri, 8.30am-12.30pm Sat. An hour online costs €6.20.

Net House (Map 6; ☎ 041 277 11 90) Campo Santo Stefano 2958-67, San Marco. Open (they claim!) 24 hours a day. You can sip cocktails, eat sandwiches, slug Irish beers and/or go online. For the latter you pay a minimum €2.60 for the first 20 minutes and €0.15 per minute thereafter.

Omniservice Internet Café (Map 3; ☎ 041 71 04 70) Fondamenta dei Tolentini 220, Santa Croce. Open 8am-10pm daily. An hour online costs €5.15.

Planet Internet (Map 3; ☎ 041 524 41 88) Rio Terrà San Leonardo 1519, Cannaregio. Open 9am-midnight daily. An hour online costs €8.25.

The Netgate (Map 6; ☎ 041 244 02 13, **W** www.thenetgate.it, Calle dei Preti Crosera 3812/a, Dorsoduro. Open 10.15am-8pm Mon-Fri, 10.15am-10am Sat, 2.15pm-10pm Sun. An hour online costs €5.15.

DIGITAL RESOURCES

The Web is a rich resource for travellers. You can research your trip, hunt down bargain air fares, book hotels, check on weather conditions or chat with locals and other travellers about the best places to visit (or avoid!).

One of the best places to start your Web explorations is the Lonely Planet Web site at **W** www.lonelyplanet.com. Other sites you might like to surf initially include:

Associazione Veneziana Albergatori
W www.doge.it
This is an hoteliers' information directory (in English and Italian), with tips on hotels and eating options, upcoming events and links to other sites dealing with Venice.

Azienda Consorzio Trasporti Veneziana (ACTV)
W www.actv.it
This site contains all the local transport details you are ever likely to want and then some.

Consorzio dei Gondolieri
W www.gondolaincoming.com
The wonderful world of gondolas and the wonderful sums you will need to pay to get on board are to be found in this site.

ENIT
W www.enit.it/uk
This is the English-language site of Italy's national tourist board, with general information and regional links.

Excite
W www.excite.com/travel/countries/italy/venice
Excite's travel pages has a farefinder and bookings, and links to maps, restaurant tips, etc.

Ombra.Net
W www.ombra.net
This is an intriguing new site where you click on a sectioned map of Venice and then search for anything from pharmacies to bars in that sector of the map. It also offers listings and a series of links on all issues Venetian. It's in English and Italian.

Rialto: The Venice Marketplace
W www.rialto.com
Want to shop in Venice without going there? This could be a site for you. Many of the city's prestigious stores (and some perhaps not so prestigious) have contributed to this site. In many cases you can see catalogues and order online. Otherwise, you can just use this Web site as an extra shopping guide for when you are in the city.

Salvaguardia di Venezia
W www.salve.it
This site, prepared by the Italian Ministry of Public Works, is dedicated to Venice's complex problems and the long history of discussion on what to do about them. It has links to related sites.

Trenitalia
W www.fs-on-line.com
This is the official site of Trenitalia, the Italian railways. You can look up fare and timetable information here, although it can be a little complicated to plough through.

VeNETia
W www.comune.venezia.it
The Venice local council official site has wide-ranging information on the city and surrounding territory as well as many links.

Veneto
W www.veneto.org
Information about the Veneto region, of which Venice is the capital, can be found here, including history, language and local news.

Venice Banana
W www.venicebanana.com
Here you can look up listings for just about anything conceivable in and around Venice. It is also a place to leave ads and look for work. At the time of writing it was in Italian only, although an English version was on the way.

Venice Incoming
W www.elmoro.com
This is a private-sector guide to the city with some potentially useful tips on eating, drinking, shopping and other activities.

Virtual Venice
W www.virtualvenice.com
This has virtual tours of the city – the rest of the information hasn't been updated in quite a while.

BOOKS

Most books are published in different editions by different publishers in different countries. Your local bookshop or library is best placed to advise you on the availability of the following recommendations.

For bookshops in Venice, see the Shopping chapter.

Lonely Planet

If you are planning wider travels in the country, get hold of *Italy*. Hikers should take a look at *Walking in Italy*. Other companion titles include *Rome*, *Florence*, *Sicily*, *Tuscany* and *Milan, Turin & Genoa*. Also published by Lonely Planet, the *Italian phrasebook* lists all the words and phrases you're likely to use.

Lonely Planet's *World Food Italy* is a full-colour book with information on the whole range of Italian food and drink, a culinary dictionary and a useful language section.

Art & Architecture

The number of books devoted to the subject of art in Italy is mind-numbing. Most people thinking of art and Italy have the Renaissance in mind. General references worth looking at include *The Penguin Book of the Renaissance*, by JH Plumb, and *Italian Painters of the Renaissance*, by Bernard Berenson. The 16th-century Florentine artist Giorgio Vasari wrote the definitive report on the art of the day in his *Lives of the Artists*.

For the narrower palette of Venice, you could try *Painting in Renaissance Venice*, by Peter Humfrey, and *Venetian Art from Bellini to Titian*, by Johannes Wilde.

A couple of illustrated paperback studies are Michael Levey's *Painting in 18th Century Venice* and David Rosand's *Painting in Sixteenth Century Venice*. Levey also wrote the introduction to Venetian art that features in *The Glory of Venice: Art in the Eighteenth Century*, edited by Jane Martineau and Andrew Robison. This is a weighty hardback tome packed with illustrations. *Treasures of Venetian Painting – The Gallerie dell'Accademia* is a marvellous illustrated work covering the best of this gallery's collection.

Patricia Fortini Brown tries to evoke a day in the life of Joe Venice four centuries ago through the prism of the city's art treasures in *Art and Life in Renaissance Venice*. It is one of several volumes she has dedicated to the study of Venetian art history.

The colour plates in *The Mosaic Decoration of San Marco, Venice*, by Otto Demus, are accompanied by knowledgeable discourse on the art form that to many observers defines the city.

People often forget that Germany's Albrecht Dürer, a prince among German Renaissance artists, spent some four years in Venice. His *Record of Journeys to Venice and the Low Countries*, a selection of the painter's letters edited by Roger Fry, gives us some insight into his time there.

The Stones of Venice, by John Ruskin, is still acclaimed by many as the greatest evocation of the city written in English. If you want more insight into Ruskin's thinking, try to track down *Ruskin's Letters from Venice, 1851–1852*. In *A History of Venetian Architecture*, Ennio Concina surveys the city from its origins to the present day.

A handy little volume you can pick up in the city (for example, at the bookshop Libreria Demetra; Map 3) is *Venice: An Architectural Guide*, by Guido Zucconi, which offers quick glosses on about 250 landmark buildings. Editions in several different languages are available. More involved, and containing a little explanatory history on the evolution of Venetian building styles, is *A Guide to the Principal Buildings*, by Antonio Salvadori. It's published by Canal & Stamperia Editrice,

which has a series of art- and architecture-related books on Venice and other cities.

If you are interested in the modern scene, have a look at Sergio Los' *Carlo Scarpa – An Architectural Guide*.

Fiction

If you were to buy just one piece of fiction concerning Venice, Thomas Mann's absorbing *Der Tod in Venedig (Death in Venice)* should be it. The city itself seems to be the main protagonist, reducing Gustav von Aschenbach, its feeble human 'hero', to a mere tragic shadow. In all its mysterious beauty, the cholera-struck city seems at the same time cloyingly infectious and coldly indifferent.

While talking of classics, Bill Shakespeare's *The Merchant of Venice*, starring Shylock and a host of colourful characters, is mandatory reading for a distant Elizabethan view of what in those days must have seemed an extraordinarily exotic and bizarre city.

Thudding heavily back to earth, Ernest Hemingway was in maudlin form when he penned *Across the River and into the Trees* in postwar Venice. It is hard not to see Hemingway seeing himself in his Colonel character – middle-aged and cantankerous.

Henry James set his *Aspern Papers*, a brief tale of a literary researcher determined to get his hands on an American poet's love letters from his aged and reclusive one-time lover, resident in the lagoon city in the 1880s. Venice is also treated in his *Italian Hours*, in which James sets out his consternation at the levelling of everything by modern culture in the late 19th century. God only knows what he'd have thought of the early 21st century!

EM Forster, best known for his Florentine introduction to *A Room With a View*, gave Venice a run in *Where Angels Fear to Tread*.

For some reason, crime writing seems to have found inspiration in Venice. Donna Leon's inspector Guido Brunetti resolves case after case in Leon's burgeoning series of detective stories, all set in the city. Try *A Venetian Reckoning*, *The Anonymous Venetian*, *Acqua Alta* and *A Sea of Troubles*. Michael Dibdin created another Venetian detective, Aurelio Zen who, however, tends to roam all over Italy.

A modern hit was Ian McEwan's book *The Comfort of Strangers*, an early novel in which an outsider rocks a marital boat. It was made into a forgettable film in 1990.

Food & Drink

The Food of Italy, by Waverley Root, is an acknowledged classic.

From fine food to the perfect Bellini, *The Harry's Bar Cookbook*, by Arrigo Cipriani, has more than 200 recipes revealing at least a few of the secrets of the success of this Venetian institution. Cipriani, son of the bar's founder, also wrote *Harry's Bar: The Life and Times of the Legendary Venice Landmark*.

Pino Agostini and Alvise Zorzi's *A Tavola con I Dogi* is an exquisite and authoritative guide to Venetian cooking.

A jolly, anecdotal tome on the subject of eating in Venice is Sally Spector's *Venice and Food*, for which she wrote the text and drew the pictures. For a local's guide to *osterie* (traditional bars/restaurants), Michela Scibilia's *Osterie & Dintorni* is a handy little pocket book.

See also the Lonely Planet heading earlier in this section.

Glass

Venetian Glass: Confections in Glass 1855–1914, by Sheldon Barr, is like a visit to a museum of the most outstanding creations from Murano at a time when mass tourism had not yet set the tone. The colour photography by John Bigelow Taylor is the main attraction of this book.

Guidebooks

If your Italian is good, the best guidebooks to the history, culture and monuments of Italy are the 23 exhaustive hardback volumes published by the Touring Club Italiano (TCI). The relevant ones in this instance are *Venezia e Dintorni* and *Veneto*.

An attractively illustrated potted guide to Venetian art, monuments and history is *Venice for Pleasure*, by JG Links.

For thematic guided strolls, try *Venice Walks*, by Chas Corner and Alessandro Giannastasio.

History & People

Italy Edward Gibbon's *History of the Decline and Fall of the Roman Empire* (available in six hardback volumes or an abridged single volume) remains the masterwork on that subject in English. Other, simpler offerings include *The Oxford History of the Roman World*, edited by John Boardman, Jasper Griffin & Oswyn Murray.

For a general look at Italy, you could do a lot worse than *History of the Italian People*, by Giuliano Procacci. Other options to help you get started include *Italy: A Short History*, by Harry Hearder, and *The Horizon Concise History of Italy*, by Vincent Cronin. *A History of Contemporary Italy: Society and Politics 1943–1988*, by Paul Ginsborg is an absorbing analysis of the country's post-WWII travails.

Venice Two great works of scholarship stand out on the subject of Venetian history. John Julius Norwich's *A History of Venice* is the better read of the two, while the heavier in terms of sheer detail (and a fair share of anecdote) is *Venice – A Maritime Republic*, by the American historian Frederic C Lane. The latter tends to concentrate on the seafaring side of Venetian life and is organised more thematically than chronologically. Less detailed but more approachable is Christopher Hibbert's *Venice: The Biography of a City*.

John Julius Norwich has also written a detailed account of the last days of the Republic, *Venice: The Greatness and the Fall*.

For a treatment of Venice's tangled relations with its imperial Eastern neighbour, traced until the fall of Byzantium to the Turks in 1453, try *Byzantium & Venice*, by Donald M Nicol.

Although the subject of Brian Pullan's *The Jews of Europe and the Inquisition of Venice, 1550–1670* covers ground beyond Venice, it sheds light on the lot of the city's Jewry. More specific to the history of Jews in the lagoon city is *Ghetto of Venice*, by Riccardo Calimani and Katherine Silberblatt Wolfthal.

Anyone interested in Giacomo Casanova's version of his own life and loves might want to read his voluminous *Memoires of Jacques Casanova de Seingalt*, translated by Arthur Machen.

Music

A close study of Venetian Renaissance music can be found in Denis Arnold's *Giovanni Gabrieli and the Music of the Venetian High Renaissance*.

Karl Heller's *Antonio Vivaldi: The Red Priest of Venice* is an insightful look into the life of the composer.

Fans of opera wanting to know about its early days might like to get hold of Ellen Rosand's *Opera in Seventeenth Century Venice: The Creation of a Genre*.

Nature

Those fascinated by Venice's watery setting, should pick up a copy of *Field Guide to Nature in Venice Lagoon*, by Giampaolo Rallo. It is published in English by Franco Muzzio Editore. The book delves into the natural and human history of the lagoon and proposes a series of excursions.

Travel

For an idea of how an assortment of writers saw the city, have a meander through *Venice: The Most Triumphant City*, compiled by George Bull.

For some, the single most powerful evocation of the city is *Venice*, by James (now Jan) Morris. Quirky, if a little irritatingly self-assured, is *Venice Observed*, by Mary McCarthy.

Jan Morris revisited the subject with *The Venetian Empire – A Sea Voyage*, in which she set out by sea from La Serenissima to explore the widely scattered dominions of the one-time trading empire.

Literary companions are all the rage nowadays and *Venice – A Traveller's Companion*, compiled by John Julius Norwich, is full of anecdotes from characters ranging from King Theodoric's envoy to Venice in 523 to Mark Twain.

French readers might like to accompany Jean Giono on his *Voyage en Italie*, a light and celebratory look at the country that covers, inevitably, Venice in its course.

FILMS

Back in the 1980s, a film archive in Venice found that the city had appeared, in one

form or another, in 380,000 films (feature films, shorts, documentaries and so on). However, the city has starred in its own right in surprisingly few great flicks, tending rather to take bit parts.

From the early 1920s, Venetians Othello and Casanova got their fair share of runs on the silver screen. A good one was the 1927 *Casanova* by Alexandre Volkoff, with scenes actually shot in the city.

As the German film industry collapsed in the wake of Hitler's rise to power, mostly shifting to Hollywood, Venice began to get a bit of a run there too. Ernst Lubitsch's *Trouble in Paradise* (1932) probably has a lot more to answer for than the director could have imagined. In his studio re-creation of the lagoon city, he has a gondolier (dubbed with the voice of Enrico Caruso) singing that great Neapolitan song *O Sole Mio*. So that's where that modern tourist request came from!

Another Hollywood Venice was constructed for *Top Hat* (1935), one of the all-time great musicals starring Fred Astaire and Ginger Rogers.

Orson Welles had a go at *Othello* in 1952, a film he shot partly in Venice but mostly in Morocco and in which he played the main man. The antithesis of this was standard Hollywood schmaltz, of which *Three Coins in the Fountain* (1954), directed by Jean Negulesco, is a fairly telling example. A year later, Katherine Hepburn fronted a somewhat more substantial production, David Lean's *Summertime*.

In 1961, Steve McQueen and a band of US sailors plan to rob the casino in *The Honeymoon Machine*. It's a fairly silly film but some of the shots of Venice are good. In 1968, the American director Mel Stuart took a gentle dig at tourists with *If It's Tuesday This Must Be Belgium*, in which Venice takes its rightful place on the list of destinations being ticked off.

Among the best known of films set in Venice is, perhaps, *Morte a Venezia* (Death in Venice), Luchino Visconti's 1971 rendition of the Thomas Mann novel, with a suitably ashen-looking Dirk Bogarde in the main role of Aschenbach. Perhaps less well known but a better film was Federico Fellini's *Casanova*

(1977), starring Donald Sutherland. In this version of the life of the self-confessed lover and adventurer, we are given a more subtle look at the unhappy soul of a man seemingly almost condemned to his role.

Donald Sutherland was no stranger to Venice when he played Casanova. In 1973 he starred with Julie Christie in Nicolas Roeg's *Don't Look Now*. Based on a Daphne du Maurier novel, it shows Venice at its crumbling, melancholy best (or worst, depending on your point of view).

More recently, Venice has made appearances in *Indiana Jones and the Last Crusade* (1989) and Woody Allen's *Everyone Says I Love You* (1996), while films set in the city include the screen version of Ian McEwan's novel *The Comfort of Strangers* (1990), Oliver Parker's *Othello* (1995) and Henry James' story of love and betrayal *Wings of the Dove* (1997). *Dangerous Beauty* (1998) centres on the life of a courtesan in 16th-century Venice. In 1999, *The Venice Project*, starring Lauren Bacall and Dennis Hopper, was released.

A charming Italian film, Silvio Soldini's *Pane e Tulipani* (Bread and Tulips; 1999) charts a housewife's unlikely escape from urban drudgery to the canals of Venice, where she embroils herself in all manner of odd occurrences.

NEWSPAPERS & MAGAZINES

You can easily find a wide selection of national daily newspapers from around Europe (including the UK) at newspaper stands all over central Venice and at strategic locations like the train and bus stations. The *International Herald Tribune*, *Time*, the *Economist*, *Le Monde*, *Der Spiegel* and a host of other international magazines are also available.

Italian National Press

There is no 'national' paper as such, but rather several important dailies published out of major cities. These include Milan's *Corriere della Sera*, Turin's *La Stampa* and Rome's *La Repubblica*. This trio forms what could be considered the nucleus of a national press, publishing local editions up and down the country.

Reading Italian papers is a curious exercise. It is unlikely you will find such a dense and constant coverage of national politics in the press of any other European country. And yet the arcane shenanigans of Italy's political class are so convoluted that even most Italians confess to understanding precious little of what they are bombarded with in the press!

Most daily papers cost €0.75, unless there is a weekly magazine *inserto* of one sort or another, in which case the cost can rise to €1.15.

Local Press

Two papers dominate the local scene. *Il Gazzettino*, which has been in business since 1887, brings out separate editions in each province across the Triveneto area (the Veneto, Friuli-Venezia Giulia and Trentino), each with a local supplement. If you are in Venice and want decent coverage of national and foreign news but with solid local content, this is probably the paper you want. Its competition is the tabloid-size *La Nuova Venezia*, a more parochial rag.

Useful Publications

Venezia News is a monthly magazine (€2.05) available at most newspaper stands. It has info on the latest events, cinema, music and the like, along with a hotchpotch of articles, some in English.

RADIO

There are three state-owned stations: RAI-1 (1332kHz AM or 89.7MHz FM), RAI-2 (846kHz AM or 91.7MHz FM) and RAI-3 (93.7MHz FM). They offer a combination of classical and light music with news broadcasts and discussion programmes. RAI-2 broadcasts news in English at three minutes past the hour from 1am to 5am daily.

Radio Vaticano (1530kHz AM, 93.3MHz FM and 105MHz FM) broadcasts the news in English at 7am, 8.30am, 6.15pm and 9.50pm. The reports usually include a rundown on what the pope is up to on any particular day.

Local stations are not very inspiring. Radio Venezia (101.1MHz FM) is among the better ones, with news and, on balance, not a bad selection of music.

You can pick up the BBC World Service on medium wave at 648kHz, on short wave at 6.195MHz, 9.410MHz, 12.095MHz and 15.575MHz, and on long wave at 198kHz, depending on where you are and the time of day. Voice of America (VOA) can usually be found on short wave at 15.205MHz.

TV

The three state-run stations, RAI-1, RAI-2 and RAI-3, are run by Radio e Televisione Italiane. Historically, each has been in the hands of one of the main political groupings in the country, although in the past few years these affiliations have become less clear-cut.

Of the three, RAI-3 tends to have some of the more interesting programmes. Generally, however, these stations and the private Canale 5, Italia 1, Rete 4 and La 7 tend to serve up a diet of indifferent news, tacky variety hours (with lots of near-naked tits and bums, appalling crooning and vaudeville humour) and game shows. Talk shows, some interesting but many nauseating, also abound.

There are also several regional channels, including Telenuovo, Italia 7, Antenna 3, TeleNordEst and Televenezia. Quality is generally indifferent at best, but all carry more news and cultural items on Venice and the Veneto than the main stations.

VIDEO SYSTEMS

If you want to record or buy video tapes to play back home, you won't get a picture if the image registration systems are different. TVs and nearly all pre-recorded videos on sale in Italy use the PAL (phase alternation line) system common to most of Western Europe and Australia but incompatible with France's SECAM system or the NTSC system used in North America and Japan. PAL videos can't be played back on a machine that lacks PAL capability.

PHOTOGRAPHY & VIDEO
Film & Equipment

A roll of film is called a *pellicola*, but you will be understood if you ask for 'film'. A 100 ASA Kodak film will cost around €4.15/5.15 for 24/36 exposures. Developing costs around €5.70/7.25 for 24/36 exposures in standard format. A roll of 36 slides *(diapositive)* costs €5.15 to buy, €4.15 to develop.

Tapes for video cameras, including V8, are often available at the same outlets, or can be found at stores selling cameras, videos and electrical goods.

A handy place for buying film and having it developed is Image Center (☎ 041 522 78 88), Rio Terrà Antonio Foscarini 879 (Map 6). It opens 9am to 1pm and 2.30pm to 7pm Monday to Saturday.

Technical Tips

Bright middle-of-the-day sun tends to bleach out your shots. You get more colour and contrast earlier and later in the day. This goes both for still photographs and video, and is even more the case in summer, when glare can be a problem – the gentler winter light gives you greater flexibility.

Restrictions

Some museums and galleries ban photography, or at least flash, and the police can be touchy about it. Video too is often prohibited.

Photographing People

It's common courtesy to ask – at least by gesture – when you want to photograph people, except perhaps when they're in some kind of public event, like a procession.

Airport Security

The major Italian airports are all fully equipped with modern inspection systems that do not damage film or other photographic material carried in hand luggage.

TIME

Italy (and hence Venice) is one hour ahead of GMT/UTC during winter, two hours during the daylight-saving period from the last Sunday in March to the last Sunday in October. Most other Western European countries are on the same time as Italy year round, the major exceptions being the UK, Ireland and Portugal, which are one hour behind.

When it's noon in Venice, it's 3am in San Francisco, 6am in New York and Toronto, 11am in London, 9pm in Sydney and 11pm in Auckland. Note that in North America

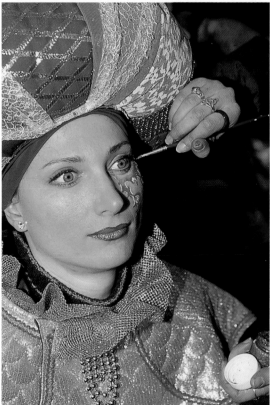

s there anybody there? Costumed revellers look blank but beautiful in the run-up to Venice's most famous wintertime celebration, the Carnevale.

ROBERTO SONCIN GEROMETTA

CHRISTOPHER GROENHOUT

DAMIEN SIMONIS

BETHUNE CARMICHAEL

Drifting down the Grand Canal (top); Giudecca waterfront (middle); the calm canals and brightly hued houses of Burano (bottom left); brass and tassel detail on a gondola (bottom right)

and Australasia, the changeover to/from daylight saving usually differs from the European date by a couple of weeks.

ELECTRICITY

Voltages & Cycles

The electric current in Venice is 220V, 50Hz, as in the rest of continental Europe. Several countries outside Europe (such as the USA and Canada) use 110V, 60Hz, which means that some appliances from those countries may perform poorly. It is always safest to use a transformer.

Plugs & Sockets

Plugs have two round pins, again as in the rest of continental Europe.

WEIGHTS & MEASURES

Italy uses the metric system. Like other continental Europeans, the Italians indicate decimals with commas and thousands with points. For a conversion chart, see the inside back cover of this book.

LAUNDRY

Self-service laundrettes are a comparative novelty in Italy and, in Venice you have the grand choice of one. Bea Vita Lavanderia (Map 3) is in Santa Croce, at Calle Chioverette 665/b. You pay €3.10 to wash 8kg and €1.55 for 15 minutes' drying time. It opens 8am to 10pm daily. If it's shut or busy and you're desperate, Laundry (Map 11), at Via Piave 41 in Mestre (about 10 minutes' walk north of the train station), is an alternative. It opens 7.30am to 11.30pm daily. It costs €2.60 to wash 8.5kg and €2.60 to dry up to 16kg.

The standard *lavanderie* (laundrettes), where you leave washing to be done, cost a small fortune (eg, €2.60 per pair of trousers).

TOILETS

Stopping at a bar or cafe for a quick coffee and then a trip to the toilet is the common solution to those sudden urges at awkward times. Make sure your bar actually has a toilet before committing yourself! Otherwise, public toilets (visitors pay €0.50, residents €0.25) are scattered about Venice – look for the 'WC Toilette' signs. They are generally open 7am to 7pm.

LEFT LUGGAGE

There are left-luggage facilities at Santa Lucia and Mestre train stations, the Piazzale Roma bus station, the Stazione Marittima (ferry port) and Marco Polo Airport. See the Getting There & Away and Getting Around chapters for more details. The cheapest service in the city itself is the one at the Piazzale Roma bus station (€2.60 for 24 hours).

HEALTH

You should encounter no particular health problems in Venice. Mild gut problems are a possibility at first if you're not used to a lot of olive oil, but most travellers experience no problems. Mosquitoes can be a bit of a nuisance, so you should take repellent with you. The water is safe to drink although most locals opt for the bottled stuff. In summer, it can get hot. Pace yourself, wear a hat, apply sunscreen and make sure you drink plenty of fluids.

Citizens of EEA countries are entitled to free or reduced cost emergency medical treatment in Italy on presentation of an E111 form. Treatment in private hospitals is not covered and charges are also likely for medication, dental work and secondary examinations, including X-rays and laboratory tests. Ask about the E111 at your local health service department a couple of weeks before you travel (in the UK, the form is available at post offices).

Australia also has a reciprocal arrangement with Italy so that emergency treatment is covered – Medicare in Australia publishes a brochure with the details. Advise medical staff of any reciprocal arrangements *before* they begin treating you.

Travel insurance is still a good idea, however. For further information, see under Documents earlier in this chapter.

For minor health problems, head to your local *farmacia* (pharmacy). Basic drugs are widely available, and indeed many items requiring prescriptions in countries such as the USA, Australia or the UK can be obtained over the counter in Italy. Travellers requiring a particular medication should take an adequate supply as well as the prescription, with the generic rather than the brand name, which will make getting replacements easier.

Tampons and condoms are available in pharmacies and supermarkets.

No vaccinations are required for entry into Italy but it is recommended that travellers keep up to date with tetanus, diphtheria and polio vaccinations.

Medical Services & Emergency

For an ambulance, call ☎ 118. The Ospedale Civile (hospital; Maps 4 & 8; ☎ 041 529 41 11) is at Campo SS Giovanni e Paolo. For emergency treatment, go straight to the *pronto soccorso* (casualty) section, where you can also get emergency dental treatment.

On the mainland, Mestre's Ospedale Umberto I (Map 11; ☎ 041 260 71 11), Via Circonvallazione 50, is a modern hospital.

For night-time call-outs (locum doctors) between 8pm and 8am on weekdays and from 10am the day before a holiday (including Sundays) until 8am the day after, call ☎ 041 529 40 60 in Venice, ☎ 041 534 44 11 in Mestre and ☎ 041 526 77 43 on the Lido.

The Italian public health system is administered by local centres generally known as Unità Sanitaria Locale (USL) or Unità Socio Sanitaria Locale (USSL), usually listed under 'U' in the telephone book (sometimes under 'A' for Azienda USL). Just for fun, the Venetian version is ULSS. Under these headings you'll find long lists of offices – look for Poliambulatorio (polyclinic) and the telephone number for Accetazione Sanitaria. You need to call this number to make an appointment – there is no point in just rolling up. Clinic opening hours vary widely, with the minimum generally being about 8am to 12.30pm Monday to Friday. Some open for a couple of hours in the afternoon and on Saturday morning too.

If your country has a consulate in Venice, staff there should be able to refer you to doctors who speak your language. However, if you have a specific health complaint, it would be wise to obtain the necessary information and referrals for treatment before leaving home.

In the USA, the non-profit International Association for Medical Assistance to Travelers (IAMAT; ☎ 716-754 4883, fax 519-836 3412), at 417 Center St, Lewiston, NY 14092, can provide a list of English-speaking doctors in Venice trained in the USA, the UK or Canada.

Pharmacies

Pharmacies in Venice are usually open 9am to 12.30pm and 3.30pm to 7.30pm. Most are closed on Saturday afternoon and Sunday. When closed, pharmacies are required to display a list of other pharmacies in the area that are open. Information on all-night pharmacies is listed in *Un Ospite di Venezia* (see Local Tourist Offices earlier in this chapter).

You can also check which pharmacies are open for 24 hours on any date at **W** www.ombra.net.

HIV, AIDS & STIs

Infection with the human immunodeficiency virus (HIV) may lead to acquired immune deficiency syndrome (AIDS), which is a fatal disease. Any exposure to blood, blood products or body fluids may put the individual at risk. The disease is often transmitted through sexual contact or dirty needles – vaccinations, acupuncture, tattooing and body piercing can be potentially as dangerous as intravenous drug use.

It is possible to get tests for AIDS and other sexually transmitted infections (STIs) done in Venice (normally you are tested for the lot in one go). Enquire at the Consultorio Familiare (Map 6; ☎ 041 529 40 04), Dorsoduro 1454. It opens 9am to 1pm Tuesday and Friday and 2.30pm to 5.30pm on Thursday. You need to book ahead for a consultation.

Blood used for transfusions in Venice hospitals is screened for human immunodeficiency virus (HIV) and should be safe.

Women's Health

For gynaecological examinations, smear tests and the like on the public health service, go to the Consultorio Familiare (see STDs & AIDS above).

WOMEN TRAVELLERS

Of the main destinations in Italy, Venice has to be the safest for women. The kind of bravado that has more southerly Italians trying it on harder with foreign women seems largely absent here. If you do get unwanted attention, whatever methods you use at home to deal with it should work.

Organisations

Centro Donna (☎ 041 534 31 86, fax 041 534 28 62), Viale G Garibaldi 155/a, in Mestre, is a women's centre that offers various facilities, including a library, and cultural events aimed at women, whether Italian or foreign.

It also operates a service for women who have been assaulted. The Centro Anti-Violenza (☎ 041 534 92 15) offers legal advice, free counselling and support to women who have been attacked, regardless of nationality. The service is free.

GAY & LESBIAN TRAVELLERS

Homosexuality is legal in Italy and well tolerated in Venice and the north in general. However, overt displays of affection by homosexual couples could attract a negative response. The legal age of consent is 16.

Gay clubs and discos and the like can be tracked down through local gay organisations (see the following section) or the national monthly gay magazine *Pride* (€3.10), which, along with the annual *Guida Gay Italia*, is available at most newspaper stands.

The *Spartacus International Gay Guide* (which sells for approximately US$32.95 or UK£19.95 and is available in bookshops worldwide) also has listings of gay venues all over Italy (and the rest of the world). *Damron Women's Traveller 2001* (available online at W www.damron.com) has information for lesbian travellers.

Organisations

The national organisations for gay men and lesbians are ArciGay and ArciLesbica (☎ 051 644 70 54, fax 051 644 67 22), Piazza di Porta Saragozza 2, 40123, Bologna.

You'll find any number of Italian gay sites on the Internet, but some are all but useless. However, ArciGay's Web site (W www.gay

.it/arcigay) has general information on the gay and lesbian scene in Italy and plenty of useful links. ArciLesbica's Web site can be found at W www.women.it/arciles.

Venice's gay association, ArciGay Dedalo (Map 11; ☎ 041 753 84 15), is at Via A Costa 38/a in Mestre.

DISABLED TRAVELLERS

ENIT, the Italian State Tourism Board in your country, may be able to provide advice on Italian associations for the disabled and what help is available in the country – see Tourist Offices Abroad, earlier, for further information. It may also carry a small brochure, *Services for Disabled Passengers*, published by the Italian state rail company, Ferrovie dello Stato (FS), which details facilities at stations and on trains. Some of the better trains, such as the ETR460 and ETR500, have a carriage for passengers in wheelchairs and their companions.

See Public Transport in the Getting Around chapter for information on getting around Venice in a wheelchair, which is possible.

Organisations

The UK-based Royal Association for Disability & Rehabilitation (RADAR; ☎ 020-7250 3222, W www.radar.org.uk), Unit 12, City Forum, 250 City Rd, London EC1V 8AS, publishes a useful guide called *European Holidays & Travel Abroad: A Guide for Disabled People*, which provides a good overview of facilities available to disabled travellers throughout Europe.

Another organisation worth contacting is Holiday Care (☎ 01293-774 535, W www .holidaycare.org.uk), 2nd floor, Imperial Buildings, Victoria Rd, Horley, Surrey RH6 7PZ. They produce an information pack on Italy for people with special needs. Tips include hotels with disabled access, where to hire equipment and tour operators dealing with the disabled.

In Italy itself, the best point of reference for disabled travellers is the Rome-based Consorzio Cooperative Integrate (CO.IN), at Via Enrico Giglioli 54/a, although it concentrates on the capital. It operates a telephone helpline (☎ 06 712 90 11) from 9am to 5pm

Monday to Friday. Information is also available online at W www.coinsociale.it or via email at e turismo@coinsociale.it.

The Associazione Italiana Assistenza Spastici (☎ 02 550 17 564), at Via S Barnaba 29, 20122 Milan, operates an information service for disabled travellers to Italy called the Sportello Vacanze Disabili.

Promotur – Accessible Italy (☎ 011 309 63 63, W www.tour-web.com/accessibleitaly), Piazza Pitagora 9, 10137 Turin, is a private company specialising in holiday services for the disabled, from tours to adapted-transport.

In Mestre, try Informahandicap (☎ 041 534 1700, e informahandicap@comune .venezia.it), based at Villa Franchin, Via Garibaldi 155.

SENIOR TRAVELLERS

Senior citizens are entitled to discounts on admission fees at some sights. It's always worth asking. The minimum qualifying age is generally 65 years. You should also seek information in your own country on travel packages and discounts for senior travellers through senior citizens' organisations and travel agents.

VENICE FOR CHILDREN

Venice isn't for art-lovers and hopeless romantics alone. The city is varied enough to keep even the most recalcitrant juniors interested at least some of the time. Some of the stuff grown-ups like, such as gondola and vaporetto rides, exploring funny corners and watching the passing parade of boats along the canals, will appeal to quite a lot of kids.

The kids will certainly enjoy a trip down the Grand Canal on vaporetto No 1. If you can't afford a gondola, at least treat them to a short trip across the canal on a traghetto. They will probably also enjoy a trip to the islands, particularly to see the glass-making demonstrations on Murano. Older kids might enjoy watching the big ships pass along the Canale della Giudecca, so take them to Gelateria Nico (Map 6) on the Fondamenta Zattere, where you can relax for half an hour or so.

Children of all ages will enjoy watching the Mori strike the hour at the Torre dell'Orologio on St Mark's Square.

Understandably most of the museums and galleries will leave kids cold but some may work. Boys should get a kick out of the boats and model ships at the Museo Storico Navale (Map 8). The sculpture garden at the Peggy Guggenheim Museum (Map 6) may prove an educational distraction while you indulge your modern art needs.

Climbing towers is usually a winner. Try the Campanile in St Mark's Square or the bell tower at San Giorgio Maggiore.

If you are having a spot of bother, or have been unkind enough to drag the little mites around just a few too many monuments for their liking, you can try a couple of things to mollify them. Both Parco Savorgnan (part of Palazzo Savorgnan, Map 3) and the Giardini Pubblici (Map 9) have swings and the like.

In summer, a trip to the beach – the Lido, Sottomarina (Chioggia) or Lido di Jesolo – should win you a few points. If you are using your own transport, remember to leave early to beat the horrible traffic jams. And forget it at weekends (except on the Lido) – whether you drive or catch buses, you'll be stuck on the roads for an eternity.

Discounts are available for children (usually aged under 12) on public transport and for admission to museums, galleries and other sights.

Before You Go

There are no particular health precautions you need to take with your children in Venice. That said, kids tend to be more affected than adults by unaccustomed heat, changes in diet and sleeping patterns, and just being in a strange place. Nappies, creams, lotions, baby foods and so on are all easily available in Venice, but if there's some particular brand you swear by, it's best to bring it with you.

Lonely Planet's *Travel with Children* has lots of practical advice on the subject, and first-hand stories from many Lonely Planet authors, and others, who have done it.

LIBRARIES

Access to the main libraries of the city generally requires a pass. You can find a list of the main libraries, with addresses, phone numbers and opening hours, in the monthly

Venezia News (see Newspapers & Magazines earlier).

UNIVERSITIES

The Università Ca' Foscari (Map 6; ☎ 041 257 81 11) is based in the *palazzo* (palace) of the same name at Dorsoduro 3246. Faculty buildings and subdivisions are scattered across the city. It began as Italy's first school of commerce in 1868 and was only made a university in 1968. There are four faculties: Economics, Foreign Languages and Literature, Literature and Philosophy, and Mathematics and Physical & Natural Sciences. The university has a Web site at W www.unive.it.

The prestigious Istituto Universitario di Architettura di Venezia (IUAV; Map 6; ☎ 041 257 11 11), set up in 1963, is based in the former convent of San Nicolò da Tolentino, Santa Croce 191. Its various departments are spread across the city and some 11,000 students flock from all over the country to attend courses here. Its Web site is at W www.iuav .unive.it.

A few foreign universities (such as Warwick University in the UK and New York University in the USA) run programmes in Venice too.

CULTURAL CENTRES

The Istituto Italiano di Cultura (IIC), with branches all over the world, is a government-sponsored organisation aimed at promoting Italian culture and language. It puts on classes in Italian and provides a library and information service. This is a good place to start your search for places to study in Italy. Try the IIC's Web sites at W www.iicmelau.org (Melbourne, Australia) or W www.iicsyd.org (Sydney, Australia), W www.iicto-ca.org/isti tuto.htm (Canada), W www.italynet.com/cul tura/istcult (France) and W www.italcultny .org (USA).

In Venice, there's a branch of the Alliance Française (Map 5; ☎ 041 522 70 79) at San Marco 4939. This French association offers classes in French, as well as organising cultural events, conferences and exhibitions.

The local representative of the Goethe Institut, Deutsch-Italienische Kulturgesellschaft (Map 4; ☎ 041 523 25 44, fax 041 524 52 75), is at Palazzo Albrizzi, Fondamenta Sant'Andrea, Cannaregio 4118. It runs courses in German, as well as a full calendar of talks, exhibitions and other cultural events.

DANGERS & ANNOYANCES

All in all, the half-awake visitor to Venice should have no problems. Still, the presence of so many foreigners inevitably encourages pickpockets and like-minded small-time criminals.

Theft & Loss

Petty crime (pickpocketing, bag-snatching and the like) is the standard problem in Venice, as indeed it is in most major tourist destinations in Italy. Overall, though, Venice is a pretty safe place. The times to be on your guard are those moments when you will probably be most distracted. Arriving at the train station and getting oriented, squeezing onto crowded vaporetti (especially when you are burdened with all your bags) and pounding the packed tourist trails (especially at certain points along the way from the train station to St Mark's Square and around the Rialto) are moments when you may be vulnerable. A modicum of awareness and keeping anything valuable well hidden should be enough protection.

Prevention is better than cure. Only walk around with the amount of cash you intend to spend that day or evening. Hidden moneybelts or pouches are useful; wearing 'bum bags' or external belt pouches makes you an easy target.

Never leave anything visible in your car and preferably leave nothing at all. Foreign

---

Lost Property

Numbers for lost property are as follows:

Trains	☎ 041 78 52 38
ACTV buses & vaporetti	☎ 041 272 21 79

Otherwise, call the local police *(vigili urbani)* on ☎ 041 522 45 76. Their lost property office is at Piazzale Roma (Map 3).

and hire cars are especially vulnerable, and there have been occasional reports of trouble at some of the car parks – in Fusina (on the mainland) in particular.

In hotels and hostels, use the safe if they have one. Try not to leave valuables in your room. If you must, then bury them deep in your luggage.

If anything does get lost or stolen, you must report it to the police and get a written statement from them if you intend to claim for them on your insurance. If your ID or passport disappears, contact your nearest consulate as early as possible to arrange for a replacement.

Rogue Taxis

A particular problem on the Isola del Tronchetto is false water-taxi drivers. These people may wear official-looking caps and badges and approach the freshly parked tourist with stories of having the only kind of vessel available to transfer people from Tronchetto to destinations elsewhere in Venice. This is rubbish, as vaporetti call here regularly. Often, unwitting victims are transported somewhere (often not where they wanted to go) for outrageous sums of money. On occasion you will be whisked away to Murano to look at someone's cousin's glass shop.

Ignore all approaches from boat captains or illegal 'taxis'. It's a racket that's gone on for years and its practitioners can become menacing – thankfully some of them do occasionally end up behind bars. The vaporetto lines 82 and 71/72 (summer only) will get you safely to most parts of Venice.

Bad Odours

In summer in particular, the smells emanating from the canals and sewers can be a little unpleasant. Put it down to local colour.

Tourists

The hordes of people meandering around the narrow *calli* (streets) of Venice and crowding onto the vaporetti can be a pain to one another and to locals. Try to be courteous. Don't amble three or more abreast down narrow streets, effectively blocking people coming up from behind who don't have all day

to gawk at things, and cutting off oncoming traffic, too. Locals go into single file when they see oncoming pedestrians or hear someone behind trying to get past.

On the vaporetti, if you must hang around the embarkation barriers to look at things, be prepared to hop off at stops to let other passengers on and off before you get back on yourself to continue your trip.

LEGAL MATTERS

The average tourist will probably have a brush with the law only if they are robbed by a bag-snatcher or pickpocket.

Drugs

Italy's drug laws are lenient on users and heavy on dealers. If you're caught with drugs that the police determine are for your own personal use, you may be let off with a warning – and, of course, the drugs will be confiscated. If, instead, it is found that you intend to sell the drugs in your possession, you could find yourself in prison. It's up to the police to determine whether or not you're a dealer, as the law is not specific about quantities.

Your Rights

Italy still has some anti-terrorism laws on its books that could make life very difficult if you happen to be detained by the police – for any alleged offence. You can be held for 48 hours without a magistrate being informed and you can be interrogated without the presence of a lawyer. It is difficult to obtain bail and you can be held legally for up to three years without being brought to trial. If arrested, contact your consulate for advice (see under Embassies & Consulates earlier in this chapter).

BUSINESS HOURS

In general, shops are open 9am to 1pm and 3.30pm to 7.30pm (or 4pm to 8pm) Monday to Saturday. They may remain closed on Monday morning or Wednesday and/or Saturday afternoon. Laws on opening hours are fairly flexible so shopkeepers have a large degree of discretion.

Big department stores, such as Coin in the Le Barche complex in Mestre (Map 11),

Police Forces

If you run into trouble in Italy, you're likely to end up dealing with either the *polizia* (police) or the *carabinieri* (military police). The polizia are a civil force and take their orders from the Ministry of the Interior, while the carabinieri fall under the Ministry of Defence. There is a considerable duplication of roles, despite a 1981 reform intended to merge the two. Both are responsible for public order and security, which means you can call either in the event of a robbery or violent attack.

The carabinieri, based in Piazzale Roma (Map 3; ☎ 041 523 53 33), wear Gucci-designed black uniforms with a red stripe and drive equally black cars with a red stripe. They are well trained and tend to be helpful.

The polizia wear powder-blue trousers with a fuchsia stripe and a navy-blue jacket, and drive light-blue cars with a white stripe and 'Polizia' written on the side. Tourists who want to report thefts and people wanting to get a residence permit will have to deal with them. They are based at the *questura* (police station; Map 8; ☎ 041 271 55 11) at Fondamenta di San Lorenzo 5053, in Castello.

Another type of police are the *vigili urbani*, who are basically traffic police. You will have to deal with them if you get a parking ticket or your car is towed away. In Venice, they can be reached on ☎ 041 274 70 70. In Mestre, call ☎ 041 274 92 67.

Lastly, the *guardia di finanza* are responsible for fighting tax evasion and drug smuggling. It is highly unlikely, but you could be stopped by one of these grey-uniformed officers if you leave a shop without a receipt for your purchase.

For a list of emergency telephone numbers, see the boxed text with that name under Telephone earlier in this chapter.

and most supermarkets are open 9am to 7.30pm Monday to Saturday. Some even open 9am to 1pm on Sunday.

Bars (in the Italian sense, ie, coffee-and-sandwich places) and cafes generally open 7.30am to 8pm, although some stay open after 8pm and turn into pub-style drinking and meeting places.

For museum and gallery opening hours, see the beginning of the Things to See & Do chapter. For bank opening hours, see Exchanging Money earlier in this chapter.

PUBLIC HOLIDAYS & SPECIAL EVENTS

The two main periods when *Veneziani* go on holiday are Settimana Santa (the week leading up to Easter Sunday) and, more noticeably, around the month of August.

Public Holidays

New Year's Day (Anno Nuovo) 1 January
Epiphany (Befana) 6 January
Good Friday (Venerdì Santo) March/April
Easter Monday (Pasquetta/Giorno dopo Pasqua) March/April
Liberation Day (Giorno della Liberazione) April 25 – marks the Allied victory in Italy and the end of the German presence and Mussolini in 1945.
Labour Day (Giorno del Lavoro) 1 May
Feast of the Assumption (Ferragosto) 15 August
All Saints' Day (Ognissanti) 1 November
Feast of the Immaculate Conception (Concezione Immaculata) 8 December
Christmas Day (Natale) 25 December
Boxing Day (Festa di Santo Stefano) 26 December

Festivals

The APT publishes a list of annual events, including the many religious festivals staged by almost every church in the city.

January

Regata delle Befana The first of more than 100 regattas on the lagoon throughout the year is held on the day of the Epiphany (6 January). Rowing Venetian-style *(la voga veneta)* involves boats somewhat resembling gondolas, whose crews row standing up.

February

Carnevale This is the major event of the year, when Venetians don spectacular masks and costumes for a week-long party in the run-up to Ash Wednesday (see the special black-and-white section 'Carry on Carnevale' following this chapter). The event was reinvented in 1979 and for some it is little more than a tacky tourist venture, albeit a popular one. Each year there is a different theme, so it is hard to pin down the programme with any precision. The starting dates for Carnevale in the next few years are: 5 February 2002, 25 February 2003 and 17 February 2004.

April

Festa di San Marco The feast day of the city's patron saint, when menfolk are supposed to give their beloved a bunch of roses, is on 25 April.

May

Vogalonga The 'long row' is a rowing regatta inspired by the Republic's glorious maritime history. This event began in November 1974, when a group of Venetians held their first race off the Isola di Burano in protest against pollution in the lagoon caused by the growing use of motorboats for business and pleasure. Since then it has developed into a friendly free-for-all, with 3000 or more participants and boats of all descriptions (powered by human muscle) participating in the 32km jaunt from the Bacino di San Marco up to Burano and back down to the Grand Canal via Cannaregio. A good spot to get a look at the latter end of the race is the Rialto area. Like quite a few events in Venice, it can't be pinned to a specific day, although it tends to be held fairly early in the month.

Festa della Sensa This feast day falls on the second Sunday of May and marks the Feast of the Ascension. Already an important day in the Catholic calendar, it takes on a special significance in Venice. Every year since Ascension Day 998, when Venetian forces left to regain control of Dalmatia, the city has celebrated the Sposalizio del Mar (Wedding with the Sea; see the boxed text 'With This Ring I Thee Wet' in the History section of the Facts about Venice chapter). These days the mayor takes on the ducal role. The fun culminates with regattas off the Lido.

Late May–Early June

Palio delle Quattro Antiche Repubbliche Marinare The former maritime republics of Amalfi, Genoa, Pisa and Venice take turns to host the colourful historical Regatta of the Four Ancient Maritime Republics, in which four galleons, crewed by eight oarsmen and one at the tiller, compete for line honours. The challenge will be held in Venice again in 2003.

June

Marciliana Since 1991, Chioggia has commemorated the siege of the city by Genoa in 1380 with a medieval pageant in late June involving parades and a competition between five *contrade*, or town quarters, that includes rowing and archery.

Sagra di San Pietro in Castello A busy local festival in the last weekend of June with music, drinking and eating at the steps of the church that was once the city's cathedral.

July

Festa del Redentore The Feast of the Redeemer is marked by yet another regatta on the Grand Canal. The main celebrations, however, take place at the Chiesa del Redentore on Isola della Giudecca on the third weekend of the month. The Senato ordered the construction of this church in 1577 in thanksgiving for the end of a bout of the plague. Every year afterwards, the doge, members of the Senato, other VIPs and many of the city's people would cross the canal on a provisional pontoon to give thanks. Nowadays, the Canale della Giudecca fills with all sorts of boats to join in the festivities as the cityfolk wander to and fro across the pontoon. The night before, people eat a traditional meal of roast duck and sit back to enjoy fireworks.

September

Regata Storica This historic gondola race along the Grand Canal is preceded by a parade of boats decorated in 15th-century style. Venetians first organised a rowing race in 1274, and have been doing it ever since. This regatta, one of the most important, is held on the first Sunday in the month. The mansions along the canal are draped in silks, flags and other festive decorations for the big day. Most of the competing boats are rowed by just two men, but in the past all sorts of vessels with crews of up to 50 competed. It may seem strange that the involvement of women used to be far greater than it is today. The race starts off at Castello and proceeds west up the canal to the former convent of Santa Chiara, where the boats turn around a *bricola* (pylon) to pound back down to the finishing line at Ca' Foscari.

Partita a Scacchi (at Marostica, in the Veneto) On the first weekend in September, the townspeople of Marostica dress as chess figures and participate in a living chess match. (See under Around Bassano del Grappa in the Excursions chapter, later.)

November

Festa della Madonna della Salute This procession over a bridge of boats across the Grand Canal to the Chiesa di Santa Maria della Salute (Map 5) on 21 November is to give thanks for the city's deliverance from plague in 1630.

Arts & Music Festivals Venice hosts some major international arts festivals and a plethora of more minor but engaging events. They include:

June–October/November

Biennale Internazionale d'Arte This major international exhibition of visual arts started in 1895 and was held every even-numbered year from the early 20th century. However, the 1992 festival was postponed until 1993 so that there would be a festival on the Biennale's 100th anniversary in 1995. It is held in permanent pavilions in the Giardini Pubblici (Map 9), and at other locations in Venice, including the Palazzo Grassi (Map 6).

August/September

Feste Musicali per San Rocco In 1608 the English traveller Thomas Coryat reported attending fine concerts in the Scuola Grande di San Rocco (St Roch) to celebrate that saint's feast day. Nowadays you can still attend concerts of Baroque and still older music in the same location. Tickets cost from €18.10 to €25.80 and proceeds help maintain and restore the Scuola Grande.

Mostra del Cinema di Venezia The Venice International Film Festival, Italy's version of Cannes, is organised by the Biennale committee and held annually at the Palazzo del Cinema on the Lido (Map 10).

DOING BUSINESS

People wishing to make the first moves towards expanding their business into Italy should get in touch with their own country's trade department (such as the DTI in the UK). The commercial department of the Italian embassy in your own country should also have information – at least on red tape.

In Italy, the trade office of your embassy can provide tips and contacts.

Business Services

A GSM mobile phone and a good laptop computer will probably be all you need to do business in Venice. However, some of the better hotels have secretarial assistance for guests. Other companies that might be of help are listed in the *Pagine Gialle* (Yellow Pages) under 'Uffici Arredati e Servizi'. Translators/ Interpreters are listed under 'Traduzioni Servizio'.

Exhibitions & Conferences

Venezia Congressi (Map 6; ☎ 041 522 84 00, fax 041 523 89 95), Dorsoduro 1056, and ENDAR (Veneto Congressi; Map 8; ☎ 041 523 85 60), Castello 4966, can assist in organising business conventions in Venice.

WORK

It is illegal for non-EU citizens to work in Italy without a *permesso di lavoro* (work permit), but trying to obtain one through your Italian consulate can be a pain. EU citizens are allowed to work in Italy, but they still need to obtain a permesso di soggiorno (residence permit) from a police station. Immigration laws require foreign workers to be 'legalised' through their employers. This applies even to cleaners and babysitters. The employers then pay pension and health insurance contributions. This doesn't mean that illegal work can't still be found.

A useful guide is *Living, Studying, and Working in Italy*, by Travis Neighbor and Monica Larner.

If you intend to look for work in Venice, you should bring along any paperwork that might help. English teachers, for instance, will need any qualification certificates and references from previous employers. Increasingly, there is cross-recognition of degrees and other tertiary qualifications, so it may be worthwhile bringing these as well. Translations validated by the Italian embassy in your country wouldn't hurt either.

Working Holidays

The best options are trying to find work in a bar, nightclub or restaurant during the tourist season. Another option is au pair work, organised before you come to Italy. A useful guide is *The Au Pair and Nanny's Guide to Working Abroad*, by Susan Griffith & Sharon Legg. Susan Griffith's *Work Your Way Around the World* is also worth looking at.

Art students and graduates might consider one other possibility. The Peggy Guggenheim Collection takes on foreign students to staff the museum, cloakroom and so on for periods of up to three months. This is most easily pursued through your art school.

Language Teaching

The easiest source of work for foreigners is teaching English (or another foreign language), but even with full qualifications, a non-EU citizen might find it difficult to secure a permanent position. Most of the larger, more reputable schools will hire only people with work and/or residence permits, but their attitude can become more flexible if demand for teachers is high and they come across someone with good qualifications.

The more professional schools will require teachers to have a Teaching English as a Foreign Language (TEFL) certificate. It is advisable to apply for work early in the year, in order to be considered for positions available in October (language-school years correspond roughly to the Italian school year: late September to the end of June).

Some schools hire people without work permits or qualifications, but the pay is usually low (around €7.75 per hour). It is more lucrative to advertise your services and pick up private students (rates vary wildly, from as low as €7.75 to up to €25.80 an hour), but of course this takes time to develop. The average rate is around €15.50. Although you may get away without qualifications or experience, bring along a few English grammar books (including exercises) to help you at least appear professional. Most people get started by placing advertisements in shop windows and on university notice boards (Map 6).

To find language schools, look up 'Scuole di Lingue' in the *Pagine Gialle* (Yellow Pages).

CARRY ON CARNEVALE

Since pre-Christian days, people have been getting up to all sorts of shenanigans to celebrate the approaching end of winter – Ancient Rome's Saturnalia are a fine example. Earliest records of the word *carnevale* date from the 12th century and scholars trace the Venetian festivities to the 15th-century Compagnie della Calza. These were private clubs whose members wore different-coloured *calze* (stockings). They began organising competing masked balls on Martedì Grasso (Ash Wednesday), during the run-up to Lent.

Over the centuries, all sorts of strange events were conceived to heighten the revellers' enjoyment. The most bizarre of these was the firing of live dogs from cannons. A chosen few Venetians would also be selected to batter a fattened cat to death – with their heads. The town authorities even allowed the running of bulls through the streets (you have to wonder how many people and bulls ended up in the canals in this Venetian version of the Hemingway scene).

By the 18th century, the twilight years of La Serenissima, the ritual had evolved into a two-month party in which, if we are to believe the contemporary accounts, few holds were barred in the licentious activities of its participants. Seemingly immune to the political and economic decay of their once-proud city empire, the Venetians revelled in carnal pleasures.

After 1797 the locals sobered up a little under foreign occupation and Carnevale lost much of its hedonistic verve. It disappeared altogether under Mussolini, who banned the wearing of masks in public.

In 1979 it took off again. 'Why?' is an interesting question. Some say it was a stunt to attract a little business in the slack winter month of February. If that is so, it worked. Carnevale is now firmly established as a must-see event, however hammed up it may seem.

Events

The festivities begin on the Friday afternoon before Ash Wednesday with La Festa delle Marie, a procession through the city. This is a precursor to the official opening on Saturday, when a traditional masked procession leaves St Mark's Square around 4pm and circulates through the streets. The next day there are jousts and other mock military tournaments.

The following Thursday is Giovedì Grasso, a festival that has always been a part of Venice's celebration of Carnevale. Friday afternoon's highlight is the Gran Ballo delle Maschere (Grand Masked Ball) in St Mark's Square. Anyone with proper costume and mask who is able to dance the quadrilles and other steps of a few centuries ago may join in.

Above:
A dressed-up duo head for the ball (Juliet Coombe)

Saturday and Sunday are given over to musical and theatrical performances in St Mark's Square. Also on the Sunday, a beautiful procession of decorated boats and gondolas bearing masked passengers wends its way serenely down the Grand Canal.

The event winds up with a parade of the Re del Carnevale (Carnival King) and the one-time guilds of the city.

During the course of the festivities, plenty goes on outside the main events – street performers fill the main thoroughfares and squares. Campo San Polo is often given over to children's theatre and jugglers. For a feel of how Carnevale was centuries ago, head for the Vecio Carnevale in Via Garibaldi.

The Grand Canal itself is the centre of the events. Throughout the Carnevale period, it is illuminated by torchlight during the evenings.

For many, the biggest events are the *balli in maschera* (masked balls). You're looking at up to €200 for a ticket, plus the outlay for hiring a costume and mask. The tourist office can tell you exactly when and where the balls are taking place and how to make a booking.

Masks & Masquerades

In such a uniquely isolated city, with its narrow streets and crowded courtyards, it's hardly surprising that a desire for privacy arose among the inhabitants. And what better way to get your yearly fix of anonymity than by donning a disguise and setting out to paint the town red? Class boundaries were dissolved and inhibitions shed, and the key to all of this rule-breaking was the humble mask. As early as 1436, the *mascareri* (mask-makers) were important enough to have their own guild, and the craft continues today. Traditional Carnevale masks are works of art made from *cartapesta* (papier-mache) or leather. They can be divided into three different styles – the old commedia dell'arte and traditional Venetian masks (see later), and modern fantasy masks, often custom-made for wealthy patrons.

Commedia dell'Arte Masks

This form of popular comedy took off in Italy during the 16th to 18th centuries. Characters such as Harlequin, Pantaloon and Columbine were used as satirical figures, and audiences became familiar with the grotesque masks that made each character instantly recognisable. The Venetians also adopted them for the Carnevale.

Left:
A reveller muses on the magic of the mask.
(Juliet Coombe)

Traditional Venetian Masks

Bauta This pointy-chinned, rather manly-looking mask was used by Venetian nobles in the 17th century and was perhaps the most common design. Always made in white, the *bauta* covered up practically the whole of the face, yet allowed the disguised man to eat or quaff to his heart's content. The mask was usually teamed with a swirling cloak and a tricorn, which completely concealed the man inside, enabling him to gamble his fortune away at the *casini* or visit his inamorata in secret. It wasn't worn only at Carnevale time, but could be used whenever the Venetian man-about-town wanted to keep his identity secret.

Moretta Perhaps the most mysterious of the traditional Venetian masks, the Moretta ('Dark') is certainly the creepiest in more ways than one. Eerily expressionless, it was only worn by women and was held in place by a button, which was clamped between the front teeth and meant that both talking and maintaining the disguise was impossible. An opportunity for Venetian Pantaloons to practise chat-up lines without fear of rejection?

Gnaga Cross-dressing is no modern invention, as the Gnaga mask shows. Men would disguise themselves as women, sometimes even going so far as to carry a baby about with them. The strange name possibly derives from *gnao*, the miaowing of a Venetian cat.

Medico della Peste This doctor costume has its wearer looking somewhat like an awkward flightless bird. Its origins, however, inspire anything but hilarity. Back in 1630, a virulent plague epidemic carried off as much as two-thirds of Venice's population. Some of the doctors who hung about to care for the sick – not that they could do much – took to wearing some very odd vestments indeed. They donned head-to-foot cloaks coated in wax, gloves and a hat, and carried a stick to lift sheets or clothing from patients for a visual examination.

The *pièce de résistance* was, however, the mask with glasses. The long beaklike protuberance contained various 'medical' essences considered helpful in avoiding infection (this was for the wearer's sake, not anyone else's). Whether or not they worked is not known, but the mask of the Medico della Peste (Plague Doctor), also known as the Medico della Morte (Doctor Death), is among the most famous of all.

Above:
Hat tricks at the February festival (Juliet Coombe)

Getting There & Away

There are direct flights to Venice from abroad and from within Italy. The city lies at the eastern end of major railway and road routes ranging across the north of the country from Milan, and it is also possible to arrive by sea – once the only way into the city.

For recommended travel agencies in Venice, see the Travel Agencies section in the Facts for the Visitor chapter.

AIR

Venice is one of Italy's smaller air traffic centres. Direct flights from major European centres and New York are available, alongside internal flights from the rest of Italy, but for most intercontinental air travel you will have to change flights at least once, either in Rome or Milan or at another major European hub.

Although Venice is hardly a discount destination, occasional good deals turn up, especially in the low-season winter months. See the following text for some examples.

Marco Polo airport is 12km from Venice, but some flights land at Treviso airport, about 35km north of the city. In the latter case, the airlines concerned sometimes provide a connecting bus to Venice. For more information on getting to and from the airports, and on facilities at the airports, see The Airports in the Getting Around chapter.

Travellers with Special Needs

If they're warned early enough, airlines can often make special arrangements for travellers, such as wheelchair assistance at airports or vegetarian meals on the flight. Children under two years old travel for 10% of the standard fare (or free on some airlines) as long as they don't occupy a seat. They don't get a baggage allowance. 'Skycots', baby food and nappies should be provided by the airline if requested in advance. Children aged between two and 12 can usually occupy a seat for half to two-thirds of the full fare, and do get a baggage allowance.

The disability-friendly Web site, W www .everybody.co.uk, has an airline directory that provides information on the facilities offered by various airlines.

Departure Tax

The departure tax payable when you leave Italy by air is factored into your airline ticket.

Other Parts of Italy

Travelling by plane is expensive within Italy and, in the northern half of the country at any rate, it makes more sense to use the efficient and considerably cheaper train and bus services. The main domestic lines are Alitalia (☎ 800 05 03 50, W www .alitalia.it) and Meridiana (☎ 199 11 13 33, W www.meridiana.it). The main airports are in Rome, Milan, Naples, Pisa, Catania and Cagliari, but there are other, smaller airports throughout Italy. Domestic flights can be booked through travel agencies.

Warning

The information in this chapter is particularly vulnerable to change: prices for international travel are volatile, schedules change, special deals come and go, and rules and visa requirements are amended. Airlines and governments seem to take a perverse pleasure in making price structures and regulations as complicated as possible. You should check directly with the airline or a travel agent to make sure you understand how a fare (and any ticket you may buy) works, and be aware of the security requirements for international travel. In addition, the travel industry is highly competitive and there are many bargains and offers to be had.

Get quotes and advice from as many airlines and travel agents as possible before you part with your hard-earned cash. The details given in this chapter should be regarded as pointers and are no substitute for your own careful, up-to-date research.

Alitalia's national network uses Rome and, to a lesser extent, Milan as hubs for most flights. A couple of direct flights also link Venice with Naples and Palermo.

One-way fares and standard returns (basically just two one-way tickets) are expensive. If you get a return, purchasing an Apex (or even better a Super Apex) fare will bring the price down considerably (up to two-thirds off) in exchange for respecting certain conditions.

The following are samples of one-way Alitalia air fares to/from Venice (travel times depend greatly on the length of stopover). Bear in mind that return Apex fares purchased two weeks in advance can cost about the same as a standard one-way ticket. Cities served by Alitalia from Venice include:

Bari Up to seven flights daily; €229 one way; three hours via Rome.
Cagliari Up to five flights daily; €206 one way; 3½ hours via Rome.
Milan Up to five flights daily; €114 one way; 55 minutes.
Naples Up to three direct flights daily; €206 one way; one hour 10 minutes.
Palermo Up to five flights daily plus occasionally one direct flight; €212 one way; three hrs via Rome/Milan or 2¾ hours direct.
Rome Up to five flights daily; €155 one way; one hour.

Meridiana offers direct flights between Venice and Olbia only. From Verona, however, the airline flies daily to Cagliari, Catania, Naples, Olbia, Palermo and Rome. Fares are similarly high – for instance, a one-way flight to Rome can cost €137 and €204 to Palermo. Apex *return* fares purchased two weeks in advance would be €149 and €205 respectively. In some cases a return fare with special conditions can actually cost *less* than a standard one-way ticket.

Before committing to anything, try out a few travel agents. Smaller airlines with scheduled flights, such as Air One (☎ 848 84 88 80, W www.flyairone.it) and Alpi Eagles (☎ 041 599 77 88, W www.alpieagles .com), occasionally seriously undercut the big names.

Other Countries

The UK & Ireland In the UK, consumer protection can be obtained by buying a ticket from an agent covered by the Air Transport Organiser's Licence (ATOL). Should the ATOL agent go bust, the Civil Aviation Authority will guarantee a refund or an alternative arrangement before travel, or will get you home if necessary, and can sometimes arrange for you to finish your holiday. For more details, see W www.atol.org.uk.

For students or for travellers aged under 26, popular travel agencies in the UK include STA Travel (telesales on ☎ 0870 160 0599, W www.statravel.co.uk), 86 Old Brompton Rd, London SW7 3LQ, which has offices throughout the UK. Usit Campus (☎ 020-7730 3402, W www.usitcampus.com), 52 Grosvenor Gardens, London SW1W 0AG, also has branches throughout the UK. Both of these agencies sell tickets to all travellers, but cater especially to young people and students.

Other recommended travel agencies include: Trailfinders (☎ 020-7937 1234 for European travel), 215 Kensington High St, London W8 6BD; and Flightbookers (☎ 020-7757 2324), 177–178 Tottenham Court Rd, London W1P 0LX. The latter has an online flight booking site called ebookers (W www.ebookers.com).

The two national airlines linking the UK and Italy are British Airways (BA; ☎ 0845-773 3377, W www.british-airways.com), 156 Regent St, London W1R 5LB, and Alitalia (☎ 0870 600 4343, W www.italia.it), 4 Portman Square, London W1H 9PS. They operate regular flights (usually several a day) to Venice. Returns with either can cost from UK£200, but with a little forward planning, you can be looking at as little as UK£140 return.

Of the several low-budget airlines operating out of the UK, only the Irish airline Ryanair (☎ 0870 156 9569 in the UK, ☎ 199 11 41 14 in Italy, W www.ryanair.ie) serves Venice (actually flying to Treviso). Fares vary wildly according to season and season. A one-way flight can cost anything from UK£45 to UK£100 or even more. The airline also operates flights to Treviso from Brussels.

GETTING THERE & AWAY

Air Travel Glossary

Alliances Many of the world's leading airlines are now intimately involved with each other, sharing everything from reservations systems and check-in to aircraft and frequent-flyer schemes. Opponents say that alliances restrict competition. Whatever the arguments, there is no doubt that big alliances are the way of the future.

Courier Fares Businesses often need to send urgent documents or freight securely and quickly. Courier companies hire people to accompany the package through customs and, in return, offer a discount ticket which is sometimes a bargain. However, you may have to surrender all your baggage allowance and take only carry-on luggage.

Fares Airlines traditionally offer 1st class (coded F), business class (coded J) and economy class (coded Y) tickets. These days there are so many promotional and discounted fares available that few passengers pay full fare.

Lost Tickets If you lose your airline ticket, an airline will usually treat it like a travellers cheque and, after inquiries, issue you with another one. Legally, however, an airline is entitled to treat it like cash and if you lose it then it's gone forever. Take very good care of your tickets.

Onward Tickets An entry requirement for many countries is that you have a ticket out of the country. If you're unsure of your next move, the easiest solution is to buy the cheapest onward ticket to a neighbouring country or a ticket from a reliable airline which can later be refunded if you do not use it.

Open-Jaw Tickets These are return tickets where you fly out to one place but return from another. If available, this can save you backtracking to your arrival point.

Overbooking Since every flight has some passengers who fail to show up, airlines often book more passengers than they have seats. Usually excess passengers make up for the no-shows, but occasionally somebody gets 'bumped' onto the next available flight. Guess who it is most likely to be? The passengers who check in late. If you do get 'bumped', you are normally offered some form of compensation.

Reconfirmation Some airlines require you to reconfirm your flight at least 72 hours prior to departure. Check your travel documents to see if this is the case.

Restrictions Discounted tickets often have various restrictions on them – such as needing to be paid for in advance and incurring a penalty to be altered or cancelled. Others are restrictions on the minimum and maximum period you must be away.

Round-the-World Tickets RTW tickets give you a limited period (usually a year) in which to circumnavigate the globe. You can go anywhere the carrying airlines go, as long as you don't backtrack. The number of stopovers or total number of separate flights is decided before you set off and they usually cost a bit more than a basic return flight.

Ticketless Travel Airlines are gradually waking up to the realisation that paper tickets are unnecessary encumbrances. On simple one-way or return trips, reservations details can be held on computer and the passenger merely shows ID to claim their seat.

Transferred Tickets Airline tickets cannot be transferred from one person to another. Travellers sometimes try to sell the return half of their ticket, but officials can ask you to prove that you are the person named on the ticket. On an international flight, tickets are compared with passports.

Go (☎ 0845 605 4321 in the UK, ☎ 848 88 77 66 in Italy, W www.go-fly.com) flies to Venice from London Stansted. Standard returns (no changes, no refunds) start at UK£100, including taxes.

Italy Sky Shuttle (☎ 020-8241 5145), 227 Shepherd's Bush Rd, London W6 7AS, specialises in charter flights to more than 20 destinations in Italy. High-season return flights from London to Venice can cost around UK£180.

The Charter Flight Centre (☎ 020-7565 6755), 15 Gillingham St, London SW1V 1HN, has charter and scheduled flights to several destinations in Italy. They had scheduled summer returns to Venice for UK£160 at the time of writing.

If you're coming from Ireland, it might be worth comparing the cost of flying direct with the cost of travelling to London first and then flying to Italy.

Continental Europe Short hops can be expensive but for longer journeys, you can often find air fares that beat overland alternatives on cost.

France If time is at a premium, flying from Paris is a fair option. There are regular flights between Paris and Venice. A return flight in June/July with Lufthansa costs €278.

The student travel agency OTU Voyages (☎ 01 40 29 12 12, W www.otu.fr) has a central Paris office at 39 ave Georges Bernanos and another 36 offices around the country. A safe bet for reasonable student and cut-price travel is Usit (☎ 0825 08 25 25, W www.usit connect.fr). They have four addresses in Paris, including 85 blvd St Michel, and other offices around the country.

Air Littoral (☎ 0803 83 48 34 in France, ☎ 035 23 30 04 in Italy, W www.air-littoral .fr) operates flights between Nice and Venice for high flyers. A return flight from Nice can cost €245. To Nice there are connections once or twice a day from other destinations within France, as well as from Barcelona, Madrid, Geneva and Munich.

AirDolomiti (☎ 08 02 02 00 30 in France, ☎ 800 01 33 66 in Italy, W www.airdolo miti.it), a regional airline in partnership with Lufthansa, operates two daily flights between Paris and Venice. Low-season return fares cost from around €229. The Italian airline Meridiana (see Other Parts of Italy earlier) has flights to Verona.

Germany Munich is a haven of budget travel outlets. Council Travel (☎ 089-39 50 22), Adalbertstrasse 32, is one of the best. STA Travel (☎ 089-39 90 96), Königstrasse 49, is also good.

In Berlin, Kilroy Travel-ARTU Reisen (☎ 030-310 00 40), Hardenbergstrasse 9, is a good travel agency. In Frankfurt am Main, you could try STA Travel (☎ 069-70 30 35), Bockenheimer Landstrasse 133.

Typically, a return to Venice from Frankfurt costs €256 in June/July. You could also try AirDolomiti (☎ 800-869 9000; mentioned earlier under France), which has flights from Cologne, Frankfurt and Munich to Venice.

Netherlands One recommended Amsterdam travel agency is Malibu Travel (☎ 020 638 6059), Damrak 30. However, compare the fare prices in the budget travel shops along Rokin before making your final decision. Holland International (☎ 070 307 6307, W www.hollandinternational.nl) has offices in most cities. At the time of writing, a high-season return flight from Amsterdam (via Brussels) to Venice cost around €250, but deals can go as low as around €205.

Spain A good travel agency in Madrid is Viajes Zeppelin (☎ 91 542 5154), Plaza de Santo Domingo 2. In Barcelona, you could try Halcón Viatges (☎ 93 412 4411), at Carrer de Pau Claris 108 (one of 25 branches in the city). Return fares start at €180 from Madrid or Barcelona and can rise steeply depending on season and flight conditions.

The USA Council Travel (☎ 800 226 8624) and STA (☎ 800 781 4040) have offices in major cities across the USA. Their Web sites are at W www.counciltravel.com and W www.statravel.com respectively. Discount travel agencies, known as consolidators, can be found by checking the weekly travel sections of the *New York Times*, the

Los Angeles Times, the *San Francisco Examiner* and the *Chicago Tribune*.

Fares vary wildly depending on season and availability. Low-season fares can occasionally drop as low as around US$550 return from Los Angeles. If you miss out on such offers, you will be looking at much more. At the time of writing, a late-November flight from Los Angeles to Venice cost US$830. Such flights involve at least one change and sometimes two (generally New York and again at Milan or another European hub). In high season, you are looking at around US$1300 to US$1500.

Prices from New York are less. In the low season you are looking at around US$550 return (sometimes as low as US$350). In summer be prepared for fares in excess of US$800. Delta Airlines was running direct flights to Venice from New York (daily in the high season) at the time of writing.

Discount and rock-bottom options from the USA include charter, stand-by and courier flights. Stand-by fares are often sold at 60% of the normal price for one-way tickets. Airhitch (freephone ☎ 1 800 326 20 09, W www.airhitch.org), 224 West 35th St, #910, New York, NY 10001, specialises in this. You will need to give a general idea of where and when you need to go, and a few days before your departure you will be presented with a choice of two or three flights.

A New York–Rome return (you won't find anything to Venice) on a courier flight can cost about US$300 (more from the west coast). Now Voyager (☎ 212-431 1616), Suite 307, 74 Varrick St, New York, NY 10013, specialises in courier flights, but you must pay an annual membership fee (around US$50) that entitles you to take as many courier flights as you like.

Also worth considering are Europe by Air coupons (☎ 1 888 387 2479). The Web site can be found at W www.eurair.com. You purchase a minimum of three US$99 coupons before leaving North America. Each coupon is valid for a one-way flight within the combined system of more than 30 participating regional airlines in Europe (exclusive of local taxes, which you will be charged when you make the flight). The coupons are valid for 120 days from the day you make your first flight. A few words of caution – using one of these coupons for a one-way flight won't always be better value than local alternatives, so check them out before committing yourself to any given flight. The same company offers two- and three-week unlimited flight passes and it sells one-off air fares too.

If you can't find a particularly cheap flight, it is always worth considering a cheap transatlantic hop to London to prowl around the discount travel agencies there. See The UK & Ireland section earlier in this chapter.

Canada Alitalia has direct flights to Rome and Milan from Toronto and Montreal. Direct flights to Venice are less likely. Scan the budget travel ads in the *Toronto Globe & Mail*, the *Toronto Star* and the *Vancouver Province*.

Travel CUTS (☎ 800 667 2887, W www .travelcuts.com), called Voyages Campus in Quebec, has offices in all major cities across Canada.

Low-season return fares from Montreal to Venice start from around C$975, while a high-season ticket could cost C$1037. From Vancouver you'd be looking at C$1063 and C$1590 respectively.

Australia STA Travel and Flight Centre are well known for cheap fares. STA Travel (☎ 1300 360 390, W www.statravel.com.au) has offices in all major cities and on many university campuses. Flight Centre (☎ 1300 362 665, W www.flightcentre.com.au) has dozens of offices throughout Australia. To find your nearest branch, call ☎ 131 600.

Heavily discounted fares can also be obtained through travel agencies. Some agencies, particularly smaller ones, advertise cheap fares in the travel sections of weekend newspapers, such as the *Age* in Melbourne and the *Sydney Morning Herald*.

Alitalia, Qantas and several other airlines fly more or less direct to Rome.

Discounted return fares on mainstream airlines through reputable agencies can be surprisingly cheap. Average low-season return fares to destinations such as Rome, Milan and Venice start at around A$1600 (although they can go lower). In the high season you could be looking at between A$2100 and A$2500.

On some flights between Australia and destinations like London, Paris and Frankfurt, a return ticket between that destination and another major European city is thrown in – you could use this to get to Venice.

For courier flights try Jupiter (☎ 02-9317 2230), Unit 3, 55 Kent Rd, Mascot, Sydney, NSW 2020.

New Zealand The *New Zealand Herald* has a travel section in which travel agencies advertise fares. Flight Centre (☎ 09-309 6171) has a large central office in Auckland at National Bank Towers (on the corner of Queen and Darby Sts) and many branches throughout the country. STA Travel (☎ 0800 874 773, **W** www.statravel.com.au) has offices in Auckland, as well as in Hamilton, Palmerston North, Wellington, Christchurch and Dunedin.

A round-the-world (RTW) ticket is sometimes cheaper than a normal return. Otherwise, you can fly from Auckland to Australia and pick up a connecting flight in Melbourne or Sydney. Return fares from New Zealand to Venice (changing in Rome) are around NZ$2500 but airlines such as Thai International or Malaysia Airlines may offer less expensive deals.

Asia Hong Kong can be a good place to buy tickets. Its discount travel centres are at least as unreliable as those of other cities. A one-way fare to Europe can cost about US$660, but shop around. Discount agencies in Bangkok can get you a one-way fare for about US$460.

STA Travel has branches in Hong Kong, Tokyo, Singapore, Bangkok and Kuala Lumpur.

Airline Offices
Airlines are listed under Linee Aeree in the *Pagine Gialle* (Yellow Pages). Generally, you won't find any offices in Venice itself. Most have reps at one or other of the airports and increasingly offer freephone numbers for you to call. The Clipper Viaggi travel agency in Mestre (Map 11) represents several airlines.

Alitalia (☎ 848 86 56 41, 041 258 12 22) Via Sansovino 7, Mestre
British Airways (freephone ☎ 800 28 72 87)
Go (☎ 848 88 77 66)
Qantas Airways (☎ 041 98 77 44) Clipper Viaggi, Via Lazzari 1, Mestre
Ryanair (☎ 199 11 41 14) Treviso airport

BUS
The bus is usually cheaper than the train, but is less comfortable for long journeys. Where rail services are poor or absent in the Veneto, bus becomes the only option. Where you can get a train, it is generally preferable to do so.

The *stazione autobus* (main bus station) is at Piazzale Roma (Map 3). Buses leave here for destinations around the Veneto, the rest of Italy and abroad. Along with ticket offices, you'll find a Telecom phone booth, hotel booking stand, bureau de change, car-hire agencies and a left-luggage office *(deposito bagagli)*. The office is open 6am to 9pm daily and charges €2.60 per item per 24 hours.

Other Parts of Italy
ACTV buses (☎ 041 528 78 86) serve the area immediately surrounding Venice, including Mestre and Chioggia.

ATVO (Azienda Trasporti Veneto Orientale; ☎ 041 520 55 30) operates buses to destinations all over the eastern part of the Veneto. Numerous other companies go farther west in the Veneto, across into Friuli-Venezia Giulia (Italy's easternmost region) and elsewhere throughout the country. Tickets and information are available at the ticket office in Piazzale Roma (Map 3).

Note, however, that for principal destinations (Padua, Vicenza, Verona and Treviso in the Veneto; Bologna, Florence, Milan, Rome and Trieste beyond) it is much easier to get the train. In the case of Vicenza and Verona, for example, you would first have to get a bus to Padua (departures every half hour or so) and then make an onward connection. The train is far more simple.

Throughout the Excursions chapter, you will find information on how to get to your destination. If a bus is suggested, board it in Piazzale Roma.

Other Countries

Eurolines, in conjunction with local bus companies across Europe, is the main international carrier. Eurolines' Web site, at W www .eurolines.com, provides links to the sites of all the national operators. In Venice, Eurolines tickets can be bought from Agenzia Brusutti (Map 3; ☎ 041 522 97 73), Piazzale Roma 497/e.

The London-based Busabout network (☎ 020-7950 1661, fax 020-7950 1662, W www.busabout.com) also covers Venice, but is of interest only to those who intend to travel a lot beyond Italy as well.

UK From London, Eurolines (☎ 0870 514 3219), 52 Grosvenor Gardens, Victoria, London SW1W 0AU, runs buses to Venice via Milan (where you must change) from two to four days per week, depending on the time of year. The trip takes 30½ hours. The one-way and return fares are, respectively, UK£75 and UK£115 (UK£68 and UK£104 for those aged under 26 and seniors) in the peak period (Easter, July–August and Christmas–New Year). Buses depart from Victoria coach station, a couple of blocks from the Eurolines office.

France Eurolines has offices in many French cities, including in the Paris bus station (☎ 01 49 72 51 51), 28 ave du Générale de Gaulle, and on the left bank at 55 rue St Jacques (☎ 01 43 54 11 99), off blvd St Germain. Passengers going to, or coming from, the UK often have to change buses here. The standard one-way/return fare to Venice is €101/164 (18 hours, four to five times per week).

Rest of Europe Eurolines also runs services direct to Venice from Amsterdam, Barcelona (with connections from Alicante and Madrid), Brussels, Bucarest, Budapest, Montpellier, Nice, Perpignan and Sofia. For buses from other European cities, you often need to change in Mestre or Padova and, depending on your destination, en route. Several long-distance services from Poland and the Ukraine pass through Mestre en route to Milan and Genoa. A weekly service runs from Istanbul via Sofia to Venice.

TRAIN

From Stazione di Santa Lucia, known in Venice simply as the *ferrovia*, you can get direct trains west to Padua, Verona, Milan and Bologna, and on into France and Switzerland. Heading east, you can travel to Trieste and on to Slovenia, Croatia, Hungary and beyond. Connections to Florence, Rome and farther south can easily be made too. There's another station in Mestre, on the mainland.

Passes & Discounts

Eurail, InterRail, Europass and Flexipass tickets are valid on the national rail network Trenitalia (formerly Ferrovie dello Stato, or FS). Possible local passes include the Railpass, Flexipass and Euro-Domino pass, all of which can be bought in Italy and abroad at most major stations and student travel outlets. They allow you unlimited rail travel for varying periods of time, although none of these passes is much use unless you plan to travel extensively in Italy or Europe. You can review passes and special deals on Eurail International's Web site at W www.eurail.com.

People aged between 12 and 25 inclusive can acquire the Carta Verde and people aged 60 and over the Carta d'Argento. Both cost €23.25, are valid for a year and entitle holders to 20% off ticket prices.

The Offerta Famiglia allows groups of three to five people travelling together to get a discount of 20% on their journey (a combined ticket for everyone travelling is issued). This offer is not valid in July, August, December, the first half of January or the period from Palm Sunday to Easter.

Information

Stazione di Santa Lucia There's a rail-travel information office inside the station opposite the APT office. It's open 7am to 9pm daily and usually has quite a queue outside.

For fare and timetable information, you can call ☎ 848 88 80 88. It's an automated service in Italian only. Train timetables are posted at Stazione di Santa Lucia. The main *orario* (timetable) displays *arrivi* (arrivals) on a white background and *partenze* (departures) on a yellow one. Impending arrivals and departures also appear on eleconic boards. You will notice a plethora of symbols and acronyms on the main timetables, some of which are useful for identifying the type of train concerned (see Types of Train in the following Other Parts of Italy section).

Occasionally you will find yearly timetables, *In Treno*, published by Trenitalia on ale at newspaper stands (€2). You can get ne for the north and centre of the country which covers the Veneto) and one for the outh. Several similar timetable guides are ublished by other companies too. A popular and reliable country-wide one is Pozzoario (€3.85). You may also be able to get free booklet covering the main lines from 'enice at the rail information office. It is alled *In Treno Triveneto* and covers main ational routes as well as all lines operating vithin the Triveneto area (ie, the Veneto, riuli-Venezia Giulia and Trentino).

Next door to the APT office in the station s an Associazione Veneziana Albergatori otel booking service.

The left-luggage office is opposite platorm 14 and opens 3.45am to 12.30am. You ay €2.60 per item for 12 hours. You'll also ind lockers on platform 1.

Opposite platform 11 there's a Change ooth, open 7am to 8.30pm daily. Change as another booth opposite platforms 4 and 5. here's also an automatic exchange machine y one of the train station exits if you are des-erate for euros outside working hours.

Just outside the Change booth at platform 1 is a credit-card pay phone; standard Tele-om phones are scattered about the station.

lestre You will find similar services at lestre station (Map 11), including rail in-ormation, a hotel booking office (see Sea-ons & Reservations at the beginning of the 'laces to Stay chapter), phones (including a redit-card phone) and a left-luggage office, pen 4.30am to 1am daily. Charges are the ame as at Stazione di Santa Lucia.

)ther Parts of Italy

ypes of Train A wide variety of trains can e found on the Italian rail network. They tart with the slow all-stops *locali*, which

generally don't travel much beyond their main city of origin or province. Next come the *regionali*, which also tend to be slow, but cover greater distances, sometimes going beyond their region of origin. *Interregionali* cover greater distances still and don't necessarily stop at every station.

From this level, there is a qualitative leap upwards to InterCity (IC) trains, faster, long-distance trains operating between major cities, for which you generally have to pay a supplement on top of the normal cost of a ticket. EuroCity (EC) trains are the international version. They can reach a top speed of 200km/h (but rarely get the chance!).

Comfort and speed on the most important lines are provided by the *pendolini*, so-called because they 'lean' up to 8° into curves to increase standard InterCity speeds by up to 35%. Pendolini and other top-of-the-range services, which on high-speed track can zip along at more than 300km/h, are collectively known as Eurostar Italia (ES). The Eurostar Italia runs once daily between Venice and Milan and takes just two hours 50 minutes. There are six services from Rome via Florence to Venice, and two from Trieste.

Other train types you may encounter are the *diretto* (D) and *espresso* (E). They are slow and are gradually disappearing.

Night trains *(notturne)* are either old *espressi* or, increasingly, InterCity Notte (ICN) services. You generally have the option of *cuccette* (couchettes) – four or six fold-down bunk beds in a compartment – or a proper bed in a *vagone letto* (sleeping car). A place in the latter is much more expensive than a simple couchette. The international version is the EuroNight (EN).

Tickets The cost of train travel is lower in Italy than in most of the rest of Western Europe, although the gap is closing.

There are many ticket possibilities. Apart from the standard division between *prima classe* and *seconda classe* (1st and 2nd class) on the faster trains (generally you can only get 2nd-class seats on locali and regionali), you usually have to pay a supplement for being on a fast train. As with tickets, the price of the supplement is calculated according to the length of the journey. You can pay the supplement separately from the ticket. Thus, if you have a 2nd-class return ticket from Venice to Milan, you might decide to avoid the supplement one way and take a slower train, but pay it on the way back to speed things up a little. Whatever you decide, you need to pay the supplement before boarding the train.

You can buy rail tickets (for major destinations on fast trains at least) at the station (often crowded) and from most travel agents. If you choose to buy them at the station, there are automatic machines that (should they be working) accept credit cards and cash. It is also possible to order tickets over the phone by credit card (☎ 199 16 61 77) and pick them up at a special counter at the station. You generally need to make the booking 24 hours in advance.

It is advisable, and in some cases obligatory, to book long-distance tickets in advance, whether international or domestic. In 1st class, booking is often mandatory (and free). Where it is optional (which is more often, but not always, the case in 2nd class), you may pay a €2.60 booking fee. Tickets can be booked at the windows in the station or at most travel agencies.

The following prices are approximate standard, 2nd-class, one-way fares (plus supplement) on InterCity trains. Pendolino and Eurostar Italia fares are higher.

destination	fare (€)	duration
Bologna	12.10	2 hours
Florence	18.75	3 hours
Milan	19.15	2¾ hours
Naples	45.15	9 hours
Rome	35.90	5½ hours

Validate your ticket by stamping it in one of the yellow machines scattered about all stations (usually with a *convalida* sign on them). Failure to do so will be rewarded with an on-the-spot fine (€5.15 to €31) if you're caught by the conductor. If you buy a return ticket, you must stamp it each way (at each end of the ticket).

The ticket you buy is valid for two months until stamped. Once stamped it is valid for 24

hours if the distance of the journey (one way) is greater than 200km, six hours if it is les The time calculated is for each one-way jou ney (so on a short return trip, you get si hours from the time of stamping on the wa out and the same on the way back).

Seats on ES trains on Friday and Sunda must be booked. On other days wagons fc unbooked seats are set aside. If you boar an ES train on Friday or Sunday without booking, you risk a €5.15 fine.

The Veneto Almost all services, from th humble locali to the high-speed Eurosta Italia trains, stop at the main centres c Mestre, Padua, Vicenza and Verona on th westward journey across the Veneto. Re member that getting an InterCity or Eurc star Italia train on short journeys such a these means paying a supplement, which i these cases will often as much as double th cost of the fare – it is up to you to decide t what extent time is money.

To other destinations in the Veneto, ra services are comparatively limited – yo can head north to Treviso and north-west t Bassano del Grappa easily, but beyon those places it becomes more sensible t work out alternatives by bus.

See the individual sections in the Excu sions chapter for information on how to ge about the Veneto.

Other Countries

The UK The Channel Tunnel allows for lan transport links between Britain and Cont nental Europe. The Eurostar passenger-trai service (☎ 0870 518 6186) travels betwee London and Paris and London and Brussel Visit its Web site at Ⓦ www.eurostar.con The Eurotunnel vehicle service travels be tween terminals in Folkestone and Calais (se the Car & Motorcycle section for details).

Alternatively, you can get a train ticke that includes the Channel crossing by ferr SeaCat or hovercraft. After that, you ca travel via Paris and southern France or b swinging from Belgium down through Ge many and Switzerland.

The cheapest standard return fare to Venic on offer at the time of writing was UK£18

Always ask about discounts. As a rule, toddlers aged under four go for free and kids aged four to 11 travel for half the adult fare. Seniors can get a Rail Europe Senior Card, which is valid for a year for trips that cross at least one border. In the UK the card costs UK£5; you must already have a Senior Railcard (UK£18), which is available to anyone who can prove they are aged 60 or over check W www.senior-railcard.co.uk or call ☎ 0845 748 4950). The pass entitles you to roughly 30% off standard fares.

For the latest fare information on journeys including the Eurostar, contact the Rail Europe Travel Centre (☎ 0870 584 8848, W www.raileurope.co.uk). Additionally, Rail Choice (☎ 020-8659 7300) is a good source of train information across Europe.

Orient Express The Venice Simplon Orient Express runs between London and Venice via Paris, Zürich and Verona two to five times per week from March to November. It departs from London at 11.05am on Thursday and Sunday, arriving in Venice at 5.28pm the following day. The fare one way costs a rather staggering UK£1200, so enjoy the luxury while it lasts.

The company that runs these trains has developed a wider range of variations on this old-world luxury theme. For instance, you can extend the London-Venice trip to Florence and Rome (this service only operates once a week), in which case you arrive in Rome at 4.30am the day after reaching Venice (with the morning spent in Florence). The one-way ticket costs UK£1500.

From Venice, you also have the choice of travelling to London via Vienna, Prague and Paris (the service doesn't operate from London). The one-way fare is a mere UK£1465.

As a rule, passengers travel one way on the Orient Express and make the outgoing or return journey by more prosaic means. The company offers packages involving a couple of nights in the destination city, the train trip and an air fare. For instance, a four-day package could involve travel to Venice, two nights there and the return to London by air. You would be looking at UK£1535 for this. For those itching to know if it's possible to

catch the Orient Express to its one-time final destination, Istanbul, the answer is yes – but not via Venice.)

Any travel agent in Venice can assist with booking tickets. Otherwise, you can get in touch with the headquarters in London (☎ 020-7805 5100, W www.orient-express trains.com).

France From Paris, about the quickest you can hope to get to Venice is in 9½ hours. This involves getting the TGV to Milan Centrale from Paris Gare de Lyon and changing there to a Eurostar Italia train for Venice. A standard, one-way, 2nd-class ticket costs from around €107, depending on the type of train connection you make in Milan. Booking is necessary.

Alternatively, but adding from two to three hours to your journey, you can travel via Lausanne in Switzerland.

Switzerland & Germany The most comfortable way in from Switzerland by rail is the modern Cisalpino (CIS) service. Most of these services terminate in Milan, coming from Basle, Bern, Geneva and Zürich. One service connects Venice directly with Geneva, via Milan. That trip costs €136.60 one way and takes about seven hours, starting in Geneva at 9.05am. There is a branch connection from Basle (€152.25).

Coming from Germany, it is possible to get a Cisalpino from Stuttgart to Milan via Zürich. Otherwise there are direct services to Venice on standard trains from Munich (three per day), Dortmund and Hamburg (one per day each).

Austria, Slovenia and Eastern Europe Three trains a day run from Vienna (Südbahnhof) to Venice (via Tarvisio in the northeast of Italy). Two direct services run every day from the Slovene capital, Ljubljana.

Other possible eastern European starting points for direct trains include Belgrade, Budapest and Zagreb (twice per day).

Spain From Spain, the only direct service is an overnight Barcelona-Milan train that runs three to seven days per week depending on the season (12¾ hours). A reclining seat costs €96.75 one way. From Milan you have to organise onward connections. A 2nd-class couchette is €119.60 and a top-class single cabin is €299.30. Total travel time to Venice (taking into account the connection in Milan) is around 17 hours.

CAR & MOTORCYCLE

To give you an idea of how many clicks you'll put behind you if travelling with your own wheels, Venice is 279km from Milan, 529km from Rome, 579km from Geneva, 1112km from Paris, 1135km from Berlin, 1515km from London and 1820km from Madrid.

Coming from the UK, you can take your vehcile across to France by ferry or on the Channel Tunnel car train, Eurotunnel (☎ 0870 241 2938, Ⓦ www.eurotunnel .com). The latter runs around the clock, with up to four crossings (35 minutes) per hour between Folkestone and Calais in the high season. You pay for the vehicle only and fares vary according to the time of day, day of the week and season; you can be looking at as much as UK£297 return (valid for a year). In the low season, you can sometimes get much cheaper offers.

The main points of entry to Italy are: the Mont Blanc tunnel from France at Chamonix (closed at the time of writing), which connects with the A5 for Turin and Milan; the Grand St Bernard tunnel from Switzerland, which also connects with the A5; and the Brenner Pass from Austria, which connects with the A22 to Bologna. Mountain passes in the Alps are often closed in winter and sometimes in autumn and spring, making the tunnels a less picturesque but more reliable way to arrive in Italy. Make sure you have snow chains in winter.

Europe is made for motorcycle touring and Italy is no exception. Motorcyclists literally swarm into the country in summer to tour the scenic routes. With a bike you rarely have to book ahead for ferries and can enter restricted traffic areas in Italian cities without any problems. Italian traffic police generally turn a blind eye to motorcycles parked on footpaths. Crash helmets are compulsory

in Italy. Clearly, you can no more get around Venice itself by bike than by car!

An interesting Web site loaded with advice for people planning to drive in Europe is Ⓦ www.ideamerge.com/motoeuropa. If you want help with route planning, check out Ⓦ www.euroshell.com.

Once in Italy, the A4 is the quickest way to reach Venice from east or west. It connects Turin with Trieste, passing through Milan and Mestre. Take the Venice exit and follow the signs for the city. The A4 is a toll road – sample prices are Venice-Padua €2.05 and Venice-Milan €10.60. Coming from the Brenner Pass, the A22 connects with the A4 near Verona. From the south, take the A13 from Bologna, which connects with the A4 at Padua. A more interesting route is to take the SS11 from Padua to Venice.

Paperwork & Preparations

Vehicles must be roadworthy, registered and insured (third party at least). The Green Card, an internationally recognised proof of insurance obtainable from your insurer, is mandatory. Also ask your insurer for a European Accident Statement form, which can simplify matters in the event of an accident.

A European breakdown assistance policy, such as the AA Five Star Service or the RAC Eurocover Motoring Assistance in the UK, is a good investment. For information on driving licences, see Documents in the Facts for the Visitor chapter.

Of course, you will not be doing any driving at all in Venice itself. For details of driving in the immediate area, as well as the hire or purchase of vehicles, see Car & Motorcycle in the Getting Around chapter.

Driving in Italy

Road Rules In general, standard European road rules apply. In built-up areas, the speed limit is usually 50km/h, rising to 90km/h on secondary roads, 110km/h on main roads (caravans 80km/h) and up to 130km/h (caravans 100km/h) on *autostrade* (toll and toll-free motorways).

Motorcyclists must use headlights at all times. Crash helmets are obligatory on bikes of 125cc or more.

Vehicles already on roundabouts often have right of way. However, this is not always the case and working out which type you are confronted with is best done by paying careful attention to local example.

The blood-alcohol limit is 0.08%. Random breath tests are conducted – penalties range from on-the-spot fines to confiscation of your driving licence.

Fines for other traffic offences are also made on the spot where foreign-registered cars are involved. You can be obliged to pay a quarter of the fine immediately. If the driver refuses to pay, the local police may confiscate the driver's licence or even the vehicle until the fine has been paid in full.

Petrol Italy is among the most expensive places in Western Europe for *benzina* (petrol); the price has been increasing steadily of late with the runaway dollar fuelling the problem. *Senza piombo* (unleaded) costs €1.10 per litre and *gasolio* (diesel) €0.85 per litre. These prices can drop by up to 3c in some service stations, especially those with *fai da te* promotions, where you serve yourself rather than wait for an attendant. Stations on motorways charge about 1c more per litre.

If you are driving a car that uses liquid petroleum gas (LPG), you will need to buy a special guide to service stations that have *gasauto* (GPL in Italy). By law these must be located in nonresidential areas and are usually in the country or on city outskirts, although you'll find plenty on the autostrade. GPL costs around €0.55 per litre.

You can pay with most credit cards at most service stations. Those on the autostrade open 24 hours per day. Otherwise, opening hours are generally around 7am to 12.30pm and 3.30pm to 7.30pm (7pm in winter). Up to 75% are closed on Sunday and public holidays; others close on Monday. Don't assume you can't get petrol if you pass a station that is closed. Quite a few have self-service pumps that accept banknotes. It is illegal to carry spare fuel in your vehicle.

Toll Roads & Highways Many of Italy's autostrade (four- to six-lane motorways) are toll roads and the tolls tend to be expensive. Some reasonable highways known as *superstrade* are toll free. More often than not, you will have the choice between a toll road and a busy *strada statale* (represented on maps as 'S' or 'SS'). These tend to pass through towns and can as much as double your travel time. The SS11 from Padua to Venice is an example. Smaller roads are known as *strade provinciali* (represented on maps as 'P' or 'SP').

Sign Language

You won't be doing any driving in Venice itself, but if you plan to drive in Italy at all, you'll save yourself some grief by learning what a few of the many road signs mean:

ENTRATA	ENTRANCE (eg, to *autostrada*)
INCROCIO	INTERSECTION/CROSSROADS
LAVORI IN CORSO	ROADWORKS AHEAD
PARCHEGGIO	CAR PARK
PASSAGGIO A LIVELLO	LEVEL CROSSING
RALLENTARE	SLOW DOWN
SENSO UNICO	ONE-WAY STREET
SENSO VIETATO	NO ENTRY
SOSTA VIETATA	NO STOPPING/PARKING
SOSTA AUTORIZZATA	PARKING PERMITTED (during times displayed)
SVOLTA	BEND
TUTTE LE DIREZIONI	ALL DIRECTIONS (useful when looking for town exit)
USCITA	EXIT (eg, from *autostrada*)

You can pay tolls by credit card (including Visa, MasterCard, AmEx and Diners Club) on most autostrade in northern Italy. Another way to pay is to buy a Viacard, available from toll booths and some service stations and tourist offices. You present it to the attendant or insert it into the appropriate Viacard machine as you exit an autostrada. Leftover credit is not refundable on leaving Italy.

Road Assistance As a rule, members of foreign motoring organisations, such as the RAC, AA (both UK) and AAA (USA), and people who arrange car insurance through them, will be provided with an emergency assistance number to use while travelling in Italy. You can also get roadside assistance from the Automobile Club Italia by calling ☎ 116. Your insurance may cover this, otherwise you'll pay a minimum fee of €82.65. In any case, it is likely that, whichever number you use, an ACI truck will arrive.

Spot Checks Theft of foreign cars is a problem in Italy, so you may well find yourself being pulled over, usually by the *carabinieri* (military police), to have your papers checked. If the car isn't yours, you need a letter from the owner that grants you permission to drive it (unless they are with you), otherwise you risk having the car impounded.

BICYCLE

If you plan to bring your own bike, check with the airline about any hidden costs. It will have to be disassembled and packed for the journey.

Once in Italy, it is possible to transport your bicycle on many trains. Those marked with a bicycle symbol on timetables have a carriage set aside for the transport of bicycles. Otherwise you need to dismantle it and pack it. You cannot take your bike on ES services requiring a booking. In all cases where you can take your bike, you must pay a supplement of €3.60.

The country around Venice is pretty flat until you start heading towards the Alps, so is potentially ideal (if not always riveting) for getting about on your bike.

UK-based cyclists planning to cycle about beyond Venice might want to contact the Cyclists' Touring Club (☎ 01483-417 217), Cotterell House, 69 Meadrow, Godalming, Surrey GU7 3HS. It has a Web site at W www.ctc.org.uk and can supply information to members on cycling conditions, itineraries and cheap insurance. Membership costs UK£25 per year.

HITCHING

Hitching is never entirely safe and we don't recommend it. Travellers who decide to hitch should understand that they are taking a small but potentially serious risk. People who do choose to hitch will be safer if they travel in pairs and let someone know where they are planning to go.

To get out of Venice, you need to start at one of the highway exits from Mestre. The chances of anyone stopping for you on autostrade are low (the practice is illegal) – try the more congested toll-free highways, such as the SS11 to Padua.

BOAT

Ferries connect Venice with Greece and Slovenia. Of course, you can reach many other parts of Italy by sea. Car ferries link ports up and down the peninsula with Albania, Corsica (France), Croatia, Greece, Malta, Spain, Tunisia, Turkey and Yugoslavia.

Detailed below are services from Venice. Tickets can be bought direct or arranged through travel agencies.

Greece

Minoan Lines (☎ 041 271 23 45), Porto Venezia, Zona Santa Marta, runs ferries to/from Greece (Corfu, Igoumenitsa and Patras) daily in summer (four times per week in winter). Passengers pay up to Dr30,600 one way for an airline-style seat, depending on the season. Minoan Lines has offices in Athens and elsewhere in Greece but you can pick up tickets from most travel agents.

Strintzis Lines (☎ 041 277 05 59), Stazione Marittima 103, operates up to four ferries per week in summer to the same destinations in Greece. A simple spot on the deck costs from Dr14,600 in the low season or up to Dr20,900 in the high season. Airline-style seats cost about the same as with Minoan Lines.

The journey with either line to Igoumenitsa takes about 27 hours. To Patras add another eight. These services all depart from the Stazione Marittima (passenger port) in Dorsoduro (Map 6). There's a left-luggage office at the back of the building.

Slovenia & Albania

Kompas Italia (☎ 041 528 65 45), San Marco 1497, operates a daily summer service from Izola (Slovenia) to Venice in summer. The trip takes 2½ hours and a round-trip ticket costs up to 14,400Sit. One way costs up to 12,000Sit. In Slovenia contact Kompas Turizem (☎ 5-617 8000), Obala 41, Portoroz. You can get to Trieste (about 150km east of Venice) by sea, depending on the political situation, from Albania. Agemar (☎ 040 36 37 37), Piazza del Duca degli Abruzzi 1/a, is a good place to inquire about this. They have several services a week to Durrés.

ORGANISED TOURS

Options for organised travel to Italy, including Venice, abound. The Italian State Tourism Board (see Tourist Offices Abroad in the Facts for the Visitor chapter) can provide a list of tour operators, noting what each specialises in. Tours can save you hassles, but they rob you of independence and generally do not come cheap.

In the UK, a couple of big specialists may be worth investigating initially, if only for the variety of tours they present: Magic of Italy (☎ 0870 546 2442), and Alitalia's subsidiary, Italiatour (☎ 01883-621 900). Magic of Italy only includes Venice in larger packages covering Florence and Rome as well.

Kirker Travel Ltd (☎ 020-7231 3333), 3 New Concordia Wharf, Mill St, London SE1 2BB, specialises in short breaks from London. Such trips start at about UK£400 per person for three nights in twin accommodation with air fare, transfers and breakfast included. Depending on the hotel you choose, the price can rise considerably. Prices also rise in summer.

UK-based art and architecture lovers might consider one of the couple of annual specialised guided tours to Venice organised by Martin Randall Travel (020-8742 3355). Call up to a year in advance as the trips are popular. You are looking at upwards of UK£800 per person.

In the USA, Breakaway Adventures (☎ 800 567 62 86, fax 202 293 04 83, W www.breakaway-adventures.com), 1312 18th St, NW, Suite 401, Washington, DC 20036, is a general tour operator that can organise trips to Venice and beyond.

In Australia, CIT Travel (☎ 02-9267 1255, fax 02-9261 4664, W www.cittravel.com.au), Level 2, 263 Clarence St, Sydney, NSW 2000, is a good general operator for trips to Italy. Another with specialist Venice knowledge is ATI Tours (☎ 02-9798 0588, freephone ☎ 1800 069 985, fax 02-9716 0891, W www.atitours.com.au), 125 Ramsay St, Haberfield NSW 2045.

Shopping around before making your final choice usually pays off. It is not unheard of for different operators to offer the same thing for considerably different prices. Hotel packages are the easiest to compare, and there's nothing worse than finding out you got the same holiday as someone else but paid much more for the pleasure.

GETTING THERE & AWAY

Getting Around

THE AIRPORTS

Most people flying into Venice will arrive at Marco Polo airport, at Tessera, just outside Mestre and about 12km from Venice. Ryanair and a few charter flights from London and a couple of other European cities land at Treviso's tiny airport, about 35km north of Venice.

Marco Polo Airport

The airport (☎ 041 260 92 60 for flight information) is just east of Mestre. The terminal building is divided into two parts. As you drive in, the first section you come to is *Arrivi* (Arrivals). Immediately beyond, in the same low building, is *Partenze* (Departures). The airport absorbs almost four million passengers a year and a new terminal building is due for completion in late 2002.

In the arrivals hall, there's a tourist office (see Local Tourist Offices in the Facts for the Visitor chapter), along with hotel booking counters, a couple of bureaux de change and a row of car-hire outlets.

More bureaux de change, banks and ATMs (all of which accept most main credit/debit cards) can be found in the departures lounge, where there are also a post office, first-aid station, shops and bars.

The left-luggage office *(deposito bagagli)* is in the arrivals hall. It's open 6am to 9pm and charges €1.80 per item per day. Next door is the *Bagagli Smarriti* (lost-luggage) office, open 9am to 8pm daily.

To/From the Airport There are several options for getting to Venice from the airport, from the super-expensive water taxi to the cheap and relatively straightforward bus. The main problem is with night flights that arrive late. Some people have found themselves at the airport faced with a long wait for public transport and no taxis.

Bus ATVO buses (Map 3; ☎ 041 520 55 30) run from the airport to Piazzale Roma via Mestre train station. The journey takes 20 minutes and costs €2.60. Also known as Fly bus, they cost €2.05 from the airport to Mestre train station. Departures are regular throughout the day (32 to Piazzale Roma; around 40 to Mestre). The first departure for Venice is at 8.30am and the last 12.30am. The first service to Mestre leaves at 7.21am.

The regular ACTV city bus No 5 also runs between the airport and Piazzale Roma (€0.75). It makes more stops and takes closer to 30 minutes. Departures are roughly every 30 minutes from Piazzale Roma, from 4.40am to 12.40am. The first departure from the airport is at 4.08am.

Boat The Alilaguna hydrofoil from the airport to Venice or the Lido costs €9.80, and to Murano it costs €4.65. Travelling to the airport, you can pick up the hydrofoil at the Zattere (Map 6) or near St Mark's Square (Piazza San Marco), in front of the Giardini ex Reali (Map 5).

Water Taxi The official rate for the ride between Piazzetta di San Marco and the airport is €44.95. To/from the Lido costs €55.25.

Taxi Just as efficient as the waterborne version, if more prosaic, are taxis with wheels. You generally pay €25.80 to get to Piazzale Roma from the airport – a trip of around 15 minutes.

Parking Marco Polo Park (☎ 041 541 59 13) allows short- and long-term parking. Short-term parking costs €1.05 for the first hour and €1.55 each hour thereafter. Leave the ticket on display.

The same company has a longer term multi-level car park. The first six hours cost €5.15 or €11.35 per day for the first six days. Thereafter the daily rate drops to €9.05 per day. There is an open-air car park too, where you pay €7.75 per day for the first three days and then the rate drops to €5.15.

Otherwise, the Brusutti car park, about 1km from the airport, charges €5.15 per day or €21/31 per week (open-air/under cover). The hitch here is that you then have to get a shuttle bus to the airport.

Treviso Airport

You are less likely to land at Treviso's minuscule San Giuseppe airport (☎ 0422 31 53 31) but if you do, don't panic! It is only about 5km south-west of Treviso.

The arrivals hall boasts a small, thinly stocked regional tourist information booth, a lost-luggage office next to it, a bureau de change and four car-hire outlets (Hertz, Avis, Maggiore and Europcar). Next door in departures, you'll find an ATM and a couple of tour and airline offices (including Ryanair). There is no left-luggage service.

To/From the Airport Those travelling from the UK or Brussels may well come on Ryanair, the low-cost Irish airline. The Eurobus service (run jointly by ATVO and Brusutti) connects with Ryanair's five daily flights. The trip to/from Piazzale Roma takes 65 minutes and costs €4.15 (€7.23 return – but the ticket is valid for one week only). If you arrive by charter, check with the charter company whether there is a special service. If all else fails, local Treviso bus No 6 stops right outside the terminal gates and goes to the main train station in Treviso. From there you can proceed to Venice by rail.

If you need to get a taxi, be prepared to pay €62 to reach Piazzale Roma. The trip can take up to one hour.

Parking Parking is provided about 300m south of the airport – follow the signs. It costs €1.05 per hour, €5.15 per day and €31 for a week. If you just need to drop someone off or pick them up, you can park beside the terminal.

PUBLIC TRANSPORT

The Azienda Consorzio Trasporti Veneziano (ACTV; ☎ 041 528 78 86, W www.actv.it) runs public transport in the Comune di Venezia (the municipality).

Public transport comprises the *vaporetti* ferry service in the city and around the lagoon, as well as buses connecting Venice

with mainland areas of the municipality and beyond (eg Mestre, Marghera and Chioggia).

You can pick up timetables and route maps for vaporetti and buses from the ACTV information office (Map 3) on Piazzale Roma.

Facilities for the Disabled

People with disabilities have not been completely left out of what is, after all, a fairly unfriendly environment for wheelchair-users or those with other mobility problems.

The map available from APT offices has areas of the city shaded in yellow to indicate that they can be negotiated without running into one of Venice's many bridges. Some of the bridges are equipped with *montascale* (lifts), which are marked on the maps. You can get hold of a key to operate these lifts from the tourist offices.

Most of the important vaporetto lines allow wheelchair access. Those that don't are Nos 13, 20 and 51/52.

Six bus lines are adapted for wheelchair-users: No 2 (Piazzale Roma to Mestre train station); No 4 (Piazzale Roma to Corso del Popolo in Mestre); No 5 (Piazzale Roma to Marco Polo airport); No 6/ (Tronchetto and Piazzale Roma to the mainland); and No 15 (a mainland service).

Gondola

See the special section 'Gondolas' following this chapter.

Vaporetto

The most common form of transport around Venice after your own two feet are the vaporetti, the town's ferries. Actually, there are at least three kinds of ferry: the standard, ponderous vaporetto (as in line No 1 down the Grand Canal), the sleeker *motoscafo*, which also runs local routes, and the *motonave* – big, inter-island boats that head for Torcello and other more distant destinations.

It's hard not to see the difference in fares for local residents and out-of-towners as a rip-off, but if you want to get around this way, there's not a lot you can do about it. You can risk it and not bother with tickets but spot checks do occasionally happen. If you are caught on a vaporetto without a ticket, you will be charged for the cost of the ticket plus an on-the-spot fine of €20.15. There are no excuses – signs are up all over the place in several languages (including English) laying down the rules.

Something to remember: the vaporetti get crowded and visitors have a habit of gathering by exits. If you are standing near one, it is common practice on reaching a stop to get off and let passengers behind you disembark before you get back on.

Warning Vaporetto stops can be confusing. Vessels making for the St Mark's Square (San Marco) area in particular can cause anguish, as most stop at one of a string of stops along Riva degli Schiavoni (Maps 5 & 8). Always keep an eye out for San Zaccaria. If your boat stops here, it is unlikely to make another San Marco stop before heading off elsewhere. The San Zaccaria area is confusing for getting away too. Study the signs at the various quays carefully otherwise you might find yourself on a vaporetto with the right number but going the wrong way!

Routes From Piazzale Roma, vaporetto No 1 zigzags up the Grand Canal to San Marco and then on to the Lido. If you aren't in a rush, it's a great introduction to Venice – see the special section 'Along the Grand Canal' for details. Ferry No 17 carries vehicles from Tronchetto, near Piazzale Roma, to the Lido.

Routes and route numbers change regularly, so the following list should be taken as a guide only. Not all routes go both ways.

No 1 Piazzale Roma–Ferrovia–Canal Grande–Lido (and back)
No 3 Fast Circular line: Tronchetto–Ferrovia–San Samuele–Accademia–San Marco–Tronchetto (summer only)
No 4 Fast Circular line in reverse direction to No 3 (summer only)
No 6 San Zaccaria–Lido (and back)
No 12 Fondamenta Nuove–Murano–Burano–Torcello–Punta Sabbioni (and back)
No 13 Fondamenta Nuove–Murano–Vignole–Treporti (and back)
No 14 San Zaccaria–Lido–Litorale del Cavallino (Punta Sabbioni). The one-way trip beyond the Lido costs an extra €2.60
No 17 Car ferry: Tronchetto–Lido (and back)

No 20 San Zaccaria–San Servolo–San Clemente (and back)
No 41 Circular line: Piazzale Roma–Sacca Fisola–Giudecca–San Zaccaria–San Pietro–Fondamente Nuove–Murano–Ferrovia
No 42 Circular line in reverse direction to No 41
No 51 Circular line: Piazzale Roma–Zattere–San Zaccaria–Lido–Ferrovia
No 52 Circular line in reverse direction to No 51
No 61 Limited-stops circular line: Ferrovia–Piazzale Roma–Zattere–Arsenale–Sant'Elena–Lido
No 62 Limited-stops circular line in reverse direction to No 61
No 71 Fast limited-stops line: San Zaccaria–Murano–Ferrovia–Piazzale Roma–Tronchetto (summer only)
No 72 Fast limited-stops line in reverse direction to No 71 (summer only)
No 82 San Zaccaria–San Marco–Grand Canal–Ferrovia–PiazzaleRoma–Tronchetto–Zattere–Giudecca–San Giorgio–Lido (summer only). A Limitato San Marco or Limitato Piazzale Roma sign means it will not go beyond those stops.
N All-stops night circuit: Lido–Giardini–San Zaccaria–Grand Canal–Ferrovia–Piazzale Roma–Tronchetto–Giudecca–San Giorgio–San Zaccaria

Tickets Tickets can be purchased from the ticket booths at most landing stations. Generally they are validated when sold to you, which means they are for immediate use. If they are not validated, or if you request them not to be (so you can use them later), you are supposed to validate them in the machines at each landing station before you get on the boat. You can buy tickets on the boat (at a slightly higher price).

You could be forgiven for feeling vexed by the sky-high cost of water transport for non-residents in Venice. The vaporetti are frequently overloaded, largely with visitors, so it is just conceivable that the high cost is partly intended to encourage people to walk where possible. On the other hand, it may well just be plain old avarice. If you're staying for a length of time, there is a way around these prices – see Passes later.

Single Tickets Unless you plan to use the vaporetti very little, a *corsa semplice* (single ticket) is poor value indeed at €3.10.

Note that if you make an extra-short trip, such as crossing from one side of the Grand

Canal to the other on the No 1 (one stop), the fare is €1.55. Another example is the ferry between Zattere and Giudecca. On the other hand, you may find yourself expected to pay double the fare if you have lots of luggage.

You can get a *carnet* of 10 single tickets for €25.80. But even this is not good value unless you plan to use the vaporetti sparingly. Should you decide to buy a one-off single, groups of three/four/five people save €0.52 each on the single tickets if they buy a *biglietto family* instead. These cost €7.75/ 10.35/12.90 respectively.

Even less likely to be of use than the above is a round-trip ticket *(biglietto di andata e ritorno)*, which costs €5.15.

Passes Those planning to use the vaporetti even moderately are advised to invest in a *biglietto a tempo*, a ticket valid on all transport (except the Alilaguna, LineaBlù and Clodia services; see the following Other Services section). They are valid for 24 hours from the first *convalida* (validation). Generally nowadays the ticket is stamped by the vendor (watch this if you are buying a ticket but don't want to start using it immediately). The ticket costs €9.30. Family versions cost €23.25/31/38.75 for three/four/five people. Schoolchildren or seniors in groups of at least 20 pay €5.15 each.

Better value still is the *biglietto tre giorni*, a three-day version that costs €18.05 (€12.90 if you have a Rolling Venice Concession Pass; see under Documents in the Facts for the Visitor chapter). A *biglietto sette giorni*, or weekly pass, costs €31.

If you intend to stay in Venice for a while, try to get an *abbonamento* – a pass valid for one month. These are available from the ACTV offices in Venice – Piazzale Roma (Map 3), Calle dei Fuseri, San Marco (Map 5) and Mestre (Map 11). You pay a one-off fee of €5.15 plus the cost of the pass, which is €23.25 (€15.50 for students). The €5.15 gets you a three-year ID card with which you can renew your abbonamento. You don't need a Carta Venezia (a pass for residents), but you will need a photo. It can take a month or so for the ID card to be prepared, but in the meantime you will be given a receipt valid for immediate use. The passes are valid for the calendar month.

Other Services Several services operate a different fare structure, including the Alilaguna hydrofoil to/from Marco Polo airport (see The Airports earlier in this chapter). This service also runs between Murano and the Lido or Piazzale Roma (both €4.40).

Tickets for the fast LineaBlù boats to the Lido from Tronchetto cost €6.20 one way and €9.30 return.

The Linea Clodia boat service to Chioggia costs €9.30 (€4.65 for kids aged under 12) for a same-day return from Venice. Cheaper is the combined boat-and-bus service (the No 11 line) to Chioggia, which costs €4.15 one way.

The 20-minute LineaFusinaZattere No 16 service between Zattere and Fusina, on the mainland (where there is a camp site), costs €4.15 one way and €7.75 return. The same company runs a summertime service four times per day direct from Fusina to the Alberoni beach on the Lido for the same price.

Biglietti turistici, valid for 12 hours, are available on three routes: the No 11 boat-and-bus route to Chioggia, No 1 (the Grand Canal) and the Laguna Nord line (Murano, Burano and Torcello). They cost €7.75.

Special tickets are available for particular events, such as soccer matches at the Stadio Penzo or congresses. Ask at ticket offices.

Transporting Cars, Motorcycles & Bicycles Passenger tickets on the *nave traghetto* style of ferry that also takes vehicles cost the same as for vaporetti. To take a car from, for example, Tronchetto to the Lido, you pay an extra €8.80 (one way) for a car under 4m or a motorcycle. From Tronchetto to Punta Sabbioni it costs €10.35 and from Alberoni (on the Lido) to Santa Maria del Mar costs €5.15.

On these and line Nos 6, 12, 13 and 14, a single ticket for you and your bicycle will cost €3.60.

Residents Permanent residents in the Comune di Venezia are entitled to massive discounts on fares. By way of example, a single ticket costs €0.75 and is valid (with as many changes as you like) for an hour. A book of 10 tickets costs €7.25. A short hop (see the section Single Tickets) costs residents €0.41.

In other words, public transport prices for locals are the same as they are for people in any other Italian city. Residents have to apply for a CartaVenezia to qualify for these fares.

Traghetto

The poor man's gondola, *traghetti* are used by locals to cross the Grand Canal where there is no nearby bridge. There is no particular limit (except common sense) on the number of passengers, who stand.

Traghetti operate from about 9am to 6pm between Campo del Traghetto (near Santa Maria del Giglio) and Calle de Lanza (Map 6); Campo San Samuele, north of the Ponte dell'Accademia, and Calle Traghetto (Map 6); Calle Mocenigo, farther north, and Calle Traghetto (Map 6); and Campo Santa Sofia and Campo della Pescaria (Map 4), near the produce market.

Several other *traghetto* routes operate from 9am to noon only. They include: Stazione di Santa Lucia to Fondamenta San Simeon (Map 3); Campo San Marcuola to Salizzada del Fondaco dei Turchi (Map 3); Fondamenta del Vin and Riva del Carbon, near the Ponte di Rialto (Map 5); Calle Vallarsso to Punta della Dogana (Map 5). Some of these may on occasion not operate at all. The ride costs €0.42 (although some locals round up the price).

Water Taxi

Water taxis (motorboats) are prohibitively expensive, with a set charge of €13.95 for the first seven minutes. Every additional 15 seconds, another €0.26 clicks on. On top of this, there are all sorts of surcharges. You pay €4.15 if you order one by telephone and a night surcharge of €4.40 between 10pm and 7am. Each piece of luggage costs €1.15. If more than four people are travelling, there is a €1.60 extra charge per head. On holidays you pay €4.65 extra (but in this case you don't pay the night surcharge).

The high prices are explained in part by the cost of the taxis themselves. The better

quality mahogany jobs cost up to €100,000 to build.

There are water-taxi stands at regular intervals along the Grand Canal. A few have been indicated on the maps. Otherwise, call one of the operating companies. Numbers include ☎ 041 522 12 65, 041 71 61 24 and 041 522 23 03.

Bus

You can't take buses anywhere around Venice itself, but there are regular runs across the bridge to Mestre. You can also use them to get up and down along the Lido. Tickets (valid for one hour from the time you validate them in the machine on the bus) cost €0.75. A carnet of 10 tickets costs €7.25. Don't rip each ticket off as you use it (they are double sided), as the whole carnet has to be shown if an inspector comes along.

You can buy tickets at the main bus station in Piazzale Roma, and from many newspaper stands and *tabacchi* (tobacconists).

Train

Pretty much every train leaving Santa Lucia station stops in Mestre. Trains run between the two stations from 5.12am to 12.38pm. The ride takes about 10 minutes and tickets (available from ticket windows and station tobacconists) cost €0.93 a pop.

For more information and details of the facilities available in both stations, see Train in the Getting There & Away chapter.

Porters

Getting from the vaporetto stop to your hotel can be difficult if you are heavily laden with luggage. There are several stands around the city where *portabagagli* (porters) can be engaged to escort you to your hotel. They charge €10.35 for one item and roughly €5.15 for each extra one. Prices virtually double to transport bags to any of the other islands, including Giudecca.

Points where porters can be found include the Ponte dell'Accademia (☎ 041 522 48 91), the train station (☎ 041 71 52 72), Piazzale Roma (☎ 041 522 35 90), the Ponte di Rialto (☎ 041 520 53 08) and San Marco (☎ 041 523 23 85).

Detail of St Mark's Basilica, with the Campanile towering behind

Houses and palaces seem to sprout from the water in this aerial vista of Venice.

The 16th-century Ponte di Rialto by moonlight

The fully clothed Scuola Varote

Renaissance drama, San Rocc

Well-wishers welcome – part of the old water system in Campo Angelo Raffaele

CAR & MOTORCYCLE

Those who insist on driving their cars right into Venice pay a hefty price for the pleasure, and not necessarily just in parking fees. On busy days (especially holiday weekends), day-trippers who drive into the city frequently find themselves stuck on the Ponte della Libertà making little forward progress and unable to go back. It is not unknown for traffic to get so jammed that the police shut the city off from the mainland. Why risk it?

Parking

Venice Driving in Venice is, of course, impossible. Once over the Ponte della Libertà from Mestre, cars must be left at one of the huge car parks in Piazzale Roma or on the island of Tronchetto.

It costs to tie up your beastie in Venice. The best value, given its proximity, is the Garage Comunale (Map 3) at Piazzale Roma, which is open 24 hours. It costs €18.60 (flat fee) per day. The nearby private Parking San Marco (Map 6) is also open all day and charges an incredible €18.05 for 12 hours or €24.80 for 24 hours. Guests of certain hotels get discounts (ask). Autopark Doge (Map 6), close to the private car park, is not much better. There you pay €5.15 for two hours or €18.05 per day (open 7am to 10pm).

At Tronchetto, farther out, you pay €15.50 for 24 hours, but of course it's not quite so handy.

There is a small area in Piazzale Roma where you can drop a car for 30 minutes (in practice, people tend to leave their cars longer). Queuing to get into one of these few spaces can be supremely frustrating, but locals generally observe the first come, first served rule.

Lido Garage Lido (Map 10; ☎ 041 526 12 800), at Via Emo 13, is open 7am to midnight and charges €23.25 for 24 hours.

Fusina You could also leave your car at Fusina, south of Mestre and Marghera, and catch the LineaFusinaZattere vaporetto (No 16) to the Zattere. You pay €7.75 for 24 hours in the guarded car park there, or you can take a risk and park near the vaporetto

landing for free. There have been reports of break-ins in the free parking area.

Mestre There are several car parks near the train station in Mestre. At Serenissima Parking, Viale Stazione 10, you pay €4.15 per day. It's open 24 hours.

Most of the street parking is metered in Mestre, although a determined hunt around the small streets around the train station may turn up a free parking space. If you choose this option, be aware that parking regulations can be pretty confusing and the local police take some pleasure in removing incorrectly parked vehicles.

Illegal Parking If you return to your car to find that it's no longer there, you can call any of the police forces, as they are all entitled to have cars towed away if they see fit. In reality, the Vigili Urbani are responsible for about 90% of cars towed. They use the national motoring association Automobile Club Italiano (ACI) to remove the vehicles, which are then dumped in one of three depots. The best number to call if you think your car has met this fate is ☎ 041 274 70 70. The Vigili Urbani staff it from 7am to midnight daily.

The cost of freeing your vehicle is a minimum of €86.75 for the tow plus €5.15 per day storage. To this is added the fine for which it was towed in the first place, which can range from €33.55 to €63.50.

Warning More worrisome than the confusion of parking legally are the thieves who tend to haunt some of the car parks, particularly those in Mestre. With so many foreign and hired cars among the prey, the temptation must often be hard to resist. Do not leave anything, of even remote value, in a parked car.

Rental

Avis has an office in Piazzale Roma (Italy-wide ☎ 199 10 01 33), as do Europcar (free-phone ☎ 800 82 80 50), Hertz (Italy-wide ☎ 199 11 22 11) and Expressway (☎ 041 522 30 00). They all have reps at Marco Polo airport too.

Purchase

Only people legally resident in Italy can buy vehicles there. The only way around this might be to get an Italian friend to buy one and put it in their name.

TAXI

If you need a land taxi to the airport or anywhere between Venice and Mestre, you can pick one up from the rank in Piazzale Roma, or call ☎ 041 523 77 74 or 041 93 62 22.

BICYCLE & MOPED

For obvious reasons, you won't have much need for a bicycle or moped for getting around Venice. Indeed, bicycle riding is officially banned in the lagoon city, although bamboozled out-of-towners can sometimes be seen sighing as they drag their two-wheelers up and down the seemingly innumerable bridges.

Cycling is a nice way to get around the Lido. See the Lido di Venezia section in the

---

From Soap St to Tits Bridge

The Venetians have always had a reputation for being relatively hard-headed and practical. So it should come as little surprise that a good number of street names, many of which have remained unchanged since a more-or-less organised effort to name streets began in 1100, have their origins in one-time everyday life.

A good number of these street names repeat themselves from one quarter of the city to another and give you a clue as to where local trade was once carried out. Around the Rialto area, for instance, we find the Fondamenta del Vin (Wine Quay) on the west bank and, opposite, the Riva del Ferro (Iron Quay) and Riva del Carbon (Coal Quay). These canalside walkways are among the few that exist along the Grand Canal and their existence serves to underline the Rialto area's historic role as the centre of Venetian commerce. The lanes around the San Polo side of the Ponte di Rialto were reserved for other particular goods and trades: Ruga dei Speziali (Spice Lane), Ruga degli Orefici (Goldsmiths' Lane), Pescaria (Fish Market), Fondamenta dell'Olio (Oil Quay), Calle del Storione (Sturgeon Street) and so on.

All over the city, you will stumble across streets with standard names like Forno (bakery), Spezier (spice shop), Magazen (warehouse), Pistor (another word for baker) and Cafetier (coffee shop). Malvasia was a sweet wine imported from Venice's Greek possessions (what Shakespeare dubbed Malmsey); streets with this name abound, and you can be sure that wherever they are, there was also once a discreet little *malvasia* (tavern) where you could quaff the stuff. Nearby you will almost always find a Calle del Forno. Sensible tipplers would pop in to pick up some bread or pastries to take down to the tavern for a bite with a soothing jar (or six) of malvasia.

Calle del Traghetto will sometimes still lead you down to one of the stops for gondolas serving as cross-Canal shuttles. Wandering down any Calle del Squero used to take you to the local gondola boatyards, most of which have now disappeared. That soap was a fairly rare product is indicated by the fact that the only streets dedicated to its production and sale (Saoneri) are clustered together in San Polo, with a few up in Cannaregio.

Perhaps one of the most colourful place names in Venice is Ponte delle Tette (Tits Bridge), on the dividing line between San Polo and Santa Croce. The bridge lay at the heart of what was made, in the 16th century, the red-light district.

Certain place names indicate the presence of an important family's residence (Venier, Correr, Morosini etc). Others designated concentrations of particular groups of people, such as Albanesi (Albanians) or traders from Ormesini (Hormuz). Still others refer to nearby churches, religious schools and the like.

If you really want to get behind the secrets of the Venetian street names, the best source is, without doubt, *Giuseppe Tassini's Curiosità Veneziane*.

Things to See & Do chapter for details of where you can hire bicycles.

WALKING

Except for when you hop onto waterborne craft, you don't really have much choice but to walk if you want to get anywhere. As you will soon notice, the streets are generally pretty narrow. Most Venetians will stick to the right when someone is coming the other way. If they are in a group, they generally move into single file so as not to block human 'traffic'. What infuriates them is that most non-Venetians don't stick to the same rules, wandering around five abreast at a snail's pace, gawping around them and completely indifferent to other peoples' attempts to get somewhere.

ORGANISED TOURS

You can join free tours for a biblical explanation of the mosaics in the Basilica di San Marco. They are arranged by the Patriarcato (the church body in Venice) and take place in Italian at 11am on Monday, Tuesday, Thursday, Friday and Saturday, and at 3pm on Wednesday. In English, the tours are at 11am on Monday, Thursday and Friday, and at the same time on Thursday in French. This timetable seems to be subject to regular change, so enquire. For more information, call ☎ 041 270 24 21.

Consult *Un Ospite di Venezia* for details of other visits to Venetian churches and sights. The APT has an updated list of authorised guides, who will take you on a walking tour of the city. Many museums can organise guided tours at a price, for example, the Palazzo Ducale. A couple of museums, such as the Museo Archeologico and the Libreria Nazionale Marciana, also offer free tours. All three places are on Map 5; see under Sestiere di San Marco in the Things to See & Do chapter for details.

Travel agencies all over central Venice can put you onto all kinds of city tours, ranging from guided walks for €23.25 to gondola rides with serenade for €31 per person. One such company is *City Sightseeing by Gondola & on Foot (Map 5; ☎ 041 520 08 44, at American Express, Salizzada San Moisè, San Marco 1471)*. You are guided through the streets of the Sestiere di San Marco and then across the Grand Canal by gondola to visit the Frari (Map 6; see under Sestieri di San Polo & Santa Croce in the Things to See & Do chapter). From there, you are taken by gondola along back canals to the Rialto. Tours (in English) last for 2½ hours and cost €28.50. They leave at 3pm daily from March to October.

Want to be guided but remain alone? A popular new option are the My Venice handheld itinerary earpieces. You rent these things (which look like long mobile phones) for anything from an hour (€3.60) to two days (€15.50). With the accompanying map, you can follow commentated itineraries to key parts of the city. Want a break? Switch it off (you can't do that with human guides!). You can hire the earpieces at the *Venice Pavilion tourist office* (Map 5). Languages catered for are Italian, English, French and German. You need to leave your passport as a guarantee that you'll return the item when you've finished.

GONDOLAS

 There was a time when the only way to get about effectively in Venice was by boat. But things have gradually changed over the past few centuries as more and more canals and other waterways have been filled in and bridges have been added. Today Venice is really a pedestrian city and not, as it's often romantically imagined, a boat town. Of course, the canals are the only way to move goods around, but your average Venetian will walk to get from A to B. Only when they have to get from one end of town to the other will they bother with *vaporetti* (ferries), while the *traghetti* (commuter gondolas) come in handy for crossing the Grand Canal at strategic points and cutting down walking detours to bridges.

This means that virtually no-one uses gondolas as a form of transport any more. Sad but true, the gondola (apart from those in service as traghetti) is pretty much a tourist activity.

Still, a gondola ride is the quintessence of romantic Venice, though the official price (€62 for 50 minutes, and €77.45 after 8pm) brings you back to reality with a bump. Rates are for a maximum of six people – less romantic but more affordable if you share the cost with a few friends. After the first 50 minutes, you pay in 25-minute increments (€31, or €38.75 after 8pm). Several travellers have reported successfully negotiating below the official rates, so get your haggling skills in order!

Some say there are few things more fake than being trundled about in a gondola, but it can be quite a pleasing experience if you do it right. The tackiest thing you can do is sign up for a *carovana*, where whole groups are loaded up onto a small fleet of gondolas and rowed about the place. You can also go the whole hog and be 'serenaded' by someone (at an extra negotiable rate).

A couple of other things are worth noting. When the tide is low, a gondola ride can be a stinky experience. If the tide is too high, it can become difficult for the gondolier to pass under certain bridges.

Gondolas are available near main canals all over the city (several *stazi*, or gondola service points, have been marked on the maps), or can be booked by telephone in the following areas: San Marco (☎ 041 520 06 85), Rialto (☎ 041 522 49 04), Piazzale Roma (☎ 041 522 11 51) and the train station (☎ 041 71 85 43). If money is no object and you don't want to rub shoulders with the hoi polloi, the last number might be useful to book a gondola to ferry yourself and your luggage to the station.

Gondola Ago-Go

Back in the 16th century, someone counted up the total number of gondolas in use in Venice and came up with the figure of 10,000. It would be interesting to know how they worked it out. At any rate, considerably

Above: Gondoliers in traditional attire (Jon Davison)

fewer ply the canals nowadays. In those distant times, their owners painted them every colour of the rainbow, and those with money to spare went to enormous lengths to bedeck them with every imaginable form of decoration. Finally, the Senato decided in 1630 that this was getting out of hand and decreed that gondoliers could paint their vessels any colour they wanted as long as it was black. Nothing has changed since.

Versions of the Vessel

No-one knows for sure the origin of the term 'gondola', but it seems probable that it came from the Near East. These people-movers don't just come in the standard size you see every day on the canals. Special ones come out to play for events such as the Vogalonga (see Public Holidays & Special Events in the Facts for the Visitor chapter) in May. These include the *dodesona* (with 12 oarsmen), the *quatordesona* (14 oarsmen) and the *disdotona* (18 oarsmen). The *gondolino da regata*, or racing gondola, is longer and flatter than the standard model.

More observant visitors will soon start to make out other types of vessel. Perhaps the most common is the *sandalo* (sandal) and its little brother, the *sandaletto*, with squared-off prow and stern. Two standing oarsmen power them along, although a skilled oarsman can row either one alone. The *vipera* is similar to the sandalo but pointed at each end – having no stern, it can be rowed in either direction. It was introduced by Austrian customs officials; if they suddenly found bandits scooting away behind them, it wasn't necessary to turn around to chase them!

Plying the canals is a series of heavy, sluggish-looking transport vessels powered with outboard motors. Known as *peate*, they are the city's work-horses and are used for everything from vegetable deliveries to house re-movals. The *bragozzo* is similar, but sometimes has sails on two masts. Typical of light lagoon-going transport vessels is the *caorlina*. It usually sports a single big sail on a long, slanted yard-arm.

The construction and maintenance of all these vessels required the ex-pertise of the *squerarioli*, master carpenters and shipbuilders. *Squeri*, the small-scale shipyards where they carried out their trade, once dotted the city. By 1612 the **squero** (Map 6), near the Chiesa di San Trovaso, employed 60 masters and scores of apprentices. It still operates today along wholly traditional lines, as does another **squero** (Map 6), farther west on Rio dell'Avogaria.

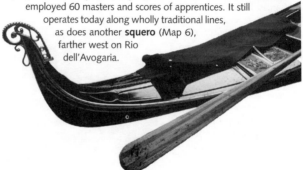

Right: A graceful gondola prow
(Paul David Hellander)

A third **shipyard** (Map 7), on Giudecca, produces gondolas by more 'pro-duction-line' methods, and their detractors claim the quality is not the same. Like most other artisans in Venice, the squerarioli had a guild and belonged to a religious confraternity *(scuola)*.

Gondola DIY

Making a good gondola is no easy task – seven different types of wood are employed to make 280 pieces for the hull alone. Also, it has to be asymmetrical. The left side has a greater curve to make up for the lateral action of the oar, and the cross section is skewed to the right to counterbalance the weight of the gondolier.

Nowadays, a master craftsman can build a gondola in about a month. Your standard model costs from €18,000. If you want more wood-carved decoration, gold leaf and other ornament, the price starts to rise. A really 'pretty' gondola can cost €50,000. Only senior and experienced gondoliers tend to go for such luxury. They do so in part as a sign of their standing within the profession, in part also in the hope of attracting more or better-off customers. A newly arrived gondolier, however, would satisfy himself with a simple, second-hand vessel to get started in the business.

A well-made gondola will last at least 30 years and often longer. One way to tell whether a gondola is old or new is to inspect the paint-work. Most gondolas get a fresh coat once a year. As coat is added to coat, the paint's thickness increases and the carvings lose their clarity.

Making the Grade as a Gondolier

Becoming a good gondolier is no easier than making a good vessel. There are just over 400 gondoliers (all men). Every year a *selezione* (se-lection) is held and, as a rule, many more candidates apply than places can be found. The trade was, by tradition, passed down from father to son, but the selezione is now open to all comers. Accusations of racism and sexism were made at the 1999 trials, when a German woman was failed after training for three years. The incentive to pass is great, as a gondolier can make a fortune in the months from Easter to September – enough to take it easy for the rest of the year.

What about those who ferry the traghetti back and forth across the Grand Canal? They are con-tracted by the city council to provide this service. As members of a cooperative, they also have an arrangement by which they run the traghetti part of the time and are otherwise free to chase their own business as independ-ent gondoliers.

Left: Gliding past the theatrical silhouette of San Giorgio Maggiore (Jon Davison)

Things to See & Do

The grandest surprise for the casual stroller in Venice is that the city is not completely teeming with outsiders in the manner of a wheat field swarming with locusts. Certainly, the main trails linking the train station to St Mark's Square (Piazza San Marco) and the *vaporetti* (ferries) of the Grand Canal are a year-round stage for the incessant and sometimes awkward pageant of international tourism. But most of Venice's visitors get little farther – many are in town too briefly to venture into the unknown; others are simply too bemused by the tangle of lanes and canals that twist and bend around the cityscape like an Escher drawing. It is an uncommon pleasure to lose yourself in the backstreets and marvel in comparative calm at the many faces of this unique creation.

Of course, most people want to poke around the great monuments and art centres as well, and these are explored in this chapter. Make some time to visit the outlying islands too – each is possessed of its own peculiar charm.

If you begin to feel like you've landed in a theme village, you may be able to gain a truer sense of the singularity of La Serenissima and, hopefully, dispel any disagreeable sentiments by exploring the mainland a little (see the Excursions chapter).

This chapter is divided into sections covering Venice's six *sestieri*, or old municipal boundaries, followed by a section on the surrounding islands. The Grand Canal is covered in a separate colour section.

In each section covering central Venice (San Marco, Dorsoduro, San Polo & Santa Croce, Cannaregio and Castello), we follow a loose walking route to take in the 'must sees', along with various curiosities. The suggested routes provide possible links from one section (and hence *sestiere*) to the next. If you kept to the order in this chapter (and no-one is suggesting you should!), you would at the end of several days' hard slog find yourself meandering west along the Riva degli Schiavoni in Castello towards the starting

---

Highlights

- Take the No 1 *vaporetto* down the length of the Grand Canal
- Tour the Gothic seat of Venetian power, the Palazzo Ducale
- Admire the Byzantine mosaics in the Cattedrale di Santa Maria Assunta on Torcello
- Sip a Bellini at Harry's Bar
- Get lost in the back lanes of the city, far from the madd(en)ing crowds of tourists
- Feast your eyes on art in the Gallerie dell'Accademia, the Peggy Guggenheim Collection and various churches in the city
- Wander among the gaily painted houses on Burano
- Allow yourself to be amazed by the wonders of St Mark's Basilica – everyone else does it too, but you can't really come to Venice and say no

---

point – Piazzetta San Marco. The routes should be viewed as suggestions for orientation. Let your imagination do the work and wander off wherever your nose leads you.

Museum Opening Hours

Check with the APT (see Local Tourist Offices in the Facts for the Visitor chapter) for the latest opening days and hours, as they can vary. Times given here are based on summer (Easter to the end of September) timetables and were correct at the time of writing. Opening hours tend to be shorter during the rest of the year (with places often closing for a couple of hours in the middle of the day). Tourist offices can provide you with a list of all monuments and their opening times.

Special Tickets

A museum pass covers entry to the Palazzo Ducale (Doge's Palace), Museo Correr, Museo Archeologico, Libreria Nazionale

A Chorus Line

An organisation called Chorus, which is involved in the upkeep of Venice's most artistically significant churches, offers visitors a special three-day ticket providing entry to all churches for €7.75.

The churches from which you can choose are, in no particular order: Santa Maria Gloriosa dei Frari, Santa Maria del Giglio, Santo Stefano, Santa Maria Formosa, Santa Maria dei Miracoli, San Polo, San Giacomo dell'Orio, San Stae, Sant'Alvise, La Madonna dell'Orto, San Pietro di Castello, Redentore and San Sebastiano. The ticket, available from any of the churches, also includes the option of visiting the *Tesoro* (Treasury) of St Mark's Basilica.

Among the more worthwhile churches to visit, if you don't want to see them all, are St Mark's (Tesoro), Santa Maria Gloriosa dei Frari, San Giacomo dell'Orio, Santo Stefano, San Polo and San Sebastiano.

Marciana, Ca' Rezzonico, Museo Vetrario on Murano, Museo del Merletto on Burano, Palazzo Mocenigo and the Casa di Goldoni (when it opens). The ticket costs €15.50 (students aged 15 to 29 pay €10.35) and can be purchased from any of these museums. It is valid for three months.

You can also buy a ticket for €9.30 (students aged 15 to 29 pay €5.15) that covers the Palazzo Ducale, Museo Correr, Museo Archeologico and Libreria Nazionale Marciana only.

Further options include a €8.25 (€4.65 for students) ticket for Ca' Rezzonico, Palazzo Mocenigo and the Casa di Goldoni, and a €6.20 (€4.15 for students) ticket for the Murano and Burano museums.

Free Admission & Reductions One week of the year (usually in spring), entry to state museums *(musei statali)* throughout Italy is made free. Since dates change, it is impossible to plan a trip around this, but keep your eyes open.

In addition, admission to all state museums is free for EU citizens under 18 and over 65.

In Venice only a few museums are concerned: the Gallerie dell'Accademia, the Ca' d'Oro and the Museo d'Arte Orientale. Admission to these museums is also free for non-EU citizens aged 12 years old and under.

A handful of museums and galleries also offer reductions for students and seniors regardless of where they are from. It never hurts to ask.

Rolling Venice Concession Pass
See Documents in the Facts for the Visitor chapter for details about this discount card.

GRAND CANAL
Nowhere can it be said more truly of a city's main thoroughfare than of Venice's Grand Canal (Canal Grande) that it is the artery along which courses the city's lifeblood. To sail its length time and again, on each occasion making new observations and 'discoveries', is a pleasure only the most insensitive souls could tire of. For the newcomer it is difficult to recommend a more appropriate introduction to the city. For a blow-by-blow itinerary, see the special section 'Along the Grand Canal'.

SESTIERE DI SAN MARCO
Piazzetta San Marco (Map 5)
Ever since the rail link with the mainland opened in the 19th century, the magical symbolism of Piazzetta San Marco has to a great extent been lost to the city's visitors.

Stand between the two **columns** bearing the emblems of Venice's patron saints – the winged lion of St Mark and the figure of the demoted St Theodore, whom St Mark replaced. The lion faces east, perhaps to signify Venice's domination of the sea, while St Theodore stands calmly on top of a crocodile-like dragon. The tip of his spear is pointed skywards, so perhaps he has killed his prey (some say the statue represents St George). He also holds a shield, as if to say Venice defends itself but does not seek to attack.

Try to imagine yourself on a galley after months at sea on a trading voyage or battle and now making your way to La Serenissima. To some observers, the lion's and dragon's tails face each other to form the crossbeam of a perennially open gate – as if to say that Venice is open to whoever visits. It must, at any rate, have been a welcome sight to Venetians returning home, and a heartening one to others arriving for the first time.

The columns were erected in 1172. In succeeding centuries, the area around them was a hive of activity with shops selling all manner of goods and food. On a more sinister note, public executions took place between the two columns.

The square is one of the lowest parts of the city – it is always the first to be covered in water when the *acqua alta* (high tide; see the boxed text 'Acque Alte' under Ecology & Environment in the Facts about Venice chapter) arrives. In fact, until the 12th century there was nothing but water here. Like so much of Venice, this area is the result of landfill. Plans to raise the level of the square, if ever put into effect, might alleviate the flooding situation.

Palazzo Ducale (Map 5)

Looking onto Piazzetta San Marco, the Palazzo Ducale *(☎ 041 522 49 51; see Special Tickets earlier; open 9am-7pm Apr-Oct, 9am-5pm Nov-Mar; ticket sales stop 1½ hrs before closing time)*, a unique example of Venetian Gothic fantasy and its simpler predecessors, was the political heart of La Serenissima for almost the entire duration of the Republic's existence. As the palace's name suggests, the doge (duke) called it home, but in its halls and dependencies were also housed all the arms of government, not to mention prisons. Infra-red radio receivers (which pick up an audio-loop commentary in each room) can be hired near the ticket desk for €5.15.

Established in the 9th century, the building began to assume its present form 500 years later, with the decision to build the massive Sala del Maggior Consiglio to house the members of the Great Council, who ranged in number from 1200 to 1700. The hall was inaugurated in 1419.

Saving Venice

Floods, neglect, pollution and other factors have contributed to the degeneration of Venice's monuments and art treasures. Since 1969, however, a group of private international organisations, under the aegis of Unesco, has been working to repair the damage.

The Joint Unesco-Private Committees Programme for the Safeguarding of Venice has raised millions of dollars for restoration work in the city. Between 1969 and 2000, more than 100 monuments and 1000 works of art were restored.

Major restoration projects which have been completed include the Chiesa di Madonna dell'Orto, the facade of the Chiesa di San Zulian, the Chiesa di San Francesco della Vigna, the Chiesa di Santa Maria Formosa, the Chiesa di San Nicolò dei Mendicoli, the Cattedrale di Santa Maria Assunta on Torcello and more recently the old Jewish cemetery on the Lido (opened to the public in 1999).

Funding for the programme comes from 29 private and charitable organisations from Italy and a dozen other countries. Apart from restoration work, the programme also finances specialist courses for trainee restorers in Venice.

Among the higher-profile groups involved in the effort is the UK's Venice in Peril Fund, chaired by Lord Norwich, perhaps the greatest historian of Venice writing in English. The sources of their funding are numerous – the UK restaurant chain Pizza Express, for example, has raised hundreds of thousands of pounds (UK£64,000 in 1999) by adding a discretionary 25p charge to its Veneziana pizzas. For UK£50 per year, you can join the Venice in Peril Fund (☎ 020-7636 6138, fax 7636 6139, W www.veniceinperil.org, Morley House, 314–322 Regent St, London W1R 5AB). The fund is presently helping to restore the Emiliana chapel on San Michele.

Important though the work of these organisations is in keeping Venice's difficulties in the public eye, more than 90% of the finance for restoration and related projects in Venice since 1966 has come from the Italian government.

THINGS TO SEE & DO

The palace's two magnificent Gothic facades in white Istrian stone and pink Veronese marble face the water and Piazzetta San Marco. Much of the building was damaged by fire in 1577, but it was successfully restored by Antonio da Ponte (who also designed the Ponte di Rialto). Thankfully, Palladio's pleas to have the burned-out hulk demolished and replaced by another of his creations fell on deaf ears. Venice's city fathers wanted their palazzo back just as it had been.

You enter the palace through the entrance facing the waterfront. Beyond the ticket office and to the left is the entrance to the **Museo dell'Opera**. It contains a total of 42 capitals that once adorned the porticoes of the palace and have at one time or another been replaced by copies to protect the originals from further deterioration. Careful observation reveals a wealth of sculptural whimsy. On one are depicted eight emperors and kings, ranging from Priam of Troy to Julius Caesar. The message appears to be that, compared with the illustrious lagoon republic, they were rather small fry.

When you leave the museum, you have no choice but to emerge into the main courtyard. Access to Antonio Rizzi's magnificent marble **Scala dei Giganti** (Giants' Staircase), at the north-eastern end of the courtyard, is closed but you can view it easily enough. It is topped by statues of Mars and Neptune by Sansovino. Behind the statues, the swearing-in ceremony of the doge traditionally took place. Here he would be presented with his ducal *zogia* (hat) and swear fidelity to the laws of the Republic. The two 16th-century wells in the middle of the courtyard are the most exquisite in the city.

To continue, climb the **Scala dei Censori** up to the **Piano delle Logge**. The floor of the loggia is a classic *terrazzo alla Veneziana* (for details, see the boxed text 'Of Floors & Walls' under Sestiere di Castello later in this chapter), of which you will see more inside the building. You wander along this gallery above the courtyard and beyond to the loggia that looks out over the Piazzetta San Marco. When you have finished here, head back to the Scala dei Censori and beyond to

Sansovino's grand **Scala d'Oro** (Golden Staircase). Just before you climb these stairs up to the next floor, you pass a *bocca della verità* ('mouth of truth'), into which people placed denunciations against those whom they considered to be wayward citizens.

Halfway up the first flight of the Scala d'Oro, turn right and then up more stairs to reach the series of rooms comprising the Appartamento del Doge (the Doge's apartments). Among these, the grand **Sala delle Mappe** is interesting. It contains maps dating from 1762 that depict the Republic's territories and the voyages of Marco Polo. Also here is the standard of the last of the doges, Manin. It is therefore also known as the Sala dello Scudo (Coat-of-Arms Room). You pass through several smaller rooms on the left wing before reaching the long hall known as the **Sala dei Filosofi**, so called because portraits of great philosophers once hung here. Of particular interest is Titian's *San Cristoforo* (St Christopher), a fresco above a side stairwell (signposted) and one of the few works to survive the 1577 fire. They say he finished this fresco in just three days. More rooms follow on the right wing. Continue through these, cross the Sala delle Mappe again and turn upstairs to the next floor.

The highest echelons of the government met in these rooms of the Palazzo. You enter the **Sala delle Quattro Porte** (The Four Doors Room, named for obvious reasons), where ambassadors would be requested to await their audience with the doge. Palladio designed the ceiling and Tintoretto added the frescoes. Titian's memorable *Il Doge Antonio Grimaldi in Ginocchio Davanti alla Fede, Presente San Marco* (Doge Antonio Grimaldi Kneels Before the Faith in the Presence of St Mark) dominates the wall by the entrance.

Off this room is the **Anticollegio**, which features four Tintorettos and the *Ratto d'Europa* (Rape of Europa) by Veronese. Through here is the splendid **Sala del Collegio**, the ceiling of which features a series of works by Veronese and a few by Tintoretto. Next is the **Sala del Senato**, graced by yet more Tintorettos. Senators met here in the presence of the doge and the Signoria (a council of 10 nen that advised the doge on policy), who at on the high tribune.

Veronese was again at work in the **Sala del Consiglio dei Dieci**. This council came to wield considerable power, acting as the Republic's main intelligence-gathering agency. The next room is known as the **Sala della Bussola** (Collection-Box Room). Note the small box in the wall. Members of the Consiglio dei Dieci picked up denunciations left here – they were poked though a hole on the other side of the wall rather like the way you post a letter.

From here you follow a set of stairs to the right that leads to the **Armeria**, what is left of the palace's once considerable collection of arms of all types. After this, you turn left down one flight of the Scala dei Censori and turn right into the **Andito del Maggior Consiglio**, a narrow L-shaped corridor (also known as the Liagò) off which is the **Sala della Quarantia Vecchia**. This body oversaw administrative matters regarding the city. In the small **Sala dell'Armamento** next door, you can see the remains of Guariento's 14th-century fresco *Paradiso* (Heaven), badly damaged in the 1577 fire.

On the other side of the corridor is the immense **Sala del Maggior Consiglio**. This is dominated at one end by Tintoretto's replacement *Paradiso*, one of the world's largest oil paintings, measuring 22m by 7m. Among the many other paintings in the hall is a masterpiece, the *Apoteosi di Venezia* (Apotheosis of Venice) by Veronese, in one of the central ceiling panels. Note the black space in the frieze on the wall depicting the first 76 doges of Venice. Doge Marin Falier would have appeared had he not been beheaded for treason in 1355.

The room off the north-western corner of the Sala del Maggior Consiglio was home to the **Quarantia Civil Nuova**, a kind of appeal court, while beyond lies the **Sala dello Scrutinio**, where elections to the Maggior Consiglio were held. It is lined with stirring and rather violent battle scenes.

From the north-eastern end, a trail of corridors leads you to the small, enclosed **Bridge of Sighs** (Ponte dei Sospiri). Before you reach the bridge, you pass through three small

rooms, the last of which contains a small collection of paintings by Hieronymus Bosch (c.1450–1516). He must have been doing drugs!

The bridge itself is split into two levels, for traffic heading into and out of the **Prigioni Nuove** (New Prisons), built on the eastern side of the Rio di Palazzo della Paglia in the 16th century to cater for the overflow from the Prigioni Vecchie (Old Prisons) within the Palazzo Ducale itself. The bridge is presumably named after the sighs that prisoners heaved as they crossed it on their way into the dungeons. You get to wind your way all over the cells of the Prigioni Nuove. They are small and dank, but not too bad by the standards of the times. Of course they are cleaned up and airy now, but wouldn't have been much fun when overcrowded with sick and unhappy prisoners on a bread-and-water diet.

Re-emerging from the prison, you recross the Bridge of Sighs to end up in the **offices** of the Avogaria Comun (Venetian magistracy) and the **Sala dello Scrigno** (Room of the Coffer). Here the Libro d'Oro (Golden Book) was kept. The Libro identified those noble families of impeccable Venetian descent who had the right to join the Maggior Consiglio. Inter-class weddings were forbidden and a vigilant watch was maintained for fraudulent attempts to pass off unsuitable persons as nobles.

The last office you pass through before arriving back in the courtyard is the **Milizia da Mar**. An office of 20 senators was set up in 1545 to organise the rapid equipping and manning of emergency war fleets whenever the need arose. The organisation began here. You then pass through a shop and downstairs to a cafe that leads onto the courtyard.

You exit the courtyard by what was traditionally the main entrance, Giovanni and Bartolomeo Bon's 15th-century **Porta della Carta** (Paper Door), to which government decrees were fixed (hence the name).

Itinerari Segreti Lesser-known areas of the palace, including the original **Prigioni Vecchie** (Old Prisons), can be visited on the 'secret itineraries' guided tour (☎ 041 522 49 51; admission €12.40; English-language tour

10am & 11.30am Apr-Oct, Italian 9.30am & 11am Apr-Oct, French 10.30am & noon Apr-Oct, tours in some or all of the above languages at 10am, 10.30am, 11.30am and noon Nov-Mar).

The 1½-hour tour is an intriguing look at the underside of the palace and the workings of government in the days of La Serenissima. You are taken first through some administrative offices, small rooms in which the Republic's civil servants beavered away. You then get to pass through a torture chamber, the **Sala dei Tre Capi del Consiglio dei Dieci** (Room of the Three Heads of the Council of Ten) and the Inquisitors' office.

After all this, the route winds upstairs to the **Piombi** (Leads), prison cells beneath the roof of the building. Here prisoners froze in winter and sweltered in summer. Giacomo Casanova got five years here for his apparently wayward and reckless lifestyle. The guide will show you how he made his escape. You also get an explanation of the engineering behind the ceiling of the immense Sala del Maggior Consiglio below.

The toughest prisoners of all ended up not in the Piombi, nor in the Prigioni Nuove (see earlier), but rather in the **Pozzi** (Wells), two bottom storeys of dank cells at water level. They are closed to the public but from all accounts, by the rather dismal standards of the Middle Ages, could have been worse.

The ticket for this tour is quite separate from the normal €9.30 ticket. Both admit you to the Palazzo Ducale, but if you want to visit the Museo Correr and other museums on the standard ticket *and* do the Itinerari Segreti, you'll have to pay for both. You need to phone ahead to book the tour.

Libreria Nazionale Marciana (Map 5)

Across the Piazzetta San Marco lies the gracious form of what Palladio once described as the most sumptuous palace ever built. Jacopo Sansovino designed it in the 16th century.

The building occupies the entire west side of the piazzetta and houses the Libreria Nazionale Marciana, or National Library of St Mark (aka Libreria Vecchia, or Old Library, and Libreria Sansoviniana, after its

architect) and the Museo Archeologico. The library extends around the corner on the waterfront into what was once **La Zecca**, the Republic's mint.

For more on the Libreria Nazionale Marciana and the Museo Archeologico, see Museo Correr later in this section. Admission to both is through that museum and included in the combined tickets described under Special Tickets at the start of this chapter.

St Mark's Square (Piazza San Marco; Map 5)

Napoleon thought of St Mark's Square as the 'finest drawing room in Europe'. Enclosed by the Basilica and the arcaded Procuratie

---

Stop the Pigeons!

If you get the impression there are more pigeons in St Mark's Square than inhabitants in the whole of Venice, you're right. Officials estimate the pesky pigeon population at around 100,000 (but how do you count them?). Anyone who has been dive-bombed by squadrons of these parasitic marauders on this most beautiful of squares will probably not be overly unhappy to hear that La Serenissima is striking back. Tests have shown that around 15% of the flock have salmonella and can pass it on to their hapless human victims, and so the city fathers have ordained a culling programme. In the past there was an attempt to sterilise them with chemically treated birdseed, but they didn't swallow it. Equally unsuccessful is the supposed ban on feeding the little beggars. There is purportedly a €51.65 fine for this activity, but to judge by the birdseed vendors and the throngs of delighted tourists allowing birdies to poop on their shoulders for that memorable St Mark's Square photo, that rule died at birth.

Worse than the poop on the people is that on the monuments – the acid in bird droppings eats away at the stone. People involved in restoration pull their hair out at the thought of the vast sums spent to restore monuments, only to see the work imperilled by the toilet habits of these gormless birds. Please don't feed them!

Vecchie and Nuove, the square plays host to competing flocks of pigeons and tourists. Stand and wait for the bronze Mori (Moors) to strike the bell of the 15th-century **Torre dell'Orologio**, which rises above the entrance to the Mercerie, the series of streets that forms the main thoroughfare from San Marco to the Rialto. Or sit and savour an expensive coffee at Florian, Quadri or Lavena, the 18th-century cafes facing each other on the piazza. On occasion, you may witness a minor military ceremony to hoist or haul in the three flags (Venice, Italy and the EU). The flagpoles have been around a lot longer than the EU, so one wonders what the third flag used to be.

St Mark's Basilica (Map 5)

No doubt some of you have skipped all the above prattling and turned straight to what for most is the number one attraction in Venice. Let's hope you have time to do it more justice than space here allows us to! To avoid the disappointment of being turned away at the door, dress appropriately for a religious building – no one with bare shoulders or knees will be admitted.

St Mark's Basilica (☎ *041 522 56 97, Piazza San Marco; open 9.30am-5pm Mon-Sat, 2pm-5pm Sun & holidays)* is at once a remarkable place of worship and a singular declaration of commercial-imperial might. The basilica embodies a magnificent blend of architectural and decorative styles, dominated by the Byzantine and ranging through Romanesque and Gothic to Renaissance. Building work on the first chapel to honour the freshly arrived corpse of the evangelist St Mark (see the boxed text 'Making His Mark' later in this section) began in AD 828, but the result disappeared in a fire in 932. The next version didn't have a much happier run, for in 1063 Doge Domenico Contarini decided it was poor in comparison to the grander Romanesque churches being raised in mainland cities and had it demolished.

The new basilica, built on the plan of a Greek cross, with five bulbous domes, was modelled on Constantinople's Church of the Twelve Apostles (later destroyed) and consecrated in 1094. It was actually built as the

doges' private chapel and remained so until it finally became Venice's cathedral in 1807. But no-one was in any doubt that this was the city's principal church. Thus symbolically tied to the power of the doge, this state of affairs was an eloquent expression of the uncomfortable position of the Church in Venice.

For more than 500 years, the doges enlarged and embellished the church, adorning it with an incredible array of treasures plundered from the East, in particular Constantinople, during the Crusades.

The arches above the doorways in the **facade** boast fine mosaics. The one at the left end, depicting the arrival of St Mark's body in Venice, was completed in 1270. Above the doorway next to it is an 18th-century mosaic depicting the doge venerating St Mark's body. The mosaics on the other side of the main doorway both date from the 17th century. The one at the right end depicts the stealing of St Mark's corpse, while next to it the Venetians receive the body of the saint. The three arches of the main doorway are decorated with Romanesque carvings dating from around 1240.

The only original entrance to the church is the one on the south side that leads to the *battistero* (baptistry). It is fronted by two pillars brought to Venice from Acre in the Holy Land in the 13th century. The Syriac sculpture, *Tetrarchi* (Tetrarchs), next to the Porta della Carta of the Palazzo Ducale (and obscured by restorers' hoardings at the time of writing), dates from the 4th century and is believed to represent Diocletian and his three co-emperors, who together ruled the Roman Empire in the 3rd century AD.

On the Loggia dei Cavalli above the main door are copies of four gilded bronze horses: the originals, on display inside, were stolen when Constantinople was sacked in 1204, during the Fourth Crusade. Napoleon removed them to Paris in 1797, but they were returned after the fall of the French Empire.

Through the doors is the **narthex**, or vestibule, its domes and arches decorated with mosaics, mainly dating from the 13th century. The oldest mosaics in the basilica, dating from around 1063, are in the niches of the bay in front of the main door from the

THINGS TO SEE & DO

ST MARK'S BASILICA

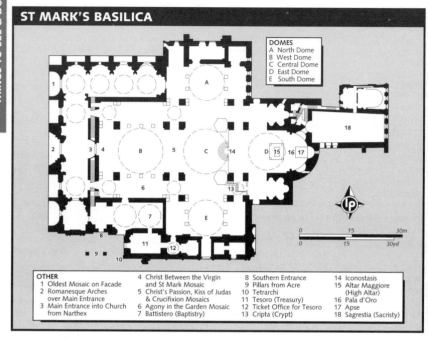

DOMES
A North Dome
B West Dome
C Central Dome
D East Dome
E South Dome

OTHER		
1 Oldest Mosaic on Facade	4 Christ Between the Virgin	8 Southern Entrance	14 Iconostasis
2 Romanesque Arches	and St Mark Mosaic	9 Pillars from Acre	15 Altar Maggiore
over Main Entrance	5 Christ's Passion, Kiss of Judas	10 Tetrarchi	(High Altar)
3 Main Entrance into Church	& Crucifixion Mosaics	11 Tesoro (Treasury)	16 Pala d'Oro
from Narthex	6 Agony in the Garden Mosaic	12 Ticket Office for Tesoro	17 Apse
	7 Battistero (Baptistry)	13 Cripta (Crypt)	18 Sagrestia (Sacristy)

narthex into the church proper. They feature the Madonna with the Apostles. Look for the red marble spot in the floor. This marks where Pope Alexander III and Barbarossa kissed and made up in 1177.

The **interior** of the basilica is dazzling: if you can take your eyes off the glitter of the mosaics, take time to admire the 12th-century marble **pavement**, an infinite variety of geometrical whimsy interspersed with floral motifs and depictions of animals. (It has subsided in places, making the floor uneven.) The lower level of the walls is lined with precious Eastern marbles, and above this decoration the extraordinary feast of gilded **mosaics** begins. Work started on the mosaics in the 11th century. Those in the baptistry and side chapels date from the 14th and 15th centuries, and as late as the 18th century, mosaics were still being added or restored.

Notable mosaics include: the 12th-century *Ascension* in the central dome; those on the arch between the central and west domes,

dating from the same period and including *Christ's Passion*, the *Kiss of Judas* and the *Crucifixion*; the early-12th-century mosaics of the Pentecost in the west dome; the 13th-century lunette over the west door depicting Christ between the Virgin and St Mark; the 13th-century *Agony in the Garden* on the wall of the right aisle; the early-12th-century mosaics in the left-transept (north) dome portraying the life of St John the Evangelist; those in the east dome depicting the Religion of Christ as foretold by the Prophets (12th century); 12th-century mosaics in the right-transept (south) dome depicting a series of saints; and those between the windows of the apse depicting St Mark and three other patron saints of Venice, which are among the earliest mosaics in the basilica.

Separating the main body of the church from the area before the high altar is a magnificent, multicoloured marble **iconostasis**. Dividing the iconostasis in two is a huge cross of bronze and silver. To each side, the

Virgin Mary and the Apostles line up. Beneath the majestic marble **altar maggiore** (high altar) lie the remains of St Mark.

Behind the altar is one of the basilica's greatest treasures, the exquisite **Pala d'Oro** *(admission €1.55)*, a gold, enamel and jewel-encrusted altarpiece made in Constantinople for Doge Pietro Orseolo I in 976. It was enriched and reworked in Constantinople in 1105, enlarged by Venetian goldsmiths in 1209 and reset in the 14th century. Among the almost 2000 precious stones that adorn it are emeralds, rubies, amethysts, sapphires and pearls.

The **Tesoro** *(Treasury; admission €2.05)*, accessible from the right transept, contains most of the booty from the 1204 raid on Constantinople, including a thorn said to be from the crown worn by Christ. The treasury is part of the Chorus scheme (see the boxed text 'A Chorus Line' earlier in this chapter).

Through a door at the far right end of the narthex is a stairway leading up to the **Galleria** *(aka Museo di San Marco;* ☎ *041 522 52 05; admission €1.55; open 9.45am-5pm daily)*, which contains the original gilded bronze horses and the **Loggia dei Cavalli**. The Galleria affords wonderful views of the church's interior, while the loggia offers equally splendid vistas of the square. Access to the crypt and baptistry is only possible if you have specific permission from the church administrators.

The mosaics are best seen when illuminated. This means weekdays from 11.30am to 12.30pm and 'all day' at weekends. This 'all day' really means when Mass is said. On Saturday, in particular, there is nothing to say the lights won't go out for a good part of the day when no service is on.

Campanile (Map 5)

The basilica's 99m-tall bell tower *(admission €5.15; open 9am-9pm late June-Aug, 9am-7pm Apr, May & Sept-Oct, 9.30am-5.30pm Nov-Mar)* was raised in the 10th century but suddenly collapsed on 14 July 1902 and was rebuilt brick by brick *(dov'era, com'era;* 'where it was and as it was'). Alterations had already been made in the 12th and 16th centuries. On the second occasion, a statuette of

---

Making His Mark

The story goes that an angel appeared to the Evangelist Mark when his boat put in at a deserted island of what would become known as the Venetian lagoon while on the way to Rome from Aquileia. The winged fellow informed the future saint that his body would rest there. When he did die some years later, it was in Alexandria, Egypt. In 828, two Venetian merchants persuaded the guardians of his Alexandrian tomb to let them have the corpse, which they then smuggled down to their ship in port.

You've got to ask yourself why they would bother with such a strange cargo. Well, in those days, any city worthy of the name had a patron saint of stature. Venice had St Theodore (San Teodoro), but poor old Theodore didn't really cut the mustard in the Christian hierarchy. An Evangelist, though, would be something quite different. Did Doge Giustinian Partecipazio order this little body-snatching mission? We will never know. Whatever the truth of this tale, it seems that *someone's* putrid corpse was transported to Venice, and that everyone rather liked to think St Mark was now in their midst. St Theodore was unceremoniously demoted and the doge ordered the construction of a chapel to house the newcomer. That church would later become the magnificent St Mark's Basilica. St Mark's symbol in the Book of Revelation (the Apocalypse) is a winged lion, and this image came to be synonymous with La Serenissima.

Legend also has it that, during the rebuilding of the basilica in 1063, the body of St Mark was hidden and then 'lost' when its hiding place was forgotten. In 1094, when the church was consecrated, the corpse (which must have been a picture of frailty by this time) broke through the column in which it had been enclosed. 'It's a miracle!' the Venetians cried. Or was it just incredibly dodgy plasterwork? St Mark had been lost and now was found. A grateful populace buried the remains in the church crypt where they now supposedly lie, beneath the basilica's high altar.

the Archangel Gabriel was positioned at the tip of the tower to serve as an elaborate weather vane. After the collapse in 1902, the tower took 10 years to rebuild. Oddly, it contains just one bell, the *marangona*, which survived the fall. You take a lift to the top, from where there are views across the entire city.

Procuratie (Map 5)

Formerly the residence and offices of the Procurators of St Mark, who were responsible for the upkeep of the basilica, the Procuratie Vecchie were designed by Mauro Codussi and occupy the entire north side of St Mark's Square. On the south side of the piazza are the Procuratie Nuove, designed by Jacopo Sansovino and completed by Vincenzo Scamozzi and Baldassare Longhena.

Ala Napoleonica (Map 5)

When Napoleon decided to make the Procuratie Nuove his official residence in Venice (not that he was ever around to enjoy it), he also decided that he needed to leave his architectural mark on the city. So he had the church of San Geminiano, at the western end of the piazza, demolished to make way for a new wing that would connect the Procuratie Nuove and Vecchie and house his ballroom.

At first glance, it seems to blend in perfectly with the Procuratie, but a slightly more attentive look soon reveals differences. The row of statues at the top is not matched anywhere else around the piazza. Just in case anyone had doubts about how Napoleon thought of himself, the statues are of Roman emperors.

Museo Correr (Map 5)

The Ala Napoleonica is now home to the Museo Correr (*☎ 041 522 56 25, Piazza San Marco; see Special Tickets earlier; open 9am-7pm Apr-Oct, 9am-5pm Nov-Mar*), dedicated to the art and history of Venice.

Once inside, you turn right into a hall lined with statuary and bas-reliefs by Canova. More of his creations adorn the following couple of rooms, collectively known as the Sale Neoclassiche (Neoclassical Rooms). Keeping the statues company is an assortment of 19th-century paintings

(including some by Hayez and others by Canova), books, documents, medallions, musical instruments and other bits and bobs.

From here you slide on into the rooms dedicated to Civiltà Veneziana (Venetian Civilisation), where you can inspect coins and standards of the Republic, model galleys, maps, navigational instruments and a display of weaponry from bygone days.

You are then encouraged to continue straight on to the **Museo Archeologico**, crammed mostly with Greek and Roman statues, along with a vast collection of ancient coins and ceramics. Some, but by no means all, of the material was collected in the Veneto. A couple of rooms are devoted to ancient Egyptian and Assyro-Babylonian objects. Free guided tours are available in English at 3pm on weekdays, and noon, 3pm and 5pm on weekends (tours are also offered in Italian and French). You will be asked to show your ticket here, as you will again in the adjoining **Libreria Nazionale Marciana**.

You enter the library, in a sense, through the back door. The Sala della Libreria is the main reading hall, built in the 16th century to house the collection of some 1000 codices left to the Republic by Cardinal Bessarione in 1468. The ceiling was decorated by a battalion of artists chosen by Titian and Sansovino, the architect. Of them, Veronese was considered the best; his three contributions form the second line of medallions after you enter.

You then pass into the Vestibolo (Vestibule). The centrepiece of the ceiling ornamentation is *Sapienza* (Wisdom) by Titian. The ancient statues cluttering the floor were part of a wider collection placed here late in the 16th century. Most were later shunted over to what would eventually become the Museo Archeologico. Finally you arrive at the top end of the fine entrance stairway – a sort of twin to the Scala d'Oro in the Palazzo Ducale across the square. Free guided tours of the Library are available in Italian and English at 10am, noon, 2pm and 4pm on weekends.

You now have to backtrack all the way to the armoury in the Museo Correr. The western corridor of the Ala Napoleonica contains further baubles relating to the Civiltà Veneziana collection. About half-way along, a stairway leads up to two other collections belonging to the Museo Correr. The modest **Museo del Risorgimento**, on the 2nd floor, traced the fall of the Venetian Republic and Italian unification. It has been closed for some years and is only opened occasionally to house a temporary exhibition. The **Arte Antica** collection is a kind of Noah's Ark of largely second-rate art, starting with 14th-century Byzantine painters and proceeding to Gothic art, with a series of rooms given over to Flemish and German paintings, and a room with eight works that came out of the Bellini workshop. A few items of interest by Carpaccio and Lorenzo Lotto dot the remaining rooms. The last of them contain porcelain and a library.

After going back downstairs, you turn left to walk through the remainder of the Civiltà Veneziana collection and so return to the ticket counter. In this section, you can view paintings of Venetian scenes, society games and a large collection of miniature bronzes, produced above all in Padua and depicting everything from frogs to gods.

West of St Mark's Square (Map 5)

Heading west from the Ala Napoleonica, you will soon find yourself on Salizzada San Moisè. Down the first street to your left, Calle Vallaresso, is a gaggle of fashion stores and Harry's Bar. Also, at No 1332, there's the closed **Teatro al Ridotto**.

In the 17th century, the Ridotto gained a name for itself as the city's premier gaming house. During the twilight years of La Serenissima, Venetian nobles were wiping out their fortunes at the gaming tables. Even if the state was getting a share, it was insufficient compensation for the ruin being brought to an already shaky local economy. In November 1774, the Ridotto was shut by the authorities *per tutti i tempi ed anni avvenire* ('for all time and years to come'). 'All time' was a relative term and less than 20 years later, it was back in operation. It remained so until the Austrians shut it for good in the early 19th century.

As you approach Campo San Moisè, you pass a busy shopping street on your right, **Frezzeria**. In medieval days, no-one would have dreamed of opening a fashion store here: the product on sale was *frecce* (arrows). All males above a certain age had to do regular archery practice and be ready to sail off to war – or at least on military escort duty for merchant convoys – when necessary. **Campo San Moisè** is dominated by the **church** of the same name. Legend has it that the first church was founded in the 8th century, but the rather unrestrained Baroque facade you see today is a product of the 1660s.

From here, the street widens into Calle Larga XXII Marzo, which was opened in 1881 and commemorates the surrender of the Austrians to Venetian rebels on 22 March 1848. The victory was short-lived, however, and it would be another 18 years before the Austrians were given their definitive marching orders. One Italian guide rather hopefully describes this as 'the City of Venice', given the presence of the Borsa (stock exchange) and several banks. Down Calle del Pestrin, which runs south off Calle Larga XXII Marzo, is the landward entrance to the **Palazzo Contarini-Fasan**. It is nothing much to look at, but legend has it that Desdemona, the wife of Othello and victim of his jealousy in Shakespeare's play, lived here.

Calle Larga XXII Marzo then contracts into Calle delle Ostreghe (Oysters St) and brings you to Campo Santa Maria del Giglio.

Chiesa di Santa Maria del Giglio (Map 6)

This church is also known as Santa Maria Zobenigo *(admission €1.55; open 10am-5pm Mon-Sat, 1pm-5pm Sun)*. Its Baroque facade features maps of European cities as they were in 1678. The facade also hides the fact that a church has stood here since the 10th century.

The church itself is a rather small affair, but quite jammed with an assortment of paintings. Of interest is Peter Paul Rubens' *Madonna col Bambino e San Giovanni* (Madonna with Child and St John), the only work of his in Venice. Behind the altar lurk

Tintoretto's typically moody depictions of the four Evangelists, and the church is stuffed with other works by lower-ranking Venetian painters.

Outside, the oddly out-of-place square brick building in the middle of the *campo* (square) was the base of the church's bell tower, knocked down in 1775 because it was in danger of falling over of its own accord.

The church is part of the Chorus scheme (see the boxed text 'A Chorus Line' earlier in this chapter).

Palazzo Corner/Ca' Grande (Map 6)

After crossing two bridges in quick succession, you could wander south towards the Grand Canal and sidle up next to this, Sansovino's 16th-century masterpiece of residential building. He built it for Jacopo Corner, a nephew of the ill-fated Caterina, the queen of Cyprus (see the boxed text 'A Queen Cornered' in the Excursions chapter). Now the seat of the Prefettura and other government offices, the mansion has apparently lost much of its lustre inside – not that you'll be able to get in and find out. From the Canal, you can tell which building it is by the two Carabinieri standing guard outside – are they awaiting a waterborne assault?

Campo San Maurizio (Map 6)

Occasionally the scene of an antiques market, the square is surrounded by elegant 14th- and 15th-century mansions, along with the church of the same name. Just off this square to the north you can sneak around to Campiello Drio la Chiesa and get a close-up look at just how much the bell tower of the Chiesa di Santo Stefano (see the next entry) is leaning. Pause, too, when you cross the bridge leading from Campo San Maurizio to Campo Santo Stefano. Looking north, you can see how the same church is in part actually built over the Rio del Santissimo.

Chiesa di Santo Stefano (Map 6)

When you walk in here, look up at possibly the finest wooden ceiling (*a carena di nave* – 'like an upturned ship's hull') of any church in Venice. The church was one of the three attached to a convent in Venice (the others were Santa Maria Gloriosa dei Frari and SS Giovanni e Paolo).

The church is part of the Chorus scheme (see the boxed text 'A Chorus Line' earlier in this chapter). You only pay here to go into the small museum *(admission €1.55; open 10am-5pm Mon-Sat, 1pm-5pm Sun)* off to the right of the altar, where a collection of Tintoretto's paintings has been crammed. Among the most notable are the *Ultima Cena* (Last Supper), *Lavanda dei Piedi* (Washing of the Feet) and *Orazione nell'Orto* (Agony in the Garden).

Unfortunately visitors cannot get into the cloisters, which are no longer church property. Outside, the bell tower has a fairly serious lean that is better appreciated from a distance (see under Campo Sant'Angelo later).

From the church, it is a brief stroll south across the grand expanse (a rare thing in Venice) that is the Campo Santo Stefano (also known as Campo Francesco Morosini after the 17th-century doge) to the Grand Canal and the Ponte dell'Accademia that spans it.

Ponte dell'Accademia (Map 6)

Built in 1930 to replace a 19th-century metal structure, the third and last of the Grand Canal bridges was supposed to be a temporary arrangement until a satisfactory design for a more permanent structure was produced. All that seems to have been forgotten, which is fine, because it is quite attractive as it is. From the middle, the views in both directions along the Grand Canal are spellbinding.

At this point you may decide to skip the rest of the Sestiere di San Marco itinerary and cross the bridge to the Sestiere di Dorsoduro. If so, brace yourself for an intense blast of high culture. Your eyes are going to have to work overtime in two of the city's most important art galleries. Proceed to the Sestiere di Dorsoduro section.

Santo Stefano to Ponte di Rialto (Maps 5 & 6)

If you decide to hang about in the San Marco area, head for the south-western end

More than Wishing Wells

Sooner or later you will probably ask yourself, as you enter one *campo* (square) or another: what are those squat stone cylinders with the metal lids firmly clamped on top? The answer is obvious enough once you think about it: they're wells.

That there are so many (some of them have been marked on the maps, in case you are wondering what we are talking about) reflects every neighbourhood's need to have its own source of drinking water in the good old days. With bridges few and far between throughout much of the history of the city, it was easier to provide each of the many *insulae* that make up the fabric of Venice with its own well than attempt to transport water.

There's a whole lot more to this system than meets the eye. In general, the well is surrounded by up to four depressions around 4m from it. Rainwater drained into these depressions and seeped into a cistern below. Sand and/or gravel inside the cistern acted as a filter for the water. In the middle of the cistern, a brick cylinder (the well) extends to the bottom. The cistern itself was sealed off with impenetrable clay to keep salty water out. Engineers also sought out relatively high spots for wells to shield them from the *acque alte* (high tides).

With the introduction of direct running water to all Venice's buildings, the wells have been closed up and are no longer in use. But it is intriguing to think of how much the city's survival depended on these ingenious structures.

of Campo Santo Stefano, where Calle Fruttarol swings off to the north-west on a twisting and winding route towards the Ponte di Rialto.

You immediately cross a narrow canal and then another, the Rio del Duca. The building on the north-west bank, with a fine facade on the Grand Canal, is the **Ca' del Duca (Map 6)** (Duke's House), so called because the duke of Milan, Francesco Sforza, bought it from the Corner family in 1461. Above the 14th-century ground floor, the rest of the mansion was rebuilt in the 19th century. At the next street, Calle del Teatro, turn left. The street name is all that remains of the Teatro San Samuele, where Carlo Goldoni (see A Ray of Gold in the Literature section of the Facts about Venice chapter) first hit the limelight.

Turn right and follow the rear side of the **Palazzo Malipiero (Map 6)**, in the wall of which you may notice a **plaque** just before you enter Salizzada Malipiero. It reminds us that in a house along this lane, Giacomo Casanova was born in 1725.

Palazzo Malipiero forms the southern limit of the quiet little Campo San Samuele on the Grand Canal. On the eastern side is the unobtrusive outline of the former Chiesa di San Samuele, and to the north is the stately

Palazzo Grassi (Map 6), frequent host to temporary art exhibitions and owned by Fiat. Massari's 1749 design clearly shows a tendency towards neoclassicism.

Wheeling around the church, we head more or less east along Calle delle Carrozze and on into Salizzada San Samuele. A number of shops, flogging everything from expensive glass to wooden sculptures of unironed shirts, line these streets. You can only wonder what Paolo Veronese, who lived at **No 3337**, would have thought of it all.

Although this itinerary barrels along towards Calle dell'Albero, unhurried strollers might like to wander down any of the several lanes around here that end at the Grand Canal. Just off Calle dell'Albero is a neat little square, the Corte dell'Albero, walled on two sides by the interesting **Casa Nardi (Map 6)** at Nos 3884–87, built in 1913 and incorporating Veneto-Byzantine architectural themes. It has a hint of the Barcelona Modernista style to it (and especially calls to mind the architect Lluís Domènech i Montaner) in its use of brick and the attempt to recycle a proud and distant design tradition.

Facing the Grand Canal at No 3877 is Codussi's **Palazzo Corner-Spinelli (Map 6)**, later reworked by Sanmicheli.

Campo Sant'Angelo (Map 6) From Calle dell'Albero, you cross a tiny canal and then head south down Calle degli Avvocati, which leads directly into Campo Sant'Angelo. You may notice that a good deal of the square is raised. The two wells clue you in that directly below is a large cistern.

The Chiesa di Sant'Angelo Michele has long since disappeared, but in the distance you can see the leaning tower of Venice – the bell tower of the Chiesa di Santo Stefano (see that section earlier in this chapter).

In 1801 the Italian musician Domenico Cimarosa died in the 15th-century **Palazzo Duodo** (No 3584), which in those days was the Albergo Tre Stelle. **Palazzo Gritti**, across the square, was built around the same period. All sorts of unpleasant things occurred in this square, according to city chronicles. In 1476 a launderer by the name of Giacomo was jailed after having taken a certain Bernardino degli Orsi under the portico of the Chiesa di Sant'Angelo Michele and raping him. In 1716 the body of a violently murdered woman was discovered in one of the wells. A Florentine was accused of assaulting, robbing and killing the poor wretch.

There's more where that came from, but enough. It's time to get a move on.

La Fenice & Campo San Fantin (Maps 5 & 6) Take Calle Caotorta and cross the first bridge you see. After the bridge, if you turn immediately left and then right, you'll end up in Calle della Fenice, a tunnel of scaffolding along the northern wall of the star-crossed opera house. A few steps along this street turn left again. The hotel on the tiny square (Campiello della Fenice; Map 6) is covered in cannon balls used by the Austrians in their campaign to retake control of the city in 1849. Follow this little arc around and you are again in Calle della Fenice. The theatre, or what is left of it, is completely hidden from view by scaffolding and hoarding. This unhappy hulk was one of the world's favourite opera houses. For more on its fate since flames destroyed it in 1996, see the boxed text 'Faltering Phoenix' in the Theatre section of the Entertainment chapter.

You now emerge into Campo San Fantin. Opposite the theatre is the **Chiesa di San Fantin (Map 5)**, whose final incarnation was wrought either by Sansovino or Pietro Lombardo.

The other main building on this square is the **Ateneo Veneto (Map 5)**, a learned society founded in Napoleon's time. Previously it had been the headquarters of the confraternity of San Girolamo and Santa Maria della Giustizia. The main charitable work of confraternity members was to accompany death-row criminals in their last moments before being executed. The confraternity's building was known as the Scuola di San Fantin or 'dei Picai' (the old Venetian version of Dead Men Walking).

To proceed, take Calle della Verona north out of the square. Just before you hit the T-junction with Calle della Mandola, you cross Rio Terrà degli Assassini. Apparently, in medieval times, this was a good place to avoid, because murder was among the more common nocturnal activities. Street crime got so bad that in 1128 the government banned the wearing of certain 'Greek style' beards that, it was said, were in vogue among wrongdoers to prevent them from being identified. It was at that time too that the first all-night lamps were set burning in the dodgier parts of town – the devotional niches you still see around were created specifically for this purpose – and the Signori di Notte (Night Masters), whose task was to deal with flourishing crime of all sorts in the dark hours, started patrolling the lanes.

Campo San Beneto (Map 6) At Calle della Mandola, we turn left then right into Rio Terrà della Mandola. This street bumps right into the side of the splendid, but rather neglected, **Palazzo Fortuny** (☎ 041 520 09 95, San Marco 3780). The building sports two rows of *hectafores*, each a series of eight connected Venetian-style windows. Mariano Fortuny y Madrazo, an eccentric Spanish painter and collector, bought the building at the beginning of the 20th century. He left his works here and, together with another 80 by the Roman artist Virgilio Guidi, they make up the bulk of the Museo

Fortuny. The palazzo was open temporarily during the Biennale in 2001, and is due to open fully to the public in 2004 after restoration work is completed.

The **Chiesa di San Beneto**, also in the square, was rebuilt in the early 17th century and is also closed.

Campo Manin (Map 5) From Campo San Beneto, drop south along Calle del Teatro Goldoni, passing the supremely ugly Cinema Rossini, and turn left at the junction into Calle della Cortesia, which leads over a bridge and into Campo Manin. At the square's centre stands the proud statue of Daniele Manin, a lion at his feet. He led the anti-Austrian revolt of 1848–49. The square also boasts a remarkably thoughtless 20th-century contribution at its eastern end, the Cassa di Risparmio di Venezia bank.

More interesting than the square itself is what lies off it. Take Calle della Vida south of the square and follow the signs to the Renaissance **Palazzo Contarini del Bovolo** (☎ 041 270 24 64, San Marco 4299; admission €2.05; open 10am-6pm), so named because of the dizzying external spiral (*bovolo* in the Venetian dialect) staircase. Built in the late 15th century, the palace still maintains a hint of the Gothic in its arches and capitals. You can enter the grounds if you wish, although the staircase is quite visible from outside.

Along the Grand Canal (Map 5) From the dead end at the Palazzo Contarini del Bovolo, our route proceeds east along Calle delle Locande to Calle dei Fuseri, which, heading north across Campo San Luca, brings us to the Grand Canal along Calle del Carbon (Coal St). Not surprisingly, Coal St leads to Coal Quay (Riva del Carbon), which until well into the 19th century was the main unloading point for the city's coal supply. Calle del Carbon, it is said, was also something of a red-light district.

To the left of Calle del Carbon are the **Palazzo Loredan** and, one street along, **Ca' Farsetti**. Both started life in the 12th century as *fondachi*. These were family houses where the ground floor, with a grand entrance on the canal, was used for the loading, unloading and storage of the merchandise upon which the wealth and standing of most of the great patrician families of Venice long depended. In some cases (as in the nearby Fondaco dei Tedeschi), a *fondaco* was more a trading house and hotel for foreign communities.

In 1826 the town hall moved its offices to the Ca' Farsetti from the Palazzo Ducale. Forty-two years later, it also acquired Palazzo Loredan. You can wander into the foyer of the latter, but generally that's as far as you'll get. On the corner of Calle del Carbon is a plaque announcing that Eleonora Lucrezia Corner Piscopia (of the family that once owned Palazzo Corner) was the first woman to receive a degree – whether the first woman *ever* or just in Venice isn't clear. Anyway, she got her piece of parchment with all the appropriate seals in 1678.

Just west of Ca' Farsetti, the Renaissance **Palazzo Grimani (Map 6)** was completed by Sanmicheli, although the 2nd floor was done later. It houses law courts.

Walking north-east towards the Ponte di Rialto from Calle del Carbon, you may notice the narrow, Gothic, 14th-century **Palazzo Dandolo**. It's just left of Bar Omnibus, a touristy restaurant that started life as a cafe in the 19th century. The house belonged to blind doge Enrico Dandolo, who led the Fourth Crusade to a famous victory over Constantinople in 1204. Never mind that the Crusaders were actually supposed to be toughing it out against the infidels in the sands of the Middle East rather than bludgeoning their fellow (albeit Orthodox) Christians in Byzantium (see History in the Facts about Venice chapter)!

Wedged in between Calle Bembo and Rio di San Salvador is the magnificent red facade of **Palazzo Bembo**. What you see is the result of 17th-century restoration of a 15th-century late-Venetian-Gothic structure. It is almost certain that Pietro Bembo, cardinal, poet, historian and founding father of the grammar of standard Italian, was born here. On the other side of Rio di San Salvador, the **Palazzo Dolfin-Manin**, easily identified by its portico, was designed by Sansovino and completed in

1573. At this point, we turn away from the Grand Canal and proceed inland a block along Calle Larga Mazzini.

Chiesa di San Salvador & Around (Map 5)

In front of you is the main entrance to the **Chiesa di San Salvador** *(admission free; open 10am-noon & 3pm-6pm Mon-Sat)*, built on a plan of three Greek crosses laid end to end. The church is among the city's oldest, although the bulk of what you see dates from later periods. The present facade was erected in 1663. Among the noteworthy works inside is Titian's *Annunciazione* (Annunciation), at the third altar on the right as you approach the main altar. Behind the main altar itself is another of his contributions, the *Trasfigurazione* (Transfiguration). To its right is the former monastery of the same name, now owned by Telecom. You can get just a glimpse of one of the cloisters by peering through the window nearest the church.

Diagonally across from the church to the north-west is the **Scuola Grande di San Teodoro**, one of the many confraternity headquarters in Venice (see the boxed text 'When School Was Cool' later in this chapter), now used frequently for music recitals and exhibitions.

Heading north-east from here, we pass the small and much interfered with **Chiesa di San Bartolomeo**, which at one time served as the parish church for the local German-merchant community based at the Fondaco dei Tedeschi (see next section). When the Republic meekly surrendered to Napoleon in 1797, an angry mob set about looting the houses of those they held responsible for such ignominy in the area around **Campo San Bartolomeo**. The Venetian militia set up cannons on the Ponte di Rialto to control the unrest – the last time the guns of San Marco were fired in anger, they spilled the blood of their own people. The statue in the middle of the square is of Carlo Goldoni, Venice's great playwright.

Fondaco dei Tedeschi (Map 5)

From the 13th century onwards, the German trading community (who enjoyed a favoured status in Venice) occupied a fondaco (or *fontego*) on

this privileged site. After a fire in 1505, the present building was erected in a little under three years (1508), not bad going for the time.

It may look a little sombre now, but you have to try to imagine the exterior adorned with frescoes by Giorgione and Titian. To help in this task, you can see some fragments in the Ca' d'Oro (see the later Sestiere di Cannaregio section).

The two artists, when they turned up at the Palazzo Ducale to pick up their payment of 150 ducats, were told their work was only worth 130 ducats. Incensed, they insisted on an independent appraisal, which confirmed the figure of 150 ducats. The artists were then told that more than 130 ducats couldn't be arranged that day, so they could take it or leave it. Perhaps such penny-pinching lay partly behind Titian's increasing tendency to accept commissions from abroad!

Inside, the building is simple but dignified. The Germans used the porticoed floors above the courtyard as lodging and offices, storing their merchandise below. They even had their own well (which remains). The courtyard was covered over in 1937 and the building now serves as the central post office.

Back to St Mark's Square (Map 5)

At this point, you are spoiled for choice of options. You could proceed north into Cannaregio (see later in this chapter) or duck around and cross the Ponte di Rialto to explore San Polo and Santa Croce (see later in this chapter). Or you could close the circle and finish up the itinerary within the Sestiere di San Marco.

To do the latter, retrace your steps to the Chiesa di San Salvador and follow the narrow shopping street around its northern flank, the Merceria San Salvador. Where the street runs into a canal, you can see the late-Gothic **Palazzo Giustinian-Faccanon**, which for a long time housed the city's main newspaper, *Il Gazzettino*.

The lanes that lead from San Salvador to the Torre dell'Orologio and into St Mark's Square are all called *merceria* (*marzaria* in Venetian dialect), referring to the merchants who traditionally lined this route. For some centuries this was one of the busiest thoroughfares in the city, directly linking St Mark's Square with Rialto (in other words, the political with the financial lungs of La Serenissima).

The arrival of the railway in the 19th century and a new axis through Cannaregio did nothing to change this. The flux of *foresti* (foreigners – ie, non-Venetians) along this narrow commercial trail remains a constant. Whether you're coming from the train station or from Rialto, the Mercerie are to this day one of the most direct routes to St Mark's Square.

It was also thus for the conspirators in the 1310 plot to overthrow Doge Pietro Gradenigo (see the boxed text below), who came a cropper in the Merceria dell'Orologio just before the Torre dell'Orologio.

Knocking Rebellion on the Head

By 1310, Venice was having some serious difficulties. Doge Pietro Gradenigo's pursuit of mainland conquest had brought upon the city a papal interdict. The pope was in no way amused by Venice's attempts to seize control of the city of Ferrara, to which the Holy See had a long-standing claim. The Venetians had been defeated in the field, and many Venetian merchants abroad had been arrested and all their goods confiscated.

Gradenigo was not without his opponents, foremost among them the Querini family. Marco Querini, who had been in command of Venetian forces at Ferrara, claimed Venice had not given him the support he needed. Marco convinced General Baiamonte Tiepolo to lead a revolt against Gradenigo. They both lived in the San Polo area, near Rialto, and so planned to send two armed columns over the bridge. Querini's would proceed down Calle dei Fabbri to St Mark's Square and Tiepolo's down the Mercerie. They would join in the piazza and combine to attack the Palazzo Ducale, at which point a third force would arrive across the lagoon from the mainland.

It might have worked, but word of the plan got out. Gradenigo and his allies gathered forces in St Mark's Square, alerted the workers of the Arsenale (dockyard), who traditionally served as a kind of ducal militia in times of uncertainty, and ordered the *podestà* (mayor) of Chioggia to intercept the invasion fleet.

Things went wrong for the rebels from the start. A storm delayed the fleet, and while Marco Querini marched on St Mark's Square, Tiepolo's troops hung about looting the public treasury at Rialto. By the time they went clattering down the Mercerie, Querini was already battling it out with ducal troopers in St Mark's Square.

Tiepolo's boys were engaged while still in the Mercerie. The decisive moment came when a local housewife, who was leaning out of her window and bombing the rebels with anything that came to hand, pelted Tiepolo's standard-bearer on the head with a mortar. The standard fell and the fight was over. Querini had already died in the fight in St Mark's Square. The leader of the fleet was captured and summarily executed on a charge of armed rebellion. Tiepolo managed to beat a hasty retreat to his home, from where he negotiated to keep his life but agreed to go into exile.

The woman who had struck the winning blow requested the right to hang the flag of the Republic from her balcony on holidays. This she received, but she was no sentimental dummy – she also asked that the rent on her house never be raised by the Procurators of St Mark, who owned the building. In 1436, the procurators actually did raise it while one of the long-deceased woman's descendants was away on military service. Thirty-two years later, he demanded, and obtained, a return to the original rent.

Today a bas-relief of the woman leaning out of her window marks the spot on Merceria dell'Orologio (just above the Sotoportego e Calle del Cappello). A simple stone with the date of the incident in Roman numerals (XV.VI.MCCCX) marks the place on the ground where the standard-bearer fell.

Where Merceria dell'Orologio begins, you can see off to the left (east) the **Chiesa di San Zulian**, supposedly founded in 829, although its actual form, covered in a layer of Istrian stone, was designed by Sansovino. Inside are a few works by Palma il Giovane.

Heading right (west) from the top of Merceria dell'Orologio over the bridge, duck right into the first little lane. In the *sotoportego* (street continuing under a building, like an extended archway) just before the T-junction, you will see on your right, at No 956/b, the entrance to the **Chiesa della Santa Croce degli Armeni**. On Sundays only, Armenian priests from the Isola di San Lazzaro celebrate a service here. The church has been active since at least the 14th century.

Return to Merceria dell'Orologio and proceed down (south) towards the Torre dell'Orologio and pass below it. You are now back in St Mark's Square.

SESTIERE DI DORSODURO

Let's assume you are now on the Ponte dell' Accademia (Map 6), having come through Campo Santo Stefano in the Sestiere di San Marco. Once you step down off the other side of the bridge, you are in Campo della Carità. Now it's time for some serious art appreciation.

Gallerie dell'Accademia (Map 6)

The first buildings you virtually bump into on crossing the Ponte dell'Accademia constitute the Gallerie dell'Accademia *(☎ 041 522 22 47; admission €6.20, audio guide €3.60, or €5.15 for two; open 8.15am-2pm Mon, 8.15am-7.15pm Tues-Sun – hrs subject to frequent change)*. This is Venice's single most important art collection. The former church and convent of Santa Maria della Carità, with additions by Palladio, houses a swathe of works that follows the progression of Venetian art from the 14th to the 18th centuries.

In 1750, the rococo painter Gian Battista Piazzetta founded the art school that later became the Accademia, Venice's official arbiter of artistic taste. The collection of paintings was assembled in 1807 and opened to the public 10 years later. The first works came from churches and other religious institutions suppressed during the brief years of Napoleonic rule. Later additions came from private collections. In 1878 the galleries were hived off from the art school and passed into state control. Acquisitions have continued ever since.

From the ticket office, you pass upstairs to Room *(Sala)* 1, where the gallery's more or less chronological display begins. You are in what was the main meeting hall of the Scuola Grande di Santa Maria della Carità, the oldest of the Scuole Grandi (see the boxed text 'When School Was Cool' later in this chapter). The magnificent timber ceiling is divided into squares, at the centre of each of which is a sculpted face – every one different – of an angel. The room is given over to the religious art, triptychs and the like, of the 14th century, including Paolo Veneziano's *Madonna col Bambino i Due Commitanti* (Madonna with Child and Two Donors).

Room 2, designed by Carlo Scarpa and with an unusual black terrazzo alla Veneziana (see the boxed text 'Of Floors & Walls' in the Sestiere di Castello section of this chapter), contains nine paintings, including a couple each by Giovanni Bellini, Vittore Carpaccio and Cima da Conegliano. Note the commonality in themes adopted by all three in their depictions of the Madonna and child, for instance the musicians at the Madonna's feet.

The most enthralling of the works is, however, Carpaccio's altarpiece *Crocifissione e Apoteosi dei 10,000 Martiri del Monte Ararat* (Crucifixion and Apotheosis of the 10,000 Martyrs of Mt Ararat). The story goes that some 10,000 Roman soldiers sent to quell rebellion in Armenia instead converted to Christianity. The Emperor was unimpressed and sent more troops. They were ordered to subject the 10,000 to the same trials that Christ had suffered if they didn't change their minds. The result was a massacre. The painting, representing a kind of collective sainthood, was a departure from the standard depiction of one or two saints in religious painting. The soldiers all have the appearance of Christ, while their executioners appear in the garb of nasty Turks – no doubt reflecting Venetian and European feelings towards the infidels of their own time. More works by Giovanni Bellini and Cima da Conegliano adorn Room 3.

In Rooms 4 and 5 you can enjoy a mixed bag, including the work of some non-Venetians. They include Andrea Mantegna's *San Giorgio* (St George) and works by Cosmè Tura, Piero della Francesca and Jacopo Bellini. In the latter's pieces, note the comparative stiffness of his characters, a faithful reflection of a painting style still crossing over from earlier Gothic tenets.

His son Giovanni has 11 paintings here and the greater suppleness and reality of expression is clear – take for instance the remarkable *Madonna col Bambino tra le Sante Caterina e Maddalena* (Madonna with Child Between Saints Catherine and Mary Magdalene).

The most striking paintings in these rooms are the two rare contributions by Giorgione, *La Tempesta* (The Storm) and *La Vecchia* (The Old Woman). Look at the latter closely. The lines and brush strokes, the look in the eyes, indeed the very subject matter, belong to another century. Its complete lack of stylisation makes it readily identifiable with 19th-century portraiture.

In Room 6 are six works each by Tintoretto and Veronese and one Titian. In Tintoretto's *La Creazione degli Animali* (The Creation of the Animals), we can see the thick splashy paint-strokes that characterised much of this Mannerist painter's work. His use of muted crimsons and blues in *Assunzione della Vergine* (Assumption of the Virgin) reminds one of El Greco. Or rather, in Tintoretto's work we can see support for the claim that El Greco took with him to Spain a good deal of what he had learned in Venice.

The main interest in Rooms 7 and 8 is Lorenzo Lotto's *Ritratto del Giovane Gentiluomo nel Suo Studio* (Portrait of a Young Gentleman in His Studio). What's the lizard doing on his desk? Others represented here are Titian, Palma il Vecchio and even Giorgio Vasari.

In Room 10 we are confronted by some major works, one of the highlights of which is Paolo Veronese's *Convito in Casa di Levi* (Feast in the House of Levi). Originally called *Ultima Cena* (Last Supper), the painting's name was changed at the behest of the Inquisition (see under Late Renaissance in the Painting section of the Facts about Venice chapter). The room also contains one of Titian's last works, *Pietà*. The almost nightmarish quality of the faces has a Goya-esque touch and reflects, perhaps, the fact that Titian was working on it during an epidemic of the plague. Finally, there are some remarkable Tintorettos dedicated to the theme of St Mark. The *Trafugamento del Corpo di San Marco* (Stealing of St Mark's Body) is a mighty example of this artist's daring with a brush.

Another fine Tintoretto is his *Crocifissione* (Crucifixion) in Room 11, where you can also admire decoration by Tiepolo saved from the Chiesa dei Scalzi after an Austrian bomb missed its target (the nearby train station) in 1915 and hit the church. His long frieze *Castigo dei Serpenti* (Punishment of the Snakes) was for many years rolled up and stashed away, which explains the damage evident today.

Room 12 contains minor 18th-century landscape painting, while Room 13 has works by Jacopo Bassano, Palma il Giovane, Tintoretto and Titian. Rooms 14, 15, 16 and 16a are of less interest, although a few minor Tiepolos appear. Room 17 is crammed with small works, including a rare (in Venice) couple by Canaletto. Francesco Guardi, Pietro Longhi, Marco Ricco and Rossalba Carriera also figure here, as do some studies by Tiepolo.

Minor Veneto landscape artists *(vedutisti)* line the walls of Room 18, while Room 19 is given over to 15th- and 16th-century artists – thus breaking the chronological order established so far.

Just as you might have thought the exhibition was losing steam and interest, you enter Room 20. The crowd scenes, splashes of red and activity pouring from the canvases in this cycle dedicated to the *Miracoli della Vera Croce* (Miracles of the True Cross) come as quite a shock. They were carried out by Vittore Carpaccio, Gentile Bellini and others for the Scuola di San Giovanni Evangelista, which is home to a relic of the True Cross. Today, much of their fascination lies in the depiction of a Venice of centuries ago, with gondolas pootling about, classic Venetian chimneys in evidence everywhere and a faithful depiction of the timber Rialto bridge that preceded the present one.

Carpaccio's extraordinary series of nine paintings recounting the life of Santa Orseola follows in Room 21.

Room 22 hosts a few neoclassical sculptures, while Room 23 is actually the former Chiesa di Santa Maria della Carità. Several works from the Bellini workshops are on display. The last room was the Sala dell'Albergo of the Scuola Grande di Santa Maria della Carità, and is dominated by an exquisite timber ceiling and Titian's *Presentazione di Maria al Tempio* (Presentation of Mary at the Temple).

In each of the rooms, there are detailed description sheets in English and Italian – remember to put them back before proceeding to the next room! When the galleries are crowded, the queues outside can be a pain – a ceiling of 300 visitors at any one time is imposed.

Galleria di Palazzo Cini & Palazzo Barbarigo (Map 6)

If you follow the signs for the Peggy Guggenheim Collection eastwards from the Gallerie dell'Accademia, you soon arrive at the relatively minor collection of the Fondazione Cini (☎ 041 521 07 55, Dorsoduro 864; admission cost changes with each temporary exhibition; opening periods are irregular – in 2001 it opened Sept-Nov only – or by appointment). Oddly, the main facade of this 16th-century building looks over the Rio di San Vio rather than the Grand Canal.

Spread out over two floors are around 30 works of Tuscan art, mostly from the 14th and 15th centuries. Among others, you will see a handful of works by Lippi, Piero della Francesca (*Madonna col Bimbo*; Madonna and Child), Botticelli (*Il Giudizio di Paride*; The Judgment of Paris) and Beato Angelico. Mixed in are some fine pieces of 15th-century Venetian furniture, porcelain collections and other odds and ends.

Cross the bridge into cute little Campo San Vio, one of the handful of small squares that back right on to the Grand Canal. Its eastern flank is occupied by the Palazzo Barbarigo, whose facade is strikingly decorated with mosaics on a base of gold. They were carried out at the behest of the Compagnia Venezia e Murano, a glass and mosaics manufacturer that moved in here towards the end of the 19th century. You can't really see it from the square, but keep an eye out when you chug up or down the Grand Canal on the vaporetto.

Peggy Guggenheim Collection (Map 6)

Calle della Chiesa and then Fondamenta Venier lead you to Venice's premier excursion into the world of contemporary art, the Peggy Guggenheim Collection (☎ 041 240 54 11, Dorsoduro 701; admission €6.20; open 10am-6pm Wed-Mon & 10am-10pm Sat Apr-Oct).

Peggy Guggenheim called the unfinished Palazzo Venier dei Leoni home for 30 years, until she died in 1979. She left behind a collection of works by her favourite modern artists, representing most of the major movements of the 20th century.

Miss Guggenheim came into her fortune in 1921 and set off for Europe with no particular aim. During the 1930s, she became quite interested in contemporary art and the avant-garde. She opened an art gallery in London in 1938, the Guggenheim Jeune, and embarked on a programme of collection that continued well into 1940. Seemingly oblivious to the war raging around her, she only decided to return to New York from Paris when the Nazis were at the gates of the city. In New York she opened the Art of this Century gallery in 1942, but five years later decided to return to Europe. By 1949 her home and museum in Venice was open to the public. The Palazzo Venier dei Leoni was so called because, it is said, the Venier family kept lions here! Peggy herself preferred the company of dogs – many of them are buried alongside her own grave in the sculpture garden.

The bulk of the collection is housed in the east wing of the palazzo. It is the pleasing result of an eclectic collector's whim. Early

Cubist paintings include Picasso's *The Poet* (1911) and *Pipe, Glass, Bottle of Vieux Marc* (1914), and Georges Braque's *The Clarinet* (1912). But the list of greats of 20th-century art is long. There are a couple of Kandinskys, including his *Upward* (1929). Interesting works from Spain include Dalí's *Birth of Liquid Desires* (1932) – a classic example of his rather psycho-sick 'eroticism' – and Miró's *Seated Woman II* (1939).

It wouldn't be right if Max Ernst, Guggenheim's husband and doyen of Surrealism, were not represented. Among his many paintings on show is the disturbing *The Antipope* (1942). Other names to look for include: Jackson Pollock, Mark Rothko, Willem de Kooning, Paul Delvaux, Alexander Calder, Juan Gris, Kurt Schwitters, Paul Klee, Francis Bacon, Giorgio de Chirico, Piet Mondrian and Marc Chagall. Outside in the sculpture garden, several sculptures by Henry Moore and Jean Arp, among others, are on display.

The rear of the mansion hosts a separate collection of Italian Futurists and other modern artists from the peninsula collected by Gianni Mattioli and now incorporated into the Guggenheim collection. Artists include Giorgio Morandi, Giacomo Balla and one early work by Amedeo Modigliani.

Temporary exhibitions are held in the new wing on the west side of the garden. A highly agreeable cafe overlooks the garden.

Palazzo Dario (Map 6)
Back on the street, we keep moving east. The next little bridge brings us into a charming, shady square. The exuberant gardens dripping over the walls, seemingly in an attempt to drop down into the water of the Rio delle Toreselle, belong to the Palazzo Dario. You can get some impression of this late-Gothic mansion from the rear, but really to appreciate it you need to see the facade from the Grand Canal – a unique Renaissance marble facing that was taken down and then later reattached in the 19th century.

Former Chiesa di San Gregorio (Map 6)
After all the bustle of the grand art galleries, it is a real pleasure to arrive in the tranquil Campo San Gregorio. The Gothic facade of the deconsecrated church of the same name boasts a graceful doorway with a Venetian pointed arch. A straggly garden on the northern flank of the square belongs to the **Palazzo Genovese**, built over part of what was once the abbey to which the church belonged.

Chiesa di Santa Maria della Salute (Map 5)
As you wander under the rough-hewn portico of Calle dell'Abbazia, Longhena's dazzling white monolith, the Chiesa di Santa Maria della Salute *(sacristy admission €1.05; open 9am-noon & 3pm-5.30pm)*, fills your entire field of vision. It is possibly the city's most familiar silhouette (viewed from Piazzetta San Marco or the Ponte dell'Accademia), but seen from so close up, it's difficult to take in.

Longhena got the commission to build the church in honour of the Virgin Mary, to whose intervention was attributed the end of an outbreak of plague in 1630 that had wiped out more than one-third of the population. The ranks of statues that festoon the outside of the church culminate in one of the Virgin Mary on top of the dome.

The octagonal form of the church is unusual. Longhena's idea was to design it in the form of a crown for the Mother of God. The interior is flooded with light pouring through windows in the walls and dome. Dominating the main body of the church is the extraordinary Baroque *altar maggiore* (high altar), into which is embedded an icon of Mary brought to Venice from Crete.

Of the paintings in the church proper, only Titian's *Pentecoste* is of particular note, but the admission price to the sacristy is worth shelling out: the ceiling is bedecked with three remarkable Titians. The figures depicted are so full of curvaceous movement they almost seem to be caught in a washing machine! The three scenes are replete with high emotion, depicting the struggles between *Caino e Abele* (Cain and Abel), *David e Golia* (David and Goliath) and finally between Abraham and his conscience in *Il Sacrificio di Isaaco* (The Sacrifice of Isaac). The eight medallions by Titian depicting saints are small but intriguing. The closer you look, the more human his saints appear. St Mark seems to be winking in amusement to himself, while you could swear that, under his swirling beard, San Girolamo is having a quiet chuckle.

The other star of the sacristy is Tintoretto's *Le Nozze di Cana* (The Wedding Feast of Cana), filled with an unusual amount of bright and cheerful light by Tintoretto's rather dark standards.

Every year, on 21 November, a procession takes place from St Mark's Square to the church to give thanks for the city's good health. The last part of the march takes place on a pontoon bridge thrown out between the Santa Maria del Giglio *traghetto* (ferry; Map 6) stop and the church.

Dogana da Mar (Map 5)

The customs offices that long occupied the low-slung Dogana have gone but nothing has replaced them. The city's plans in the late 1990s to establish a new art gallery here in conjunction with the Guggenheim Foundation are now dead and buried.

To stand at dawn on the **Punta della Dogana**, which marks the split between the Grand Canal and the Canale della Giudecca, is to feel oneself on the prow of a proud fighting vessel putting out to sea. Waxing lyrical, do you think? Not really. Giuseppe Benoni, who designed it in 1677, was hoping for just that effect. On top of the little tower behind you at the tip of the Dogana da Mar buildings, two bronze Atlases bend beneath the weight of the world. Above them twists and turns capricious Fortune, an elaborate weather vane.

The Zattere to I Gesuati (Maps 5, 6 & 7)

The Fondamenta Zattere runs the length of the south side of Dorsoduro along the Canale della Giudecca from Punta della Dogana to the Stazione Marittima. Not surprisingly, it is a popular spot to indulge in a lingering *passeggiata* (the afternoon or Sunday stroll that is something of an institution in Italian life).

Saloni Ex-Magazzini del Sale (Map 7)

The first buildings of any note as you begin to walk west are the city's one-time salt warehouses. Although the facade (hard to appreciate from the street because you are standing so close) is a neoclassical job from the 1830s, the warehouses were built in the 14th century. It was only in the early 1900s that the salt was moved elsewhere. The buildings are now used in part by rowing clubs and as exhibition space for the Biennale.

Chiesa di Santo Spirito (Map 7)

The modest Renaissance facade of this small church is not overly remarkable. But it is from here that boats are lined up to create a bridge across the Canale della Giudecca for the Festa del Redentore in July (see Public Holidays & Special Events in the Facts for the Visitor chapter).

Ospedale degli Incurabili (Map 6)

Put up in the 16th century, this is where incurable syphilis sufferers, who had a tendency to end up quite potty, used to be parked. Later it was used as an orphanage and it is now the seat of the Minors' Court.

Chiesa dei Gesuati (Map 6)

After crossing a couple of bridges, you end up in front of the imposing 18th-century church built for the Dominicans by a collective of architects led by Giorgio Massari. Also known as the Chiesa di Santa Maria del Rosario *(admission €1.55; open 8am-noon & 5pm-7pm)*, the church contains ceiling frescoes by Tiepolo telling the story of St Dominic. The statues lining the interior are by Gian Maria Morlaiter (1699–1781).

Little-visited **Chiesa di Santa Maria della Visitazione** *(open 8am-12.30pm & 3pm-7pm)* next door has a curious 15th-century chessboard timber ceiling bearing row upon row of scenes depicting the Visitation and a series of portraits of saints and prophets.

Rio di San Trovaso (Map 6)

One of the most attractive of Venice's waterways, the Rio di San Trovaso is also home to the most important of the few remaining *squeri* (gondola workshops) in the city – the **Squero di San Trovaso**. From the right bank you look across and see vessels in various states of (dis)repair.

The leafy square behind the squero is backed by the **Chiesa di San Trovaso** *(admission free; open 8am-11am & 3.30pm-6.30pm Mon-Sat, 8.30am-noon Sun)*, rebuilt in the 16th century on the site of its 9th-century predecessor. The associated *scuola* (school; community and religious association) was home to the confraternity of *squerarioli*, or gondola-builders. Inside the church are a couple of Tintorettos.

Before continuing with the itinerary, a brief stroll west along Fondamenta Bontini towards the former Chiesa di Ognissanti (now part of a medical centre) is worthwhile, if only to get a glimpse across the canal into the pretty gardens of the mansions that front the Zattere.

Chiesa di San Barnaba (Map 6)

A walk of a few hundred metres north brings you to this fairly unprepossessing 18th-century reconstruction. The church *(open 9am-6pm Wed-Mon)* hosts a handful of paintings, including one Veronese and a couple by Palma il Giovane. Opening times become uncertain if there is no temporary exhibition on.

Ca' Rezzonico (Map 6)

This superb 17th- to 18th-century mansion, facing the Grand Canal, houses the **Museo del Settecento Veneziano** *(Museum of the 18th Century;* ☎ *041 241 01 00, Dorsoduro 3136; admission €6.70, included in combined ticket – see Special Tickets at start of chapter; open 10am-6pm Wed-Mon)*. Designed by Longhena and completed in the 1750s by Massari, it was home to several notables over the years, including the poet Robert Browning, who died here.

The museum houses a collection of 18th-century art and furniture and is also worth visiting for the views over the Grand Canal.

A broad staircase by Massari ascends from the ground floor to the *piano nobile* (main floor). This leads to the Salone da Ballo (Ballroom), a splendid hall dripping with frescoes and richly furnished with 18th-century couches, tables and statues in ebony.

There follows a series of rooms jammed with period furniture and *objets d'art*, and plenty of paintings. Particularly noteworthy is Tiepolo's ceiling fresco in the Sala del Trono (Throne Room), the *Allegoria del Merito tra Nobiltà e Virtù* (Allegory of Merit Between Nobility and Virtue). Tiepolo contributed several other frescoes and paintings, as did his son Giandomenico (look out for his fresco cycle taken from the Tiepolo house at Zianigo, near Mira on the mainland). Other artists include Pietro Longhi, Francesco Guardi, Rosalba Carriera and Canaletto.

Ca' Foscari (Map 6)

North of Ca' Rezzonico, this late-Gothic structure was commissioned by Doge Francesco Foscari and is now the seat of the university. Although one of the finest mansions in the city, it has fallen into quite a state of disrepair. In mid-1999, a deceptively realistic mock facade was unveiled to hide restoration work that will take until at least 2002 to complete.

Campo Santa Margherita (Map 6)

This is a real people's *Platz*. Sure, any number of tourists or foreign students can be heard at the tables of the many restaurants and bars, but in the afternoon, when all the local kids come out to play, it takes on a special, *living* air. Henry James' words spring to mind, when he speaks of '... that queer air of sociability, of cousinship and family life, which makes up half the expression of Venice. Without streets and vehicles, the uproar of wheels, the brutality of horses, and with its little winding ways where people crowd together, where voices sound as in the corridors of a house... the place has the character of an immense collective apartment.'

The square is headed at its northern end by what little is left of a former church, long ago swallowed up by residential buildings. The squat little object at its southern end was one of the city's many *scuole*, or religious confraternities, the **Scuola Varoteri**.

Scuola Grande dei Carmini Proceed west of the square, as it tapers away from the buzz.

Just before you bump into the church of the same name, you pass on the right the Scuola Grande dei Carmini (☎ 041 528 94 20, Dorsoduro 2617; admission €4.15; open 9am-6pm Mon-Sat, 9am-4pm Sun), with paintings by Tiepolo inside.

The facades have been attributed to Longhena. In its heyday, this was probably the most powerful of the religious confraternities, with a membership of 75,000 in 1675 – not bad in a city where the entire population was not much more than twice that! For more on scuole, see the boxed text 'When School Was Cool' later.

Of its numerous works of art, the nine ceiling paintings by Tiepolo in the Salone Superiore (upstairs) depict the virtues surrounding the Virgin in Glory. Restored in the late 1980s, they suffered a blow in 2000 when one of the panels collapsed from the ceiling, partly eaten away by a woodworm-like bug. It was hoped that work in 2001 would head off any further damage.

Chiesa dei Carmini What remains of the original 14th-century Byzantine and then Gothic Chiesa dei Carmini (open 7.30am-noon & 2.30pm-7.10pm Mon-Sat, 7.30am-noon & 2.30pm-4.30pm Sun) sits a little uneasily side by side with the richer, and perhaps less digestible, ornament of the 16th and 17th centuries. Among the paintings on view are several works by Cima da Conegliano.

Palazzo Zenobio (Map 6)

Stride across the small campo in front of the main facade of the church and head southwest along Fondamenta del Soccorso. The dominating mansion on your left is the Palazzo Zenobio, since the mid-19th century the headquarters of the Collegio Armeno dei Padri Mechitaristi (Armenian College of Mechitarist Fathers). The Baroque structure is the handiwork of Antonio Gaspari, but apart from the grand curved tympanum, the exterior of the building tells you little. Ad hoc tourist visits are not welcome, but if you could only sneak in and see the Sala della Musica, you would witness Gaspari's voluptuous decor at its Baroque extreme. You *can* get in if and

when guided visits are organised, usually from June to September. You need to call ahead (☎ 041 522 87 70) to find out.

Chiesa di San Sebastiano (Map 6)

Continue past Palazzo Zenobio and round the canal to the left. Cross at the second bridge and you have before you the Renaissance reconstruction (Scarpagnino's work?) of Paolo Veronese's parish church (admission €1.55; open 10am-5pm Mon-Sat), which became his final resting place too.

Veronese went to town here, decorating the inside of the church with frescoes and canvases that cover a good deal of space on the ceiling and walls. The organ is his work too, with depictions of scenes from Christ's life on its shutters. The ceiling paintings together seem to exude a pallid, yellowish light. The sacristy, which also contains some of his work, was tightly shut at the time of writing.

Titian left a notable item behind here too – his *San Nicolò*, first up on the right as soon as you enter the church.

The church is part of the Chorus scheme (see the boxed text 'A Chorus Line' earlier in this chapter).

Santa Marta Area & Back to Campo Santa Margherita (Map 6)

When you walk out of the church, don't do what just about everyone else does and head back towards Zattere or Campo Santa Margherita. Wander around the back through the interlinked squares that take you to the Chiesa di San Basilio, better known as **Angelo Raffaele**. The uneven squares, with clumps of grass pressing up between the flagstones, are intriguingly quiet during the day, but take on an evening buzz as locals take their places at the local trattorias.

As you cross the bridge north of Angelo Raffaele and look left (west), you'll espy the bell tower of the **Chiesa di San Nicolò dei Mendicoli**. Although it has been fiddled with over the centuries, the church still preserves elements of the 13th-century original. The portico attached to one side was used to shelter the poor. The whole area was fairly downtrodden and known for its *mendicoli*, or beggars. The church's tiny square, bound in by the canals and featuring a pylon bearing the winged lion of St Mark (one of the few not to have been destroyed under Napoleon), is at the heart of one of the oldest parishes in Venice. They say it was established in the 7th century.

Across the Rio delle Terese was the **Chiesa di Santa Teresa** and its attached convent, of which nothing much can be seen. A stroll up to Fondamenta Santa Marta and west into the quarter of the same name reveals a curious contrast to the Venice of monuments. It's a working-class district with orderly housing blocks and broad walkways. Just beyond, across the Canale Scomenzera (Map 2), you can watch the desultory activity of Venice's commercial port, now much overshadowed by the monster of Marghera.

You could then follow our suggested route back towards Campo Santa Margherita via Fondamenta delle Procuratie. Along here and the parallel Fondamenta dei Cereri, rental housing was built as early as the 16th century by the Procurators of St Mark for the less well off. It has remained largely unchanged since.

Campo San Pantalon (Map 6)

A short walk north from Campo Santa Margherita along Calle della Chiesa and over the bridge will bring you into Campo San Pantalon (which leads you on to the Scuola Grande di San Rocco and the Chiesa di Santa Maria Gloriosa dei Frari in Sestiere di San Polo – see the following section).

The stark, unfinished and now seriously cracked brick facade of the **Chiesa di San Pantalon** *(open 4pm-6pm Mon-Sat)* dominates the small square. It dates from the 17th century, although a church was here as early as the 11th century. Inside, the greatest impact comes from the 40 canvases representing the *Martirio e Gloria di San Pantaleone* (Martyrdom and Glory of St Pantaleone), painted for the ceiling by Giovanni Antonio Fumiani. The artist died in a fall from the scaffolding as he was finishing the painting and is buried in the church. Veronese, Vivarini and Palma Il Giovane have works in here too. Head for the Cappella del Sacro Chiodo (Chapel of the

Holy Nail) to see the greatest concentration of works. To observe the ceiling and Veronese's *San Pantaleone Risana un Fanciullo* (St Pantaleone Heals a Boy) better, stick coins into the slot machine to turn on the lights.

SESTIERI DI SAN POLO & SANTA CROCE (SANTA CROSE)

These two sestieri have been lumped together because they form a neat whole – more than with any other two sestieri, you will probably find yourself crossing from one to the other frequently.

From Campo San Pantalon (see the previous section), follow the *calle* (street) around to the right of the church and keep heading north over the next bridge. You will emerge in Campo San Rocco. In front of you rises the brooding Gothic apse of the Chiesa di Santa Maria Gloriosa dei Frari. On your left, the Scuola Grande di San Rocco and the church of the same name face each other at an angle. Between them they contain a formidable concentration of Venetian art.

Scuola Grande di San Rocco (Map 6)

Antonio Scarpagnino's (c.1505–49) Renaissance facade (exhibiting a hint of the Baroque to come), with its white marble columns and overbearing magnificence, seems uncomfortably squeezed into the tight space of the narrow square below it. Whatever you make of the exterior of this scuola dedicated to St Roch *(☎ 041 523 48 64, Dorsoduro 3052; admission €5.15; open 9am-5.30pm Easter-Oct, 10am-4pm Nov-Easter)*, nothing can prepare you for what lies inside.

St Roch, by the way, was born in 1295 in Montpellier (France) and at the age of 20 began wandering through southern France and Italy helping plague victims. He died in 1327 and a cult soon grew around him. His body was transferred to Venice as a kind of plague-prevention measure in 1485.

After winning a competition (Veronese was among his rivals), Tintoretto went on to devote 23 years of his life to decorating the school. The overwhelming concentration of more than 50 paintings by the master is altogether too much for the average human to digest. Chronologically speaking, you should start upstairs (Scarpagnino designed the staircase) in the Sala Grande Superiore. Here you can pick up mirrors to carry around to avoid getting a sore neck while inspecting the ceiling paintings (which depict Old Testament episodes). Around the walls are scenes from the New Testament. A handful of works by other artists (such as Titian, Giorgione and Tiepolo) can also be seen. To give your eyes a rest from the paintings, inspect the woodwork below them – it is studded with curious designs, including a false book collection.

Downstairs, the walls of the confraternity's assembly hall feature a series on the life of the Virgin Mary, starting on the left wall with the *Annunciazione* and ending with the *Assunzione* opposite.

Chiesa di San Rocco (Map 6)

You are likely to wander out of the Scuola Grande di San Rocco wondering what hit you. Maybe that's why there's no charge to enter the church across the street. Although built at about the same time as the scuola, the church *(open 7.30am-12.30pm & 3pm-5pm)* was completely overhauled in the 18th century – hence the Baroque facade (easily identified by all the statues in niches and wall sculpture). It has a somewhat neglected feel inside, but it contains several paintings of interest to those who have not overdosed. These include some by Tintoretto on the main-entrance wall and around the altar.

Detour to Campo San Tomà (Map 6)

A brief walk towards the Grand Canal from the Campo San Rocco along Calle Larga Prima brings you to this charming little square, closed off at the far end by the **Chiesa di San Tomà**, whose facade dates from 1742. On the San Rocco side of the square is the **Scuola dei Calegheri**, the shoemakers' confraternity. Veering around to the right of the church, you reach the San Tomà vaporetto stop.

Across Rio di San Tomà is Palazzo Centani, now known better as the **Casa di Goldoni** *(☎ 041 523 63 53, Calle Nomboli 2794; admission included in combined ticket – see Special Tickets at start of chapter)*, for this is where Venice's greatest playwright, Carlo Goldoni, was born in 1707. His house was due to open to the public in late 2001.

When School Was Cool

The name *scuola* as applied to the great confraternities in Venice is perhaps misleading to a modern reader. In an era when the welfare state had not even been dreamed of, the scuola served as a community and religious association. Its lay members formed a brotherhood *(confraternita)* under a patron saint and, apart from acting as a religion-based club, it dealt with such matters as financial assistance to the families of members fallen on hard times. The scuola, along with the parish church, formed the backbone of local social life.

The division between the big six (the Scuole Grandi, dedicated to San Marco, San Rocco, San Teodoro, San Giovanni Evangelista, Santa Maria della Misericordia and Santa Maria della Carità – the latter swallowed up into the Accademia in the 18th century) and the rest (the Scuole Minori) was decreed in the 15th century. The smaller scuole totalled about 400, many without a church or even a fixed headquarters. Pretty much all the city's workers' and artisans' guilds had their own scuola and patron saint, with whom they identified strongly. As club, welfare centre and rallying point for the big parades and religious events in the city, the role of the scuola in Venetian society cannot be underestimated.

Early in the 19th century, most of the *scuole*, as religious institutions, were suppressed by Napoleon's administrators. Some of the richer ones (and they were indeed rather well endowed) lost a good number of their works of art and precious artefacts. Only a few of the scuole were later resurrected. Some are now used, among other things, to host exhibitions and concerts.

A Hitchcock moment on the wintry Grand Canal (above); and the same waterway under the spell of a Venetian summer sunset (below)

DAMIEN SIMONIS

Stop to gape at Giacomo Rizzo's dazzling displays of perfect pasta.

DAMIEN SIMONIS

Ceramics on sale in Santa Croce

ALAN BENSON

Just three bits of foccacia, give them to me...

Chiesa di Santa Maria Gloriosa dei Frari (Map 6)

If you have seen Notre Dame in Paris, Cologne's Dom or even Milan's Duomo, you will probably be asking yourself what is so Gothic about the Frari *(admission €1.55; open 9am-6pm Mon-Sat, 1pm-6pm Sun)*. Built for the Franciscans in the 14th and 15th centuries of brick rather than stone, and bereft of flying buttresses, pinnacles, gargoyles and virtually any other sign of decoration inside or out, it is indeed a singular interpretation of the style. Nevertheless, some features give it away, among them the Latin-cross plan (with three naves and a transept), the high vaulted ceiling, and its sheer size. In any case, you should not let appearances deceive you – even if you are not struck by the church's exterior, a look inside is a must on any art lover's tour of the city.

A curious element is the presence in the middle of the central nave of the *coro* (or choir stalls). A common feature in Spain, the stalls in most churches beyond the Iberian Peninsula tend to be kept out of the way (behind the altar, off to the side or high up at the bottom end of the cross floor plan). Was the idea an import or is it coincidence?

The simplicity of the interior (red and white marble floor, with the same colours dominating the walls and ceiling) is more than offset by the extravagance of decoration in the form of paintings and funereal monuments.

While Tintoretto is the star of San Rocco, Titian is the main attraction of the Frari. His dramatic *Assunta* (Assumption; 1518) over the high altar, praised unreservedly by all and sundry as a work of inspired genius, represents a key moment in his rise as one of the city's greatest artists.

Another of his masterpieces, the *Madonna di Ca' Pesaro* (Madonna of Ca' Pesaro), hangs above the Pesaro altar (in the left-hand aisle, near the choir stalls). Also of note are: Giovanni Bellini's triptych, in the apse of the sacristy; Donatello's statue of *Giovanni Battista* (John the Baptist), in the first chapel to the right of the high altar; and Vivarini's *Sant'Ambrogio in Trono e Santi* (St Ambrose Enthroned and Saints), in the second-last chapel to the left of the high altar.

The church is part of the Chorus scheme (see the boxed text 'A Chorus Line' earlier in this chapter).

Archivio di Stato (Map 6)

Next to the Frari spread the buildings and peaceful cloisters of the former Convento dei Frari, suppressed in 1810 by Napoleon. Since 1815 it has housed the Archivio di Stato, the city's archives. It is a treasure-trove, containing some 15 million documents covering the breadth of Venice's history from the 9th century on. Wandering in is not a problem during office hours, but you are unlikely to make it even to the first of the three cloisters unless you are here on official business.

Scuola Grande di San Giovanni Evangelista (Maps 3 & 6)

Cross the Rio dei Frari, turn left and cross the next bridge. Veer left around the block and you end up in the nondescript Campo San Stin. Take the western exit off the campo and turn right. Almost immediately on the left you will be struck by what seems like an iconostasis. Behind it, two impressive facades give onto a courtyard.

On the southern side is the **Chiesa di San Giovanni Evangelista (Map 6)**, raised in 970 but subsequently rebuilt several times. Opposite is one of the six major Venetian scuole, dedicated to the same saint **(Map 3)**. Codussi designed the interior. Like San Rocco, the plan is typical of the big schools, with an assembly hall (here divided in two by a line of columns) and a grand staircase up to the 1st-floor hall (*☎ 041 71 82 34, San Polo 2454; guided tour €2.60; open by appointment only)*, which contains an altar used for religious services. Massari restyled this hall in sumptuous fashion in 1727. Many of the major works of art once housed here have been moved to the Gallerie dell'Accademia.

From Rio Marin to Piazzale Roma (Maps 3 & 6)

Back on Calle dell'Olio, we proceed north to the canal and turn left (you have no choice about this). Cross the first bridge over the Rio

Marin and head along the bank to Calle della Croce. Our itinerary takes us right down this street and on to Campo San Giacomo dell' Orio. See the next section to go there directly.

Beforehand, a few words on some minor but noteworthy items between here and the western end of the Sestiere di Santa Croce. Right across Rio Marin you are facing the **Palazzo Soranzo-Cappello (Map 3)**, a 16th-century mansion graced with what must have been a beautiful (but now unruly) garden. It is slowly being restored. From the same period is the **Palazzo Gradenigo (Map 3)**, farther north-west, by the last bridge over the canal. Were you to walk up to that bridge and look to your right, you'd see the tiny **Chiesa di San Simeon Grande (Map 3)**. Of ancient origins, it was heavily restored in the 18th century. Inside you can see an *Ultima Cena* (Last Supper) by Tintoretto.

Across the bridge, you end up on Calle Bergami. Turn right at its end and head for the high-arched **Ponte dei Scalzi (Map 3)**, one of three bridges across the Grand Canal. Built in 1934, it replaced an iron bridge built by the Austrians in 1858. Crossing over this bridge puts you on our route through the Sestiere di Cannaregio – see that section later for details.

If you turn left before the bridge and follow Fondamenta San Simeon Piccolo south-west, you'll pass the **church (Map 3)** of the same name (the present version was built from 1718 to 1738). Its outstanding feature is the bronze dome. At the next bridge, turn left down Fondamenta dei Tolentini. The modern facade on the bend is the entrance to the **Istituto Universitario di Architettura di Venezia (Map 6)** (IUAV), designed by Carlo Scarpa. The institute is one of the country's most prestigious architecture schools. Beside it, the late-16th-century **Chiesa di San Nicolò da Tolentino** houses quite a few works by Palma il Giovane.

The **Giardini Papadopoli (Maps 3 & 6)** *(open 8am-7.30pm summer, 8am-5.30pm winter)* across the canal seems almost an afterthought. The park was actually quite a deal more impressive until in 1932 the Rio Nuovo was slammed through. Beyond the park lies Piazzale Roma, home to the unlovely bus station and car parks. A wander around it and along Canale di Santa Chiara (Map 3) is a sobering reminder of how even the most beautiful of cities contain pockets of neglect.

Beyond the canal lies the now little-used merchant-shipping harbour and then the Isola del Tronchetto – a giant car park and temporary home to the Fenice theatre.

Chiesa di San Giacomo dell'Orio (Map 3)

Let's say you decided against going west of Rio Marin. Head east down Calle della Croce, turn right and left into Campo San Nazario Sauro, and keep heading east down Ruga Bella, which takes you into Campo San Giacomo dell'Orio.

This charming, leafy square is graced by the modest outline of one of Venice's few good examples of Romanesque architecture (see also Architecture in the Facts about Venice chapter), the Chiesa di San Giacomo dell'Orio *(admission €1.55; open 10am-5pm Mon-Sat, 1pm-5pm Sun)*. The initial 9th-century church was replaced in 1225. The main Gothic addition (14th century) is the remarkable wooden ceiling *a carena di nave* (in the style of an upturned ship's hull). It is one of several examples in Venice and, for anyone who has tramped around the great

---

Food for Thought

From Calle della Croce, you can make a detour to one of the rare strips of footpath actually on the Grand Canal. Turn left (north) up Calle Larga dei Bari, right along Lista dei Bari and left (north) along Ramo Zen then Calle Zen to the Riva di Biasio. A couple of the mansions here are interesting enough to behold and the views to the other side of the canal are more impressive still.

But the prize goes to a tale we all hope is taller than true. A sausage-maker by the name of Biagio (Biasio) Cargnio had a shop here in the 16th century. They say he was sent to the next world on charges of having sausages made of – wait for it – children.

churches of Spain, starkly reminiscent of the Muslim-influenced *artesonado* ceilings.

Among the intriguing jumble of works of art are a Byzantine column in green marble, a 13th-century baptismal font and a Lombard pulpit perched on a 6th-century column from Ravenna. In front of the main altar is a wooden crucifix by Veronese, and on the wall at the rear of the central apse, a rare work by Lorenzo Lotto, *Madonna col Bambino e Santi* (Madonna with Child and Saints).

The church is part of the Chorus scheme (see the boxed text 'A Chorus Line' earlier in this chapter).

From San Giacomo dell'Orio to Rialto via Campo San Polo (Maps 3, 5 & 6)

At this point, two separate routes suggest themselves to get you to the Ponte di Rialto. This first one follows a trail largely ignored by tourists. The other, via Campo San Stae (see the following section), is busier, but still loaded with interest. You can also join them together into a circular route that would bring you right back into this square. From here you could then backtrack to Rio Marin and go on to the Ponte dei Scalzi to pick up our route through Cannaregio.

From Campo San Giacomo dell'Orio, follow Calle del Tintor south-east, cross the bridge and continue until you hit a T-junction. As you turn left into Rio Terrà Secondo, note on the right-hand side, opposite the Gothic **Palazzo Soranzo-Pisani**, the building in which Aldo Manuzio got his **Aldine Press (Map 3)** started up and so revolutionised the world of European letters (see Literature in the Facts about Venice chapter). His was an address much frequented by learned fellows from across the Continent.

Head north-east and turn right into Calle del Scaleter. At Da Fiore (one of only two restaurants with a Michelin star in all Venice), turn left into Calle del Cristo, cross the bridge and take the second right (Ramo Agnello). Follow it straight over the bridge and stop at the second bridge.

It's hard to tell now, but this was long the centre of Venice's cheaper red-light zone. The bridge is known as **Ponte delle Tette (Map 3)** (Tits Bridge), because a city ordinance stipulated that the whores who worked here should hang about in windows and doorways barebreasted to encourage business. Pardon? Back in the 14th century, the city fathers had in fact tried to clamp down on prostitution in Venice, but by the late 15th century found it the only hope of reviving the ardour of Venetian men, who were apparently adopting imported Eastern habits of sodomising each other. La Serenissima took a far dimmer view of this than prostitution, so much so that anyone successfully prosecuted for sodomy, under a law of 1482, found themselves executed and incinerated between the two columns on Piazzetta San Marco.

Beyond the bridge is Rio Terrà delle Carampane. The name originally came from a noble family's house in the area (Ca' Rampani), and at some point the ladies of the night working here came to be known as *carampane*. The word is now a colourful part of standard Italian and describes the muttondressed-up-as-lamb brand of loose woman.

From the Ponte delle Tette, look south down Rio di San Cassiano and you will notice a high wrought-iron walkway linking **Palazzo Albrizzi (Map 3)** to its own private gardens. Inside the 16th-century mansion, Isabella Teotochi Albrizzi held her literary salon around the end of the 18th century, with sculptor Antonio Canova and writer Ugo Foscolo among the lucky guests.

We now backtrack to the Da Fiore restaurant. Here turn left (south-east) across the bridge and along Calle Bernardo (the fine Gothic **mansion** of the same name is best seen from the bridge), which brings you into the broad and leafy expanse of Campo San Polo (Map 6), one of the most attractive squares in the city. Among the several fine mansions facing onto the square are **Palazzo Corner**, designed by Michele Sanmicheli in the 16th century, and the Gothic **Palazzi Soranzo (both Map 6)**.

Chiesa di San Polo (Map 6) Although of Byzantine origin, the church *(admission €1.55; open 10am-5pm Mon-Sat, 1pm-5pm Sun)* has lost much of its attraction through repeated interference and renovation. Worst

The Oldest Profession

Accounts of prostitution in Venice make interesting reading. Although generally allowing it to go on, and in some cases encouraging it, the attitude towards the practice and its practitioners was always ambiguous.

In 1358, local authorities were instructed to select an area of Rialto to set aside for prostitution. This they did and a group of houses was soon occupied by prostitutes and their matrons, who took care of the till and paid the women a wage at the end of the month. Prostitutes were not allowed on the streets after a certain hour and were forbidden to work on religious holidays. This restricted area of houses of ill repute, kept under surveillance by six guardians, came to be known as Il Castelletto (Little Castle). The atmosphere must have been oppressive, for prostitutes began to spread out across the city, especially to the Carampane area. At first, attempts were made to force them back into Il Castelletto, but in the end the authorities gave in to the situation and even proclaimed laws obliging the girls to display their wares to attract business.

By the 1640s, however, various regulations were in place to put a brake on prostitution. Prostitutes could not enter churches or potter around in two-oared boats (only 'ladies' could be taken about in such a manner). They were not to adorn themselves with gold or other jewellery. They could not testify in criminal court cases, nor could they prosecute when services rendered were not paid for (which was generally where pimps came in). Your average street whore was made to feel very much like a second-class citizen.

Different strokes for different folks: there was a whole other class of prostitution. In the 16th century the myth of the *cortigiane* (courtesans) began to take shape. These were women of distinction, not simply better-paid, better-looking bimbos. Schooled in the arts, fluent in Latin, handy with a harpsichord, they were women of keen intellect and talent not fortunate enough to have been born into nobility. For such daughters of middle-class families, working for a high-class escort service seemed the only way to acquire independence and well-being.

In 1535, when the Venetian populace totalled about 120,000 and some 11,000 prostitutes were registered, a very handy tourist guide was published: *Questo si è il Catalogo de tutte le principal, et più honorate Cortigiane di Venetia* ('This Is the Catalogue of the Main and Most Honoured Courtesans of Venice'). It contained names, rates and useful addresses. No wonder the city had such a lascivious reputation.

of all, the pile-up of houses between it and the Rio di San Polo has completely obscured its facade. It is, however, worth your time to wander inside if you enjoy the art of Tiepolo. A whole cycle of his, the *Via Crucis* (Stations of the Cross), has been stacked rather unceremoniously along the walls of the sacristy.

The church is part of the Chorus scheme (see the boxed text 'A Chorus Line' earlier in this chapter).

On to Rialto A glance at the map will show we have almost completed a circuit to the Frari. You could head down that way and beyond into Dorsoduro (see earlier in this chapter), or stroll eastwards towards Rialto and the Grand Canal.

From Campo San Polo, take Calle della Madonnetta and follow it to Campo Sant' Aponal. On the way, duck down Calle Malvasia to peer enviously through the gates at the gardens of the **Palazzo Papadopoli (Map 6)**. It seems almost unfair that such luxuriant greenery should be the preserve of the Istituto per lo Studio della Dinamica delle Grandi Masse (Institute for the Study of the Dynamics of Large Masses)!

The former **Chiesa di Sant'Aponal (Map 6)** has a simple Gothic facade topped by five statues, and its free-standing bell tower is Romanesque. From here, Calle dell'Olio takes you around the right side of the church. Turn right down Rio Terrà San Silvestro and you pass the unremarkable early-20th-century facade of the **Chiesa di San Silvestro (Map 6)**. Turn onto the former wine docks on the Grand Canal, the Fondamenta del Vin (Map 5), and the Ponte di Rialto is clearly in view ahead. The restaurants along here make a tempting spot for a break, but you'll pay €2.60 for a cup of coffee. For more on the Rialto area, see later in this chapter.

From San Giacomo dell'Orio to Rialto via Campo San Stae (Maps 3, 4 & 5)

Follow the signs north from the square along Calle Larga (turning off at the canal) to reach the **Fondaco dei Turchi (Map 3)** *(☎ 041 524 08 85, Santa Croce 1730)*, a 12th-century building used as a warehouse by Turkish merchants and now housing the Museo Civico di Storia Naturale (Natural History Museum).

In Venice and across the Middle East and beyond, these warehouses were set up both to house foreign merchants and to store their goods. The word *fondaco* spread, and where Western merchants stayed and worked came to be known in Arabic as a *funduq*, from Aleppo in Syria to Alexandria in Egypt. The Venetian dialect word, which you may also encounter, is *fontego*. In Arab countries, funduq has come simply to mean hotel.

The building was only rented out to the Turkish trading community in 1621 (they remained until 1858, long after the demise of La Serenissima). Previously it had belonged to a series of private owners and the dukes of Ferrara. Although it dates to the 12th and 13th centuries, the place was restored in appalling taste in the mid-19th century. It was a little like plastic surgery gone wrong. Original features in the facade were sacrificed to the architectural fancies of the time – the odd crenellations are, for example, an unhappy addition.

The museum has been closed for years but is due to reopen in 2003 – if it does, take the kids there to see the impressive 12m-long crocodile.

Palazzo Mocenigo & San Stae (Map 3)

From the fondaco return to the canal, cross it and take Calle del Tintor east. Interesting shops line this route to Campo San Cassiano.

At Salizzada di San Stae, turn left (northeast). On the right is the Palazzo Mocenigo *(☎ 041 721 17 98, Santa Croce 1992; admission €4.15 or included in combined ticket – see Special Tickets at start of chapter; open 10am-5pm Tues-Sun)*, which belonged to one of the most important families of the Republic. It now houses a modest museum, with clothes, period furnishings, accessories and the like. It is interesting for the hints it gives you of how the other half lived in the twilight years of La Serenissima.

At the end of the street is the tiny canalside Campo San Stae (St Eustace Square) and vaporetto stop, named after the Baroque **church** *(admission €1.55; open 10am-5pm Mon-Sat, 1pm-5pm Sun)* that closes off the southern end of the square. It is a fairly simple little house of worship, although the facade (finished in 1709) might lead you to think otherwise. Among its art treasures are Tiepolo's *Il Martirio di San Bartolomeo* (The Martyrdom of St Bartholomew).

The church is part of the Chorus scheme (see the boxed text 'A Chorus Line' earlier in this chapter).

Next door to the left (No 1980) is the **Scuola dei Tiraoro e Battioro**, the former seat of the goldsmith confraternity's scuola.

Ca' Pesaro (Map 3) At Campo San Stae, cross the bridge, turn right then left, cross another bridge and you arrive directly at the land entrance to this Baroque mansion. Its main facade faces the Grand Canal and inside it has housed the **Galleria d'Arte Moderna** *(☎ 041 524 06 95, Santa Croce 2076)* on the ground floor since 1902. The collection includes works purchased from the Biennale art festival and is one of the largest collections of modern art in Italy. You can enjoy works by De Chirico, Miró, Chagall, Kandinsky, Klee, Klimt, Moore and others. Closed for almost 20 years, the gallery was due to open in 2002.

The **Museo d'Arte Orientale** *(☎ 041 524 11 73, Santa Croce 2070; admission €2.05; open 8.15am-2pm Tues-Sun)*, in the same building on the top floor, features Asian and Eastern oddments, including important collections of Edo-period art from Japan and Chinese porcelain.

The building itself is considered one of the more important ones on the Grand Canal, started by Longhena and completed in 1710 by Gaspari. Longhena died worrying about the cost!

To Campo delle Beccarie (Map 3) Walk south-west, away from Ca' Pesaro, and on the corner of the second street on the right, you could be forgiven for completely missing the **Chiesa di Santa Maria Mater Domini**. Sansovino supposedly had a hand in it and inside (if you happen to find it open) is an early work by Tintoretto, the *Invenzione della Croce* (Invention of the Cross).

Campo Santa Maria Mater Domini is an intriguing little square, with well-preserved late-Byzantine and Gothic buildings. No 2174 dates from the 13th century. Cross the square and turn left (north) into Calle della Regina. At the end of the street, looking onto the Grand Canal, is the **Palazzo Corner della Regina**. The Corners, one of the most powerful trading families in Venice, had mansions all over town. On this site lived Caterina, a woman who ended up on the throne of Venetian-controlled Cyprus in the late 15th century, only to be unceremoniously obliged by the schemers of San Marco to abdicate. In exchange, she got Asolo and its lovely countryside (see the boxed text 'A Queen Cornered' in the Excursions chapter). The building as it stands today was actually remodelled in the early 18th century.

Tintoretto fans may want to stop off at the **Chiesa di San Cassiano** *(open 9am-noon Tues-Sat)* in the campo of the same name. The sanctuary is decorated with three of his paintings, the *Crocifissione* (Crucifixion), the *Risurrezione* (Resurrection) and the *Discesa al Limbo* (Descent into Limbo). Make a quick detour towards the Grand Canal along Calle del Campanile and duck into **Corte de Ca' Michiel**. This was once known as Calle del Teatro, reputedly the site of one of the city's first theatres in 1580. It didn't last too long, as the Inquisition (not an overly popular institution in Venice) shut it down for what it claimed were the lewd goings-on.

Rialto (Map 4)

A couple of streets on from Chiesa di San Cassiano, you arrive at Campo delle Beccarie. Welcome to the nerve centre of Venice. Rivoalto (later contracted), the highest spot in the collection of islets that formed the initial nucleus of the lagoon city, was the area of first settlement. It became a centre of trade and banking for the Republic, and while political power resided over in San Marco, this is where dosh traded hands, voyages were bankrolled and news (sometimes hard to disentangle from fishwives' gossip) was exchanged. While in Campo delle Beccarie, spare a thought for the Querini family. One wing of their house still looks onto the square, but the rest was demolished in 1310 in reprisal for having backed the revolt against Doge Pietro Gradenigo.

Today, the area continues to buzz with the activity of the daily produce and fish **markets** – why break the habit of 1000 years? The **Fabbriche Vecchie**, along the Ruga degli Orefici and in the shadow of the **Palazzo dei Dieci Savi** (Palace of the 10 Wise Men), were created by Scarpagnino in 1522. They were designed to accommodate markets at ground level and house offices in the upper levels. The Dieci Savi administered taxes (the building now houses the Magistrato alle Acque, or water administration). The **Fabbriche Nuove**, running along the Grand Canal, went up in 1555 to designs by Sansovino and became home to magistrates' courts. Other magistrates, the 'chamberlains', were housed in a separate Renaissance edifice, the **Palazzo dei Camerlenghi**, designed by Guglielmo dei Grigi. At ground level were prisons for common offenders.

The **Pescaria**, the site of the fish market (which extends into Campo delle Beccarie), was rebuilt in neo-Gothic style in 1907. They have been selling fresh fish here since 1300.

From the docks all around here, Crusader fleets set sail. While men and provisions were gathered, various knights and other notables stayed in hostels just behind the Fabbriche Nuove. Many others camped out on Giudecca or around the Chiesa di San Nicolò on the Lido. Before heading off, they heard their last Mass on land for some time in the

Chiesa di San Giacomo di Rialto. Virtually in the middle of the market, off the Ruga degli Orefici, it was supposedly founded on 25 March 421, the same day as the city.

Ponte di Rialto (Map 4) Given Rialto's importance from the earliest days of the Republic, it is hardly surprising that the city's first bridge over the Grand Canal was built here.

The crossing had quite a chequered history before Antonio da Ponte (Anthony of the Bridge) built this robust marble version. Commissioned in 1588, the present bridge cost 250,000 ducats, which was an enormous sum in those days. When it was finally completed in 1592, all concerned must have been happy with the result – which has lasted very nicely in the four centuries since.

The first bridge was little more than a dodgy pontoon arrangement thrown across the canal around 1180. A more permanent wooden structure was built in 1265, but it was cut in two in 1310 as Baiamonte Tiepolo and his fellow rebels beat a hasty retreat on horseback (see the boxed text 'Knocking Rebellion on the Head' earlier in this chapter). It was repaired, but collapsed in a heap in 1444 under the weight of a crowd straining to watch the wedding procession of the marquis of Ferrara. It was again rebuilt, as a timber drawbridge, before finally being dismantled and replaced by da Ponte's version. You can cross here into the Sestiere di San Marco.

Alternatively, as mentioned earlier, you can follow one of the two routes between Rialto and Campo San Giacomo dell'Orio back to the latter square, and then make a brisk dash for Rio Marin and the Ponte dei Scalzi to cross the Grand Canal and arrive in Cannaregio.

SESTIERE DI CANNAREGIO

This was long the swampiest part of Venice and unpleasantly malarial to boot. It owes its name to the reeds *(canna)* that grew in abundance here.

Most people first arrive here off the train, but for the sake of argument, let's assume you have just stumbled over Ponte dei Scalzi after following our routes around Santa Croce and San Polo. A glance at the map will confirm that it virtually amounts to the same thing anyway.

Stazione di Santa Lucia to Ponte delle Guglie (Map 3)

The long thoroughfare connecting the train station and St Mark's Square crawls with tourists heading from one to the other – few venture off it into the peaceful back lanes.

The first sight of any significance you lay eyes on is the Carmelite **Chiesa dei Scalzi** *(literally 'barefoot'; admission free; open 7am-11.45am & 4pm-6.45pm Mon-Sat, 7.45am-12.30pm & 4pm-7pm Sun & holidays)*, virtually next to the train station. There are damaged frescoes by Tiepolo in the vaults of two of the side chapels. Longhena designed the church but the Baroque facade was done by Giuseppe Sardi. The abundance of columns and statues in niches is a deliberate echo of the particularly extravagant Baroque style often employed in Rome. Apparently the Carmelites, who had moved here from Rome several years before, specifically requested that it be so. The voluptuous decorative spin continues within – the altar is a good example of Baroque clearly heading for the extremes of rococo.

At the north-eastern end of Rio Terrà Lista di Spagna, the otherwise uninspiring 18th-century **Chiesa di San Geremia** contains the body of St Lucy (Santa Lucia), who was martyred in Syracuse in AD 304. Her body was stolen by Venetian merchants from Constantinople in 1204 and moved to San Geremia after the Palladian church of Santa Lucia was demolished in the 19th century to make way for the train station. The bell tower is a Romanesque leftover from an earlier church on the same spot. Facing the square at right angles to the church, the **Palazzo Labia** *(☎ 041 78 12 77, Cannaregio 275; admission free; open 3pm-4pm Wed-Fri)* is a fine 17th-century residence. Now the Venice office of the RAI, Italy's national radio and TV organisation, it boasts some Tiepolo frescoes inside. Phone ahead to arrange a visit.

At the **Ponte delle Guglie** (Bridge of the Needles), so called because of the obelisks at each end, the itinerary splits into two. The

THINGS TO SEE & DO

first option takes us to the Sestiere di San Marco via the Ghetto. The second is a more meandering stroll through many of the backstreets and canals of Cannaregio that brings us to Campo SS Giovanni e Paolo in Castello.

Itinerary I: Ponte delle Guglie to Sestiere di San Marco

The Ghetto (Map 3) Cross the Ponte delle Guglie and turn left. Just before you do, you may want to poke around the daily **fish and produce market** on Rio Terrà San Leonardo.

Turn off the Fondamenta di Cannaregio at Calle del Ghetto Vecchio (you'll recognise it by the Gam Gam kosher restaurant). On emerging into the small square, you will see two of the Ghetto's five synagogues, also known as *schole* because they were used for scripture studies. The existence of five places of worship within the Ghetto reflected in part the density of the Jewish population and also liturgical variations between the different communities. The **Schola Spagnola** is at the square's southern end (look for the plaque commemorating Italian Jewish victims of the Holocaust). It and the **Schola Levantina**, opposite, were erected by Jews from the Iberian Peninsula. You can visit the latter as part

The Jews of Venice

The first records of Jews in Venice go back to the 10th century. Even at this early point, acquiring Venetian citizenship was all but impossible, and so outsiders had to content themselves with regularly renewing their residence permits. The early Jews were Ashkenazi of German and Eastern European origins. In 1382, the Maggior Consiglio decreed that Jews could operate as moneylenders. In fact, it encouraged them.

As refugees of various nationalities crowded into Venice during the dark days of the League of Cambrai (see History in the Facts about Venice chapter), the Republic decided on 29 March 1516 that all Jews residing in Venice should be moved to one area. The Getto Novo (New Foundry) was considered ideal, being far from the city's power centres and surrounded by water – a natural prison. The Ashkenazis' harsh Germanic pronunciation gave us the word ghetto.

Jews could move freely through the city only if they wore a yellow cap or badge. At midnight, a curfew was imposed. Gates around the Ghetto Nuovo were shut by Christian guards paid for by the Jewish community and reopened at dawn.

Deliberately excluded from most professions, Jews had few career options. Most tried to get along as moneylenders or in the rag trade. Two of the 'banks' from which moneylenders used to operate remain in evidence on Campo di Ghetto Nuovo, the **Banco Rosso** and **Banco Verde (Map 3)**. A third option was medicine. Jews who had lived in Muslim Spain or in the Middle East had benefited from the advances in the Arab world on this front and were considered better doctors than their Christian counterparts. Jewish doctors were allowed, in emergencies, to leave the Ghetto during curfew. It sounds bad, but everything is relative. Jews who made it to Venice were not persecuted and were free to practise their religion. Compared with their brethren in much of the rest of Europe, Venice's Jews were doing OK.

A quick look around will show you how small the Ghetto was. And the population, in its thousands, was growing. In 1541, waves of Levantine Jews from Spain and Portugal finally made their way into Venice. Here there was a difference – they came with money, as many were wealthy and successful merchants with contacts in the Near East.

Extreme overcrowding combined with building-height restrictions had already created 'skyscrapers' around the Campo di Ghetto Nuovo – some apartment blocks have as many as seven storeys, but with very low ceilings. On top of three of them were built three modest *schole*. The **Schola Tedesca** (German Synagogue) is above the building that now houses the Museo Ebraico. Virtually next door is the **Schola Canton** (Corner Synagogue) and farther around is the **Schola Italiana**

of a tour starting at the Museo Ebraico (see towards the end of this section). The interior betrays a hefty rococo influence, best seen in the decor of the pulpit. The Schola Levantina is used for Saturday prayers in winter (it has heating) while the Schola Spagnola (which can't be visited) is used in summer.

Calle del Ghetto Vecchio proceeds northeast over a bridge into the heart of Venice's Jewish community, Campo di Ghetto Nuovo.

Museo Ebraico (Map 3) A modest collection of Jewish religious silverware can be found at the Jewish Museum (☎ *041 71 53 59, Campo di Ghetto Nuovo, Cannaregio 2902/b; admission €2.60; open 10am-7pm Sun-Fri except Jewish holidays; guided tours of Ghetto & synagogues €6.20 including museum admission; tours hourly 10.30am-5.30pm Sun-Fri except Jewish holidays).* The guided tours (in Italian or English; other languages if booked in advance) of the Ghetto and three of its synagogues (Schola Canton, Schola Italiana and Schola Levantina) that leave from the museum are highly recommended. Enquire also at the museum about guided tours to the Antico Cimitero Israelitico (old Jewish cemetery) on the Lido.

The Jews of Venice

(Italian Synagogue; all on Map 3). This latter is the simplest. The largely destitute Italian Jews concerned had come from Spanish-controlled southern Italy. From the outside, the synagogues could be distinguished from the residential housing by the small domes that indicate the position of the pulpit. In the case of the German and Italian ones, the rows of five larger windows are another giveaway sign.

When the Levantine Jews began to arrive, even the town authorities had to admit there was no more space and ceded another small area to the Jews – the Getto Vecio (Old Foundry). So of course it came to be known as the Old Ghetto, although the converse was true (the foundry was old but the Jewish community was new). Here the Spanish and Portuguese built their two synagogues, mentioned in The Ghetto section earlier. They are considered the most beautiful synagogues in northern Italy.

A final small territorial concession was wrung from the town authorities when a street south of the Ghetto Nuovo, subsequently known as the Calle del Ghetto Nuovissimo (Very New Ghetto Street), was granted to the Jews.

From 1541 until 1553, the Jewish community thrived. Their money and trade were welcome in Venice, and the community also built a reputation for book printing. Then Pope Julian banned such activities. From then on, things started to go downhill. To top it off, the plague of 1630 left fewer than 3000 Jews alive.

In 1797 Napoleon abolished all restrictions on Jews. Later, under the Austrians, they enjoyed considerable freedom, if not complete freedom from prejudice. After Venice was annexed to the Italian kingdom in 1866, all minorities were guaranteed full equality before the law and freedom of religious expression.

Mussolini's rise to power spelled trying times for the Jews in Italy. The 1938 race laws imposed restrictions, but the real torment came in November 1943, when the puppet Fascist government of Salò declared Jews enemies of the state. Of Venice's 1670 remaining Jews, quite a few were rounded up and sent to the Italian concentration camp of Fossoli (outside Modena). They were even marched out of the **Casa Israelitica di Riposo** (rest home; Map 3) on Campo di Ghetto Nuovo. The home's wall bears a memorial to the victims. The next stop for about 200 was a death camp in Poland. Altogether, about 8000 Italian Jews were killed in the Holocaust.

Of the 500 or so Jews still living in Venice, only about 30 remain in the Ghetto. You can contact the local Jewish community on ☎ 041 71 50 12. For more on the ghetto, you can also look online at ⓦ www.ghetto.it.

To Ca' d'Oro (Map 3) Leave the Ghetto by the portico that leads across the canal to Calle Farnese. This was one of the Ghetto gates that used to be locked at midnight. Proceed straight to Rio Terrà Farsetti and turn right, then duck down Rio Terrà del Cristo to look at the **Chiesa di San Marcuola** and the Grand Canal. Although a church has been here since the 9th century, what you see was cobbled together (and not quite completed) in the 18th century by Massari and Gaspari. Inside (you may only be able to get in during Mass) is an *Ultima Cena* (Last Supper) by Tintoretto. His Christ and apostles are spotlighted against a black background, giving the meal an extraordinary air.

Heading east across Rio di San Marcuola, you will come up against the **Palazzo Vendramin-Calergi**. The canalside facade is a masterpiece of restrained Renaissance elegance. The composer Richard Wagner expired here in 1883. It's now the home of the casino: you can wander into the ground-floor area but have to fork out to see the gaming rooms, where formal dress is obligatory.

From here, return to the main drag (at this point called Rio Terrà della Maddalena – you'll know you've hit it when you are sucked up into the crowds again). Proceed a couple of blocks eastwards, then head off to the right (south): in a quiet little campo is the quite unique, circular **Chiesa della Maddalena**. The pretty square is flanked by houses with their upper parts poking over heavy timber barbicans. Notice anything yet? Like you are about the only one to have sufficient curiosity to get off the strip and have a quick look here? Try jumping back into the flood of passers-by and then jumping out again. Amazing, isn't it?

Now you could go around the back of the church and follow Calle del Forno around to a dead end right on the Grand Canal. It's a little mucky but it is always interesting to get another view of the canal.

By backtracking and then taking Calle Correr, you end up back on the strip. The bronze statue on the square opposite you is of Paolo Sarpi, La Serenissima's greatest philosopher (some might suggest only). He

took on the papacy in 1606 and won (see Decline in the History section of the Facts about Venice chapter). You could make a little detour at this point and scurry northeastwards across a couple of bridges to get to the **Chiesa di San Marziale**. If it's open, have a peek inside at all the Baroque baubles.

Otherwise skip it and head southeastwards along the main street. It's called Strada Nova (or Nuova) here and was bulldozed through the area some years after the rail link was opened in the 19th century. On your right you pass a veritable parade of Venetian mansions, but you'd never know it – they only present their photogenic profile to the Grand Canal. The second of them after you cross the Rio di San Felice (named after the church you pass on the left just before the bridge) is the Ca' d'Oro.

Ca' d'Oro (Map 4) This magnificent Gothic structure (☎ 041 523 87 90, *Calle di Ca' d'Oro 3931, Cannaregio; admission €3.10; open 8.15am-2pm Mon, 8.15am-7.15pm Tues-Sun*), built in the 15th century, got its name (Golden House) from the gilding that originally decorated the sculptural details of the facade. The facade, which is visible from the Grand Canal, stands out quite remarkably from the remainder of the edifice, which is rather drab by comparison.

Ca' d'Oro houses the **Galleria Franchetti**, an impressive collection of bronzes, tapestries and paintings. The 1st floor is devoted mainly to religious painting, sculpture and bronzes from the 15th and early 16th centuries. One of the first items you see is a polyptych recounting the martyrdom of St Bartholomew (San Bartolomeo). Take a closer look at the detail. The violence is quite remarkable, as is the saintly indifference with which Bartholomew seems to accept his torment! Much of what you see on this floor is Venetian, but one room has been set aside principally for Tuscan art.

On the 2nd floor, you can see a series of fragments of frescoes saved from the outside of the Fondaco dei Tedeschi (see the earlier Sestiere di San Marco section). All but one are by Titian. The other, a nude by Giorgione, is the most striking, however. Also on this floor is a mixed collection, including works by Tintoretto, Titian, Carpaccio, Mantegna, Vivarini, Signorelli and van Eyck.

A big incentive for visiting is the chance to lean out from the balconies over the Grand Canal on the 1st and 2nd floors. Staff will start hustling you out half an hour before actual closing time.

To Sestiere di San Marco (Map 4) The Strada Nuova leads into the pleasing **Campo dei SS Apostoli**. The church of the same name *(open 7.30am-11.30am & 5pm-7pm Mon-Sat, 8.30am-noon & 4pm-6.30pm Sun)* is worth visiting for a look at the 15th-century Cappella Corner by Mauro Codussi, which features a painting of Santa Lucia by Tiepolo.

Keep following the crowd over the next two bridges and on the left is the rather curious **Chiesa di San Giovanni Grisostomo** *(open 8.15am-12.15pm & 3pm-7pm Mon-Sat, 10.15am-12.15pm & 3pm-7pm Sun & holidays)*. It was remodelled on a Greek-cross plan by Codussi in 1504. Since 1977, it has housed an icon of the Virgin Mary that attracts a lot of the local faithful. What with burning incense and candles, to wander in here is to feel yourself in a mysterious church of the Orthodox East. Notable is Giovanni Bellini's *San Gerolamo e Due Santi* (St Jerome and Two Saints).

Around the back, Corte Prima del Milion leads into a chain of brief streets, *sotoporteghi* (streets continuing under buildings, like extended archways) and squares. At No 5845 in Corte Seconda del Milion, you are supposedly looking at what we are commonly told was **Marco Polo's house**. That's one theory. Another (apparently more reliable) suggests the Polo family house disappeared to make way for the **Teatro Malibran** in 1677. During the restoration work on the theatre, which ended in 2001, traces of the Polo residence were unearthed. Return to the Chiesa di San Giovanni Grisostomo and head south. The next canal marks the boundary between the sestieri of Cannaregio and San Marco. The building you are looking at is the Fondaco dei Tedeschi (see the earlier Sestiere di San Marco section).

Itinerary II: Ponte delle Guglie to Castello

To Chiesa della Madonna dell'Orto

(Map 3) For this second ramble, we don't even cross the Ponte delle Guglie, choosing instead to head north-west along Fondamenta Venier, named after the late-18th-century neoclassical **mansion** of the same name. Farther up, **Palazzo Savorgnan's** big draw is its garden, now a public park with slides and other traditional amusements for the kiddies.

Beyond the palace, the character of the area changes quickly – it's clearly a working-class district. It was perhaps not always thus. Across the canal, just before you reach the last bridge (Ponte di Tre Archi), the 17th-century **Palazzo Surian** stands out. During the last century of the Republic, the French moved their embassy in here and Jean Jacques Rousseau managed to blag his way into a job as secretary to the ambassador.

To the left, down along Rio di San Giobbe, the rather ordinary **church** of the same name boasts a remarkable ceiling faced with multicoloured glazed terracotta. Of the one-time neighbouring convent, little remains but one portico.

Before crossing the Ponte di Tre Archi, you might like to stroll to the end of Fondamenta di San Giobbe. The enormous complex at the end here was the **Macello Comunale**, the city's abattoir. Le Corbusier designed a hospital for the site, but (much to the annoyance of many citizens) it got the thumbs down in 1964. Since then, not a lot has been made of the site. The Università Ca' Foscari operates in part of it and rowing clubs use the lagoon side as a launch pad.

Across the bridge, towards the end of Fondamenta di Cannaregio, the former **Chiesa di Santa Maria delle Penitenti** was one of the seemingly abundant religious institutions set up to take in wayward women who were anxious to put their wicked past behind them.

The winding walk along Calle Ferau and through the Sacca di San Girolamo area, an unpretentious residential district, takes you past the barely noticeable **Chiesa delle Cappuccine** on the left and the ugly hulk of the

Chiesa di San Girolamo on the right across the canal. Apart from soaking up the peace and quiet of the area, your objective is the **Chiesa di Sant'Alvise** *(admission €1.55; open 10am-5pm Mon-Sat, 1pm-5pm Sun)*. Built in 1388, it plays host to a noteworthy Tiepolo, the *Salita al Calvario* (Climb to Calvary), a distressingly human depiction of one of Christ's falls under the weight of the cross. The ceiling frescoes are an unexpected riot of colour. The church is part of the Chorus scheme (see the boxed text 'A Chorus Line' earlier in this chapter).

To reach the next stop, there is no choice but to make a detour across the canal and then a little way along Fondamenta della Sensa and back up Calle Loredan to Fondamenta Madonna dell'Orto. The long courtyard on the left as you head east is called Corte del Cavallo (Horse Court) because here the bronze was melted down for the great equestrian statue to Colleoni in Campo SS Giovanni e Paolo (see the following Sestiere di Castello section).

Chiesa della Madonna dell'Orto (Map 3)

Architecture fans should find the exterior of this church *(admission €1.55; open 10am-5pm Mon-Sat, 1pm-5pm Sun)* intriguing. Elements of Romanesque remain (the inner arch over the main entrance, for instance) in what is largely a 14th-century Gothic structure in brick. That changes were made a century later is fairly clear from the series of statues in niches above the two lower wings of the facade and from the triangular finish at the top. The five statues crowning the facade were actually added in the 18th century.

Tintoretto was a local parishioner, and although he used a good deal of his creative genius filling the Scuola di San Rocco (in San Polo) with his paintings, he found the time to execute some works for this church too. Among them are the *Giudizio Finale* (Last Judgment), *Adorazione del Vitello d'Oro* (Adoration of the Golden Calf) and the *Apparizione della Croce a San Pietro* (Vision of the Cross to St Peter). On the wall at the end of the right aisle is the *Presentazione di Maria al Tempio* (Presentation of Mary at the Temple). Tintoretto is buried with other family members in the church.

In the Cappella di San Mauro is the white stone statue of the *Madonna col Bambino* (Madonna and Child) after which the church is named. The statue was supposedly found in a nearby garden in 1377 and brought here amid considerable excitement.

The church is part of the Chorus scheme (see the boxed text 'A Chorus Line' earlier in this chapter).

If you cross the first bridge to the east of the church, you will end up in Calle dei Mori. Follow it to the next canal and turn left down Fondamenta dei Mori. Almost immediately you will see on your left a plaque noting that Tintoretto lived in this **house** (No 3399) until his death. The strange statue of a man with a huge turban that sticks out of the wall next door on **Palazzo Mastelli** is one of four spread out along here and around the corner on Corte dei Mori. The street names here (dei Mori) mean 'of the Moors' and refer to these strange statues, traditionally said to represent members of the Mastelli family, 12th-century merchants from the Morea (one of La Serenissima's most important Greek possessions). The building on which they appear is also known as the Palazzo del Cammello, because of the distinctive bas-relief depicting this animal on the facade overlooking Rio della Madonna dell'Orto.

To the Gesuiti (Map 4) Backtrack to the Chiesa della Madonna dell'Orto and continue south-east along Fondamenta Gasparo Contarini, named after the **Palazzo Contarini del Zaffo**, which extends to the end of the street. A narrow wooden quay protrudes out into the little protected bay off the lagoon. Locals use it for sunbathing and from here you enjoy good views across to the islands of San Michele and Murano. Behind the palazzo spread luxuriant private gardens leading to an isolated little building on the lagoon, the so-called **Casino degli Spiriti**, where in the 16th century students, literati and glitterati with the right contacts would gather for learned chit-chat and a few drinks.

There is little choice here but to cross Rio della Madonna dell'Orto and follow Corte

Vecchia south-west to Rio della Sensa. Before turning left to continue south-east, turn around to the right and you'll see a rare (and run-down) example of a **squero**, or gondola-building yard, complete with slipways into Rio dei Muti.

The next stop of importance is the Gesuiti, the massive hulk erected by the Jesuits. To get there, we pass down Fondamenta dell'Abbazia under the portico of the **Scuola Vecchia della Misericordia**, once the seat of one of the city's grand religious confraternities. It later moved into the immense **Scuola Nuova della Misericordia**, designed by Sansovino in the 1530s, on the southern side of Rio della Sensa. Next to the Scuola Vecchia, on the pretty little campo that overlooks the busy Canale della Misericordia, is the **Chiesa di Santa Maria della Misericordia**, established in the 10th century and altered in the 13th.

A series of bridges takes you into Calle della Racchetta. To get to the Gesuiti, follow this street north-east to Fondamenta Santa Caterina and head east until you reach Campo dei Gesuiti.

The Gesuiti & Around (Map 4) The Jesuits took over this church *(open 10am-noon & 4pm-6pm)*, more properly known as the Chiesa di Santa Maria Assunta, in 1657 and ordered its reconstruction in the Roman Baroque style. The conversion was completed by 1730. The facade is impressive enough – in fact, as is often the case with such sights in Venice (see also the Scuola di San Rocco in San Polo), it seems out of place, as though it were bursting for more space to allow a greater appreciation of its splendour.

No-one could accuse the Jesuits of sober tastes. Inside, the church is lavishly decorated with white and gold stucco, white and green marble floors, and marble flourishes filling in any empty slots.

Tintoretto's *Assunzione della Vergine* (Assumption of the Virgin), in the north transept, is a remarkable exception to the rule – think of the darkness of his images in the Scuola di San Rocco and you wonder where all the lightness and joy came from in this representation of the Assumption.

Maybe there was some role-swapping going on, as Titian's *Martirio di San Lorenzo* (Martyrdom of St Lawrence) is an uncharacteristically stormy and gloomy piece (it's the first painting on the left as you enter the church). Of course the subjects of each painting make the respective results quite logical.

On the subject of Titian, fans can find his **house** by walking up to the Fondamente Nuove, heading south-east as far as Calle delle Croci and penetrating the web of lanes in search of Corte della Carità. North of this square, a narrow dead-end lane is your objective – at the end of it on the right is Titian's place.

Chiesa di Santa Maria dei Miracoli (Map 4) From Corte della Carità, you can trace a path down along Calle del Fumo, past the 17th-century **Palazzo Widman** and down the narrow calle of the same name. You will emerge on Campo Santa Maria Nova. Off to the right (north-west) is the **Chiesa di San Canciano**. Although here since the 9th century, what you see is the result of intervention by Massari and Gaspari.

The real stunner around here is off to the left (south-east). The Chiesa di Santa Maria dei Miracoli *(admission €1.55; open 10am-5pm Mon-Sat, 1pm-5pm Sun)* looks like an elaborate box containing the most refined of all imaginable chocolates. Pietro Lombardo was responsible for this Renaissance jewel, which is fully carapaced inside and out in marble, bas-reliefs and statues. The result is intense, but lacks the flowery motifs that would come later with Baroque. The timber ceiling is also eye-catching. Pietro and Tullio Lombardo executed the carvings on the choir.

The church is part of the Chorus scheme (see the boxed text 'A Chorus Line' earlier in this chapter).

From the church, you can turn left (east) along Calle Castelli (which continues over the canal as Calle delle Erbe). Once over the next bridge, you are obliged to swing left and arrive in Campo SS Giovanni e Paolo. You are now in the city's easternmost sestiere: Castello.

SESTIERE DI CASTELLO
Chiesa dei SS Giovanni e Paolo
& Around (Map 4)

This huge Gothic church *(open 7.30am-12.30pm & 3.30pm-7pm Mon-Sat, 3pm-6pm Sun)*, founded by the Dominicans, rivals the Franciscans' Frari in size and grandeur. Work started on it in 1333, but it was not consecrated until 1430. The similarities between the two are all too evident. The use of brick and modest white stone refinements around

The Infamy of Famagusta

Keep an eye out for the monument to Marcantonio Bragadin in the Chiesa dei SS Giovanni e Paolo (Map 4). It is on the wall of the south aisle, virtually opposite the westernmost pillar. The monument is singular for its content, rather than for any artistic merit.

Bragadin was the commander of the Famagusta garrison in Cyprus, the last to fall to the Turks in 1570. Promised honourable terms of surrender after having endured a long siege, Bragadin decided to call on the Turkish commander Mustafa and present him the keys of the city. Mustafa lost, as it were, his head, and lopped off Bragadin's ears and nose. Several hundred Christians in the vicinity also lost their heads, rather more literally. The post-battle massacre that until now had been avoided suddenly swept like a storm across the city.

While the population of Famagusta was decimated, Bragadin rotted for a couple of weeks in prison. He was then hauled about the town under the crushing weight of sacks of stone and earth. After various other humiliations, he was tied to a stake in the execution square and skinned alive. According to one account, he only passed out when they reached his waist. The corpse was then beheaded and quartered, and the skin stuffed with straw and paraded about town. Mustafa then took it home as a trophy to present to the sultan. Some years later, a Venetian trader with considerable courage managed to steal it from the arsenal of Constantinople and return it to the Bragadin family in Venice. The remains have been in the Chiesa dei SS Giovanni e Paolo since 1596.

windows and doorways is a clear point they have in common. A particular departure here, however, is the way in which three chapels, each of different dimensions, have been tacked – it seems almost willy-nilly – onto the church's southern flank.

The vast interior, like that of the Frari, is divided simply into an enormous central nave and two aisles, separated by graceful, soaring arches. The red and white chessboard floor is a further demonstration of the contemporaneity of the two buildings.

A beautiful stained-glass window made in Murano in the 15th century fills the southern arm of the transept with light. A host of artists contributed to its design, including Bartolomeo Vivarini, Cima da Conegliano and Girolamo Mocetto. It owes some of its brilliance to restoration carried out in the 1980s. Below the window and just to the right is a fine *pala* (altarpiece) by Lorenzo Lotto. On the opposite aisle wall, below the organ, is a triptych by Bartolomeo Vivarini. Noteworthy, too, are the five late-Gothic apses, graced by long and slender windows. Look out for Giovanni Bellini's polyptych of St Vincent Ferrer (San Vincenzo Ferreri) over the second altar of the right aisle.

In the Cappella del Rosario, off the northern arm of the transept, is a series of paintings by Paolo Veronese, including ceiling panels and an *Adorazione dei Pastori* (Adoration of the Shepherds) on the west wall.

The church is a veritable ducal pantheon. Around the walls, many of the 25 tombs of doges were sculpted by prominent Gothic and Renaissance artists, in particular Pietro and Tullio Lombardo.

At right angles to the main facade of the church is the rather more eye-catching (well, not while the scaffolding stays up!) marble frontage of the former **Scuola Grande di San Marco**. Pietro Lombardo and his sons all worked on what was once one of the most important of Venice's religious confraternities. Codussi put the finishing touches on this Renaissance gem. Have a closer look and, apart from the predictably magnificent lions, you will notice the sculpted trompe l'oeil perspectives covering much of the lower half of the facade. Nowadays the scuola is the entrance to the Ospedale Civile. You are free to enter the scuola itself – the timber beams of the ceiling are held up by two ranks of five columns. The staircase to the upper storey is closed. Beyond, in what were the Convento dei Domenicani and the Chiesa di San Lazzaro dei Mendicanti, is the hospital proper.

Presiding over the Campo di SS Giovanni e Paolo is the most impressive of the city's few **equestrian statues**, by the Florentine Verrocchio (1435–88). It is dedicated to the *condottiero* (professional mercenary commander) Bartolomeo Colleoni, who from 1448 commanded mercenary armies in the name of the Republic. Although he was of the school of mercenaries that tended to organise things so that they lived to fight another day, he remained faithful to La Serenissima. On his death in 1474, Colleoni bequeathed 216,000 gold and silver ducats and considerably more in property to Venice, on one condition – that the city erect a commemorative statue to him in St Mark's Square. The Senato took the money but cheated, placing the grand statue here instead. Still, Colleoni can rest easy that the Republic didn't scrimp on the statue itself.

Ospedaletto (Map 8)

Just east of the campo, Longhena's Baroque Chiesa di Santa Maria dei Derelitti *(also known as the Ospedaletto, or Little Hospital; ☎ 041 270 24 64, Castello 6691; open 3.30pm-6.30pm Thur-Sat)* is the focal point of a hospital for elderly and poor patients that was built in the 17th century. In an annexe is the elegantly frescoed **Sala da Musica** *(admission €1.55; open same hours)*, where patients performed concerts.

Chiesa di San Francesco della Vigna (Map 8)

After a quiet stroll east along residential streets, you emerge in Campo San Francesco della Vigna, where the sudden appearance of the massive Palladian facade of this church *(open 8am-12.30pm & 3pm-7pm)* comes as a bit of a shock.

The remainder of the church, which takes its name from the vineyard that once thrived on the site, was designed by Sansovino for the Franciscans. At the back is the bell tower – to all intents and purposes the twin of the Campanile in St Mark's Square.

Inside, just to the left of the main door, is a triptych of saints by Antonio Vivarini. The Cappella dei Giustiniani, to the left of the main altar, is decorated with splendid reliefs by Pietro Lombardo and his school. Off the left (northern) arm of the transept, you can enter the Cappella Santa, which houses a *Madonna col Bambino e Santi* (Madonna and Child with Saints) by Giovanni Bellini. From here you can admire the leafy cloisters too.

Scuola di San Giorgio degli Schiavoni (Map 8)

Proceeding east around the south flank of San Francesco della Vigna, you'll end up in Campo della Celestia. Follow the only lane exiting off it across the canal and into Campo San Ternità. Calle Dona veers to the left (east) off this square. After the canal, turn right (south-west) and almost immediately on your left is **Casa Magno**, a unique example of Gothic housing. Now head straight down to and across Campo Do Pozzi. You'll end up on Calle degli Scudi, at which point you turn right (north-west) and cross the canal into Campo delle Gatte. A quick dogleg and you will run into Rio di San Lorenzo. Just before the bridge, on the right, is the Scuola di San Giorgio degli Schiavoni *(☎ 041 522 88 28, Castello 3259/a; admission €2.60; open 9.30am-12.30pm & 3.30pm-6.30pm Tues-Sat, 9.30am-12.30pm Sun)*.

Venice's Dalmatian community established this religious school in the 15th century and the building was erected in the 16th century. The main attraction is on the ground floor, where the walls are graced by a series of superb paintings by Vittore Carpaccio depicting events in the lives of the three patron saints of Dalmatia: George, Tryphone and Jerome. The image of St George dispatching the dragon to the next life is a particularly graphic scene. Scattered about before the dragon are remnants of its victims – various limbs, the half-eaten corpse of a young woman and an assortment of bones.

Members of the scuola gathered upstairs for meetings and religious services. Delicate timber decor and the heavy exposed beams of the ceilings complete the scene.

From here, proceed south along the canal and at the Chiesa Sant'Antonin follow the main street south into Campo Bandiera e Moro.

Campo Bandiera e Moro (Map 8)

This quiet square is named after the brothers Bandiera and the Venetian Domenico Moro, who were executed by troops of the Bourbon Kingdom of the Two Sicilies after a hopelessly failed pro-unity insurrection in Cosenza (Calabria) in 1844. It is fronted in the south-eastern corner by the **Chiesa di San Giovanni in Bragora**, where Antonio Vivaldi was baptised.

Among the works of art inside is a restored triptych by Bartolomeo Vivarini, the *Madonna in Trono tra I Santi Andrea e Giovanni Battista* (Enthroned Madonna with St Andrew and John the Baptist). In the peaceful square just south of the church, **Campiello del Piovan**, the architect Giorgio Massari was born at No 3752.

Arsenale (Maps 8 & 9)

From the Chiesa di San Giovanni in Bragora, follow Calle Crosera to the east. About the shortest route to what was once the military powerhouse of the Republic takes us up Calle Erizzo past the Renaissance **palazzo** of the same name and across the bridge to the **Chiesa di San Martino (Map 8)**. The church is a 16th-century Sansovino design on the site of a 7th-century predecessor that was built by mainland refugees fleeing Lombard invaders. Across the canal are the walls of the Arsenale. To reach its entrance, walk along Fondamenta di Fronte until you reach the Rio dell' Arsenale.

The city's huge dockyards are said to have been founded in 1104, although some historians think it may have happened a century later. What became known as the Arsenale Vecchio (Old Arsenal) is the core of the complex. Within it was a special storage area for the *bucintoro*, the great ceremonial galley used by the doge on important occasions, such as the Sposalizio del Mar (see the boxed text 'With This Ring I Thee Wet'

in the History section of the Facts about Venice chapter).

As the Republic's maritime needs grew and shipbuilding requirements changed, so the Arsenale was enlarged. In 1303–04 came the first expansion, known as La Tana. It occupies almost the whole length of the southern side of the Arsenale (it was refashioned in 1579 by Antonio da Ponte). The **Arsenale Nuovo (Map 9)** (New Arsenal) was added in 1325, followed in 1473 by the **Arsenale Nuovissimo (Map 2)** (Very New Arsenal). When, in the 16th century, production of much larger war vessels with a deeper draught *(galeazze)* got under way, further workshops and **construction sheds (Map 2)** were added, along with the Canale delle Galeazze (Map 8). The whole was unsurprisingly walled in and top secret. The *arsenaloti*, or shipyard workers, were relatively well paid and tended throughout the history of the Republic to be faithful to the doge and the State. This was proven on several occasions when they were called to arms in times of unrest or rebellion.

The Arsenale was as close as Venice (or anyone for that matter, until the 18th century) came to industrial production. And to late-medieval eyes, it must have made an enormous impression, with all its boiling black pitch, metalworking and timber cutting. Dante was so awestruck he used it as a model scene for Hell in his *Divina Commedia* (Canto XXI, lines 7–21).

The Arsenale had another function. An emergency reserve fleet of at least 25 vessels was always to be kept ready to sail from inside it, either as a war fleet or as merchant ships. As the centuries progressed, although the shortage of raw materials (especially timber) became a problem, more often than not the Republic's difficulty was finding crews. Eventually, it was obliged to employ slaves, prisoners and press gangs to fill the personnel gaps.

The Arsenale at its peak covered 46 hectares, was home to 300 shipping companies and employed up to 16,000 people. In 1570, when requested to produce as many ships as possible for an emergency fleet, the Arsenale put out an astounding 100 galleys in just two months. The following year at the

Battle of Lepanto, the last great sea struggle fought mainly with oar power and a stunning defeat of the Turks, more than half the allied Christian fleet (which included Imperial Spain) was provided by Venice.

For most of its history, Venice relied on one form or other of rowing vessel, often combined with sail. In battle, such galleys were often more manoeuvrable. By the 17th century, however, the nimble, all-sail vessels being produced in England and Holland began to show their superiority. The Arsenale never fully made the switch and when it tried its products often proved inferior. By this time, Venetians were increasingly turning away from the sea anyway, and the practice of buying or renting foreign vessels (and sometimes their crews) grew more common. Venice was growing soft and its people becoming landlubbers. By the time La Serenissima fell in 1797, naval production had all but ceased. Various minor modifications were made in the course of the 19th century and the whole area is now naval property, although they do little with it.

The land gateway, surmounted by the lion of St Mark, is considered by many to be the earliest example of Renaissance architecture in Venice; it was probably executed in 1460. Later, a plaque was installed commemorating the victory at Lepanto in 1571. The fenced-in terrace was added in 1692. At the foot of the statues (each with allegorical meaning) is a row of carved lions of varying size and type. The biggest of them, in regally seated pose, was taken as booty by Francesco Morosini from the Greek port of Piraeus. This must have required quite an effort. On its right flank is a series of Viking runes. Attempts to decipher them have brought mixed results, although by one account they are an 11th-century 'Harold was here'-style piece of graffiti left behind by Norwegian mercenaries who apparently took control of Piraeus at the time.

The No 52 vaporetto used to ply the Rio dell'Arsenale, Darsena Arsenale Vecchio and Canale delle Galeazze, but alas no more. On the way through you could see 15th- and 16th-century workshops and the storage area for the bucintoro. The best you can do today is enter the vestibule at the pedestrian entrance and peer through. It can be open as early as 7am and is generally shut by 5pm. It is only open at all to let navy personnel in and out.

Museo Storico Navale & Beyond

A short walk down Fondamenta dell'Arsenale, towards the Canale di San Marco, brings us to this former grain silo turned museum **(Map 8)** (☎ *041 520 02 76, Castello 2148; admission €1.55; open 8.45am-1pm Mon-Fri, 8.45am-1.30pm Sat)*.

Spread over four floors, this museum traces the maritime history of the city and of Italy. There are some wonderfully complex models of all sorts of Venetian vessels, but also ancient triremes, Asian warships, WWII battleships and ocean liners. The ground floor is devoted mainly to weaponry (the usual stuff – cannons, blunderbusses, swords and sabres). Most curious are the 17th-century diorama maps of Venetian ports and forts across the city's one-time Adriatic and Mediterranean possessions.

On the 1st floor is a model of the sumptuous bucintoro, the doge's ceremonial barge, in among the many large-scale model sailing vessels. Napoleon's French troops destroyed the real thing in 1798. The 2nd floor is mostly given over to Italian naval history and memorabilia, from unification to the present day, and includes many models of modern warships. Up on the 3rd floor is a room containing a few gondolas, including Peggy Guggenheim's. A small room set above the 3rd floor is given over to – wait for it – Swedish naval history. Curious.

The ticket also gets you entrance to the **Padiglione delle Navi (Map 8)** (Ships Pavilion), on Fondamenta della Madonna near the entrance to the Arsenale. Of the various boats on display, the most outstanding is the *Scalé Reale*, an early-19th-century ceremonial vessel last used in 1959 to bring the body of the Venetian Pope Pius X to rest at St Mark's Basilica. It had been used to bring King Vittorio Emanuele to St Mark's Square in 1866 when Venice joined the nascent Italian kingdom.

If you proceed east, you are entering Very-Few-Tourists Territory. Follow the street round behind the museum and past the ugly Palazzetto dello Sport to Campo della Tana. Here you are again faced by the walls of the Arsenale. Follow them, cross the bridge and take Fondamenta della Tana, turning right down Calle di San Francesco di Paola – you'll hit the broad Via Giuseppe Garibaldi. The **Chiesa di San Francesco di Paola (Map 9)** is a fairly uninteresting 18th-century remake of the 16th-century original.

Follow the road east and cross the last bridge northwards across the Rio di Sant'Anna (named after the ruined church that looks out over the Canale di San Pietro). Proceed north across Campo di Ruga and take the last lane on the right (east). The bridge at the end of it takes you across to the Isola di San Pietro.

There is no need to rush through. An aimless wander through the simple grid pattern of residential streets allows you to immerse yourself in the simple, gritty, everyday life of ordinary Venetians. No sights, just life.

San Pietro (Map 9)

Although overshadowed by St Mark's Basilica in the heart of town, the **Cattedrale di San Pietro di Castello** *(admission €1.55; open 10am-5pm Mon-Sat, 1pm-5pm Sun)*, on the island of San Pietro, was in fact Venice's cathedral from 1451 to 1807. Indeed, the island was among the first areas to be inhabited.

In 775 the original church here was the seat of a bishopric. Between then and the 16th century, the church underwent several transformations. Its present appearance is basically a post-Palladian job, taking its cue in part from Giudecca's Chiesa del Redentore. Inside, various hands were at work at one point or another, including Longhena, responsible, among other things, for the Baroque main altar.

Although this was officially Venice's cathedral for so long, St Mark's Basilica to all intents and purposes was the senior church. The doges no doubt liked it that way. The splendour of their chapel, as it were, thus outshone even ecclesiastical power. The Church never really did get its own way in the Republic.

Today San Pietro rests in easy retirement on this quiet islet, its blinding white **campanile** (bell tower), made of Istrian stone by Codussi, leaning at an odd angle and the **former patriarchate** dozily crumbling away next door. The latter was for a while used as a barracks.

San Pietro is part of the Chorus scheme (see the boxed text 'A Chorus Line' earlier in this chapter).

Giardini Pubblici & Biennale (Map 9)

The only other way off the Isola di San Pietro is by the more southerly of the two bridges, which brings us back to the ruins of Sant'Anna. Walk past them (heading west) and duck down Calle Correra. Cross the broad Secco Marina, keep on down Corte del Solda and cross the bridge. A stroll past the **Chiesa di San Giuseppe di Castello** will bring us into the somewhat tatty Giardini Pubblici, one of the city's few public parks. You may have noticed during your Venetian strolls that a surprising amount of greenery shoots out at all sorts of angles (except in winter), but it is mostly in the form of private gardens (so much so that someone has even published a coffee-table book entitled *Secret Gardens in Venice*).

There are few opportunities for enjoying parks, and about the best on offer are the Giardini Pubblici and their extension across to Sant'Elena (see the next section). In the gardens you'll find shaded benches, a few *giostre* (swings and other kids' rides) and a snack bar/restaurant.

Also here are the various national pavilions of the **Biennale Internazionale d'Arte**, an arts fest held every two years from June to the end of the year. Together the pavilions form a kind of mini-compendium of 20th-century architectural thinking. Standing well away from the historic centre and thus uninhibited by concerns about clashing with it, the site's pavilions are the work of a veritable legion of architects. Carlo Scarpa contributed in one way or another from 1948 to 1972, continually updating the Italian Pavilion and building the Venezuelan one (1954). He also did the Biglietteria (ticket office) and entrance courtyard. Other interesting contributions are James Stirling's 1991 Padiglione del Libro (Book Pavilion), Gerrit Rietveld's Dutch Pavilion (1954), Josef Hoffman's Austrian Pavilion (1934) and Peter Cox's Australian Pavilion (1988).

Sant'Elena (Maps 2 & 9)

From the Biennale, you can wander over the Rio dei Giardini to what is probably the quietest and leafiest residential corner of Venice. Housing construction began in 1925, before which there was little here but an abandoned pilgrims' hospice and the closed Chiesa di Sant'Elena. The arrival of riot police and armies of football supporters occasionally snap it out of its usual (and not unpleasant) torpor. The crowds make for the **Stadio Penzo (Map 2)** to see the home side struggle to get itself off the bottom of the table.

Just past the stadium is the humble **Chiesa di Sant'Elena (Map 2)**. It's a small Gothic number that was abandoned in 1806 and reopened in 1928 when people started moving into the new residential district nearby.

Towards San Marco (Maps 8 & 9)

At this point the weary could get the No 42 or No 52 circle line vaporetto from the Sant'Elena stop (Map 2) to San Zaccaria (Map 8) to continue this itinerary; or they could hop on the No 1 and potter up the Grand Canal to do something else altogether.

Otherwise, it is a pleasant and leafy walk from the Chiesa di Sant'Elena through the Parco delle Rimembranze and then the Giardini Pubblici along the waterfront. If you do choose to amble, you will approach Venice almost as it should be done – by sea (that is, you are coming from the appropriate direction – it's just that you are on land rather than seaborne). The idea is a borrowed one: cheers Thomas Mann et al!

The waterside walkway west from Rio Ca' di Dio and on to the Palazzo Ducale in San Marco is known as the **Riva degli Schiavoni (Map 8)**, a word for Slavs that referred to Dalmatian fishermen who, from medieval times, used to cast their nets off this waterfront. For centuries, vessels would dock here amid all the chaos you might expect from a busy harbour. Boat crews, waterfront merchants, nobles, gendarmes and crooks, dressed in all manner of garb reflecting the passing parade of Greeks, Turks, Slavs, Arabs, Africans and Europeans, all jostled about these docks. It is perhaps hard to imagine the sight of seemingly chaotic rows of galleys, galleons and, later on, sailing vessels competing for dock space or moored farther out in the Canale di San Marco. Or the confusion of rigging and containers of all sorts, the babble of languages, the clang and clatter of arms and cooking pots as locals or seafarers prepared impromptu meals for those just arrived. The assault on all the senses must have been quite something.

Today it remains busy, but the actors have changed. The galleons of yore have been replaced by ferries, the exotic crews and merchants by gondoliers and not-so-exotic tourists. Instead of impromptu food stalls and the smell of cooking meat, there are ice-cream stands and tourist tat. The linguistic babble remains as confusing as ever. And now some of the grand old mansions function as pricey hotels for the well-heeled out-of-towner.

One of Italy's greatest writers, Francesco Petrarca (Petrarch), for a time found lodgings at No 4175, east of Rio della Pietà.

Just at the point where we will turn inland, away from the lagoon, is the Chiesa di Santa Maria della Pietà, simply known as **La Pietà (Map 8)**, where concerts are held regularly. Vivaldi was concert-master here in the early 18th century. Look for the ceiling fresco by Tiepolo.

San Giorgio dei Greci (Map 8)

A short walk north brings you to the rear side of the Chiesa di San Giorgio dei Greci *(open 9am-1pm & 3pm-4.30pm Wed-Sat & Mon, 9am-1pm Sun)*. Walk around it to reach the main entrance alongside Rio dei Greci. Here, Greek Orthodox refugees were allowed to raise a church in 1526, interesting for the richness of the Byzantine icons, iconostasis and other works inside.

Attached to the church is the **Museo delle Icone** *(aka Museo dei Dipinti Sacri Bizantini; ☎ 041 522 65 81, Castello 3412;*

admission €3.60; open 9am-12.30pm & 2pm-4.30pm Mon-Sat, 10am-5pm Sun) of the Istituto Ellenico, where you can further explore the curiosities of Orthodox religious art. On display are some 80 works of art and a series of other items, including the letter from Doge Leonardo Loredan granting the Greeks permission to build their church. Foremost among the artworks are two 14th-century Byzantine icons, one representing Christ in Glory and the other the Virgin Mary with Child and Apostles. Much of the remaining works were produced by or for the Greeks in Venice and elsewhere in northern Italy.

Campo San Lorenzo (Map 8)

As you leave San Giorgio and cross the bridge to the west, take Fondamenta di San Lorenzo north. At the second bridge across the canal is Campo San Lorenzo, dominated by the rather shaky-looking brick facade of the **church** of the same name. It is an odd structure, divided down the middle to form a section for the general public and another for members of a Benedictine nunnery that has long since ceased to exist. The church is closed for restoration.

Campo Santa Maria Formosa & Around (Map 5)

This square is one of the most appealing in Venice, full of local life, eateries, benches where you can take the weight off your feet and some interesting buildings. There was a time when all sorts of popular festivals were played out here (chasing bulls around the square was one of the less sensible activities). One of Venice's best-remembered courtesans, Veronica Franco, lived in a house on this campo. Poet, friend of Tintoretto and lover, however briefly, of France's King Henry III, Miss Franco was listed in the city's 16th-century guidebook to high-class escorts as: *Vero. Franco a Santa Mar. Formosa. Pieza so mare. Scudi 2.* The last bit is the base price for her services, which ranged from intelligent conversation to horizontal folk-dancing.

Perhaps there was always a little ribaldry in the air around here. The **Chiesa di Santa Maria Formosa** *(admission €1.55; open*

10am-5pm Mon-Sat, 1pm-5pm Sun) was rebuilt in 1492 by Mauro Codussi on the site of a 7th-century church. The name stems from the legend behind its initial foundation. San Magno, bishop of Oderzo, is said to have had a vision of the Virgin Mary on this spot. Not just any old vision, however. In this instance she was *formosa* (beautiful, curvy). The inside was damaged when an Austrian bomb went off in 1916. Among the works of art on display is an altarpiece by Palma il Vecchio depicting St Barbara.

The church is part of the Chorus scheme (see the boxed text 'A Chorus Line' earlier in this chapter).

Among the ageing mansions facing onto the square, **Palazzo Vitturi** is a good example of the Veneto-Byzantine style, while the buildings making up the **Palazzi Donà** are a mix of Gothic and late Gothic. While you're here, a further quick circuit suggests itself. Leave the square and head north-west. Don't cross the canal – veer right instead along Calle del Dose and then left along Calle Pindemonte. You end up in Campo Santa Marina **(Map 4)**, faced by the 13th-century **Palazzo Dolfin Bollani** and the Lombardstyle **Palazzo Loredan**. A side lane off the square leads you to the 15th-century **Palazzo Bragadin-Carabba**, restored by Sanmicheli.

Coming out of the square to the west, head south along Calle Carminati, which brings you into Campo San Lio **(Map 5)**. A brief detour farther south down Calle della Fava brings you to the square of the same name and the **Chiesa di Santa Maria della Fava**. It was begun by Gaspari and finished off in 1753 by Massari. Inside, the first painting on your right after you enter is Tiepolo's *Educazione della Vergine* (The Virgin's Education). Back outside, you can get a good view across Rio della Fava of the late Gothic Palazzo Giustinian-Faccanon, over in the Sestiere di San Marco.

Scurrying back to Campo San Lio, turn right (more or less east) down the busy Salizzada San Lio. The street retains some intriguing examples of Byzantine housing. More interesting still, though, is **Calle del Paradiso**, which branches off it back in the direction of Campo Santa Maria Formosa. It is marked by the Gothic arch beneath which you enter this street, which gives you a pretty good idea of what a typical Gothic-period street in Venice looked like. On the ground floor were shops of various types. Jutting out above them on heavy timber barbicans are the upper storeys, which were offices and living quarters. At the end of the street is another arch, this one more elaborate. Known as the Arco del Paradiso (Heaven's Arch), it depicts the Virgin Mary and bears the standards of the families who financed it.

Palazzo Querini-Stampalia (Map 5)

Once back in Campo Santa Maria Formosa, walk around the church. Behind it, a private bridge leads you to this mansion. The outside shell dates from the first half of the 16th century. The last of this branch of the Querini ordained that the building should be home to a foundation of the same name, and it has been since the 1860s.

The inside of the mansion could not be more surprising. In the 1940s Carlo Scarpa

was commissioned to design the entrance and garden, and again in 1959 to rethink the 1st floor (which houses the foundation's library). Scarpa decided to have some disciplined fun with shape, and, in the garden in particular, took some inspiration from the Arab emphasis on geometrical patterns. It may or may not appeal, but it does make a refreshing change in one sense – there is very little that is 'modern' in Venice.

On the 2nd floor is the **Museo della Fondazione Querini-Stampalia** (☎ *041 271 14 11, Castello 4778; admission €6.20; open 10am-1pm & 3pm-6pm Tues-Sun Oct-Apr, 10am-1pm & 3pm-6pm Tues-Thur & Sun, 10am-1pm & 3pm-10pm Fri & Sat May-Sept).* The core of the collection is made up of period furniture that mostly belonged to the Querinis, portraits of some of the more illustrious family members and various of their papers. The collection of paintings consists mostly of minor works, although there is an interesting *Presentazione di Gesù al Tempio* (Presentation of Jesus at the Temple) by Giovanni Bellini. The poor child

---

Of Floors & Walls

As you wander about the Palazzo Querini-Stampalia, observe the floor. The smooth speckled surface, a classic *terrazzo alla Veneziana*, could almost be a mottled carpet if it weren't a little more solid than pile. In fact it's the result of combining finely fragmented marble chips with plaster and then laying this mixture down.

Why not straight marble floors? Virtually the entire city is built on foundations of timber pylons and has all the resulting problems of subsidence that you would expect. Movement is often greater than in more stable mainland environments. Great slabs of marble have no give – they would just crack open. This mixture, when hardened, has all the feel and solidity of marble, but greater elasticity. And when cracks do appear, all you need to do is mix up a batch of the marble-plaster goo, smooth it over and allow it to dry. You don't want it to dry out, though. At least once-yearly treatment with linseed oil is needed to keep it in good shape and to allow it to be polished up.

You will no doubt have noticed this type of floor in the Palazzo Ducale, Museo Correr and some other sites – you may well have it in your hotel room!

It is not so apparent in this building, but if you get to see inside other houses or manage to stay in a hotel or mansion of sufficient history, you will often see how much these floors undulate with time – a lot better than breaking up altogether.

While on the subject of home-handyman issues, you may also have noticed that the classic Venetian colour is a reddish-burned orange. Innumerable houses are 'painted' this way. Except it isn't really paint. A straight coat of red paint quickly fades and streaks with all the rain and humidity inevitable in the lagoon. Traditionally, the outside walls of houses were coated in a mixture of paint and crushed up red bricks. Once applied and dry, it lasts much longer than standard wall paint.

looks like a long-suffering mummy, standing up improbably in his tightly wrapped swaddling clothes. And what's the guy on the right looking at? Well you, actually.

Just before you get to the Bellini is a small annexe of a large hall. It is given over to a long series of paintings by Gabriele Bella (1730–99) depicting *Scene di Vita Veneziana* (Scenes of Venetian Life). The style of painting is rather naive, if not downright childlike, but the series does provide an intriguing set of snapshots of life under the doges. It is a curious exercise to try to blend these images in your mind's eye with places you have seen in order to capture some idea of what Venice must have been like in the last decadent century of the Republic.

Another room towards the end of the permanent exhibition is devoted to works of Pietro Longhi. It also contains some good examples of traditional Venetian furniture, characteristic for its engraved and lacquered wood with painted floral motifs. Quite a few hotels around town have adopted a watered-down version of the style to furnish their rooms.

Admission to the museum is somewhat steep, but on Friday and Saturday evenings in summer, short concerts are put on at 5pm and 8.30pm that are free to those visiting the museum.

Museo Diocesano d'Arte Sacra (Map 5)

From Palazzo Querini-Stampalia, our route winds south past the former **Chiesa di San Giovanni Novo** (now used occasionally as exhibition space) and eventually across the Rio del Vin to the Chiesa di San Zaccaria. A quick detour to the Museo Diocesano d'Arte Sacra (☎ 041 522 91 66, Fondamenta di Sant'Apollonia 4312, Castello; admission free, but voluntary contributions welcome; open 10.30am-12.30pm Mon-Sat), south-west of Campo SS Filippo e Giacomo, is worthwhile, especially for fans of Romanesque architecture.

Housed in a former Benedictine monastery dedicated to Sant'Apollonia, the museum has a fairly predictable collection of religious art. More interesting is the little Romanesque cloister you cross in order to get to the museum. It is a rare example of the genre in Venice. The cloister is often open much longer hours.

The building next door was a church until 1906. It now houses exhibition spaces.

Back on the main street, instead of turning left (west) for St Mark's Square, head in the opposite direction down Salizzada San Provolo.

Chiesa di San Zaccaria (Map 8)

You'll know you've struck pay dirt when you pass under a Gothic arch depicting the Virgin Mary and Jesus, thought to have been crafted by a sculptor from Tuscany in around 1430.

Beyond it, you arrive in the Campo San Zaccaria. The Renaissance facade of the church *(open 10am-noon & 4pm-6pm)* before us is the handiwork of Antonio Gambello and Codussi. Gambello started off in a Gothic vein but was already influenced by Renaissance thinking. The lower part of the facade in marble is his work. When Codussi took over, he favoured white Istrian stone and the clean curves at the top that mark his take on the Renaissance.

Inside, the mix of styles could not be clearer. Against a backdrop of classic Gothic apses, the high cross vaulting of the main body of the church is a clear leap of faith into the Renaissance.

On the second altar to the left after you enter the church is Giovanni Bellini's *La Vergine in Trono col Bambino, un Angelo Suonatore e Santi* (The Virgin Enthroned with Jesus, an Angel Musician & Saints). You cannot miss it. It exudes a light and freshness that the surrounding paintings seem deliberately to lack.

The Cappella di Sant'Atanasio *(admission €1.05)* is off to the right. It holds some works by Tintoretto and Tiepolo, as well as some magnificently crafted choir stalls. You then pass through another chapel to reach the Cappella di San Tarasion (also called Cappella d'Oro) in the apse. Its vaults are covered in frescoes and the walls are decorated with Gothic polyptychs. You can wander downstairs to the Romanesque crypt, left over from an earlier church on the site.

To Piazzetta San Marco (Map 5)

When you exit the church, head south off the square and you emerge through a sotoportego onto Riva degli Schiavoni again, not far from where we left it earlier.

Turn right (west) to cross the Ponte del Vin; the building immediately on the right is the Palazzo Dandolo, better known to most as the Danieli, one Venice's most prestigious hotels. For a curious tale about the origins of the hideous Danieli extension on the other side of Calle delle Rasse, see the boxed text 'A Dogey Death' in the Places to Stay chapter.

Calle delle Rasse takes its name from the word *rascia* or *rassa*, a rough woollen material sold along this street for use as protective covers for gondolas. The material came from what is now Serbia, known to the Venetians centuries ago as Rascia. The next street, Calle degli Albanesi, was so named because an Albanian community lived on and around it. Interesting choice of address when you consider that the prisons line its western side.

Walking past the **prisons**, which you may have visited while touring the Palazzo Ducale (see the earlier Sestiere di San Marco section), we arrive at the bridge that marks the boundary between the sestieri of San Marco and Castello. Look north at the unassuming closed passage linking the Palazzo Ducale with the prisons. Yes folks, this is it, the bridge you've all been waiting for: the **Bridge of Sighs** (Ponte dei Sospiri). Now you can breathe a sigh of relief that you've seen it. Some people walk away inconsolably despondent that the bridge in no way corresponds to all their romantic imaginings.

The pink and white walls of the Palazzo Ducale lead us back to the Piazzetta San Marco, the gateway to Venice, where we finally complete our long and tortuous circuit of the lagoon city that for more than 1000 years was the Most Serene Republic. Perhaps now is an opportune moment to again gaze out over the Bacino di San Marco and let your by now well-primed imagination do a little wandering.

On the other hand, maybe it's time for a drink. Why not loosen the old purse strings and pop across to Harry's Bar for a soothing cocktail?

AROUND THE LAGOON

Venice goes beyond the six sestieri. Indeed, it did not even begin on the islands that constitute them. Although the bulk of the city's visitors don't bother, it is a more than worthwhile exercise to get out to at least some of the islands and even onto the mainland. The remainder of this chapter and the Excursions chapter towards the end of the book should set you on your way.

Isola della Giudecca (Map 7)

Originally known as *spina longa* (long fishbone) because of its shape, Giudecca's present name probably derives from the word Zudega (from *giudicato* – the judged), applied to rebellious nobles banished from Venice proper. There are variations on this story – the most likely seems to be that as early as the 9th century, families that had been exiled earlier (and one assumes unjustly) were given land on Giudecca by way of compensation. Until that time, the only inhabitants had been a handful of fishermen and their families.

By the 16th century, the island had been extended through land reclamation to reach something approaching its present form. Merchants set up warehouses and a flourishing local commercial life made Giudecca a prime piece of real estate. Elite families (such as the Dandolos, Mocenigos and Vendramins) bought up land to build their homes-away-from-home facing Venice to the north and ending in luxuriant gardens looking south to the open lagoon. Several religious orders also established convents and monasteries here.

With the fall of the Republic in 1797, everything changed. The noble families slipped away as their fortunes declined. The religious orders were suppressed and the convents closed. The face of the island gradually changed through the 19th century. Replacing the pleasure domes and religious retreats came prisons, barracks and factories, and, with the latter, working-class housing grids. Descendants of the workers who powered the factories remain in the modest low-level housing, but most of the factories have long since been closed down.

Giudecca is a strangely melancholy place. A few boatyards keep busy with repair work, while a handful of shops and eateries survive on a modest local trade and the few tourists who stop long enough to want to eat here. The women's prison (until 1857 it had been a convent for reformed prostitutes) is still in operation. Mild building activity suggests that perhaps more life will some day come to Giudecca.

Molino Stucky The striking hulk of the best-known factory complex on the island, the Molino Stucky, was built in the late 19th century. The windowless brick structure looks for all the world like a cathedral to industry and is hard to miss when looking across to Giudecca from the western end of the Zattere. It was shut in 1954 and has long sat in dignified silence. The buildings have been saved from the wrecking ball and are being restored in a project destined to convert them into a complex of 120 apartments with a hotel and a congress centre.

Chiesa di Sant'Eufemia A simple Veneto-Byzantine structure of the 11th century, the church's main portico was actually added in the 18th and 19th centuries. Down Fondamenta Rio Sant'Eufemia are the one-time church and convent of **SS Cosma e Damiano**. They were turned into a factory and the bell tower into a smokestack!

Chiesa del Redentore With the passing of a bout of plague in 1577, the Senato commissioned Palladio to design a church of thanksgiving. The following year, the doge, members of the Senato and a host of citizens made the first pilgrimage of thanksgiving, crossing from Zattere on a pontoon bridge of boats and rafts.

Work on this magnificent edifice *(admission €1.55; open 10am-5pm Mon-Sat, 1pm-5pm Sun)* was completed under Antonio da Ponte (better known for his Ponte di Rialto) in 1592. The long church was designed to accommodate the large numbers of pilgrims who, from 1578 onwards, made the annual excursion. Even now, on the third Saturday in July, the pilgrimage takes place and it remains one of the most important events on Venice's calendar.

Inside are a few works by Tintoretto, Veronese and Vivarini, but it is the powerful facade that most inspires observers. Indeed, although it is uncertain why the site was chosen, there is no doubt that its open position makes the church easy to observe and admire from just about anywhere on the Fondamenta Zattere across the Canale della Giudecca. The simple cleanness of the design reminds one, if on a considerably grander scale, of the Venetian villas on the mainland (see the Excursions chapter).

Chiesa delle Zitelle Also designed by Palladio in the late 16th century, the Chiesa di Santa Maria della Presentazione *(open 10am-noon Fri-Sat)*, known as the Zitelle, was conceived as a church and hospice for poor young women *(zitelle* means 'old maids', which is presumably what many of these unfortunates remained). It is now used as a conference centre.

Isola di San Giorgio Maggiore (Map 7)

On the island of the same name, Palladio's **Chiesa di San Giorgio Maggiore** *(bell-tower lift €2.60; church admission free; open 9.30am-12.30pm & 2.30pm-6.30pm)* has one of the most prominent positions in Venice and, although it inspired mixed reactions among the architect's contemporaries, it had a significant influence on Renaissance architecture. Built between 1565 and 1580, it is possibly Palladio's most imposing structure in Venice. The facade, although not erected until the following century, is believed to conform with Palladio's wishes. The massive columns on high plinths, the crowning tympanum and the statues all contain an element of sculptural chiaroscuro, if such a term is permissible, casting strong shadows and reinforcing the impression of strength. Indeed facing the Bacino di San Marco and the heart of Venice, its effect is deliberately theatrical.

Inside, the sculptural decoration is sparse, the open space regimented by powerful clusters of columns and covered by luminous vaults.

San Giorgio Maggiore's art treasures include works by Tintoretto: an *Ultima Cena* (Last Supper) and the *Raccolta della Manna* (Shower of Manna) on the walls of the high altar, and a *Deposizione* (Deposition) in the Cappella dei Morti. Take the lift to the top of the 60m-high bell tower for an extraordinary view.

Behind the church extend the grounds of the former monastery. Established as long ago as the 10th century by the Benedictines, it was rebuilt in the 13th century and then restructured and expanded in a series of projects that spanned the 16th century, finishing with the library built by Longhena in the 1640s. Unfortunately, little or none of this can be seen, as the Fondazione Cini bought it in 1951 (saving it from a slow death by neglect, it should be added). The foundation operates various scholarly centres here. The open-air Teatro Verdi, at the bottom end of the islet, has been off limits for many years.

Isola di San Michele (Map 2)

The city's **cemetery** *(open 7.30am-4pm Oct-Mar, 7.30am-6pm Apr-Sept)* was established on San Michele under Napoleon (even the Venetians can't complain that the diminutive Corsican did nothing for them) and is maintained by the Franciscans. The **Chiesa di San Michele in Isola**, begun by Codussi in 1469, was among the city's first Renaissance buildings. The quiet cloister is attractive and worth a peek. Among those pushing up daisies here are Ezra Pound, Sergei Diaghilev and Igor Stravinsky. Look for the graves in the northeast sector of the island (sign-posted). They are in the 'acatholic' (read Protestant and Orthodox) sections.

Vaporetto lines 12 and 13 from Fondamente Nuove stop here, as do the circle line vaporetto Nos 41 and 42.

Murano

The people of Venice have been making crystal and glass (the difference between the two lies in the amount of lead used) since as early as the 10th century, when the secrets of the art were brought back from the East by merchants. The bulk of the industry was moved to the island of Murano

in 1291 because of the danger of fire posed by the glass-working furnaces.

Venice had a virtual monopoly on the production of what is now known as Murano glass and the methods of the craft were such a well-guarded secret that it was considered treason for a glass-worker to leave the city.

The incredibly elaborate pieces produced by the artisans can range from the beautiful to the grotesque – but, as the Italians would say, *i gusti son gusti* (each to his own). Watching the glass-workers in action in shops and factories around the island is certainly interesting. You can see them in several outlets along Fondamenta dei Vetrai and a couple on Viale Garibaldi. Look for the sign 'Fornace' (furnace).

The **Museo Vetrario** *(☎ 041 73 95 86, Fondamenta Giustinian 8; admission €5.15 or included in combined ticket – see Special Tickets at start of chapter; open 10am-5pm Thur-Tues)* has some exquisite pieces. Across Canale di San Donato is one of the few private mansions of any note on the island, the 16th-century **Palazzo Trevisan**.

The nearby **Chiesa dei SS Maria e Donato** is a fascinating example of Veneto-Byzantine architecture. Looking at the apse, however, it is impossible not to see Romanesque influences too. Founded in the 7th century and rebuilt 500 years later, the church was originally dedicated to the Virgin Mary. It was rededicated to St Donato after his bones were brought here from Cephalonia, along with those of a dragon he had supposedly killed (four of the 'dragon' bones are hanging behind the altar). The church's magnificent mosaic pavement (a very Byzantine touch) was laid in the 12th century, and the impressive mosaic of the Virgin Mary in the apse dates from the same period. **Palazzo da Mula**, just over the Ponte Vivarini, the only bridge to span the Canal Grande di Murano, is sometimes host to exhibitions. More often than not the subject is... glass.

The island can be reached on vaporetto No 12, 13 or 42 (41 the other way) from Fondamente Nuove in Cannaregio (No 42 also leaves from San Zaccaria in Castello

MURANO

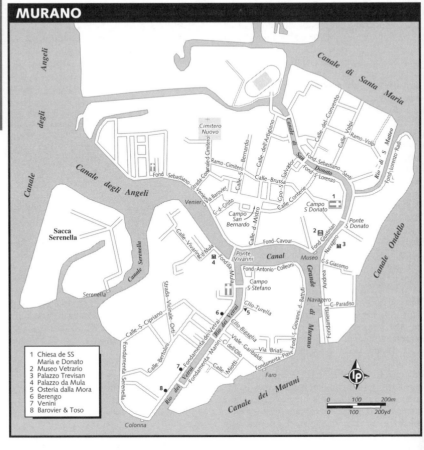

1 Chiesa de SS
  Maria e Donato
2 Museo Vetrario
3 Palazzo Trevisan
4 Palazzo da Mula
5 Osteria dalla Mora
6 Berengo
7 Venini
8 Barovier & Toso

and Piazzale Roma in Santa Croce). No 72 (71 the other way) also chugs there between Piazzale Roma and San Zaccaria.

Burano

Famous for its lace industry, Burano is a pretty fishing village, its streets and canals lined with bright, pastel-coloured houses. They say the bonbon colours have their origins in the fishermen's desire to be able to see their own houses when heading home from a day at sea. Regardless of the reasons, the bright, gay colours are engaging. Given the island's distance from Venice (around 40

minutes by ferry), you really do get the feeling of having arrived somewhere only fleetingly touched by La Serenissima.

If you go to the effort of coming (most people couple the excursion with stops in Murano and Torcello), try to give yourself time to wander into the quietest corners and shady parks. Walk over the wooden bridge to neighbouring **Mazzorbo**, a larger island with little more than a few houses, a couple of trattorias and open green space. A snooze in the grass takes you light years away from the marvels of Venice and somehow puts them into a harmonious perspective.

The **Museo del Merletto** (☎ 041 73 00 34, Piazza Galuppi 187; admission €4.15 or included in combined ticket – see Special Tickets at start of chapter; open 10am-5pm Wed-Mon, ticket window shut from 3.30pm) is a lace-making museum. If you plan to buy lace on the island, choose with care and discretion, as these days much of the cheaper stuff is imported from Asia (see also the Shopping chapter). That said, you can still occasionally see women working away at lace-making in the shade of their homes and in the parks.

Take vaporetto No 12 from Fondamente Nuove (Cannaregio). Note that this ferry stops at San Michele, Murano, Mazzorbo, Burano and Torcello (some don't go on to Torcello – ask). That same ferry on the way back from Torcello doesn't generally stop at Burano, but it does call in at Mazzorbo (from where you can walk to Burano). This priceless piece of information is for those who want to go to Torcello first and then Burano.

Torcello

This delightful little island, with its overgrown main square and sparse, scruffy-looking buildings and monuments, was at its peak from the mid-7th century to the 13th century, when it was the seat of the bishop of mainland Altinum (modern Altino) and home to some 20,000 people. Rivalry with Venice and a succession of malaria epidemics systematically reduced the island's splendour and population. Today, fewer than 80 people call Torcello home.

When you get off the vaporetto, you have little choice but to follow the path along the canal that leads to the heart of the island in a leisurely 10 minutes. Around the central square is huddled all that remains of old Torcello – the lasting homes of the clergy and the island's secular rulers.

To get here, take the No 12 boat from Fondamente Nuove in Cannaregio (via Murano and Burano; see the previous Burano section for details).

Cattedrale di Santa Maria Assunta The island's Veneto-Byzantine cathedral (admission €2.60, plus €2.05 to climb bell tower, or €5.15 for ticket that also includes Museo di Torcello – see later; cathedral open 10am-5.30pm) was founded in the 7th century and was Venice's first. Visitors to Venice tend to forget that the first important settlement in the lagoon was right here in Torcello. In its now abandoned state, the island gives us some idea of how things must have looked at the outset of settlement on the other islands too.

What you see of Santa Maria Assunta today dates from the first expansion of the church in 824 and rebuilding in 1008. It is therefore about the oldest Venetian monument to have remained relatively untampered with. This we probably owe to the fact that by 1008 the settlement was already well on the road to decline.

The three apses (the central one dates back to the original 7th-century structure) could be Romanesque and a certain intermarriage of building styles seems likely. A jewel of simple, early-medieval architecture, the interior is still more fascinating for its magnificent Byzantine mosaics.

On the western wall of the cathedral is a vast mosaic depicting the Last Judgment. Hell (lower right side) doesn't look any fun at all. Late-20th-century sceptics may grin, but such images probably inspired sheer terror in the average resident of Torcello back in the 12th and 13th centuries when the mosaics were put together.

The greatest treasure is the mosaic of the Madonna in the half-dome of the central apse. Starkly set on a pure gold background, the figure is one of the most stunning works of Byzantine art you will see in Italy. And if you needed more confirmation of the church's Eastern influences, have a look at the iconostasis set well before the altar. The entry fee includes an informative audio tape. You can also climb the bell tower.

Around Santa Maria Assunta The adjacent tiny **Chiesa di Santa Fosca** was founded in the 11th century to house the body of Santa Fosca. In front of the cathedral entrance are the excavated remains of the 7th-century circular baptistry. Steps lead down into what was a kind of pool, a standard early-Christian model for baptistries. It was later demolished

THINGS TO SEE & DO

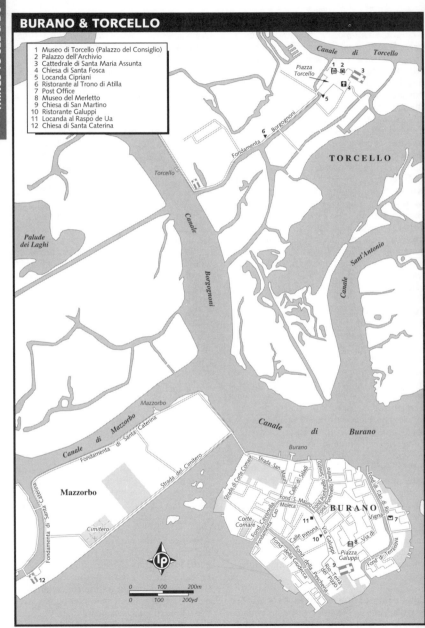

BURANO & TORCELLO

1 Museo di Torcello (Palazzo del Consiglio)
2 Palazzo dell'Archivio
3 Cattedrale di Santa Maria Assunta
4 Chiesa di Santa Fosca
5 Locanda Cipriani
6 Ristorante al Trono di Atilla
7 Post Office
8 Museo del Merletto
9 Chiesa di San Martino
10 Ristorante Galuppi
11 Locanda al Raspo de Ua
12 Chiesa di Santa Caterina

and replaced several times until in the 19th century these remains were uncovered. Fragmentary remains of construction on the site of the baptistry go back to the 4th century, indicating that the island was already inhabited under the Roman Empire.

Across the square, in the Palazzo del Consiglio, is the **Museo di Torcello** (☎ 041 73 07 61; admission €1.55; open 10.30am-5.30pm Tues-Sun), which tells the history of the island. Part of the collection is in the adjacent **Palazzo dell'Archivio**. Both buildings date from the 13th century and together formed the nerve centre of temporal power in Torcello.

The rough-hewn stone chair outside is known as the **Sedia di Attila** (Attila's Seat). Why is anyone's guess, and even the use to which the seat was put is a bit of a mystery. It is surmised that magistrates sat here to pass judgment.

Lido di Venezia (Map 10)

The main draw here is the beach, but the water ain't great and the public areas of the waterfront can be less than attractive. You pay a small fortune (between €10.35 and €41.30) to rent a chair, umbrella and changing cabin in the more easily accessible and cleaner areas of the beach. This said, it is not entirely clear what, if anything, is done if you choose to plonk your towel close to the water's edge (a town ordinance technically forbids obstruction of the open beach area between the rows of cabins and the water).

The Lido forms a land barrier between the lagoon and the Adriatic Sea. For centuries, the doges trekked out here to fulfil Venice's Marriage to the Sea ceremony by dropping a ring into the shallows, celebrating the city's close relationship with the tides. This was done just off the **Chiesa di San Nicolò**, at the northern end of the island. After the ceremony, everyone headed to the church to hear Mass. The church today is a relatively uninteresting 17th-century structure. Nearby was one of the city's defensive forts.

A few hundred metres to the south of the church lies the **Antico Cimitero Israelitico** (former Jewish cemetery; guided visits in Italian & English €6.20; visits 10.30am Fri, 2.30pm Wed & Sun). You can turn up at the gates or buy tickets in advance at the Museo Ebraico in Cannaregio (see earlier in this chapter) to tour the burial ground, said to be the second oldest Jewish cemetery in Europe after that in Worms (Germany).

The Lido became a fashionable seaside resort at the end of the 19th century and its more glorious days are depicted in Thomas Mann's novel *Der Tod in Venedig* (Death in Venice). A wander around the streets between the Adriatic and the vaporetto stop will turn up occasional Art Nouveau (what the Italians refer to as 'Liberty style') and even Art Deco villas. Today the island is fairly laid back for most of the year, although it can get crowded on summer weekends with local and foreign sun-seekers. The beaches are better on the northern coast of the mainland (Cavallino, Jesolo and farther along the coast as far as Bibione), but the Lido is easier to reach. The place fills up for the Mostra del Cinema di Venezia, which takes place every year from late August to September. The cinema-fest is hosted in the snappy **Palazzo della Mostra del Cinema**.

On the lagoon side, you can see the nearby Isola di San Lazzaro degli Armeni (see the following Minor Islands section). Closer to the shore is the former leper colony of **Lazzaretto Vecchio**.

Bus B from Gran Viale Santa Maria Elisabetta or your bicycle will take you to Malamocco, in the south of the island. Arranged across a chain of squares and some canals, the old heart of this town is far more reminiscent of Venice than the late-19th-century seaside conceits at the northern end of the island. The original settlement of Malamocco, besieged by Pepin in the early years of the lagoon republic, is believed to have been an island off the Lido and has long since disappeared.

You can reach the Lido by vaporetto Nos 1, 6, 14, 51, 52, 61, 62 and 82 and the vehicle ferry (No 17) from the Isola del Tronchetto. The first thing you should do is hire a bike at one of a couple of *bicycle hire places* just off Gran Viale Santa Maria Elisabetta, a couple of minutes from the main vaporetto stop. It costs €7.75 per day and will allow you to explore the whole island, as well

THINGS TO SEE & DO

as (for the energetic) Pellestrina and even Chioggia to the south.

Pellestrina (Map 1)

Separated from the southern tip of the Lido by the Porto di Malamocco, one of the three sea gates between the Adriatic and the lagoon, Pellestrina is shaped like an 11km-long razor blade.

Small villages of farmers and fishing families are spread out along the island, protected on the seaward side by the Murazzi, a remarkable feat of 18th-century engineering, although they don't look much to the modern eye. These sea walls, designed to keep the power of the sea over the lagoon in check, once extended without interruption some 20km from the southern tip of Pellestrina to a point well over halfway up the coast of the Lido. The Pellestrina stretch and part of the Lido wall remain. They were heavily damaged during the 1966 floods and partially restored in the 1970s. Long stretches of sparsely populated grey sand beaches separate the Murazzi from the sea on calm days.

You get to Pellestrina using the No 11 Lido-Chioggia bus-and-ferry line. If you've hired a bicycle, you can take it across on the ferry for €1.05 (plus the passenger fare of €3.10 if you haven't got a day ticket).

Minor Islands

San Francesco del Deserto (Map 1) The Franciscans built themselves a **monastery** (☎ *041 528 68 63; admission free, donation appreciated; open 9am-11am & 3pm-5pm Tues-Sun*) on this island about 1km south of Burano to keep away from it all. The island is otherwise deserted and it makes an enchanting detour while exploring the islands of the lagoon. Legend has it that Francis of Assisi himself landed here, seeking shelter after a journey to Palestine in 1220. The Franciscans left in 1420, as conditions were difficult and malaria was rampant. Pope Pius II then granted the island to another order, the Minori Osservanti. Except for an interruption under Napoleon, they have remained ever since.

The only way there is to hire a private boat or taxi from Burano. Ask around at the

ferry stop. You will be looking at about €77.50 for up to four passengers for the return trip and a 40-minute wait time. You could try negotiating the price. If no-one is around, try calling ☎ 041 73 00 01 or 041 73 54 20.

Le Vignole & Sant'Erasmo (Map 1)

Together these islands almost equal Venice in size, but any comparison ends there. Sparsely inhabited, they offer nothing in terms of sights, but for those curious enough to get a glimpse of little-known sides of Venice and its lagoon, they are not without interest. Both are largely rural, and covered in fields and groves.

The south-western part of Le Vignole is owned by the military and contains the best preserved of a scattering of old forts, the **Forte Sant'Andrea**, which can only be seen from the sea. The island long produced the bulk of the doge's wine, and its 50-or-so inhabitants still live mainly from agriculture.

Together with Le Vignole, Sant'Erasmo was long-known as the *orto di Venezia* (Venice's garden) and has never been densely inhabited. About 1000 people are resident on the island, many around the Chiesa ferry stop. Historically, it has always been agricultural, although the Roman chronicler Martial records the presence of holiday villas belonging to the well-to-do of the now-disappeared mainland centre of Altinum. Until the 1800s, the island faced the Adriatic. Construction of dikes at the Bocca del Lido favoured the build-up of sediment that created Punta Sabbioni and this largely closed the island off from the sea.

If you can get your hands on a hire bicycle, a spin among the fields takes you about as far from the atmosphere of Venice as is possible. Otherwise it is about a half-hour walk from the Chiesa stop to the more southern Capannone stop, and another 15 minutes out to what remains of the round **Torre Massimiliana**, a 19th-century Austrian defensive fort.

The No 13 ferry runs to Le Vignole and Sant'Erasmo from Fondamente Nuove (Cannaregio) and Murano (Faro stop).

Isola di San Clemente, Isola di San Servolo and Isola di San Lazzaro degli Armeni

The Isola di San Clemente (Map 1) was once the site of a hospice for pilgrims returning from the Middle East. Later, a convent was built and from 1522 it was a quarantine station. The plague that devastated Venice in 1630 was blamed by some on a carpenter who worked on San Clemente, became infected and brought the disease over to the city. The Austrians turned the building into a mental hospital for women and, until recently, it still operated in part as a psychiatric hospital.

The Isola di San Servolo (Map 1) shared these mental hospital functions from the 18th century until 1978. From the 7th to the 17th centuries Benedictine monks had a monastery here, bits of which still remain in the former hospital. Now the island is home to various cultural institutions.

Of the islets scattered about south of Venice, the most important is the Isola di San Lazzaro degli Armeni (Map 11). In 1717 the Armenian order of the Mechitarist fathers was granted use of the island, which centuries before had been a leper colony. The Mechitarists founded a monastery (☎ 041 526 01 04; adult/child €5.15/2.60; entry by guided tour only 3.25pm-5pm) that became an important centre of learning, which it remains to this day. Visitors can see the 18th-century refectory, church, library, museum and pinacoteca (art gallery). A mix of Venetian and Armenian art is on show, along with a room dedicated to Lord Byron, who often stayed on the island. True to his eccentric nature, he could often be seen swimming from the island to the Grand Canal. Considerable damage was done to the complex by fire in 1975.

You can reach the islands by vaporetto No 20 from San Zaccaria (in Castello). Look for the stop in front of the equestrian statue of Vittorio Emanuele.

Isola di Poveglia

Lying less than 1km off Malamocco, at the southern end of the Lido, this long-abandoned island is one of several up for auction. The CTS travel organisation had expressed an interest in turning it into a youth tourism centre but has pulled out,

leaving the fate of the island as uncertain as before.

Chioggia (Map 1)

The most important town in the Comune di Venezia after Venice itself, Chioggia lies at the southern end of the lagoon.

Invaded and destroyed by the Venetian Republic's maritime rival, Genoa, in the late 14th century, the medieval core of modern Chioggia is a crumbly but not uninteresting counterpoint to its more illustrious patron to the north. In no way cute like Murano or Burano, Chioggia is a firmly practical town, its big sea-fishing fleet everywhere in evidence.

Information The APT office (☎ 041 554 04 66), Lungomare Adriatico 101, is on the waterfront towards the northern end of Sottomarina. In summer it opens 8.30am to 6.30pm daily. Hours are slightly reduced in winter.

Things to See & Do On the assumption you arrive via the Lido and Pellestrina – by far the most enchanting way to get here – you'll find yourself at the northern end of Main St Chioggia (actually Corso del Popolo) as soon as you set foot on dry land. Before you do anything else, head left down Calle della Santa Croce to the **Chiesa di San Domenico**, whose main claim to fame is the painting of San Paolo (St Paul), said to be Vittore Carpaccio's last-known work.

Return to Corso del Popolo. A brisk walk down this cobblestoned and largely pedestrianised thoroughfare and you are in the heart of the old town. Along the way, you reach the **cathedral**. Rebuilt in the 17th century to a design by Longhena, about all that remains of the earlier structure is the campanile (bell tower), raised in 1350.

The historic centre of Chioggia is in fact an island and transferred here from its original position in what is today Sottomarina, on the coast, after the Genoese siege of 1379–80. The reasoning was simple enough. Just as water was Venice's best defence, so it would be for Chioggia. People only began to populate the Sottomarina area again three centuries later.

Through the middle of the island runs the ever-so-Venetian Canale della Vena, complete with little bridges. On either side it is protected by the Canale Lombardo and Canale di San Domenico. Beyond the latter (after crossing another narrow islet), the Ponte Translagunare bridges the lagoon to link Chioggia with Sottomarina and thus the Adriatic beaches.

More interesting than the monuments is simply pottering about, ducking down the alleys that branch off like ribs to the east and west from the spinal cord of Corso del Popolo. The **fish market** *(mercato ittico; closed Sun & Mon mornings)*, alongside Canale di San Domenico where the Ponte Translagunare reaches into Chioggia, is an eye-opener if you can get there at about 6am.

If you want a swim, the **beaches** at Sottomarina are pretty clean, although the water can be murky. It's a typical seaside scene, with cheap hotels, bouncy castles for kids, snack bars, tat and even the odd tacky disco.

Getting There & Away If your time is limited in Venice, you can live without seeing Chioggia – the trip can take about two hours each way.

Bus No 11 leaves from Gran Viale Santa Maria Elisabetta, outside the tourist office on the Lido; it boards the car ferry at Alberoni and then connects with a steamer at Pellestrina that will take you to Chioggia. Or you can catch a bus from Piazzale Roma in Santa Croce.

Once you're in the town, city bus Nos 1, 2, 6 and 7 connect Chioggia with Sottomarina (a 15-minute walk), the town's beach.

ACTIVITIES
Swimming
If you feel the need to do a few laps rather than wallow in the Adriatic, try the **Piscina Comunale A Chimisso (Map 2)** *(☎ 041 528 54 30, Sacca S Biagio; swim €3.85; open Sept-June)*, west of Giudecca on Sacca Fisola. Hours are limited and complicated. Another pool, open less often, is the **Piscina Comunale di Sant'Alvise (Map 2)** *(☎ 041 71 35 67, Campo Sant'Alvise, Cannaregio 3161; swim €4.15; open mid-Sept–mid-July)*.

Jogging
If you can't live without a run, the best places to do it are around the Giardini Pubblici and Isola di Sant'Elena (both in Castello).

COURSES
Language
The *Istituto Italiano di Cultura* (IIC; Italian Cultural Institute), a government-sponsored organisation aimed at promoting Italian culture and language, is a good place to research courses in Italy. It has branches all over the world, including Australia (Sydney), Canada (Montreal), the UK (London) and the USA (Los Angeles, New York and Washington).

Venice has a couple of other institutions which offer Italian lessons.

Società Dante Alighieri *(☎ 041 528 91 27, fax 041 523 08 57,* **e** *venicedantealigheri@libero.it, Istituto Paolo Sarpi, Castello 2821)* **Map 8** The society offers courses in Italian at all levels.

Istituto Venezia *(☎ 041 522 43 31, fax 041 528 56 28,* **w** *www.virtualvenice.net, istitutovenezia, Campo Santa Margherita, Dorsoduro 3116/a)* **Map 6** The Venice Institute offers language and one- and two-week cooking courses. It also does a course in Venetian history and art, involving 12 guided tours of the city. Four weeks (80 hours) of intensive language classes cost €510.

Other
InformaGiovani (see Tourist Offices in the Facts for the Visitor chapter) can provide some ideas on the kinds of course available in Venice.

Fondazione Cini *(☎ 041 528 99 00, fax 041 523 85 40, Isola di San Giorgio Maggiore)* **Map 7** The foundation organises seminars on subjects relating to the city, in particular music and art.

Università Internazionale dell'Arte *(☎ 041 528 70 90, fax 041 528 70 94,* **e** *uave@tim.it, Calle Michelangelo 54/p, Giudecca, 30033 Venice)* **Map 7** This institution runs full courses on art history. For more information, write or email.

ALONG THE GRAND CANAL

Main St, Venice, is a river, or rather the extension of one. Centuries before people realised that the islets of Rivoalto would be a cosy place to found a city, the River Brenta (it is believed) had been carving a path through the mud flats and shallow waters of the Venetian lagoon towards the Adriatic Sea. After ducking and weaving its way past the islets, it widens into what the Venetians subsequently called the Canale di San Marco or Canal Grande (Grand Canal), and then heads on to the sea.

Like any self-respecting central boulevard, the Grand Canal is lined with classy hotels, grand old churches and fine *palazzi* (mansions) dating from the 12th to the 18th centuries. An inverted 'S' 3.5km long, the canal is only 6m deep. Its width ranges from 40m to 100m. In the city's glory days, the warehouses along its banks were constantly busy with the transfer of goods from all over the known world. Back in the 15th century, the French writer Philippe de Commines declared the Grand Canal 'the finest street in the world, with the finest houses'.

Today, the trading may have stopped, but the canal is as busy as ever. Traffic jams are not as much of a problem as in other cities, but the riot of colour and noise as *vaporetti* (ferries), private runabouts, taxis, ambulances, fire department vessels, delivery boats and gondolas churn their way up, down and across it makes the Grand Canal hectic enough.

Prime Venetian real estate has always included canal views. It follows that many of the jewels of centuries of Venetian architecture face the canal. Often, the only way to see them up close is from the water. On the assumption that you don't walk on the stuff and don't wish to shell out a sizeable wad of notes for a gondola, the best way to get a look is on *vaporetto* No 1 – the all-stops Grand Canal 'omnibus'.

The pages that follow briefly detail the notable bridges, churches and palazzi along the way, starting at the uninspiring north-western end, by Stazione di Santa Lucia, and winding down towards St Mark's Square. The number refers to the map location, while an asterisk indicates that there is more detailed information in the Things to See & Do chapter, in which we sidle up to the buildings on foot as best we can!

Below:
A peaceful moment on the Grand Canal
(John Hay)

All you need to do now is jump on board the No 1 at Ferrovia (the train station stop) and try to grab a deck seat at the back.

AGC1

LEFT BANK

As you pull away from the landing, you leave behind (for a while any-way) the lowering form of **Stazione di Santa Lucia (1)**. Originally built in 1865 on the site of a convent dedicated to the same saint, the station was remodelled in 1954.

The Baroque chocolate-cake facade just beyond the station fronts the **Chiesa dei Scalzi (2*)**, a building that was originally designed by Longhena, although its facade was done by Giuseppe Sardi. On the other side of the **Ponte dei Scalzi (3*)**, one of only three bridges over the Grand Canal, is the **Palazzo Calbo-Crotta (4)**. Much remodelled, it retains some of the original 15th-century Gothic elements. A couple of smaller buildings to its right are also late Gothic.

RIGHT BANK

As on the left bank, things get off to a desultory start, but that's probably a good thing: it'll give you time to get yourself sorted out for the visual feast

that appears farther down the line. **Palazzo Emo-Diedo (5)** is a mod-est late-17th-century building attributed to Andrea Tirali. A couple of streets farther on is the unmistakable out-line of the **Chiesa di San Simeon Piccolo (6*)** with its distinctive brass dome. Shortly after-wards, **Palazzo Foscari-Contarini (7)** is a 15th-century reconstruction of a 12th-century mansion, in which it is thought Doge Francesco Foscari was born in 1375.

Railway Buildings (late 19th century)

Ponte della Libertà

Piazzale Roma

Giardini Papadopoli

Piazzale Roma

0 50 100m
0 50 100yd

Ferrovia Scalzi

Ferrovia Santa Lucia

Rio del Taronco

Rio Nuovo

Rio Marin

Below:
Boats and elegant buildings lined up along the waterfront (Neil Setchfield)

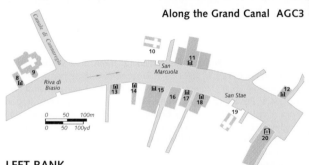

LEFT BANK

Just before the hulking 18th-century **Chiesa di San Geremia (9*)** is the four-storied **Palazzo Flangini (8)** (1682), designed by Giuseppe Sardi. A row of 17th- and 18th-century palazzi then stretches up to the **Chiesa di San Marcuola (10*)**. After this house of God, you pass the canal of the same name and then a house of the devil, the Renaissance **Palazzo Vendramin-Calergi (11*)**, winter seat of the casino. On the left corner of Rio di Noale is **Palazzo Gussoni-Grimani della Vida (12)**, attributed to Sanmicheli. Tintoretto added frescoes that have since faded away.

RIGHT BANK

Shortly after Canale di Cannaregio, the elegant 15th-century **Palazzo Giovanelli (13)** emerges on the right. Next follows **Casa Correr (14)**, a modest 17th-century house where Teodoro Correr started the collection that would form the basis of Museo Correr (in St Mark's Square).

The **Fondaco dei Turchi (15*)**, or Turkish emporium, has recently been stripped of restorers' scaffolding. Across the *rio* (canal) is the 15th-century **Deposito del Megio (16)**, the main grain silo of La Serenissima. The serious-looking lion is a later copy of the one removed after Napoleon arrived in 1797. (Venice had been covered in lions, but the Corsican felt that such symbols were out of place in his brave new world and had them all destroyed.) The next building, topped by what look like two spear tips, is a 17th-century creation of the very busy Longhena, **Palazzo Belloni Battaglia (17)**. **Ca' Tron (18)** went up a century earlier and is now part of the university. Farther along, you can't miss the Baroque facade of the **Chiesa di San Stae (19*)**. **Ca' Pesaro (20*)** is an important example of canalside Baroque, started by Longhena and finished by Gaspari.

Below:
Woman crossing the canal by *traghetto* (Dennis Jones)

LEFT BANK

The pink **Palazzo Fontana-Rezzonico (21)** was built in the style of Sansovino's buildings. In 1693 Carlo Rezzonico was born here – he went on to become Pope Clement XIII. A couple of houses along is **Ca' d'Oro (22*)**. **Ca' Pesaro (23)**, just on the other side of the vaporetto stop, is a nicely restored 15th-century Gothic house, not to be confused with Longhena's building of the same name. It is immediately followed by the still older **Palazzo Sagredo (24)**, built in the Byzantine style and later given a Gothic overhaul.

Just past the Rio dei SS Apostoli, approaching the bend, is the medieval **Ca' da Mosto (25)**, once home to one of the oldest hotels in Venice.

When you've almost reached the **Ponte di Rialto (27*)**, you'll see the former trading house and present-day post office, **Fondaco dei Tedeschi (26*)**.

RIGHT BANK

Begun in 1724, the present version of **Palazzo Corner della Regina (28*)** appeared centuries after Caterina Corner, short-lived queen of Cyprus, had passed into history. The bijou 14th-century **Ca' Favretto (29)** is now a hotel.

When you chug by the neogothic arches of the **Pescaria (30*)**, you have reached what was long the commercial heart of Venice – Rialto. The produce markets still do a brisk trade, but the bankers have long since been replaced by tourist-tat stalls. The long buildings are the **Fabbriche Nuove (31*)** and **Fabbriche Vecchie (32*)**. They are followed by the Renaissance **Palazzo dei Camerlenghi (33*)**, just before the Ponte di Rialto, and the **Palazzo dei Dieci Savi (34*)**, just beyond it.

Below:
The slanting arcades of the Ponte di Rialto (Bethune Carmichael)

LEFT BANK

A couple of blocks south of the Ponte di Rialto are **Palazzo Dolfin-Manin (35*)**, designed by Jacopo Sansovino, and **Palazzo Bembo (36*)**. Look for the narrow, early-Gothic **Palazzo Dandolo (37*)**, four houses along. Just past Calle del Carbon stand two fine Veneto-Byzantine trading houses *(fondachi)*, **Palazzo Loredan (38*)** and **Ca' Farsetti (39*)**. The grand entrances onto the canal were once opened to goods from all over the world; they now house the city council.

The third building along from here is the imposing Renaissance **Palazzo Grimani (40*)**, designed by Sanmicheli just before his death in 1559.

On the other side of Rio di San Luca are clustered several Gothic edifices, among them the 15th-century **Palazzo Tron (41)**, followed farther down by **Palazzo Corner-Spinelli (42*)**, which was the work of Codussi.

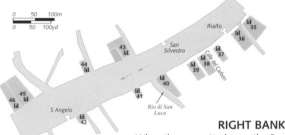

RIGHT BANK

When the vaporetto leaves the San Silvestro stop, **Palazzo Papadopoli (43*)** is the mansion after the first canal on the right. More than anything else, it is locally renowned for its lush, but unfortunately private, gardens. Just past the next canal is **Palazzo Bernardo (44)**, a fine Gothic structure whose tracery on the upper main floor is copied from the Palazzo Ducale's loggia. Also worthy of note is **Palazzo Pisani-Moretta (45)**, dating from about the same period. Next door, the 16th-century **Palazzo Tiepolo (46)** still boasts some original (if faded) frescoes.

Below: View of the canal from the Ponte di Rialto (Jon Davison)

LEFT BANK

Shortly before the next bend in the canal, four mansions, the **Palazzi Mocenigo (47)**, belonging to the powerful family of the same name, abut against one another. The two outside houses were originally Gothic, but all four were substantially made over in the following centuries. The detached **Palazzo Contarini dalle Figure (48)** is a fine Renaissance house where Palladio lived for a while.

A couple of Gothic mansions lie between Palazzo Contarini and **Palazzo Moro-Lin (49)**, a stout house raised by the Tuscan architect Sebastiano Mazzoni in 1670. Larger still is the **Palazzo Grassi (50*)**. In a backstreet next to the **Palazzo Malipiero (51*)**, Giacomo Casanova was born in 1725. **Ca' del Duca (52*)** is the next major building down the canal. It is swiftly followed by **Palazzo Giustinian-Lolin (53)**, a 14th-century pile reworked by Longhena in 1630.

RIGHT BANK

Down at **Palazzo Balbi (54)**, on the northern side of Rio di Ca' Foscari, we can see some tentative early-Baroque touches on an essentially Renaissance structure. Across the canal is **Ca' Foscari (55*)**. Since mid-1999, a deceptively realistic mock facade has been in place to disguise the restoration activity that has been going on for years.

At the next vaporetto stop is the 17th-century **Ca' Rezzonico (56*)**. The fourth mansion along from here, **Palazzo Loredan dell'Ambasciatore (57)**, is so called because in the 18th century Habsburg imperial ambassadors lived here.

Below:
Full speed ahead – a motorboat overtakes slower craft (Jon Davison)

Just across Rio di San Trovaso, **Palazzo Contarini degli Scrigni (58)** is an interesting hybrid composed of a late-Gothic structure with an early-17th-century add-on. The original nucleus of the art collection that would later end up in the Gallerie dell'Accademia was housed here. Moving it can't have been too onerous, as the **Gallerie dell'Accademia (59*)** are about 100m to the south-east. In front of the Gallerie, the last of the Grand Canal's three bridges, the **Ponte dell'Accademia (60*)**, links Dorsoduro on the right bank with the Sestiere di San Marco on the left.

LEFT BANK

Past the Ponte dell'Accademia, the next edifice of substance on the left bank is Sansovino's imposing **Palazzo Corner (61*)**, also known as Ca' Grande. The 15th-century Gothic **Palazzo Pisani-Gritti (62)** was altered in the 19th century and is now a luxury hotel. The rather narrow **Palazzo Contarini-Fasan (63*)** is an ornate Gothic building raised in the second half of the 15th century. **Palazzo Giustinian (64)** was built in 1474 in late-Gothic style. At this point, the No 1 ferry calls in at the San Marco stop.

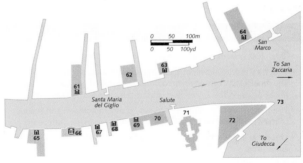

RIGHT BANK

What distinguishes **Palazzo Barbarigo (65*)** are the mosaics added towards the end of the 19th century. Next up is the Palazzo Venier dei Leoni, which houses the **Peggy Guggenheim Collection (66*)**,

followed a block later by the lopsided **Palazzo Dario (67*)**, with its early-Renaissance marble facade.

Just on the other side of the next canal, **Palazzo Salviati (68)**, with its exuberant mosaic decoration, is hard to miss. The Salviati glass firm added this touch, recently by Venetian standards (in 1924).

Don't be fooled by the seemingly Gothic grandeur of **Palazzo Genovese (69)**. It is actually a neogothic whim erected late in the 19th century. Much of the former **Abbazia di San Gregorio (70)** was destroyed to make way for it. What is left dates from the 12th century, although it has been so often remodelled that you'd never know. It presents a rather forlorn picture on the canal today. All the more so since this part of Dorsoduro is completely dominated by the Baroque splendour of Longhena's **Chiesa di Santa Maria della Salute (71*)**.

Next to it are former seminary buildings and then the long low structure of the **Dogana da Mar (72*)**, where for centuries traders paid customs duty on seaborne imports. Like a ship's prow, Dorsoduro ends here in a point known as the **Punta della Dogana (73*)**.

The No 1 vaporetto continues on its way to San Marco, San Zaccaria and beyond.

Did You Know?

- Over 100 palaces line the banks of the Grand Canal.

- The stripy poles *(bricole)* outside the mansions are used to moor boats. The municipality caused an uproar recently when it replaced traditional oak poles on the Zattere with plastic ones in a bid to save money.

- The contents of the canal drained away completely, leaving an avenue of thick sludge, when it was hit by an earthquake in the 14th century.

- The canal divides the city very neatly in two – with three *sestieri* on either side.

- When Lord Byron slipped and fell into the Grand Canal on the way to a romantic rendezvous, he wasn't going to let a bit of water stop him. He hurried on to his lover's house and wooed her all evening in soggy clothes.

Below: Sunset and silhouettes on the Grand Canal (Jon Davison)

Places to Stay

It will come as no great surprise to hear that Venice is an expensive place to stay, in spite of the huge choice of accommodation. Even in the depths of the low season, you're unlikely to pay less than €36.15/51.65 for a single/double without private bathroom. In the high season, only a handful of hotels offer such prices. Expect to pay from €77.45 upwards for a decent budget double with bathroom (which often means shower, washbasin and toilet). In the high season, as the prices below show, you can be looking at higher rates still.

Lone travellers are particularly penalised. Most hotels have few, if any, single rooms. When they do, such rooms are usually rather poky. One upset tourist complained of having found herself shoved into a hastily reconverted storage room (the hotel concerned is not in this guide). You will generally be offered a double at two-thirds to three-quarters of the price two people would pay.

Many places offer triple, quad and even quintuple rates. Usually, this means extra beds in a fairly spacious double. Still, if you are in a group, it works out more economically. Most hotel proprietors pad out the bill by including a compulsory breakfast in the price. The (in)famous continental breakfast in these cases generally consists of a lavishly laid-out stale bread roll, accompanied by little packets of butter and jam and a pot of weak instant coffee. If you have the cash, you may as well view this as an optional arrangement and get a proper cup of coffee in a bar.

Hotels go by various names. An *albergo* is a hotel. A *pensione* or *locanda* is generally a smaller, simpler, family-run establishment, although frequently there is little to distinguish them from lower-end hotels.

Budget travellers have the choice of the youth hostel on Giudecca or a handful of other dormitory-style possibilities, some of them religious institutions. They are mostly open in summer only.

Most of the top hotels are around the San Marco area and along the Grand Canal, but it is still possible to find 'bargains' (the concept is, of course, relative) tucked away in tiny streets and on side canals in the heart of the city. There are lots of hotels near the train station, but it is a good 30-minute walk from there to San Marco. The Dorsoduro area is quiet and relatively free of tourists.

As the influx of tourists steadily rises, so do prices – well beyond the natural increments caused by inflation. In Venice more than elsewhere, hotel rates vary wildly for a range of other reasons. Some hotels have the same prices year-round, while others drop them when things are slow (rare). 'Low season' for the average Venetian hotelier means November, early December and January. *Lowish* season for some hotels comes in the July-August period, when Italian tourists tend to head for the seaside and leave the cities to the foreigners. That's it. Some of the more expensive hotels operate further price differentials: weekend rates can be higher than weekday rates, and rooms with views (especially of the Grand Canal) are generally more expensive than others. If you are there in the low season and/or staying for several days, it never hurts to ask for a discount before simply agreeing to a room price. Of course, in busy periods the only reaction you're likely to get is a pitying smile.

The prices that follow should be regarded as a guide and are based on high season rates.

If things are looking tight, you could consider using Padua as a base (it's only 37km away, or about 30 minutes on most trains), perhaps for a day or two while you get oriented in Venice, giving yourself time to find and book a place that suits.

Seasons & Reservations

It is advisable to book in advance year-round in Venice, particularly for Christmas, Easter and Carnevale, in May, June and September and for weekends. Remember that, unless you pay a deposit, many smaller hotels won't feel obliged to hold a room for you all day unless you call to confirm on the day. Some hoteliers overbook in the way airlines do. If you haven't sent a fax with confirmation and/or paid some form of deposit, you risk losing the room if you turn up late in the evening.

The Associazione Veneziana Albergatori has offices at Santa Lucia train station (Map 3; ☎ 041 71 52 88, fax 041 522 12 42), two in Piazzale Roma, at the Tronchetto car park and at the airport. Staff can book you a room in a wide range of hotels (they have more than 200 on their books). You pay a booking fee, ranging from €0.52 at the train station to €2.05 at Piazzale Roma. The train-station branch is the main one, open 8am to 10pm daily in summer (understood as Easter to the end of October). It closes one hour earlier in winter. It also has 'last-minute' booking numbers: from within Italy, the number is freephone ☎ 800 84 30 06; from abroad dial ☎ 041 522 22 64.

The Consorzio Alberghi della Terraferma Veneziana (Map 11; ☎ 041 93 01 33, fax 041 93 15 70) is a separate organisation based in Mestre train station (platform 1). If you arrive in Mestre and are worried Venice may be full, these people can put you in a hotel in Mestre – be warned, though, that they have been known to be a little less than frank about the situation in Venice. They have about 40 Mestre hotels on their books. The booking fee is €2.05 and the office opens 8.30am to 7.30pm Monday to Saturday, and sometimes from noon to 5pm on Sunday.

PLACES TO STAY – BUDGET

You have already been warned. Cheap options are close to nonexistent. Apart from camping, hostels and other dorm possibilities, only a handful of places charge 'low' rates. We have included places running up to as much as €118.80 for a high-season double with toilet and shower/bath in this category. That may sound absurd, but wait until you see the prices for mid-range and top-end digs!

Camping

There are numerous camp sites, many with bungalows, on the Litorale del Cavallino, the coast along the Adriatic Sea, north-east of the city. You can also stay at one of several along the rather tacky beach at Sottomarina, Chioggia. Neither of these options puts you very close to Venice. If you want to camp or park your trailer a little nearer to the city, there are several possibilities. None are truly great, but some are OK. The tourist office in St Mark's Square has a full list. In all cases, you will be paying roughly €5.15 per person and €10.35 per tent space (which includes room to park one car). Add the inconvenience of getting to and from Venice and you may find this is not really such a hot option.

Marina di Venezia (☎ *041 96 61 46, fax 041 96 60 36,* **w** *www.cavallino.net/marinave, Via Montello 6, Punta Sabbioni)* **Map 1** Sites per person €7.50, per tent €13.50-18.60. Open late Apr-end Sept. This camp site has just about everything, from a private beach to a shop, cinema and kiddies' playground. You can get the No 12 vaporetto to Fondamente Nuove (Cannaregio) via Burano and Murano or the No 14 to San Zaccaria via the Lido.

Serenissima (☎ *041 92 18 50, fax 041 92 02 86,* **w** *www.campingserenissima.com, Via Padana 334/a, Località Oriago)* **Map 1** Sites per person/tent €6.20/10.35. Open mid-Apr–mid-Nov. Bus 53 from Piazzale Roma. If you do want to stay closer to Venice, this is possibly the best bet. Set in a fairly leafy locale on the Venice-Padua bus route, the site has a shop, restaurant, laundry facilities and table tennis.

Campeggio Fusina (☎ *041 547 00 55, fax 041 547 00 50, Via Moranzani 79, Località Fusina)* **Map 1** Sites per person €5.15, per tent €7.75-10.35. Open year-round. This place is reasonably well equipped and you can get the LineaFusina vaporetto straight into Venice (Zattere). It's a private charter, though, so you need to buy separate tickets (€4.15 one way, €7.75 return). The bus also passes close by. Some travellers have reported being disturbed at night by summertime discos in the area.

Hostels

Ostello Venezia (☎ *041 523 82 11, fax 041 523 56 89, Fondamenta della Croce 86)* **Map 7** B&B €15.50. Open 7am-9.30am &

2pm-11.30pm. Vaporetto No 41, 42 or 82 from train station or Piazzale Roma to Zitelle. This Hostelling International (HI) property is on Giudecca. It's open to members only, although you can buy a card there (see Documents in the Facts for the Visitor chapter). Evening meals are available for €7.75. The hostel is on HI's computerised International Booking Network (IBN).

Istituto Canossiano (☎/fax 041 522 21 57, Fondamenta di Ponte Piccolo 428) **Map 7** Singles/doubles €56.80/87.80, beds in triple or quad €38.75. Open June-Sept. Vaporetto No 41, 42 or 82 to Sant'Eufemia on Giudecca. Near the Ostello Venezia, this place, clearly no longer a budget option but included here because it is run as a hostel, is for women only.

Ostello Santa Fosca (☎/fax 041 71 57 75, Fondamenta Canal 2372, Cannaregio) **Map 3** Dorm beds €18.05, beds in double €20.65. This is a fairly no-nonsense hostel for young people but the setting is peaceful enough, with a garden. From July to September, guests have use of kitchen facilities too.

Foresteria Valdese (☎/fax 041 528 67 97, Castello 5150) **Map 8** Dorm beds €18.60, doubles €51.65-67.15. This is in a rambling old mansion near Campo Santa Maria Formosa (Map 5). Head east from the square on Calle Lunga, cross the small bridge and the Foresteria is in front of you. Double rates depend on the room and whether or not it has a bathroom. Breakfast is included. Book well ahead.

Domus Civica (☎ 041 72 11 03, fax 041 522 71 39, Calle Campazzo 3082) **Map 6** Open mid-June–early Sept. Dorm beds/doubles €25.80/46.50. This place has student-dorm-style beds and doubles, and is not bad for what it is. The location is fine and not too far from the train station.

Bed & Breakfast

The APT has a modest list of about 20 houses offering bed & breakfast. You can be looking at anything from €36.15 in low season to €103.30 in the high season for a double (in a couple of cases considerably more). None are listed here as, in general, they only offer a couple of rooms.

Hotels & Pensioni

San Marco Despite being the most touristy part of Venice, the San Marco area contains a few places that offer comparatively good value for money.

Hotel ai do Mori (☎ 041 520 48 17, fax 041 520 53 28, Calle Larga San Marco 658) **Map 5** Doubles without/with bathroom up to €82.65/118.80. This hotel is just off St Mark's Square. It has pleasant rooms, some of which offer views of the Basilica. The pick of the crop is without doubt the cosy little double at the top that comes with a terrace attached. The hotel also offers accommodation for groups of three, four and five people.

✗*Locanda Casa Petrarca (☎/fax 041 520 04 30, San Marco 4386)* **Map 5** Singles/doubles without bathroom €41.30/77.45, doubles with toilet & shower €98.15. This is one of the nicest places to stay in this area. Breakfast is extra (€5.15). It's a bit of a family affair and the cheerful owner speaks English. To get here, find Campo San Luca, follow Calle dei Fuseri, take the second left and then turn right into Calle Schiavone.

Pensione al Gazzettino (☎ 041 528 65 23, fax 041 522 33 14, San Marco 4971) **Map 5** Singles without bathroom €51.65, doubles with bathroom up to €113.65. This is not as good as some of the previous listings, but is quite acceptable. The position by the canal is enticing and it has a decent restaurant (see the following Places to Eat chapter). It offers straightforward, comfortable doubles. The only single is a fairly tiny affair on the top floor.

Locanda Fiorita (☎ 041 523 47 54, fax 041 522 80 43, ℮ locafior@tin.it, San Marco 3457/a) **Map 6** Singles without bathroom up to €72.30, doubles with bathroom up to €108.45. This place is set on a wonderful little square a spit away from the broad Campo Santo Stefano. The rooms in this old Venetian pile are simple but well maintained, and it is hard to complain about the prices. This is one of those inexplicable gems that makes you ask why they can't all be so.

Dorsoduro *Antica Locanda Montin (☎ 041 522 71 51, fax 041 520 02 55, ℮ lo candamontin@libero.it, Fondamenta di*

PLACES TO STAY

Borgo 1147) **Map 6** Singles/doubles without bathroom €67.15/103.30, doubles with bathroom up to €129.10. Ezra Pound favoured this small and comfortable place. It has a popular if pricey restaurant (see the following Places to Eat chapter).

Albergo Antico Capon (☎/fax 041 528 52 92, e hotelanticocapon@hotmail.com, Campo Santa Margherita 3004/b) **Map 6** Rooms up to €85.20. This place is right on the liveliest square in Dorsoduro and has a variety of rooms. The beds are wide and firm, the rooms in which they stand bright and airy.

Hotel Galleria (☎/fax 041 520 41 72, w www.hotelgalleria.it, Accademia 878/a) **Map 6** Singles/doubles from €51.65/87.80, largest double €124. This is the only one-star hotel right on the Grand Canal, near the Ponte dell'Accademia. The place was an old private mansion before being converted into the modest and warm-feeling hotel it is now. Space is a little tight, but the decor is welcoming. If you can get one of the rooms on the canal, how can you possibly complain?

Santa Croce & San Polo *Hotel ai Tolentini (☎ 041 523 67 61, fax 041 522 81 88, Corte di Amai 197/g, Santa Croce)* **Map 6** High season singles/doubles with bathroom €75.90/101.25, low season €18.05-20.65 less. This place is a couple of minutes' walk from Piazzale Roma. It has just seven rooms (five with bathroom), all with TV and phone. This is one of the few places where breakfast is not included.

Albergo Casa Peron (☎ 041 71 00 21, fax 041 71 10 38, Salizzada San Pantalon 85, Santa Croce) **Map 6** Singles/doubles with shower €43.90/67.15, with toilet & shower €20.65-25.80 more. This is a small but characterful place, with rooms tucked around corners and up stairs.

Hotel dalla Mora (☎ 041 71 07 03, fax 041 72 30 06, Santa Croce 42/a) **Map 6** Singles/doubles with bathroom up to €56.80/82.65. This hotel is on a small canal just off Salizzada San Pantalon. It has clean, airy rooms, some (such as No 5) with lovely canàl views, and there is a terrace. Bookings are a must.

Pensione Guerrato (☎ 041 522 71 31, fax 041 528 59 27, e hguerrat@tin.it, Ruga due Mori 240/a, San Polo) **Map 4** Doubles without/with bathroom €87.80/108.45. This pensione, amid the Rialto markets, is a gem, a one-star place that has rooms with at least glimpses of the Grand Canal. It is housed in a former convent, which before (so they say) had served as a hostel for knights heading off on the Third Crusade. The friendly managers run a tight ship. They are usually booked pretty solid.

Cannaregio There is plenty to choose from here, with many hotels just a stone's throw from the train station.

Archies (☎ 041 72 08 84, Rio Terrà del Cristo 1814/b) **Map 3** Dorm beds from €10.35, doubles €20.65. This is about the cheapest place in town and rooms are very basic. Run by a Chinese family (with ads up for cheap Chinese food around town), it's a crumbling doss, reminiscent of dives on the overland trails in Asia or Africa, but you can't really argue with the prices.

Hotel Santa Lucia (☎/fax 041 71 51 80, Calle della Misericordia 358) **Map 3** Singles/doubles without bathroom €51.65/77.45, doubles with bathroom €98.15. Off the Rio Terrà Lista di Spagna, this hotel is in a newish building with clean, spacious and well-kept rooms.

Hotel Villa Rosa (☎ 041 71 89 76, fax 041 71 65 69, e villarosa@ve.nettuno.it, Calle della Misericordia 389) **Map 3** High season singles/doubles €82.65/103.30, low season singles from €41.30. Just up the road, this hotel has 33 comfortable rooms with bathroom, TV and phone. Out the back is a quiet little garden terrace where you can take your compulsory breakfast.

Hotel Minerva & Nettuno (☎ 041 71 59 68, fax 041 524 21 39, e lchecchi@tin.it, Rio Terrà Lista di Spagna 230) **Map 3** Singles/doubles without bathroom up to €41.30/53.20, singles/doubles with bathroom €56.80/82.65. This hotel is a tad more economical. The rooms are generally a good size, some looking onto the noisy street, others over internal courtyards. Some are actually in a building across the street.

Hotel Adua (☎ 041 71 61 84, fax 041 244 01 62, Rio Terrà Lista di Spagna 233/a) **Map 3** Doubles without/with bathroom €72.30/108.50. Renovated in 1999, this place is not a bad deal. The theme is blinding white but it's clean and comfortable. Single occupancy of rooms costs a little less.

Hotel Rossi (☎ 041 71 51 64, fax 041 71 77 84, Calle delle Procuratie 262) **Map 3** Singles/doubles without bathroom up to €46.50/69.70, doubles with bathroom €85.20. Set in a tiny lane off the Rio Terrà Lista di Spagna, this hotel's rooms are pleasant enough, with wood panelling, fans and heating. The location is nice and quiet while still handy for the train station. Breakfast is included.

Hotel al Gobbo (☎ 041 71 50 01, fax 041 71 47 65, Campo di San Geremia 312) **Map 3** Singles/doubles without bathroom €46.50/67.15, singles/doubles with bathroom €69.70/85.20. The rooms here are pleasantly decorated and comfortable. While not exciting, it is a reliable option.

Hotel San Geremia (☎ 041 71 62 45, fax 041 524 23 42, Campo di San Geremia 290/a) **Map 3** Doubles without/with bathroom €87.80/118.80. This is a friendly establishment. The rooms are standard, with phone and TV. Some have views of the square and a couple up top have little terrace arrangements, although these are usually rented as triples. The prices are inflated in comparison with neighbouring places, but if you have no luck finding accommodation around here, it's a reasonable option for people travelling in pairs.

Alloggi Calderan & Casa Gerotto (☎ 041 71 53 61, Campo di San Geremia 283) **Map 3** Dorm beds €18.05, doubles without/with bathroom €67/93. This twin family pack is the pick of the crop on this square for a simple, budget deal. They have combined to offer a whole range of rooms. The handful of bright singles are hard to come by as they are generally occupied by long-term residents. The dorms are single sex. Triples are also available and most rooms have pleasing views over the square. Prices can drop by about one-third in slow periods.

Hotel Silva & Ariel (☎ 041 71 47 73, fax 041 72 03 26, Calle della Masena 1391/a) **Map 3** Doubles without/with bathroom €77.45/98.15. Hidden away in a narrow lane leading into the Ghetto, this is not a bad little place, where you can sit in a diminutive back garden. The owners also have some apartments available that could be handy for groups of up to six. Rooms are about €20 less if taken as singles.

Castello This area to the east of San Marco, although close to the piazza, is less touristy. From the train station, catch vaporetto No 1 and get off at San Zaccaria.

Hotel Doni (☎/fax 041 522 42 67, Fondamenta del Vin 4656) **Map 5** Singles/doubles without bathroom €46.50/72.30, doubles with bathroom €98.15. A stone's throw east of San Marco is this delightful little establishment to rival the Fiorita (see the earlier San Marco section). It's an 18th-century mansion (although they say the ground floor is 200 years older still). It has been a hotel for more than a century, originally as the Minerva until it changed hands in 1947. It is well maintained and a pleasure to be in. The 12 rooms are mostly spacious and in one, the ceiling is adorned with a fine fresco dating from 1850.

Albergo Corona (☎ 041 522 91 74, Calle Corona 4464) **Map 5** Singles/doubles €43.90/54.25. This is an odd place. You climb mountains of stairs to get to indifferent rooms (although the electric baggage-carrier may take a load off your shoulders if it works). The breakfast area is quirkily decorated (check out the wooden parrot). What can we say? It's about as cheap as it gets around here.

Locanda Silva (☎ 041 522 76 43, fax 041 528 68 17, ✉ albergosilva@libero.it, Fondamenta del Rimedio 4423) **Map 5** Singles/doubles without bathroom €43.90/72.30, singles/doubles with shower & toilet €62/98.15. This place, south of Campo Santa Maria Formosa, is a preferable rival to Albergo Corona. It doesn't have any of the odd character, but the modest rooms are clean and pleasant enough. A few look onto the narrow canal.

PLACES TO STAY

Hotel Riva (☎ *041 522 70 34, fax 041 528 55 51, Ponte dell'Angelo 5310)* **Map 5** Doubles without/with bathroom €72.30/103.30. This hotel is on a lovely side canal. With a little persuasion, you can get the rate shaved a little for single occupancy.

Casa Linger (☎ *041 528 59 20, fax 041 528 48 51, Salizzada Sant'Antonin 3541)* **Map 8** Singles/doubles with bathroom €72.30/103.30. The loquacious (if you speak Italian) proprietor lends this fairly pedestrian locanda a little animation. If you like climbing stairs, this is definitely the spot for you. Still it's not too bad and the place is quiet. Forget about the rabbit hole they call a single room.

Locanda Sant'Anna (☎/fax *041 528 64 66,* e *hsantanna@tin.it, Corte del Bianco 269)* **Map 9** Single/doubles without bathroom up to €54.25/64.55, doubles with bathroom €93. Hidden away right in the east of Castello, you can't get much farther away from the heart of Venice and still be there! This is a real residential quarter and may appeal to some for that reason alone. Rooms are modest but comfortable.

Lido *Pensione La Pergola* (☎ *041 526 07 84, Via Cipro 15)* **Map 10** Singles/doubles with bathroom €38.75/77.45. This pensione, just off Gran Viale Santa Maria Elisabetta, has a range of rooms. Prices can be halved in the low season. The rooms are simple but pleasant enough. It's about as cheap as you'll find on the Lido in summer.

Burano For details of how to get to Burano, see under Around the Lagoon in the Things to See & Do chapter.

Locanda Al Raspo de Ua (☎/fax *041 73 00 95, Via Galuppi 560)* **See Map p156** Doubles without bathroom from €46.50. This is a modest locanda on the island's main drag. It is the only place to stay here and could make your Venetian visit a quite different experience. After the last of the tourists head back to Venice at night, it's just you and the locals on this pretty islet.

Mestre Only 10 to 15 minutes away on city bus Nos 2 and 7 (the former passes Mestre train station) or by train, Mestre is a drab, if sometimes necessary, alternative to staying in Venice. There are a number of good hotels, as well as plenty of cafes and places to eat around the main square.

Albergo Roberta (☎ *041 92 93 55, fax 041 93 09 83, Via Sernaglia 21)* **Map 11** Singles without bathroom €43.90, singles/doubles with bathroom €62/93. This place has good-sized, clean rooms. Breakfast is included.

Hotel Giovannina (☎ *041 92 63 96, fax 041 538 84 42,* w *www.hotelgiovannina.it, Via Dante 113)* **Map 11** Singles without bathroom €33.55, doubles up to €67.15. This is a cheaper alternative to the Albergo Roberta and is perfectly acceptable. Breakfast is included. Downstairs you can chow down at a couple of no-nonsense restaurants.

Hotel Monte Piana (☎ *041 92 62 42, fax 041 92 28 55, Via Monte San Michele 17)* **Map 11** Doubles €82.65. This hotel is similar in quality to the Giovannina and is also close to the station, but in a quiet residential street. It has some on-site parking.

PLACES TO STAY – MID-RANGE
San Marco

The San Marco area is generally not so great for good-value, mid-range hotels, and in any case is so thronged with tourists that it is hard to think of a reason for staying in the area. Attractive alternatives abound in other parts of town that really aren't so far away.

Al Gambero (☎ *041 522 43 84, fax 041 520 04 31,* e *hotgambero@tin.it, Calle dei Fabbri 4687)* **Map 5** Singles/doubles without bathroom €49/82.65, singles/doubles with bathroom €93/124. This hotel is in a great location north of St Mark's Square and can be recommended. Clean, comfortable rooms come with TV, phone and that very Italian consideration, a hairdryer in the bathroom.

Serenissima (☎ *041 520 00 11, fax 041 522 32 92,* e *serenhtl@tin.it, Calle Goldoni 4486)* **Map 5** Singles/doubles €108.45/162.70. If you must stay in the area, this place, tucked away between San Marco and the Ponte di Rialto, is not a bad option. They have a few cheaper rooms with private bathrooms.

Dorsoduro

Albergo Accademia Villa Maravege (☎ 041 521 01 88, fax 041 523 91 52, ⓦ www.pensioneaccademia.it, Fondamenta Bollani 1058) **Map 6** Singles/doubles up to €113.65/ 217. This popular hotel is set in lovely gardens, with views of the Grand Canal.

Pensione Seguso (☎ 041 528 68 58, fax 041 522 23 40, Fondamenta Zattere ai Gesuati 779) **Map 6** Singles/doubles without bathroom up to €100/142, singles/doubles with bathroom €129/160. Open Mar-Nov. This pensione is in a lovely quiet position facing the Canale della Giudecca. Book ahead.

La Calcina (☎ 041 520 64 66, fax 041 522 70 45, ⓦ www.lacalcina.com, Fondamenta Zattere ai Gesuati 780) **Map 6** Singles/ doubles €93/155. John Ruskin wrote *The Stones of Venice* in this charming little hotel, which has a smidgen of garden attached.

Hotel Messner (☎ 041 522 74 43, fax 041 522 72 66, ⓔ messner@doge.it, Rio Terrà del Spezier 216) **Map 6** Singles/doubles up to €93/129. The Messner is tucked away on a tiny street. It was fairly recently overhauled and boasts an inviting bar and courtyard.

Hotel alla Salute da Cici (☎ 041 523 54 04, fax 041 522 22 71, Fondamenta di Ca' Balà 222) **Map 6** Singles/doubles €119/129. Just around the corner from the Messner, this is another comfortable spot in a well-kept old Venetian house. Some rooms look onto the canal and they have a couple of cheap singles (€72.30) without bathroom. They cut prices a little in July and August.

Albergo agli Alboretti (☎ 041 523 00 58, fax 041 521 01 58, ⓔ alborett@gpnet.it, Rio Terrà Antonio Foscarini 884) **Map 6** Singles/doubles up to €90.40/139.45. This is a charming hotel that almost feels like an inviting mountain chalet when you step inside. In its category, it is one of Venice's star choices. The management is friendly and the rooms tastefully arranged. The restaurant is also of a high standard.

Locanda San Barnaba (☎/fax 041 241 12 33, ⓦ www.locanda-sanbarnaba.com, Calle del Traghetto 2785–6). **Map 6** Singles €103.30, doubles €165.30-206.60. This charming new 13-room hotel has been elegantly carved out of a fine mansion. Rooms are well equipped and some face onto the canal. A small terrace graces the top of the building, as well as a small canalside garden for breakfast or evening drinks. Americans rush to the place, which can be booked out months in advance.

Santa Croce & San Polo

Hotel Canal (☎ 041 523 84 80, fax 041 523 91 06, ⓦ www.hotelcanal.com, Fondamenta San Simeon Piccolo 553, Santa Croce) **Map 3** Singles/doubles up to €180.75/201.45. Although this area is not the most picturesque in Venice, this hotel, a few minutes' walk from Piazzale Roma, overlooks the Grand Canal. Chop off one-third of the rates here in the low season.

Hotel San Cassiano (☎ 041 524 17 68, fax 041 72 10 33, ⓦ www.sancassiano.it, Calle del Rosa 2232, Santa Croce) **Map 3** Singles/doubles €196.30/284. The 14th-century Ca' Favretto houses a mixed selection of rooms, the better ones high-ceilinged doubles overlooking the Grand Canal. The building is a wonderful old pile (which the managers continue to refurbish), with stone doorways along the staircases. If you're up early, you can grab one of a couple of tables for breakfast on the balcony on the Grand Canal.

Locanda Sturion (☎ 041 523 62 43, fax 041 522 83 78, ⓦ www.locandasturion.com, Calle Sturion 679, San Polo) **Map 5** Singles/doubles from €108.45/175.60. This locanda is two minutes from the Ponte di Rialto. It has been a hotel on and off since the 13th century and has superb rooms loaded with character.

Cannaregio

Hotel Abbazia (☎ 041 71 73 33, fax 041 71 79 49, Calle Priuli detta dei Cavalletti 68) **Map 3** Singles/doubles up to €176.65/ 196.30. This hotel is in a restored abbey, a one-minute walk from the train station. Many of the lovely rooms face onto a central garden. Prices drop considerably out of season. Breakfast is included.

Hotel Tre Archi (☎ 041 524 43 56, fax 041 524 43 68, ⓦ www.hoteltrearchi.com, Fondamenta di Cannaregio 923) **Map 3** Singles/doubles €196/207. Set away from the tourist rush, this attractive little hotel of 24 rooms, opened in mid-2001, is in a bit of the 'real Venice'. The place is furnished and decorated in classical Venetian style. Some rooms (a couple with small terraces) look over the Canale di Cannaregio, while others are around the internal garden, where you can take breakfast in summer. In slow periods the same rooms can go for less than half price.

Locanda Leon Bianco (☎ *041 523 35 72, fax 041 241 63 92, Campiello Leon Bianco 5629)* **Map 4** Doubles €144.60, small rooms without canal views €118.80. No singles. This is a fine option, although your initial impression may not be too positive as you enter the tiny, lightless courtyard. To find the locanda, cross Rio dei SS Apostoli (heading towards San Marco) and turn right. Pass the high staircase on your left and head straight into the dead-end courtyard. Go up two flights of stairs in which medieval-style flaming torches would be at home and you are there. The best three rooms (of eight) look right onto the Grand Canal. The undulating *terrazzo alla Veneziana* floors (see the boxed text 'Of Floors & Walls' in the Things to See & Do chapter) and heavy timber doors with their original locks lend the rooms real charm. All but one have bathrooms. Breakfast is served in the rooms. The house next door is the 12th-century Ca' da Mosto. Owned from the beginning by a renowned family of Venetian navigators, from the 16th to the 18th centuries it also housed Venice's first and most famed hotel, Del Leon Bianco.

Hotel Giorgione (☎ *041 522 58 10, fax 041 523 90 92,* e *giorgione@hotelgiorgione .com, Calle Larga dei Proverbi 4587)* **Map 4** Singles €93, doubles up to €305. In this welcoming hotel you will find comfortable, if in some cases rather small, rooms mostly in a 15th-century mansion (part of the building is modern). At the centre of the hotel is a peaceful courtyard. You can take breakfast outside and sip drinks on the 1st-floor terrace. Some of the best top floor rooms have little terraces.

Castello

Castello offers a broad palette on the accommodation front in this range, with a couple of gems and some worthy runners-up.

Hotel Bridge (☎ *041 520 52 87, fax 041 520 22 97,* w *www.hotelbridge.com, Calle Sagrestia 4498)* **Map 5** Doubles with bathroom up to €201.45. The better rooms here are furnished in typical period Venetian style (creamy painted woodwork with floral decorations). All is modern and clean but space is a bit of a problem.

Locanda Al Piave (☎ *041 528 51 74, fax 041 523 85 12,* e *hotel.alpiave@iol.it, Ruga Giuffa 4838–40)* **Map 5** Doubles up to €154.95. Single occupancy €92.95. This locanda has fine and, in most cases, spacious rooms, furnished with muted elegance. All have shower and TV and are spotlessly clean.

Hotel da Bruno (☎ *041 523 04 52, fax 041 522 11 57, Salizzada San Lio 5726)* **Map 5** Singles/doubles up to €118.80/154.95. This hotel is just west of Campo Santa Maria Formosa. The rooms are a reasonable size and have bathroom and TV.

Pensione Bucintoro (☎ *041 522 32 40, fax 041 523 52 24, Riva San Biagio 2135)* **Map 8** Singles/doubles without bathroom €67/124, singles/doubles with bathroom €85/152.35. The big advantage of this pensione is that all rooms look onto the lagoon and are well kept. They shave off about €5 per person in slack periods.

Albergo Paganelli (☎ *041 522 43 24, fax 041 523 92 67,* e *hotelpag@tin.it, Riva degli Schiavoni 4182)* **Map 8** Singles/ doubles up to €114/180.75. This place is a good deal if you get one of the three waterfront rooms. It has been a hotel since the mid-19th century. The most expensive rooms have views over the lagoon. Others, including some without their own bathroom, can be almost half the cost. Breakfast is included.

Albergo al Nuovo Teson (☎/fax *041 520 55 55, Ramo Pescaria 3980)* **Map 8** Singles/ doubles up to €108.45/118.80. Secreted away on a square with a real local flavour, this hotel is a good option. Sure, there is a passing trade in tourists, but here you feel you have moved away from the glitz and into a grittier side of Venice. There's nothing particularly gritty about the rooms, elegantly furnished and equipped with shower, TV and phone. Again, loners get a rough deal.

La Residenza (☎ *041 528 53 15, fax 041 523 88 59,* W *www.venicelaresidenza.com, Campo Bandiera e Moro 3608)* **Map 8** Singles/doubles up to €93/145. If you can live without watery views, head inland to this delightful 15th-century mansion. It is also known as Palazzo Gritti-Badoer, after two of the families who have owned it. The main hall upstairs makes quite an impression with its candelabras, elaborate decoration and distinguished furniture. The rooms are rather more restrained, but fine value.

Locanda Remedio (☎ *041 520 62 32, fax 041 521 04 85, Calle del Rimedio 4412)* **Map 5** Singles/doubles up to €93/154.95. This is indeed something of a remedy – after the streaming, screaming masses of visitors thronging around San Marco just a few minutes away. It's hard to imagine them so close to the tranquil little courtyard in which this inn is hidden. The building dates from the 16th century and belonged to the Rimedio family. In the same courtyard was a *malvasia*, a tavern where wine of the same name, imported from the Venetian-controlled Greek islands, could be had. In a nice play of words, the building came to be known by the name *remedio* (remedy) towards the end of the 16th century – the medicinal qualities of malvasia were thought to ward off the plague. Try for the front double, the ceiling of which is graced with a mid-16th-century fresco by Andrea Medolla.

Hotel Scandinavia (☎ *041 522 35 07, fax 041 523 52 32, Campo Santa Maria Formosa 5240)* **Map 5** Doubles €180-310. This 15th-century converted mansion is not a bad choice. The heavy timber beams and period furnishings give the rooms a cosy touch – the best ones look onto the square. Rates vary considerably. As usual, however, count on the bad news rather than the good. They have a few not-so-inspiring singles.

Mestre

Hotel Vivit (☎ *041 95 13 85, fax 041 95 88 91,* e *hotelvivit@libero.it, Piazza Ferretto 75)* **Map 11** Singles/doubles €72.30/110.55. This is a somewhat drab and cumbersome-looking place, but the functional rooms are quite OK. If you have to be in Mestre, at least here you are in the heart of town and on a lively pedestrianised square. Breakfast is included.

Tritone (☎ *041 538 31 25, fax 041 538 30 45,* e *info@httritone.com, Viale Stazione 16)* **Map 11** Singles/doubles up to €93/119. This three-star property is quite comfortable and has the obvious advantage of being right by the station – ideal for quick getaways to the lagoon. Breakfast is included.

PLACES TO STAY – TOP END
San Marco

Gritti Palace (☎ *041 79 46 11, fax 041 520 09 42,* e *reso73.grittipalace@luxury collection.com, Campo Traghetto 2467)* **Map 6** Doubles up to €980. This luxury property, the facade of which fronts the Grand Canal, is one of the most famous hotels in Venice. If you can afford to pay top rates, you'll be mixing with royalty. A good portion of Hemingway's *Across the River and into the Trees* is set in the hotel.

Bauer (☎ *041 520 70 22, fax 041 520 75 57,* W *www.bauervenezia.it, Campo San Moisè, San Marco 1459)* **Map 5** Singles/doubles up to €465/1085. This is, for some people, a better address still. Don't mind the awful 1949 Soviet-style entrance – the canalside neogothic frontage of the palazzo is sufficiently elegant. Views from some rooms across the Grand Canal towards Santa Maria della Salute (the most expensive) are hard to beat, and you're a stone's throw from St Mark's Square. The elegant rooms on the 2nd floor drip Carrara marble and Murano glass.

Dorsoduro

Ca' Pisani Hotel (☎ *041 277 14 78, fax 041 277 10 61,* W *www.capisanihotel.it, Rio Terrà Antonio Foscarini 979/a)* **Map 6** High-season rooms €240-310. Named after the hero of the siege of Chioggia in 1310, this centuries-old building houses a curious new departure in the Venetian hotel scene – a self-conscious design hotel, filled with 1930s and 1940s furnishings, as well as items specially made for the hotel. The rooms, some with exposed beam ceilings, are elegant, well equipped and full of pleasing decorative touches.

Cannaregio

Grand Hotel Palazzo dei Dogi (☎ *041 220 81 11, fax 041 72 22 78,* e *grandhoteldeidogi@ italyhotel.com, Fondamenta Madonna dell'Orto 3500)* **Map 3** Singles/doubles up to €284/387.35. A cut above and apart, this hotel stands in splendid isolation right up in the north-west of the city. The rooms are well

A Dogey Death

When Doge Vitale Michiel returned to Venice with the sorry remains of his fleet in May 1172, he must have known things weren't going to go well for him. He had set off in September of the year before with a war fleet of 120 vessels to avenge assaults on Venetians carried out in Constantinople. Unfortunately, he decided to agree to talks.

While his negotiators got bogged down in ultimately fruitless chitchat, his idle fleet at the Greek island of Chios collapsed as plague broke out. By the time it had become clear that Constantinople had no intention of continuing serious negotiations, the fleet was in no condition to fight. And so Michiel had little alternative but to go home – taking the plague with him.

As he gave his sorry report to the assembly in the Palazzo Ducale, he realised from the mounting anger that he would have to flee. He didn't get far. Scampering east along the Riva degli Schiavoni, he was met by the mob and killed. (A conflicting version of events says Michiel was on his way to the Chiesa di San Zaccaria for Mass when he was struck down.)

When things had settled a little, the city's leaders searched for, tried and executed the assassin. If anyone was going to do the killing around here, it was the State. The man's house was found to be at Calle delle Rasse, virtually next to the spot where Michiel met his end, and was flattened. It was decreed that in future no building of stone should be raised on the site. The decree was respected until 1948. When it was finally repealed, the silent vacuum of reproach was filled with the rather Mussolini-esque expansion of the Hotel Danieli, an ugly sister that sits rather uncomfortably beside Palazzo Dandolo, the hotel's main home.

appointed, and if you want luxury while feeling nicely out of the way, this could be the place for you.

Castello

Some of the city's finest hotels are on the Riva degli Schiavoni.

Londra Palace (☎ *041 520 05 33, fax 041 522 50 32,* e *info@hotellondra.it, Riva degli Schiavoni 4171)* **Map 8** Doubles up to €570. Most rooms in this four-star property have views over the water. Renovated in 1998, the rooms feature 19th-century period furniture, jacuzzis and marble bathrooms.

Hotel Danieli (☎ *041 522 64 80, fax 041 520 02 08,* w *www.starwood.com/westin, Riva degli Schiavoni 4196, Castello)* **Map 5** Singles/doubles up to €413/878. Most of the rooms in this top-ranking hotel look out across the water to Santa Maria della Salute and San Giorgio Maggiore. It opened as a hotel in 1822 in the Palazzo Dandolo, built in the 14th century.

Giudecca

Cipriani (☎ *041 520 77 44, fax 041 520 39 30,* e *info@hotelcipriani.it, Giudecca 10)* **Map 7** High-season suites up to €1085. This place is set in the one-time villa of the Mocenigo family and is surrounded by lavish grounds, with unbeatable views across to San Marco. Prices drop considerably in the low season. The hotel runs a private boat from San Marco.

Lido

Villa Mabapa (☎ *041 526 05 90, fax 041 526 94 41,* w *www.villamabapa.com, Riviera San Nicolò 16)* **Map 10** Singles/ doubles up to €182/284. This is a pleasant hideaway handy for the vaporetto stop. A grand old residence, it is frequently booked out in summer and for the cinema festival in September.

Grand Hotel Des Bains (☎ *041 526 59 21, fax 041 526 01 13,* w *www.starwood.com/ sheraton, Lungomare Guglielmo Marconi 17)* **Map 10** Doubles around €400. This is the top address for Thomas Mann fans. Take a room at the 'tale' end of the season to enjoy the fully melancholy effect.

Excelsior (☎ 041 526 02 01, fax 041 526 72 76, W www.starwood.com/westin, Lungomare Guglielmo Marconi 41) **Map 10** Doubles around €475. A fanciful Moorish-style property, this is the top address on the Lido.

LONG-TERM RENTALS

Few of us can afford to hang around even the cheapest hotel indefinitely. You could try cutting a deal for cheaper long-term accommodation in a bed & breakfast or *affittacamere*, private households that rent out rooms and operate more or less as little pensioni.

A cheaper option, but not an easy one to set up, is to share an apartment. In Italy, only students tend to do this, so start by heading to the Università Ca' Foscari notice boards at Calle Larga Foscari in San Polo and next to Chiesa di San Sebastiano in Dorsoduro (both Map 6). You can put up your own ad here. You could also try for an apartment to rent alone. As a rule, it's possible to get a room in a shared place for about €260 a month. To rent even a studio for yourself, you could be looking at €1030. Another approach is to ask small-hotel owners if they know of anything – sometimes they can quickly find a place for you to rent.

Venetian Apartments (☎ 020-8878 1130, fax 8878 0982, W www.venice-rentals.com, 408 Parkway House, Sheen Lane, London SW14 8LS) Two-person apartments from around UK£600 per week. This organisation in the UK arranges accommodation in flats.

You can find many other such dealers on the Web. Online at W www.wotspot.com/venice, you can find flats in the Santa Croce area for as little as €60 per day. Euroflats (W www.ccsrl.com) has flats sleeping up to four from €700 per week. For luxury apartments, you could also try Guest in Italy (W www.guestinitaly.com).

Finally, another route to go might be time-share. You buy time in a property (minimum one week) for annual use. You don't have to use it yourself, but could sublet or simply not bother with it. Theoretically at least, it should be like investing in property – you could sell your share further down the line. Immobiliare Sviluppo (Map 4; ☎ 041 523 01 24, fax 041 522 67 16, W www.perleveneziane.it), Campo dei SS Apostoli, Cannaregio 4438, is a time-share company based in Venice. It calls its programme Perle Veneziane (Venetian Pearls).

PLACES TO STAY

Places to Eat

FOOD

If you've enjoyed the cuisines of Tuscany and Emilia-Romagna, the 'down-home' style of a Roman meal or the Sicilians' gift for seasoned fantasies, you might find the fare in Venice a bit disappointing. Indeed, other Italians tend to be rather disparaging about La Serenissima's attempts in the kitchen, lamenting that *si spende tanto e si mangia male* ('you spend a lot and eat badly'), but then they are rather fastidious about their food. For the rest of us, Venice isn't really that bad. Even that august collective of self-appointed foodies in Italy, Slow Food, have found about 20 places to stick into their annual *Osterie d' Italia* guide. Chowing down in Venice is, however, pricey.

Search out the little eateries tucked away in the side alleys and squares, since many of the restaurants immediately around San Marco, near the train station and along main thoroughfares are tourist traps. Read the fine print if you want to eat seafood, as most fish is sold by weight. When considering a set-price menu, make sure you know whether or not all service charges are included – often they are not.

When to Eat

Breakfast *(colazione)* is generally a quick affair, taken on the hop in a bar on the way to work.

For lunch *(pranzo)*, restaurants usually open from 12.30pm to 3pm, but many are not keen to take orders after 2pm. In the evening, opening hours for dinner *(cena)* vary, but people start sitting down to dine at around 7.30pm. You'll be hard pressed to find a place still serving after 10.30pm.

Cafes and bars, which also serve hot drinks and sandwiches, generally open from 7.30am to 8pm, although some stay open after 8pm and turn into pub-style drinking and meeting places.

Restaurants and bars are generally closed one day each week; the day varies depending on the establishment. Closing days (where applicable) are listed but opening times are only mentioned where they vary substantially from the norm.

Where to Eat

The standard name for a restaurant is *ristorante*. Often you will come across something known as a *trattoria*, a cheaper, simpler version of a ristorante (by tradition, at least). In Venice particularly, you will also come across another phenomenon – the *osteria*, originally a wine bar offering snacks and a small selection of dishes. For specific examples, see the boxed text 'Osteria 'Opping' later in this chapter. The *pizzeria*, however, needs no explanation.

The problem with all this is that nowadays the names seem to have become interchangeable. It would appear that restaurant owners consider it more enticing to punters to call their places osteria (or even *hostaria*, reflecting an olde-worlde approach). Don't judge an eatery by its tablecloth. You may well have your best meal at the dingiest little establishment you can find.

In all cases, it is best to check the menu – usually posted by the door – for prices. Occasionally you will find places with no written menu. This usually means they change their offerings daily. Inside there may be a blackboard or the waiter will tell you what's on – fine if you speak Italian, a little disconcerting if you don't. Try to think of it as a surprise. If you encounter this situation in an overtly touristy area, you should have your rip-off antennae up.

Most eating establishments have a cover charge, ranging from €0.75 up to €5.15. On top of this you have to factor in the service charge of 10% to 15%.

Better areas to look include the back streets of Dorsoduro, Santa Croce, San Polo and Castello.

Where Not to Eat

Feeding tourists second-rate meals is something of a sport in Venice. As a rule, places with a set-price *menù turistico* are to be avoided if you want to eat at all well (see the next section). Places displaying a menu in languages other than Italian can be dodgy too, although that is not always the case. One fairly clear warning sign is whole tour groups chomping together on identical meals – usually a sorry-looking plate of pasta with a tomato sauce, a side order of wilting salad and maybe even chips. Anyone who takes up a waiter/tout's invitation to step inside and enjoy their food deserves everything they get.

The worst areas are in Cannaregio – along the route from the train station towards San Marco – and in the San Marco zone itself. This is not to say you can't find good places in either of these areas – just that they have more than their fair share of bad 'uns.

What to Eat

Breakfast Italians rarely eat a sit-down breakfast. They tend to drink a cappuccino, usually warm (*tiepido*), and eat a croissant (*cornetto*) or other type of pastry (generically known as *pastine*, which elsewhere in northern Italy you'd call *brioches*) while standing at a bar.

Snacks Many bars serve filling snacks with lunch-time and pre-dinner drinks. Most also have a wide range of *panini* (sandwiches or filled bread rolls), with every imaginable filling. *Tramezzi* (sandwich triangles) and huge bread rolls cost from €0.75 to €2.60 if you eat them standing up. You'll also find numerous outlets where you can buy pizza by the slice (*a taglio*).

Another option is to go to an *alimentari* (grocery shop) and ask them to make a *panino* with the filling of your choice. At a *pasticceria* you can buy pastries, cakes and biscuits.

A further alternative are *osterie* (also known in their more straightforward, old-fashioned bar form as *bacari*), a cross between bars and cheap restaurants. They serve local wines by the glass (sometimes known by the traditional name of *ombra*) and snacks (*cicheti*), mostly of the seafood variety. Some also act as restaurants (see the boxed text 'Osteria 'Opping' later in this chapter).

Lunch & Dinner Traditionally, the main meal of the day is lunch, and some shops and businesses close for two or three hours every afternoon to accommodate it.

A full meal will consist of an *antipasto*, which can vary from fried vegetables to a small offering of fried seafood. Next comes the *primo piatto*, generally a pasta or risotto, followed by the *secondo piatto* of meat or fish. This does not usually come with vegetables and Italians will order a vegetable dish (*contorno*) to go with it. Salads (*insalate*) have a strange position in the order here. They are usually ordered as separate dishes and, in some cases, serve as a replacement for the primo piatto – although there is nothing to stop you ordering a salad as a side order to a main (second) course, Italians don't seem to do so as a rule.

Although most restaurants offer a range of desserts, Italians sometimes prefer to round off the meal with fruit then *caffè*, often at a bar on the way back to work.

Numerous restaurants offer a menù turistico or *menù a prezzo fisso*, a set-price lunch costing an average of €10.35 to €15.50 (not including drinks). Generally, choice is limited and the food is breathtakingly unspectacular. Sometimes it's bloody awful. From your taste buds' point of view (and as long as you are not overly hungry), you'd be better off settling for a plate of pasta, some salad and wine at a decent restaurant.

The evening meal, which follows a similar pattern, was traditionally a simpler affair, but habits are changing because of the inconvenience of travelling home or going out for lunch every day.

Note It appears certain culinary stereotypes have gone too far. Many people seem to believe that *parmigiano* (parmesan cheese) should be scattered on top of all pasta dishes, no matter what the sauce. Nothing could be further from the truth. You should never use it with any kind of seafood sauce, for the simple reason that the cheese kills the flavour rather than enhancing it! If your waiter doesn't offer you the cheese, 99 times out of 100 there will be a perfectly good reason for this. It seems some dinner guests feel they are being ripped off if they don't get their parmesan and badger their waiters into providing the cheese against their own better judgment!

Gelato At the tail end of lunch and dinner, you can opt for a house dessert, but at least once or twice you should head for the nearest *gelateria* (ice-cream shop) to round off the meal with a *gelato*, followed perhaps by a *digestivo* (digestive liqueur) at a bar. Italians tend to see ice cream as a summertime treat and/or something for the kids. But that's their problem. Studies published in Italy affirm that a gelato a day can actually be good for you – now that's heartening news!

Food Vocabulary For essential food vocabulary, see the Language chapter at the end of this book.

Venetian Cuisine

Some commentators, such as Venice's own Alvise Zorzi (a historian and writer of some note in the lagoon city), claim that true Venetian cuisine has all but disappeared. Whether or not this is quite accurate is open to debate, and one hopes that Zorzi's faith in the rebirth of interest in good cooking (and eating!) will save any traditions that might have been on the verge of extinction. At any rate, his introduction to *A Tavola Con I Dogi*, an elaborate tome devoted to fine Venetian cuisine, makes interesting reading.

Staples The basic staple in north-eastern Italian cuisine is a humble thing indeed – polenta. This maize-based stodge is to Venetians what couscous is to North Africans. It comes in different forms, although generally it arrives at the table in yellow slabs, lightly grilled. A less common version is made of a fine maize and has the colour and consistency of porridge. By itself, it really is a little sad, but used to soak up sauces and the like during a meal, it can be quite tasty.

No-one could be expected to live on polenta alone. Two dishes form the next basic rung up, not only in Venice but across the Veneto, and you will see them often on the menu. *Risi e bisi* is a kind of risotto broth with

---

In Praise of Polenta

If you have any doubts about what the natives think of polenta, that rather stodgy culinary invention of theirs, just have a read of Carlo Goldoni's 1743 play *La Donna di Garbo*. He considered it important enough to lift it to literary heights, as one character, Rosaura, explains to Arlecchino (Harlequin) how to prepare a slap-up dish of the stuff. Mmm.

---

peas. Despite the often lurid green appearance, it is really very tasty when properly prepared. Sometimes it's served with ham and parmesan cheese. In the Veneto, people take their peas seriously – some towns even stage Pea Parties *(Sagra dei Bisi)*. It takes all sorts.

Perhaps even more common is *pasta e fagioli* (in Venetian dialect, *pasta e fasioi*). This is 'poor' cuisine, a peasant dish *par excellence* that people unable to afford much meat have been munching for centuries. It is not restricted to the Veneto – indeed, you can find it all over Italy and across the Adriatic in the former Yugoslavia. To the basic mix of short pasta, dry fava beans, onion, olive oil and salt and pepper, you can add pretty much what you want to make it more interesting. Other vegetables (carrots, peas, potatoes) and various kinds of sausage and meat are all options.

Snacks & Starters *Cicheti* and *antipasti*, or snacks and starters, are Venetian specialities. A classic snack or starter is *sarde in saor*, sardines fried up in an onion marinade, a favourite since the 13th century. Anything fishy fried up in saor tastes pretty good. The secret is in the saor marinade, which comes out extra tasty with a few pine nuts thrown in. Onions played a big part in traditional Venetian cuisine, especially for those at sea, as a preventative measure against scurvy.

Variations on the *baccalà* (dried cod) theme are also legion. It is good served up with polenta, which absorbs some of the fish's natural saltiness. A classic cod dish is *baccalà mantecato*, cod prepared in garlic and parsley.

Another delicacy, at their best from October to December, are *granseole*, large crabs that live at the bottom of the Mediterranean and the Adriatic. *Cape sante*, or *coquilles St Jacques*, often feature with pasta, but as a snack are fried in olive oil and garlic, with parsley, lemon and a little white wine added at the last minute. *Peoci* (mussels, known as *cozze* in Italian) and other shellfish all feature prominently, and the list of bite-size seafood items served up for cicheti is as long as the sea is deep. The Venetians also tend to have their own names for everything – the best advice is to get in there and pick and choose. Among the meat starters are *cotechino*, a type of pork sausage served up with mustard.

Vegetables fried in breadcrumbs *(verdure fritte)* are also good. A particular Venetian obsession is artichokes (*carciofi* in Italian, *articiochi* in Venetian dialect). If you hang around produce markets, you may well see buckets of carefully cut-out artichoke hearts *(fondi di articiochi)* in water. Locals swear that, fried up with parsley and garlic and accompanied by a slab of steak, articiochi will send your taste buds to heaven.

Primi Piatti Beyond the two classics named above (risi e bisi and pasta e fagioli), you will come across a wide range of first courses, split fairly evenly between risotto and pasta.

Risotto, which is basically a rice-based stew (think of the Spanish paella and you'll begin to get the idea), comes in many varieties in the Veneto. Among the possible ingredients served up with your risotto are mushrooms, courgettes (zucchini), sausage, quail, trout and other seafood, chicken and spring vegetables. Not to be missed is *risotto nero*, coloured and flavoured with the ink of cuttlefish *(seppia)*. Many restaurants that offer risotto will only serve it to a minimum of two people. So, yet again, the lone traveller gets it in the neck.

One thing to note about pasta is that only a few types really have any long standing in the Venetian tradition. In Venetian restaurants today, you can eat good pasta first courses, but often they have their origins in other regions. So although *spaghetti alle vongole* (spaghetti with clams) may be a delicious dish and readily available in many restaurants, it's not Venetian. In fact, it's Neapolitan.

One type of pasta that is Venetian is *bigoli*, a kind of rough, thick spaghetti. Its texture makes it ideal for seafood sauces, which stick to it better than to other pastas. A classic is bigoli or spaghetti *alla busara* – with scampi and a very mild red sauce. Unfortunately, if you talk to the Milanese about bigoli they will giggle like school kids – for them, a bigolo is slang for a boy's naughty bit. Gnocchi, made of potato, are strictly speaking a Veronese speciality, but have been absorbed into the Venetian tradition.

Among the soups, the best known is *sopa de pesse* (which in Italian is *zuppa di pesce*, fish soup). When it's good, it's very good – especially on a cold winter's night.

Secondi Piatti Seafood is popular but also often expensive. Remember that the prices you see for some fish are price per *etto* (100g). Look at the fine print – otherwise you might get an unpleasant surprise. The cost of fresh fish is high, so cheap fish meals generally mean frozen fish is used.

Try seppia with polenta. The most common fish types you will be offered include *branzino* (sea bass; good when boiled), *orata* (bream) and *sogliola* (sole). *Masanete* and *moleche* are variations on the crab theme (both of which just translate to *granchio* in Italian).

Those not keen on seafood will on occasion be frustrated in Venice, as many osterie and restaurants specialise in watery delights and offer few, and in some cases no, meat alternatives.

This is not to say meat dishes do not exist. Of land-going critters, pork and its derivatives figure high in the more traditional foods, along with items such as liver *(fegato)* and even spleen (*milza*; an acquired taste) or cow udder *(mammella di vacca)*. Don't worry – all the more standard cuts of beef *(manzo)*, lamb *(agnello)*, veal *(vitello)* and so on are available. Or try boiled meats with bitter red lettuce *(radicchio trevisano)* eaten baked, in risotto or with pasta.

If you were to try only one meat dish in Venice that you had never had before (or even if you had), it would have to be *carpaccio*. We all know that the Bellini was invented in Harry's Bar (see the boxed text 'The Cocktail Circuit' later in this chapter), but less well known is that the idea to serve up plates of very finely sliced raw beef in a simple sauce was also 'cooked up' chez Cipriani. The sauce is a mix of mayonnaise, crushed tomato, cream, mustard and a dash of Worcestershire sauce. The Ciprianis named it after Vittore Carpaccio, because at the time the artist was the subject of a big exhibition in Venice. A common variation on the theme sees the beef slices bathed in lemon, *rucola* (rocket) and shavings of *grana* cheese.

Dolci Apart from the classic gelato (see the earlier What to Eat section), you will find no shortage of house desserts *(dolci)*.

Tiramisù, a rich dessert with mascarpone, is a favourite here, and supposedly originated in Venice. All sorts of light biscuits have also been dreamed up over the centuries in Venice – start looking in cake-shop windows. They come with such names as *baicoli*, *ossi da morto* and *bigarani* and are supposed to be taken with dessert wine.

In Venice, more than elsewhere in Italy, you may well be offered *sorbetto* (a lemon sorbet) at the end of the main course. It is designed to clean your palate before dessert, but for many makes a good dessert on its own account. An alcoholic version with vodka and a dash of milk, called a *sgroppino*, will be more to the liking of some.

Foreign Cuisine
The availability of non-Italian cuisine in Venice is conspicuous by its almost total absence, aside from the ubiquitous Chinese option.

Among the restaurants listed in this chapter you will notice one Indian place, a couple of Arab spots, a burritos option and sushi. That's about as far as it goes here.

Vegetarian Food
Vegetarian restaurants as such seem nonexistent in Venice. This may not cause huge problems, as many starters, pasta dishes and side orders *(contorni)* are all-vegetable affairs.

(Osteria La Zucca, in particular, has wonderful and generous contorni – see Santa Croce & San Polo in the Budget section later in this chapter.)

DRINKS
Nonalcoholic
Water While tap water is reliable, most Italians prefer bottled mineral water *(acqua minerale)*. It comes either sparkling *(frizzante* or *gasata)* or still *(naturale)*, and you will be asked in restaurants and bars which you prefer. If you want a glass of tap water, ask for *acqua dal rubinetto*.

Coffee The first-time visitor to Italy is likely to be confused by the many ways in which the locals consume their caffeine. As in other Latin countries, Italians take their coffee seriously. Consequently they also make it complicated!

First, there's a pure and simple *espresso* – a small cup of very strong black coffee. A *doppio espresso* is a double shot of the same. You could also ask for a *caffè lungo*, but this may end up being more like the watered-down, instant version with which foreigners will be more familiar. If you want to be quite sure of getting the watery version, ask for a *caffè Americano*.

Enter the milk. A *caffellatte* is coffee with a reasonable amount of milk. To most locals, it is a breakfast drink only. The stronger version is a *caffè macchiato*, basically an espresso with a dash of milk. Alternatively, you can have *latte macchiato*, a glass of hot milk with a dash of coffee. *Cappuccino* is a frothy version of caffè latte. You can ask for it *senza schiuma* (without the froth, which is scraped off the top). It tends to come lukewarm, so if you want it hot, ask for it to be *molto caldo*.

In summer, the local version of an iced coffee is a *caffè freddo*, a long glass with cold coffee, sometimes helped along with ice cubes.

To warm up on those winter nights, a *corretto* might be for you – an espresso 'corrected' with a dash of *grappa* (grape liqueur) or some other spirit. Some locals have it first thing in the morning.

After lunch and dinner it wouldn't occur to Italians to order either caffè latte or cappuccino – espresso, macchiato and corretto are perfectly acceptable. Of course, if you want a cappuccino, there's no problem – but you might have to repeat your request a couple of times to convince the disbelieving waiters that they have heard correctly.

An espresso or macchiato can cost from an Italy-wide standard of €0.70 or €0.75 standing at a bar to €1.55 sitting at your average outside table. Along the Grand Canal

(around Ponte di Rialto) the price will be more like €2.60, and expect €5.15 or more in a place such as Caffè Florian on St Mark's Square.

Tea Italians don't drink a lot of tea *(tè)* and then generally only in the late afternoon, when they might take a cup with a few *pasticcini* (small cakes). You can order tea in bars, although it will usually arrive in the form of a cup of warm water with an accompanying tea bag. If this doesn't suit your taste, ask for the water *molto caldo* or *bollente* (boiling). Good-quality packaged teas, such as Twinings tea bags and leaves, as well as packaged herbal teas, such as camomile, are often sold in alimentari (grocery stores) and sometimes in bars. You can find a wide range of herbal teas in a herbalist's shop *(erboristeria)*, which will sometimes also stock health foods.

Granita *Granita* is a drink made of crushed ice with fresh lemon or other fruit juices. In origin, it is a Sicilian speciality, but you'll see it in Venice in the summer months. It's not like the old days, though, when you could get delicious hand-crushed granita. Nowadays, it's all standard mass-produced stuff.

Soft Drinks The usual range of international soft drinks is available in Venice, although they tend to be expensive. There are some local versions too, along with the rather bitter Chinotto, an acquired taste.

Alcoholic

Beer The main Italian brands are Peroni, Dreher and Moretti, all very drinkable and cheaper than the imported varieties. Italy imports beers from throughout Europe and the rest of the world. Several German beers, for instance, are available in bottles or cans; English beers and Guinness are often found on tap *(alla spina)* in *birrerie* (bars specialising in beer). You can even find Australia's XXXX, if you are so inclined. The UK and Irish cause is being spread with the growth of the pseudo-Irish-pub phenomenon, to which not even Venice is immune.

The Cocktail Circuit

Back in the 1950s, behind the bar at Harry's, a new sensation was born. It was deceptively simple – mix *prosecco* (bubbly white wine) with peach nectar, and you have a Bellini. Of course, they will tell you there is more to it than that – the quality of the ingredients and, more importantly, the proportions. Whatever – it is good.

You don't have to shell out the €11.90 for one at Harry's Bar, as Bellinis and other cocktails are popular at *aperitivo* time (that loose early-evening, pre-dinner period) all over town. Still, if you can afford a drink or two at Harry's, it's worth it. Apart from the Bellini they do some other mean mixes. These guys have been practising the art of the Martini for as long as they have been open.

Truman Capote called a good Martini a Silver Bullet. What's in it? Good gin and a drop of Martini Dry. But of course the amount of the latter varies according to taste. For a strong, dry Martini, 'rinse' the glass with Martini and then pour in freezing gin. Hemingway, who set part of his book *Across the River and into the Trees* at Harry's, had his own recipe – pour freezing-cold gin into a glass dipped in ice and sit it next to a bottle of Martini for a moment before drinking!

More emblematic of everyday Venice is the *spritz*. This is one part sparkling white wine, one part soda water and one part bitter (Campari, Amaro, Aperol or Select), topped with a slice of lemon and, if you wish, an olive. They say this drink dates from the days of the Austrian occupation in the 19th century.

Wine Wine *(vino)* is an essential accompaniment to any Italian meal. Italians are justifiably proud of their wines and it would be surprising for dinner-time conversation not to touch on the subject, at least for a moment.

Prices are reasonable and you will rarely pay more than €8 for a good bottle of wine, although they can range up to more than €20 for the better stuff. Wine tends to be more expensive in Venice than elsewhere in Italy because of added transport costs.

Wine is graded according to three main classifications – DOCG *(denominazione d'origine controllata e garantita)*, DOC *(denominazione d'origine controllata)* and table wine *(vino da tavola)* – which are marked on the label. A DOC wine is produced subject to certain specifications, although the label does not certify quality. DOCG is subject to the same requirements as normal DOC, but it is also tested by government inspectors for quality.

Your average trattoria will generally stock only a limited range of bottled wines, but quite a few of the better restaurants (some of which are listed in this chapter) offer a carefully chosen selection of wines from around the country. Most people order the house wine *(vino della casa)* or the local wine *(vino locale)* when they go out to dinner and generally this is perfectly OK.

For fairly obvious reasons, Venice itself produces no wines. Nor is the Veneto Italy's prime wine-making region. That said, some good ones are produced around Verona, including Soave (white), Valpolicella (red) and Bardolino (red and rosé). Nosiola, another white, is not bad. The Vicenza area is also dotted with wineries. Wines from the Friuli-Venezia Giulia area, Italy's easternmost region, are often good and are readily available. The Pinot Grigio (white) and Pinot Nero (red) are both promising.

A Venetian wanting a quick drink in a bar will quite likely ask for a *prosecco*, a lightly bubbly white wine, produced all over the Veneto. The average price is €1.30. Otherwise, a simple ombra of local house *bianco* (white) or *rosso* (red) will do.

Another regional curiosity is the very sweet *fragolino*. This strawberry-flavoured red isn't strictly wine and cannot be sold as such commercially, though you'll occasionally come across it in bars in Venice and elsewhere in the Veneto. You can sometimes find a white version too. You can be fairly sure you are drinking the real thing if it is served in unlabelled bottles. Many stores have taken to selling a fizzy 'wine' they call fragolino. This is a travesty – it is little more than poor wine with strawberry flavouring added – it is *not* the real McCoy (if it were, they couldn't sell it).

Liquors & Liqueurs For an after-dinner digestivo, try a shot of grappa, a strong, clear brew made from grapes. It comes from the nearby Grappa region, on the mainland. Or you could go for an *amaro*, a dark liqueur prepared from herbs. If you prefer a sweeter liqueur, try an almond-flavoured *amaretto* or the sweet aniseed *sambuca*.

PLACES TO EAT – BUDGET

One diner's idea of a budget meal will be the next guy's once-a-month splurge, so it's a little difficult to come up with a hard-and-fast category. The bad news is that truly dirt-cheap places are thin on the ground.

This category covers you up to around €26 – you could easily spend more at most of these places, which thus could equally be considered mid-range. On the other hand, if you stick to one course and a side order, combined with house wine, you can often get away with spending around €15.50 or less, which also goes for many places listed as mid-range.

At lunch time, in particular, sticking to pizzas or other snacks, such as sandwiches, can save you loads. The average panino, often with ham, cheese and salad, and a can of pop may cost you around €6.70 – a filling and inexpensive way to kill midday growls. You can stick to the pizza formula at night (the average pizza will cost from €4 to €10 depending on place and size of pizza). By the slice it is cheaper still.

By the way, when looking at menus and working out what you might spend, remember that almost invariably you will pay separately for vegetables or salad to go with your main course. So a main advertised at €11 will be more like €15 when you add in some vegetables.

A final tip if you are scrimping and scraping but would like to splurge is that you can save pennies by cutting down on the frills. A post-prandial cup of coffee in a restaurant will cost double or more than you would pay for the same thing at a bar across the street. The same goes for dessert. If you want gelato, go to a gelateria – the walk will do you good anyway!

Restaurants, Cafes & Bars

San Marco *Ai Rusteghi (☎ 041 523 22 05, Calletta della Bissa 5529)* **Map 5** Snacks around €1.55-2.60. Open 9.30am-3pm & 5pm-8.30pm Mon-Sat. For a great range in mini-panini, pop into this place. They also offer good wines. There's nothing better than an ombra or two and a couple of panini as a quick lunch-time snack.

Vino Vino (☎ 041 523 70 27, Calle del Cafetier, San Marco 2007) **Map 5** Pasta or risotto €5.65, mains €8.25, sarde in saor €8.25. Open Wed-Mon. This is a popular bar/osteria at Ponte Veste, near Teatro La Fenice. The menu changes daily and the pre-prepared food is of a reasonable quality. There is a good selection of vegetables. Wine is sold by the glass for €1.05.

Osteria al Bacareto (☎ 041 528 93 36, San Marco 3447) **Map 6** Meals around €23. Open Mon-Fri. The search for a good traditional trattoria in this corner of San Marco is over when you reach Al Bacareto. Since it doubles as an osteria, you can opt for a plateful of cicheti with a glass of wine.

Dorsoduro *Osteria da Toni (☎ 041 528 68 99, Fondamenta di San Basilio 1642)* **Map 6** Meals around €21. Open Tues-Sun. This is a popular workers' haunt. You can eat great seafood at relatively low prices or just sip wine. When the sun shines, take your place by the canal.

Trattoria ai Cugnai (☎ 041 528 92 38, Piscina Forner 857) **Map 6** Meals around €26 per person. Open Tues-Sun. This is a simple little place with solid home cooking – their various soups are great in winter.

Arca (☎ 041 524 22 36, Calle San Pantalon 3757) **Map 6** Pizza & pasta €4.65-7.75. Open Mon-Sat. There's live music Tuesday nights, usually of a light jazz variety to accompany the cheap and cheerful chow, which attracts a predominantly student clientele.

Trattoria Dona Onesta (☎ 041 71 05 86, Calle Dona Onesta 3922) **Map 6** Pasta €5.15-6.20, mains €6.20-12.40. This is a straightforward eatery with no frills. The food is OK but the main attraction is the modesty in price.

Santa Croce & San Polo This is a great area for small, cosy places to eat.

Trattoria al Ponte (☎ 041 71 97 77, Ponte del Megio 1666) **Map 3** Meals around €26. Open Mon-Fri & lunch Sat. Arrive early here and try to grab one of the few canalside tables. This simple, down-home little eatery tends to specialise in fish, but other options are available. The food is solid and the prices reasonable.

Osteria La Zucca (☎ 041 524 15 70, Calle del Tintor 1762) **Map 3** Meals €31. Open Mon-Sat. Just over the bridge, this is an excellent alternative. It seems like just another Venetian trattoria, but the menu (which changes daily) is an enticing mix of Mediterranean themes. The vegetable side orders (€3.60) alone are inspired (try the *peperonata alle melanzane*, a cool stew of capsicum and aubergine), while the mains (around €10) are substantial. You won't need to order pasta (€6.20) as well, and that will bring the cost down.

PLACES TO EAT

Old Well Pub (☎ *041 524 27 60, Corte Canal 656)* **Map 3** Pizzas from €5.15. Open daily. The good thing about this place is that the pizzas are decent and the kitchen is open late by local standards – you can eat as late as midnight (and drink until 2am)!

Cannaregio Numerous bars along the main thoroughfare between the train station and San Marco serve sandwiches and snacks.

For restaurants, it is best to head for the side streets to look for little trattorias and pizzerias, but there are a couple of OK spots on the main thoroughfare.

La Colombina (☎ *041 275 06 22, Campiello del Pegolotto 1828, Cannaregio)* **Map 3** Meals around €31. Open Tues-Sat. An excellent wine list (including a few foreign drops) accompanies a delicious range of dishes and snacks. Ownership changed in September 2001, so the verdict remains open.

Gam Gam (☎ *041 71 52 84, Calle del Ghetto Vecchio 1123)* **Map 3** Pasta around €7.75, mains €12.90. Open noon-10pm Sun-Thur & lunch Fri. Gam Gam is great for your taste buds if you like Israeli-style falafels and other Middle-Eastern delicacies. This place is fully kosher and presents a diverse menu, ranging from Red Sea spaghetti to couscous (with choice of meat, fish or vegetable sauce) and from houmous to that arch-Venetian side order of *fondi di carciofi* (artichoke hearts).

Da Marisa (☎ *041 72 02 11, Fondamenta San Giobbe 652/b)* **Map 3** Meals around €26. They are not especially fond of tourists here so you may need to work up some Italian credentials to squeeze in. For all that, it's a great low-price eating experience in Venice and worth the effort.

Anice Stellato (☎ *041 72 07 44, Fondamenta della Sensa, Cannaregio 3272)* **Map 3** Meals €31. Open Tues-Sun. Awaiting you in the guise of a doorman is a huge wine *damigiana* (demijohn) by the entrance. Inside, the heavy timber tables and wooden chairs seemingly invite a chatty, convivial meal. The pasta dishes are excellent and the mains imaginative, including the occasional use of curry and other spices not immediately associated with either local or national cuisine.

Fondamenta della Misericordia is something of a foodies' street where locals crowd into several trattorias and bars.

Paradiso Perduto (☎ *041 72 05 81, Fondamenta della Misericordia 2539)* **Map 3** Meals around €21. Open Mon, Tues & Thur-Sat. Young people will enjoy this restaurant/bar, which has live music and tables outside in summer. The *lasagna ai carciofi* (artichoke lasagne) is great and the bar snacks are also enticing. It gets pretty packed.

Sahara (☎ *041 72 10 77, Fondamenta della Misericordia 2520)* **Map 3** Mains €9.30. Open Tues-Sun. For a Middle-Eastern touch, try this place. It serves up good Syrian food and you can even clap along to a not-so-authentic display of belly dancing.

Iguana (☎ *041 71 35 61, Fondamenta della Misericordia 2515)* **Map 3** Burritos, quesadillas & tacos €4.15-7.25. Open 6pm-1am Tues-Sat. You could opt for the Tex-Mex flavour at this, Venice's first Latin-American experiment, next door to Sahara. The low, wood-beam ceiling makes for a warm atmosphere, plus the food is OK and moderately priced.

Pizzeria Casa Mia (☎ *041 28 55 90, Calle dell'Oca 4430)* **Map 4** Pizzas €3.85-€6.20, pasta around €6.20, mains around €13. Open Wed-Mon. Venice is covered in pizzerias but this welcoming little place, hidden just out of sight of the hubbub, is a good spot for generous pizzas prepared the way they should be.

Ostaria al Ponte (☎ *041 528 61 57, Calle Larga G Gallina 6378)* **Map 4** Open 8am-3.30pm & 4.30pm-8.30pm Mon-Sat. On the 'frontier' with Sestiere di Castello is this aptly named and highly recommended snack bar. It is a rather tiny spot where you can nibble on cicheti and indulge in good wines.

Castello *Al Vecchio Penasa* (☎ *041 523 72 02, Calle delle Rasse, Castello 4587)* **Map 5** Sandwiches €1.30. Open 6.30am-11.30pm. Between Riva degli Schiavoni and Campo SS Filippo e Giacomo, this remains a good spot for its excellent selection of sandwiches and snacks at reasonable prices.

Alla Rivetta (☎ *041 528 73 02, Ponte San Provolo 4625)* **Map 5** Mains €9.30-11.35.

Open Tues-Sun. This is one of the few restaurants near St Mark's Square that is recommended. It has long been on the tourist list of musts as a place to eat, but you can still get edible seafood for not unreasonable prices.

Trattoria agli Artisti (☎ *041 277 02 90, Ruga Giuffa 4625*) **Map 5** Set menu up to €14.45. Open Thur-Tues. For cheap and cheerful food, this trattoria is an acceptable stop. It has two set menus, and you can't complain about the prices!

Trattoria da Remigio (☎ *041 523 00 89, Salizzada dei Greci 3416*) **Map 8** Pasta €5.15, mains €7.75-13. Open Wed-Sun & lunch Mon. It is not often you find a restaurant that in the early evening can post a sign in the window saying *completo* (full), as though it were a hotel, but this place can. It has a mixed menu, featuring Venetian fish dishes and some meat options. It's clearly busy and you'll need to book to be sure of a spot.

Tokyo Sushi Restaurant (☎ *041 277 04 20, Calle Casselleria 5281*) **Map 5** Sushi around €10. Don't get too excited as this is not the best sushi you will ever eat. It is, however, about the *only* sushi you'll find in Venice. And that's about all we can say.

Hostaria da Franz (☎ *041 522 08 61, Fondamenta San Giuseppe 755*) **Map 9** Meals about €36-46.50. Open Wed-Mon. If you end up in the eastern end of Castello, past the Arsenale, you will be in a distinct minority. The only spot in this neighbourhood really worth considering is this homely place. It specialises in crustaceous creatures.

Ristorante Paradiso (☎ *041 523 11 66, Castello 1260*) **Map 9** Pasta €6.20, mains €8.25. Open Tues-Sun. This restaurant-cum-snack-bar is best for a soothing drink or quick bite while wandering around the green tranquillity of this end of Venice. You can also sit down to a full meal of average quality.

Sant'Elena *Trattoria dal Pampo* (☎ *041 520 84 19, Calle Gen Chinotto*) **Map 9** Meals around €23. Open Sat-Thur. This is a real locals' place for wine and snacks, but you can also sit down and have a full meal. Set opposite a charming little park in this, the quietest end of the city, it comes well recommended.

Giudecca *Ai Tre Scaini* (☎ *041 522 47 90, Calle Michelangelo 53/c*) **Map 7** Meals with wine about €23. Open noon-2.30pm & 6pm-1am Mon-Sat. This is *the* popular local eatery. It's a no-nonsense place for seafood and other goodies and you can dine in the garden out the back.

Lido *Trattoria da Scarso* (☎ *041 77 08 34, Piazzale Malamocco 4*) **Off Map 10** Average meal approximately €26. Open Tues-Sun. This is a simple trattoria with a pleasant pergola. Set in the tiny old Venetian settlement of Malamocco, it isn't too heavily frequented by *foresti* (foreigners). Local colour alone makes it an attractive stop.

Murano *Osteria dalla Mora* (☎ *041 527 46 06, Fondamenta Manin 75*) **See Map p154** Meals around €28. Open Sat-Thur. This place looks out over one of the island's canals and is worth considering for lunch or dinner. The *frittura mista*, or mixed fried seafood dish, is a popular request.

Chioggia Several options suggest themselves in central Chioggia, all just off or near Corso del Popolo.

Ristorante Vecio Foghero (☎ *041 40 46 79, Calle Scopici 91*) Meals around €21. Open Wed-Mon. This place has good pizzas and seafood. The *tagliolini al salmone* (ribbon pasta with salmon sauce, €6.20) is tempting. It is one of a few cheap restaurant options that puts its Venetian counterparts to shame, at least in relative terms of quality and wallet damage.

Ostaria da Pupi (☎ *041 40 47 95, Calle Fattorini 255*) Meals around €23. Open Tues-Sun. This ostaria is another good one to look for. They have half-a-dozen tables in air-con comfort upstairs and another five on the lane. The limited seafood menu is good. Try the *tagliolini al granchio* (ribbon pasta with crab, €5.15) followed by a *grigliata mista* (mixed seafood grill, €12.90).

Ristorante El Fontego (☎ *041 550 09 53, Piazzetta XX Settembre 497*) Meals €23. Open Tues-Sun. The setting here is a little brassier but equally popular. The restaurant offers a broad range of vegetarian and 'cream

PLACES TO EAT

pizzas' (with a brie cheese base, €7.25). Actually, they're not bad. They also have vegetarian pizzas for €6.20.

Osteria Penzo *(☎ 041 40 09 92, Calle Larga Bersaglio 526)* Meals around €26 excluding wine. Open Wed-Mon. Once, all you would get here was wine and basic snacks, but now staff prepare good local dishes based entirely on the fleet's catch.

Mestre *Da Bepi Venesian* *(☎ 041 92 93 57, Via Sernaglia 27)* **Map 11** Meals around €26. Open Tues-Sun. A couple of blocks from the train station, Da Bepi serves traditional dishes. The place is huge – with four dining areas – and specialises in fish. Try the *seppie con polenta* (cuttlefish with polenta).

Osteria La Pergola *(☎ 041 97 49 32, Via Fiume 42)* **Map 11** Meals under €21. Open Mon-Fri & dinner Sat. At this osteria you could be served a delicious plate of *pappardelle all'anatra* (thick ribbon pasta with duck) below the vines of the garden pergola.

Chains

Those on a tight budget, in particular, may want to keep an eye out for these cheaper eateries. Several Italian firms have taken the fast-food concept and put a local spin on it. The result is a cut way above the McDonald's of this world (we have indicated one of these in Cannaregio, on Map 4, for those who need a fix – three others lurk in Sestiere San Marco and one at Mestre train station), at an affordable price.

Brek *(☎ 041 244 01 58, Rio Terrà Lista di Spagna 124)* **Map 3** 1st/2nd courses about €3.35/5.15. Open 7.30am-10.30pm daily. If you have to do cheap fast-ish food, you could do a lot worse than take a break here. For what you pay, the grub's not bad – light years from hamburgers and hotdogs! The restaurant area is open normal hours for lunch and dinner but you can get snacks at the bar all day. There is another branch in Mestre *(Via Carducci 54)* **Map 11**.

Spizzico *(Campo San Luca 4475–6)* **Map 5** Pizza slices around €3.10. Open 9am-11pm, sometimes closed Sun. For quick slices of pizza, this place isn't bad – the chain is quite popular across northern

Italy. If you want burgers instead, a ***Burger King*** is located on the same premises.

Self-Catering

Making your own snacks is the cheapest way to keep body and soul together. The best ***markets*** take place on the San Polo side of the Ponte di Rialto (Map 8).

For salami, cheese and wine, shop in alimentari or *salumerie*, which are a cross between grocery stores and delicatessens. Fresh bread is available at a *forno* or *panetteria* (bakeries which sell bread, pastries and sometimes groceries) and usually at alimentari. You'll find a concentration of these around Campo Beccarie, which happens to lie next to the city's main fish market (Map 4).

Standa Supermarket *(Strada Nuova, Cannaregio)* **Map 3** Open 9am-7.30pm daily. This supermarket is a reasonably well-stocked option for self-caterers.

Billa Supermarket *(Fondamenta Zattere al Ponte Lungo)* **Map 6** Open 8.30am-8pm Mon-Sat, 9am-8pm Sun. Near the Stazione Marittima, this is a big place where you can stock up before hitting the high seas for Greece.

Coop Supermarket *(Rio Terrà dei SS Apostoli 4662, Cannaregio)* **Map 4** Open 9am-1pm & 4pm-7.30pm Mon-Sat. This is also a good place to hunt for nutrients and other useful items.

Mini-Coop *(Campo San Giacomo dell' Orio 1492)* **Map 3** Open 9am-1pm & 4pm-7.30pm Mon-Sat. This is another option for self-caterers.

PLACES TO EAT – MID-RANGE

We take this to mean a fairly broad range, up to around €55 per head. By London standards, for instance, this is not an unreasonable sum to pay, especially if the chow on offer is good. If you've landed in Venice from the USA or Australasia and haven't acclimatised your purse to the European fiscal free-for-all, this may seem a little shocking. Such is life.

Restaurants, Cafes & Bars

San Marco *Ristorante da Ivo* *(☎ 041 528 50 04, San Marco 1809)* **Map 5** Meals

€46.50-51.65. Open Mon-Sat. This Venice dining classic specialises in seafood as well as offering a mix of Venetian and Tuscan meat dishes. Consequently it's not cheap – depending on your choices from the menu, the bill could easily top the €55 mark.

Ristorante ai Barbacani (☎ *041 521 02 34, Calle del Paradiso 5746)* **Map 5** Set lunch menu €18, mains €15.50. Open Tues-Sun. This restaurant, right by a canal bridge, is a delightful spot if you can grab a waterside seat – but don't fall in! As for the food, it's fine without being Venice's best.

Ristorante al Gazzettino (☎ *041 522 33 14, San Marco 4971)* **Map 5** Meals around €36. Open Tues-Sun. Since 1953, this restaurant, below the *pensione* (small hotel) of the same name, has been a well-known favourite in central Venice. Until 1977, journos and printers from *Il Gazzettino* newspaper, then based in the nearby Ca' Faccanon, made it their regular. As if in tribute to the good ol' days, the present owners have plastered the walls with pages from *Il Gazzettino* past – if you can read Italian, you'll find it hard not to let your food go cold.

Dorsoduro *L'Incontro* (☎ *041 522 24 04, Rio Terrà Canal 3062)* **Map 6** Meals around €26. Open 12.30pm-3pm & 7.30pm-1am Tues-Sun. Typical regional fare is served at this place, between Campo San Barnaba and Campo Santa Margherita. The menu alters daily.

Osteria ai Carmini (☎ *041 523 11 15, Calle delle Pazienze 2894/a)* **Map 6** Meals around €31. Open 9.30am-11pm Mon-Sat. For fresh fish and seafood, this is one of the best spots to seek out around Campo Santa Margherita.

Riviera (☎ *041 522 76 21, Fondamenta Zattere al Ponte Lungo 1473)* **Map 6** Meals around €36. Open Tues-Sun lunch. Sit by candlelight on the promenade that looks across to Giudecca, and dine on good seafood cooking. Or you can drop by for breakfast.

Santa Croce & San Polo *Trattoria alla Madonna* (☎ *041 522 38 24, Calle della Madonna, San Polo 594)* **Map 5** Meals from €31. Open Thur-Tues. This place, which is

a few streets west of the Rialto off Fondamenta del Vin, is an excellent trattoria specialising in seafood. Prices are reasonable.

Al Nono Risorto (☎ *041 524 11 69, Sotoportego de Siora Bettina)* **Map 3** Pasta around €7.75, mains €12.90-16.50. Open Thur-Tues. Stop in here if only to luxuriate in the canalside garden. This is a good place for pizza (up to €7.75) or you could opt for the lunch-time *menu del giorno* at €15.

Vecio Fritolin (☎ *041 522 28 81, Calle della Regina 226)* **Map 3** Set lunch menu €21.70, pasta €12.90, mains €18. Open Tues-Sat & Sun lunch. A *fritolin* traditionally was an eatery where diners sat at a common table bedecked with bits of fried seafood and polenta and simply dug in (or they wrapped it up in paper and took it away, a tradition that goes back to the early 1800s). Things have greatly changed since the place came under new management in 2000. You can now sit down to meticulous cooking, with local and Italian dishes. The *pappardelle con scampi e fagioli* (thick ribbon pasta with prawns and white beans) is an enticing first course. The quality is high and the service friendly. With the fish and produce markets of Rialto close by, you can be sure of the freshness of the ingredients.

Ganesh Ji (☎ *041 71 90 84, Fondamenta Rio Marin, San Polo 2426)* **Map 3** Set menu €22.20. Open Thur-Tues. Fancy a quick curry? Forget it. But a good slow one can be had on the pleasant little canalside terrace of

Light on the Heart of Darkness

If you pass under the *sotoportego* (a street that continues under a building) to the east of the Vecio Fritolin, you'll notice on the left an altar in the wall. In fact, you may already have seen them scattered about town; there are some 500 in all. Their purpose was not just to encourage passers-by to stop for a moment of prayer and contemplation. Apart from helping to bring light to the darkness of tormented souls, the candles or oil lamps kept alight in the altars also served as a form of street lighting in medieval times.

this place. Danilo and his charmingly chaotic staff serve up authentic dishes at reasonable prices – particularly pleased guests have scribbled their appreciation on the walls. They even do takeaways.

Cannaregio *Fiaschetteria Toscana (☎ 041 528 52 81, Calle Grisostomo 5719)* **Map 4** Full meals around €46.50. Open Wed-Sun & lunch Mon. This is about as Tuscan as a gondola. Rather they serve up solid Venetian food to be washed down with a choice of wines from an impressive list which includes tipples from around the country. The *frittura della Serenissima*, a mixed fried seafood platter, is memorable.

Trattoria al Vagon (☎ 041 523 75 88, Cannaregio 5596) **Map 4** Meals around €36. Open Wed-Mon. This trattoria, overlooking the Rio dei SS Apostoli, is wonderful for its canalside dining under the porticoes. The food is OK without being spectacular and the prices are a little elevated – you're paying for the location rather than the salivation here.

Vini da Gigio (☎ 041 528 51 40, Fondamenta della Chiesa 3628/a) **Map 4** Meals around €41.30. Open Tues-Sun. This is a wine-drinker's home away from heaven. A selection of fine whites and reds from the Veneto and beyond (ranging from €18 to €31 a bottle) help wash down some fine cooking – how about the *gnocchi con burro fuso e ricotta affumicata* (little dumplings bathed in melted butter and smoked ricotta cheese)?

Osteria alla Frasca (☎ 041 528 54 33, Corte della Carità 5176) **Map 4** Meals around €41. The dishes on offer are fairly standard, favouring seafood, and a smidgen pricey for what you get. However, the setting, with tables spilling out into the charming campiello rarely touched by tourist

---

Osteria 'Opping

Venice's *osterie* (aka *bacari*) are a cross between bars and *trattorie* (cheap restaurants), where you can sample *cicheti* (small finger-food snacks such as stuffed olives and vegetables deep-fried in batter), washed down with an *ombra* (glass of wine). They say the name, which means 'shade', comes from the days when people would go to stands set up in the shade in the local square for an afternoon tipple. Locals often bar hop from osteria to osteria, munching cicheti as they go. It's a great way for visitors to experience a more down-to-earth side of Venice. Some osterie serve full meals.

Enoteca Il Volto (☎ 041 522 89 45, Calle Cavalli 4081, San Marco) **Map 5** Open Mon-Sat. Near Campiello San Luca, this spot has an excellent wine selection and good snacks.

Cantina Do Mori (☎ 041 522 54 01, Sotoportego dei do Mori 429, San Polo) **Map 4** Open Mon-Sat. Hidden away near the Ponte di Rialto, this is something of a traditional institution. Unfortunately, the local consensus is that the prices have gone up unreasonably. Shame, because it is an enticing place, oozing history and still attracting a lot of local custom for such items as its *francobolli* ('stamps'), tiny little stuffed bread snacks.

Cantina Do Spade (☎ 041 521 05 74, Calle do Spade 860, San Polo) **Map 3** Meals €31. Open Mon-Sat. Welcome to Venice's oldest eating house, where the emphasis is more on the full meals than hanging about the bar for snacks.

All'Arco (☎ 041 520 56 66, Calle dell'Arco 436, San Polo) **Map 4** Open Mon-Sat. If what you were looking for around here was cicheti and a glass or two of wine, then All'Arco, a few steps away from Cantina Do Spade, is the place for you.

Osteria alla Patatina (☎ 041 523 72 38, Calle Saoneri 2741/a, San Polo) **Map 6** Open Mon-Fri & lunch Sat. Here is a straight-up-and-down local eatery where the cicheti are tasty and the simple first courses go down well with a glass of red or two. It retains a traditional air.

Al Prosecco (☎ 041 524 02 22, Campo San Giacomo dell'Orio 1503, Santa Croce) **Map 3** Open Mon-Sat. Al Prosecco is the ideal place to prop up the bar and load up on cicheti, washing them down with, well, the bubbly white wine *prosecco*.

caravans, is a winner. The locals like it too and you'll often see a few chatting over a glass of wine.

Castello *Al Covo* (☎ *041 522 38 12, Campiello della Pescaria 3968*) **Map 8** Mains over €13, meals around €41, set lunch €30. Open Fri-Tues. Closer to the centre of things is this place. Anyone who can afford to shut their doors twice a week must feel pretty confident about their product. Al Covo has quite a name among Venetians and the cuisine is resolutely local. Credit cards are not accepted.

Trattoria Corte Sconta (☎ *041 522 70 24, Calle del Pestrin 3886*) **Map 8** Meals with wine around €46.50. Open Tues-Sat. This trattoria is hidden well away, off even the unbeaten track. The chefs almost exclusively prepare seafood, served up to you inside or in a charming little garden. Try the *risotto* *ai scampi* (€14.50), for instance. The owners cannot guarantee that on any given day all the dishes on the menu will be available for the simple reason that they use only the fish and other sea critters they find fresh at the market that day. Who can carp at such a policy?

Al Nuovo Galeon (☎ *041 520 46 56, Via Giuseppe Garibaldi 1308*) **Map 9** Meals around €31-52. Open Wed-Sun. This place not only has a boat jammed inside it, but it feels as if you are in the cabin of a great Venetian merchant ship. There aren't too many fine dining choices around this part of town, so it can get a little packed – booking ahead is advisable. It specialises in fish dishes. Just out of interest, next door is the entrance to the former Ospeal de le Pute. You might initially think this means the Whores' Hospice. In fact the word in Venetian dialect just means 'girls'.

Osteria 'Opping

Osteria dalla Vedova (☎ *041 528 53 24, Calle del Pistor 3912, Cannaregio*) **Map 4** Meals around €23. Open Mon-Wed & Fri-Sat. The 'Widow's Hostelry', off Strada Nova, is also called Trattoria Ca d'Or and is one of the oldest osterie in Venice. The food is good and modestly priced.

Cantina Vecia Carbonera (☎ *041 71 03 76, Ponte Sant'Antonio 2329, Cannaregio*) **Map 3** Meals around €21. Open Tues-Sun. You can prop up the bar and treat yourself to an glass of wine and a few snacks, or sit down for a full meal in this ageless osteria. On some nights things get quite busy, especially if a little live music has been organised.

Alla Fontana (☎ *041 71 50 77, Fondamenta di Cannaregio 1102, Cannaregio*) **Map 3** Mains €12.90. Open Tues-Sat. Close to the Jewish ghetto, this little osteria has been dispensing wines to local tipplers for more than 100 years. For many, it is a place to chat over house wine (all of it from the surrounding Veneto and Friuli regions) and cold meats and cheese. It also offers a limited menu of mains.

Osteria da Alberto (☎ *041 523 81 53, Calle Larga G Gallina 5401, Cannaregio*) **Map 4** Open Mon-Sat. Another hidden Venetian jewel is run by Alberto, a well-known figure in the business of serving up traditional food in Venice. Be aware that they close the kitchen by about 9pm here. The dried cod is good.

Osteria al Mascaron (☎ *041 522 59 95, Calle Lunga Santa Maria Formosa 5525, Castello*) **Map 5** Meals around €31-36. Open Mon-Sat. Located east of Campo Santa Maria Formosa, this is a bar/osteria and trattoria. The cicheti are good, but meals are overpriced.

La Mascareta (☎ *041 523 07 44, Calle Lunga Santa Maria Formosa 5138, Castello*) **Map 5** Open Mon-Sat. A few steps away from the Mascaron (the 'big mask') is this 'little mask', a perfectly genial tavern for the sipping of wine accompanied by a limited but tempting range of cicheti.

Al Portego (☎ *041 522 90 38, San Lio 6015, Castello*) **Map 5** Open Mon-Sat. Situated beneath the portico that gives this osteria its name, Al Portego is an inviting stop for cicheti and wine, along with some robust meals. Try the thick pasta *bigoli*, whatever sauce they come with.

Giudecca *Harry's Dolci (☎ 041 522 48 44, Fondamenta San Biagio 773)* **Map 7** Pasta from €17.55, mains from €29. Open Wed-Mon Apr-Oct. This place, run by the Hotel Cipriani and with its tables by the Canale della Giudecca looking across to Venice, has fantastic desserts (which is the main reason for stopping by). Should you want a full meal, they can also accommodate you – at elevated prices. There's a snack bar too.

All'Altanella (☎ 041 522 77 80, Calle delle Erbe 268) **Map 7** Pasta €8.25, mains €12.90. Open Wed-Sun. For the average pocket, this is the best deal on the island. Seafood is the speciality. Romantic candle-lit dinners in winter or outside by the canal in summer are the order of the evening.

Burano The island is pretty, but the restaurant prices are less so.

Ristorante Galuppi (☎ 041 73 00 81, Via B Galuppi 470) **See Map p156** Meals about €23. Open Fri-Wed (daily in summer). This is one of the better choices – look for the dolls in the windows.

Torcello *Al Trono di Attila (☎ 041 73 00 94, Fondamenta Borgognoni 7/a)* **See Map p156** Pasta €5.15-7.75, mains €10.85-15.50. Open Tues-Sun. Unless you plan to blow your budget at the famous Locanda Cipriani (see Places to Eat – Top End), try this place, between the ferry stop and the cathedral. The atmosphere is suitably bucolic and you will want to dine in the charming garden with pergola. Try the *gnocchetti con rucola e scampi* (small gnocchi with rocket and shrimps). Generally it opens for lunch only, unless you book ahead for dinner.

Mestre *Da Luca (☎ 041 95 71 22, Via Monte Grappa 42)* **Map 11** Full meals up to €46.50. Possibly the best restaurant in Mestre, the owners take you down a unique culinary path combining Venetian favourites with some good examples of Japanese cooking – clearly a fishy affair.

PLACES TO EAT – TOP END

Using €55 per head as the artificial marker, wherever you can be reasonably sure of busting that limit without trying has been slotted in here.

Restaurants

San Marco *Harry's Bar (☎ 041 528 57 77, Calle Vallaresso 1323)* **Map 5** Meals from €77.50. Open noon-11pm daily. Harry's is off Salizzada San Moisè, a quick stroll west of St Mark's Square. The Cipriani family, who started the bar in 1931, claims to have invented many Venetian specialities, including the Bellini cocktail (€11.90). A meal is expensive but it is one of only two restaurants in the city to have been awarded a Michelin star. Toscanini, Chaplin, Hemingway and just about everyone who was anyone (and quite a few who were definitely no-one) have eaten and drunk here.

San Polo *Da Fiore (☎ 041 72 13 08, Calle del Scaleter 2202)* **Map 3** Meals from €83. Open Tues-Sat. This is the other recipient of a Michelin star. The unprepossessing shopfront appearance belies an Art Deco interior and some traditional dishes, such as *risotto di scampi* and *bigoli in salsa*, prepared with optimum care. They have a good wine selection. The prices don't deter people and the place can easily be booked out for dinner weeks in advance. It's easier to get in for lunch.

Trattoria Poste Vecie (☎ 041 72 10 37, Pescaria 1608) **Map 4** Meals around €52. Open Wed-Mon. Closer to Rialto, this trattoria claims to be the oldest eating house in Venice (disputing the honour with the Cantina Do Spade, mentioned earlier). It is definitely inviting, but the euros you spend will be for the location more than the food. The name, which means 'old post office', refers to the days when many states and cities took care of their own post and thus had offices across Venice for the use of their own citizens. After the fall of the Venetian Republic, many offices were converted to wine cellars.

Torcello *Locanda Cipriani (☎ 041 73 01 50, Piazza Santa Fosca 29)* **See Map p156** Meals from €52. Open lunch Wed-Mon & dinner Sat. This truly exclusive culinary hideaway was established in 1946. Ernest

Iemingway, more readily associated with Spain, set down his bags here in 1948 and wrote part of his *Across the River and into the Trees*. They don't let out rooms in this rustic retreat any more, but it's an enticing place to splash out on your rumbling tum.

Cafes

If you can cope with the idea of paying €6.45 for a cappuccino (and up to €12.90 for an Irish coffee), spend an hour or so sitting at an outdoor table at Florian, Quadri or Lavena, enjoying the atmosphere in St Mark's Square. Oh, and we musn't forget €3.60 for the music! All three cafes have bars, where you can pay less extravagant prices for a coffee or a drink (taken on your feet) and still enjoy the elegant surroundings.

In summer they go to the trouble of having quartets playing under awnings on the square – they seem to compete with one another for attention, one striking up some stirring Vivaldi and the other countering with a little modern stuff. They usually have the courtesy to play in turns – if you stand in the middle of the square when they aren't being so gentlemanly, the effect is more cacophonous than melodious. Which is reassuring – even when trying to outdo itself in refined elegance, Venice can occasionally be humanly lacking in finesse.

Caffè Florian (☎ 041 520 56 41, Piazza San Marco 56/59) **Map 5** This is the most famous of the three – its plush interior has seen the likes of Lord Byron and Henry James taking breakfast (separately) before they crossed the piazza to Caffè Quadri for lunch. Venetians started paying exorbitant sums for the pleasure of drinking here in 1720.

Caffè Quadri (☎ 041 522 21 05, Piazza San Marco 120) **Map 5** Restaurant open Wed-Sun. Quadri is in much the same league as Florian, and equally steeped in history. Indeed, it actually opened its doors well before its better known competitor, in 1683.

Lavena (☎ 041 522 40 70, Piazza San Marco 133) **Map 5** Open daily Apr-Sept, Wed-Mon Oct-Mar. Founded in 1750 and a

little less renowned, Lavena is in the same vein. Wagner was among its more visible customers but, historically, gondoliers and *codega* (see the boxed text 'Shining Path') also hung out here.

SWEETS
Gelato

Prices range from about €1.05 for a small cup to €2.05 for a big cone. Prices don't vary much but the generosity of the portions can.

Gelateria Millefoglie da Tarcisio (San Polo 3034) **Map 6** This gelateria, behind the Chiesa di Santa Maria Gloriosa dei Frari, is an excellent ice-cream stop.

Gelateria Nico (Fondamenta Zattere ai Gesuati 922) **Map 6** Head here for the best ice cream in Venice. The locals take their evening stroll along the fondamenta while eating their heavily laden cones.

Gelateria il Doge (Campo Santa Margherita) **Map 6** This place also has excellent *gelati*.

Cake and Pastries

Pasticceria Marchini (Calle Spezier 2769) **Map 6** Open 9.30am-8.30pm Wed-Mon. You will be spellbound by the offerings in the window of this, one of Venice's most illustrious cake shops.

Entertainment

The Venice Carnevale (see the black-and-white special section 'Carry on Carnevale' after the Facts for the Visitor chapter) is one of Italy's best-known parties, but exhibitions, theatre and musical events continue throughout the year. Information is available in *Un Ospite di Venezia*, and the tourist office also has brochures listing events and performances for the entire year. Also keep your eyes on the monthly *Venezia News*.

A handy centralised ticket outlet is *Box Office*, which has two agents in Venice. One is the travel agency *Gran Canal Viaggi* (☎ *041 271 21 11, Ponte dell'Ovo, San Marco 4759/4760)* (Map 5), and the other the CD shop *Parole e Musica (☎ 041 523 50 10, Salizzada San Lio 5673)* (Map 5). You can also book tickets with credit cards on the phone by calling Milan on ☎ 02 5 42 71 from 10am to 5pm, Monday to Saturday. A Web ticket service, Ticket One (W www.ticketone.it), allows you to book tickets for theatre, football and other events on the Internet. It also provides a list of outlets around town (and the rest of Italy) where you can pick up tickets in person. To find out where the nearest outlet is you can also call Ticket One in Milan at ☎ 02 39 22 61.

For some major events, you can also pick up tickets at *Vela (☎ 041 271 47 47, freephone 800 40 08 88, W www.velaspa.com)* outlets, which are part of the ACTV city transport body. They have a phone ticketing service (watch the charges) on ☎ 899 90 90 90. Two Vela points operate by the train station. They also sell vaporetto tickets and Rolling Venice passes (see the Facts for the Visitor chapter).

BARS

Drinking in Venice (or anywhere else in Italy for that matter) is not a particularly cheap business. The equivalent of a pint of beer generally costs around €4.15, while cocktails and mixed drinks often cost around €5.15. A glass of wine or *prosecco* (a light, sparkling white that is *the* standard drink in Venice) is generally the most economical tipple, starting at around €1.30.

San Marco

Black Jack Bar (☎ 041 522 25 18, Campo San Luca) Map 5 Open 7.45am-8.45pm Mon-Sat. This bar serves a decent Bellini among other cocktails, for the early evening ritual.

Vino Vino (☎ 041 523 70 27, Calle de Cafetier, San Marco 2007) Map 5 Open Wed-Mon. This place (see the Places to Eat chapter) is great just for sipping wine if you want to forget the food.

Le Bistrot de Venise (☎ 041 523 66 51, Calle dei Fabbri, San Marco 4685) Map 5 Open 10am-1am. As much restaurant as bar the bistro is an elegant setting for a little wine-tasting accompanied by nibbles, particularly Italian and French cheeses.

Devil's Forest (☎ 041 520 00 23, Calle dei Stagneri 5185) Map 5 Open 10am-1pm & 5pm-12.30am Mon-Sat. This is a reasonable imitation of a UK pub, complete with old red telephone box and Irish beers on tap (Kilkenny and Harp).

Inishark (☎ 041 523 53 00, Calle Mondo Nuovo 5788) Map 5 Open Mon-Sat. This is yet another little twist on the Irish pub theme 'Nuff said.

Bacaro Jazz (☎ 041 528 52 49, Salizzada del Fondaco dei Tedeschi 5546) Map 5 Open 11am-2am Thur-Tues; happy hour 2pm-7.30pm. This place also likes to sell itself as an eatery – a rather pricey one. It won't be to everyone's taste, being a little brash and too close to the tourist route for comfort, but a drink's a drink.

Torino@Notte (☎ 041 522 39 14, Campo San Luca 459, San Marco) Map 5 Open 10pm-2am Tues-Sat. This unlikely looking spot (during the day) livens up at night as a young student set settles in for mixed drinks music and occasionally even a live act.

Martini Scala (☎ 041 522 41 21, San Marco 1501) Map 5 Open 9pm-3.30am Wed-Mon. If you like the piano-bar scene, maybe this is for you. It's a little cheesy and very pricey, but then the options aren't bountiful (especially this late at night), are they?

Harry's Bar (☎ *041 528 57 77, Calle Valaresso 1323*) **Map 5** Cocktails for €9.30-11.90. Open noon-11pm. As well as being one of the city's more notable restaurants (see the Places to Eat chapter), Harry's is, of course, first and foremost known as a bar. Everyone who is anyone passing through Venice usually ends up here sooner or later. The Aga Khan lounged around here and other characters as diverse as Orson Welles, Ernest Hemingway and Truman Capote have all sipped on a cocktail or two at Harry's.

Dorsoduro

Caffè Blue (☎ *041 523 72 27, Dorsoduro 3778*) **Map 6** Open 8am-2pm & 5pm-2am Mon-Sat. This is a coolish student bar with live music on Friday. It can be a little quiet on some evenings.

Café Noir (☎ *041 71 09 25, Calle San Pantalon 3805, Dorsoduro*) **Map 6** Open 7am-2am Mon-Sat. Cocktails €3.60. You start the day with breakfast in here, pop in for some time online with one of the handful of computers or hang out into the night with a mixed crowd of Italian students and foreigners. The place has a laid back, underground feel about it.

Capo Horn (☎ *041 524 21 77, Calle San Pantalon 3740, Dorsoduro*) **Map 6** Open 8pm-2am Mon-Sat. A few steps away from Café Noir, the Capo Horn is decked out as an 18th-century sailing vessel. It has recently been renovated, and isn't a bad bar to hang out in for beer and whisky (of which they have a wide variety). Very happy hour is 6pm to 8pm, when a *spritz* costs €0.50.

Taverna da Baffo (☎ *041 520 88 62, Campiello Sant'Agostin 2346*) **Map 3** Open 7am-2am Mon-Sat. Named after Casanova's licentious poet pal, Giorgio Baffo, and lined with his rhymes in praise of 'the round arse' and other parts of the female body, this bar has a young, chirpy feel. In summer the tables outside are an especially pleasant spot to sip on a spritz or two.

Cantina di Vini già Schiavi (☎ *041 523 00 34, Fondamenta Maravegie 992*) **Map 6**

Open Mon-Sat. This is a fusty old wine bar across from the Chiesa di San Trovaso. Wander in for a glass of prosecco beneath the bar's low-slung rafters and in the wavering light provided by dodgy bulbs. Alternatively, you could just buy a bottle of whatever takes your fancy and take it away.

Campo Santa Margherita is lined with a collection of places for drinking and snacking that keep busy until about 2am.

Green Pub (☎ *041 520 59 76, Campo Santa Margherita 3053/a*) **Map 6** Open Fri-Wed. This spot is good for a Guinness, which many will say is good for you. They also have snacks.

Caffè (☎ *041 528 79 98, Campo Santa Margherita 2693*) **Map 6** Open Mon-Sat. A lively, hip, student bar with snacks, it is known to locals affectionately as the *caffè rosso* because of the red sign.

Margaret Duchamp (☎ *041 528 62 55, Campo Santa Margherita 3019*) **Map 6** Open daily. Across the square, this is also a highly popular spot for a spritz and chat until the early hours.

Round Midnight (☎ *041 523 20 56, Fondamenta dello Squero 3102, Dorsoduro*) **Map 6** Open 7pm-4am Mon-Sat Sept-May. After you're through hanging about and soaking up the atmosphere on Campo Santa Margherita, head around to this little drink-and-dance cove on a nearby back canal. You can sip on all sorts of cocktails and even get a snack. The music tends towards acid jazz and latin.

Santa Croce & San Polo

Ai Postali (☎ *041 71 51 76, Fondamenta Rio Marin 821*) **Map 3** Open to 2am, sometimes later, Mon-Sat. This is a buzzy little locals' bar along the Rio Marin. Roberto gave up flying for Alitalia to pilot this place.

Pizzeria Jazz Club 900 (☎ *041 522 65 65, Campiello Sansoni 900, San Polo*) **Map 3** Open 11.30am-4pm & 7pm-2am Tues-Sun. Decked out in early 1900s fashion, this little spot, hidden away on a tiny square, is a north point for jazz musicians in Venice. On those evenings when a performance is on, you can listen to jazz while munching on a pizza.

ENTERTAINMENT

Fill 'Er Up

Yes, it's all very fine sitting about posturing in fine restaurants and paying high prices, but sometimes you just want some plonk to have at home. And there's the question of cost – not everyone can afford to go out and invest in great-name labels.

Fortunately, apart from the wonderful option of sipping wines in a local osteria or *bacaro* (traditional Venetian bar), a fine take-home tradition persists in Venice. Every now and then you will stumble across a wine shop. You'll know you've hit one if you find it crammed with huge glass containers (the kind of 'bottle' even Hercules would have trouble slugging from) known as *damigiane*. From these monsters, each containing a sea of simple and quite acceptable Veneto table wine, you make a choice and have it poured into whatever you bring – used wine or mineral-water bottles – it's up to you. The stuff is siphoned (much as you would siphon petrol from a car) into your bottle and you will be charged, on average, €1.95 per litre.

A chain called Nave de Oro has at least five branches in Venice (listed below) and one each on the Lido and Murano. A handful of other places along the same lines can also be found:

Cantina del Baffo
Map 3; Fondamenta degli Ormesini, Cannaregio 2678
   Open 8.30am-1pm & 4.30pm-7.30pm (afternoon only Wed)

Nave de Oro
Map 3; Rio Terrà San Leonardo, Cannaregio 1370
   Open 8am-1pm & 4.30pm-7.30pm (afternoon only Wed)

Map 4; Rio Terrà dei SS Apostoli 4657
   Open 9am-1pm & 4pm-7.45pm Mon-Sat (morning only Wed)

Map 5; Calle Mondo Nuovo, Castello 5786/b
   Open 9am-1pm & 5pm-7.45pm (morning only Wed)

Map 6; Campo Santa Margherita, Dorsoduro 3664
   Open 9am-1pm & 5pm-7.30pm (morning only Wed)

Map 8; Calle Santa Maria Formosa 5179
   Open 9am-1pm & 5pm-7.45pm (morning only Wed)

Wine Shops (Nameless)
Map 3; Fondamenta di Cannaregio 1116
   Open 8.30am-12.30pm & 4.30pm-7.30pm (morning only Wed)

Map 6; Campo Santa Margherita, Dorsoduro 2897
   Open 8.30am-12.30pm & 5pm-7.30pm (morning only Wed)

Cannaregio
Paradiso Perduto (☎ *041 72 05 81, Fondamenta della Misericordia 2539*) **Map 3** Open Thur-Sat & Mon-Tues. This hip joint (see the Places to Eat chapter) sometimes has live music.

The Fiddler's Elbow (☎ *041 523 99 30, Corte dei Pali 3847*) **Map 4** Open 5pm-1am Thur-Tues. On the Irish scene, this place is representative of the genre.

Osteria agli Ormesini (☎ *041 71 38 34, Fondamenta degli Ormesini 2710*) **Map 3** Open to 2am Mon-Sat. Oodles of wine and 120 types of bottled beer in one knockabout little place? Perhaps you should get along to this osteria. It's something of a student haunt and tipplers spill out onto the fondamenta to enjoy their grog.

La Fondamenta (☎ *041 71 73 15, Fondamenta della Misericordia 2578*) **Map 3**

pen 11am-3pm & 5pm-2am Wed-Mon.
his is a cheap and cheerful restaurant that is
othing special but people tend to use it as a
ar as well later in the evening.

LUBS & DISCOS

he club and dancing scene in Venice is vir-
ually zero. One or two possibilities are avail-
ble, but if you are looking for action, do not
ome to Venice.

Things look up a little in summer, when a
andful of places open on the Lido, but the
al action is at Jesolo, on the coast to the
orth-east of Venice. Remember that, though
e word *discoteca* may conjure up images of
ell-bottoms and big hair, it's the Italian
quivalent of what others regard as clubs. A
lub' to an Italian could be anything from a
cal bingo association to a sleazy night spot
here people with bald pates, bad-smelling
gars and chest carpets buy drinks for them-
lves and their recently acquired girlfriends.

In Italy, the in clubs for the young, student-
ge set tend to be placed well out of the way,
the countryside or small towns. Generally,
e only way to get to them is to drive, and
ou need to be right up to date with what's in
nd what's out. The same is true in Venice
nd around. Get hold of *Venezia News* for
me specific ideas.

Expect to pay €5.15 to €10.30 (occasion-
ly more) to get into a club. This may include
e first drink. A few options are given here.

orsoduro

iccolo Mondo (☎ *041 520 03 71, San
arco 1506)* **Map 6** Open to 4am Tues-Sun.
his teensy little disco and bar is a bit on the
imy side, but perfectly all right in its own
ide-lapel fashion. It pulls a 30s-plus crowd.

annaregio

asanova (☎ *041 275 01 99, Rio Terrà Lista
Spagna 158/a, Cannaregio)* **Map 3** Open
m-4am Tues & Thur-Sat. A quick stumble
om the train station, this is it, about the only
lace in Venice that can vaguely call itself a
isco (and it really is more disco than club).
ach night has its own musical theme, from
ck revival on Thursday through Latin on
riday and thumping techno on Saturday.

Mestre

The Zoo (☎ *348 989 70 17, Via Ca'Zorzi 2)*
Off Map 11 Admission up to €12.90. Open
11pm-4am Fri & Sat. The best offering in
the Mestre area is this venue, out in Tessera,
virtually opposite Marco Polo airport. In
four dance spaces you can weave from
house to Latin rhythms or mainstream pop.

Metrò (☎ *041 95 92 62, Via Einaudi 19)*
Map 11 Open 10pm-4am Mon-Sat. In the
centre of town, you can sip cocktails and listen to good music here. The latter depends on
the day and ranges from 80s through Latin to
house. You might want to skip karaoke night
on Tuesday.

Chioggia

In summer, especially, a row of beach-front
discos cranks up for the local holiday crowd
in Sottomarina. It's not really practical from
Venice, though.

Jesolo Lido

About one hour's drive from Venice, this
seaside resort is where the nightlife really is,
from June to September. ATVO bus No 10a
from Piazzale Roma takes about 70 minutes
and costs €3.35. The problem is getting back
home. Even in summer, the last bus leaves at
11.20pm. Locals seem to compete to see who
will be killed first on the roads. Perhaps
sleeping the night off on the beach would be
safer! If you find a taxi, you are looking at
€72.30 or more, depending on the traffic.

Sound Garden (☎ *0421 37 23 45,* W *www
.soundgardencafe.com, Via Aleardi/Piazza
Mazzini)* Open 10pm-4am. Sound Garden
concentrates on rock (sometimes of the hard
variety) and features live bands on Friday.

Dolce Vita (☎ *348 360 80 01, Via Mameli
115)* Admission up to €15.50. Open 10pm-
5am Thur-Sat. For some hard-hitting, deaf-
ening clubland action, this is one of the
hipper Jesolo options. House predominates.

Cuba Libre Cafe (☎ *0421 37 16 48, Via
Buonarroti 15)* Open 8.30pm-4am. You can
start the evening here with pizza and other
snacks to accompany the first tipples or hang
about later. The music selection is varied.

Il Muretto (☎ *0421 37 13 10 or 348 410
11 20,* W *www.ilmuretto.net, Via Roma destra*

120/d) Admission up to €20.65. Open 10pm-5am Sat. This was the hippest nocturnal dance locale of the 2001 season. An army of DJs spins mostly house. Flyers for this place can be seen floating around as far away as bars in Padua. A couple of other spots are located on the same road.

MUSIC
Classical & Baroque
Several groups of musicians perform regular concerts of classical or Baroque music throughout most of the year. These are aimed at tourists and can be a little cheesy, but the quality is really not bad.

Chiesa di Santa Maria della Pietà (La Pietà; Riva degli Schiavoni) **Map 8** This has been a popular venue for classical music recitals, especially anything involving Vivaldi, over the past few years.

Other classical and Baroque music venues are *Chiesa di San Bartolomeo* **(Map 5)** near the Ponte di Rialto; the *Chiesa delle Zitelle* **(Map 7)** on Giudecca; the *Scuola Grande di San Teodoro* **(Map 5)** in San Marco; and the *Scuola Grande di San Giovanni Evangelista* **(Map 3)**. The following figure among the performers.

The two standard Venetians, Vivaldi and Albinoni, figure in the repertoire of the Musici Veneziani (☎ 041 521 02 94, 🌐 www.imusiciveneziani.com), who go the period-costume route. The music may not be seriously highbrow, but it's OK. Following them down the period-costume path is the Orchestra di Venezia (☎ 041 522 81 25, 🌐 www.orchestra.venezia.it).

The Concerti della Venezia Musica group (☎ 041 523 10 96, 🌐 www.vivaldi.it) perform Vivaldi's music regularly at the Chiesa di Santa Maria della Pietà, May to September.

The Concerto in Gondola (☎ 041 521 02 94, 🌐 www.concertingondola.com) play yet another version. From May to September you board one of a fleet of gondolas, some of which are occupied by musicians and singers in 18th-century garb who present a mixed selection of light classical music and opera. Tickets cost up to €43.90.

Information and tickets for these and other similar performances can be had from

Agenzia Kele & Teo (☎ 041 520 87 2 Ponte dei Baratteri, San Marco) **(Map 5** Expect to pay €20.65 to €31 a head for mo performances.

Contemporary
With the exception of jazz, blues and th like, intermittently on offer at a handful o places such as *Paradiso Perduto*, *Caffè Blu* and *Pizzeria Jazz Club 900* (see the earlie Bars section), there's not much happening.

Very occasionally you can see bands pla in Venice. If you really want to see band you'll need to go to Mestre or even Padu. If you can get hold of the monthly bookl *Press Music* (you can sometimes find lying around in Caffè – see the earlier Ba section), you'll see most of the action tak place well beyond the city limits. Even i Mestre the offerings aren't fabulous.

In summer, occasional concerts are o ganised in Jesolo – watch the local press. big rock event is Jesolo Beach Bum (th Italian rendering of the English 'boom' usually held over a weekend at the begin ning of July. In Mestre's Forte Marghe area, the big annual event is Marghera E tate Village (the name changes from on year to the next), a programme of night live music, from rock to ethnic, that ru from late June right through the summer.

A Contemporary Music Festival is he annually in October at the Teatro Goldo (see the Theatre section later).

CINEMAS
The city doesn't have an English-langua cinema. The time to see foreign cinema the original language is during the Veni International Film Festival in Septembe (see Festivals under Public Holidays Special Events in the Facts for the Visit chapter). You generally pay around €6.2 to see a flick.

Summer Arena Open July-Aug. Th cinema-under-the-stars in Campo San Po features British and American films, b they are generally dubbed.

If you have a hankering for the movi and can cope with dubbing into Italian, se eral cinemas (overleaf) screen decent film

Cinema Accademia d'Essai (☎ 041 528 77 06, Calle Corfu, Dorsoduro 1018) **Map 6** This is a fusty old place with indifferent screen quality, but they choose quality flicks.

Cinema Giorgione Movie d'Essai (☎ 041 522 62 98, Cannaregio 4612) **Map 4** A modern cinema, the Giorgione also frequently presents quality movies.

Cinema Dante d'Essai (☎ 041 538 16 55, Via Sernaglia 12) **Map 11** This is the best bet in Mestre.

THEATRE

Teatro Goldoni (☎ 041 520 75 83, Calle Teatro Goldoni 4650/b) **Map 5** Named after the city's greatest playwright, this is, rather unsurprisingly, the main theatre in the centre of town. It's not unusual for Goldoni's plays to be performed – what more appropriate location?

OPERA & BALLET
La Fenice

Teatro La Fenice (Campo San Fantin, San Marco 1970) **Map 6** Until it was destroyed by fire in January 1996 (see the boxed text 'Faltering Phoenix' below), this was Venice's premier opera stage. Performances of opera and ballet are still organised but held in alternative venues.

The bulk of the Fenice performances are held at the circus-style big top called the

---

Faltering Phoenix

From as far off as the Ponte della Libertà, the bridge linking Venice to the mainland, scarlet flames could be seen shooting into the night sky as the pride of the city, the Teatro La Fenice, burned to the ground on 29 January 1996.

The blaze began at about 8pm and five fire-brigade squads were rushed in to avert disaster – in vain. Fate would have it that the canals in the immediate area had been temporarily drained so that they could be unsilted. This lack of water close to hand proved fatal. Firemen managed to prevent the blaze spreading, but the theatre was utterly destroyed. It had been closed since the previous August for refurbishment and was due to reopen shortly.

Built in 1792, the theatre was a tangible link with the final days of the Venetian Republic. The horseshoe-shaped auditorium created exquisite acoustics. Prior to a fire in 1836, various opera greats had made their mark here – Rossini, Bellini and Donizetti, to name a few. Rebuilt within two years, the theatre's halcyon days came with the years of close association between La Fenice and Giuseppe Verdi, who presented many of his most outstanding operas here in the 1850s. As the 19th century wore into the 20th, a more international flavour came to pervade the Venetian operatic scene, with works by such diverse composers as Britten and Prokofiev staged. All the greats have graced its stage, from Callas to Pavarotti.

If the manner of the theatre's demise in 1996 was lamentable, the story of its return to brilliance is perhaps even more so. The then mayor, Massimo Cacciari, and just about everyone who is anyone in Venetian politics, vowed to have the theatre back in action *dov'era, com'era* ('where it was and as it was') in time for the opera season in 2000. (The bon mot was a phrase borrowed from the 1902 collapse of the Campanile in St Mark's Square, or Piazza San Marco, which was, in fact, rebuilt exactly as it had been.)

The date came and went and not a great deal happened. The circumstances of the fire and subsequent irregularities in the awarding of contracts to rebuild the theatre brought everything to a halt. In June 2001, the newly appointed Under Secretary for Culture, Vittorio Sgarbi, rather dramatically announced that the central government would wade in and assured that the Fenice would be rebuilt by mid-2003. The present mayor, Paolo Costa, welcomed the announcement but no-one is holding their breath.

In the meantime, opera-goers have to content themselves with the 'big-top' circus tents known as the PalaFenice, on the Isola del Tronchetto, and one or two other theatres as interim alternative venues.

ENTERTAINMENT

PalaFenice (☎ *041 78 65 01, Isola del Tronchetto*) **(Map 2)**.

Teatro Malibran (☎ *041 78 65 20, San Marco 5870)* **Map 4** Reopened in May 2001 after years of restoration, this charming little theatre is earmarked as an alternative to the PalaFenice. It first opened in early 1678.

Tickets for Fenice performances are available from the *Cassa di Risparmio di Venezia bank* **(Map 5)** (☎ *041 521 01 61, Campo San Luca)*, open 8.30am to 1.30pm Monday to Friday, or from the theatres an hour before the show starts. You can look up the programme and book on the internet at **W** www.teatrolafenice.it. At the same online address, you can also find details of booking agents in your country. The cost of tickets ranges up to €31 for a decent seat at the opera. The performances are frequently by quality international artists, although we are not at the heights of Milan's La Scala here.

CASINO
People under the age of 18 are not allowed in to the following gambling dens.

Casinò Municipale di Venezia (☎ *041 529 71 11, Palazzo Vendramin-Calergi, Cannaregio 2040)* **Map 3** Vaporetto No 1 or 82, alight at San Marcuola stop. Open 3pm-3am Oct-May. All the old gamblers' favourites, from slot machines to black jack, are available to contribute to your fiscal demise.

Venice Casino (☎ *041 529 71 11, Ca' Noghera, Via Triestina 222, 30030 Tessera)* Admission €2.60 Sun-Thur, €5.20 Fri & Sat. Open 11am-4.45am Sun-Fri, 11am-6am Sat, every day except 24 and 25 Dec. This brand-spanking-new casino complex on the mainland has a more casual dress code.

FOOTBALL
Like anywhere else in Italy, *il calcio* reigns supreme in the hearts and minds of many a Venetian. Venezia, or the *arancioneroverde* (orange, black and greens), are a middling team rarely touched by the ultimate pleasure of competition victory. Indeed, they suffered the indignity of going down to 2nd division (Serie B) in 2000, but managed to re-emerge in the top division for the 2001-2002 season.

The team plays at the Stadio Penzo, on Isola di Sant'Elena (Map 2), at the far eastern end of the lagoon city. The uniqueness of the team's home town makes for some interesting logistics when the side plays at home. Special ferry services are laid on between Tronchetto car park and Sant'Elena – normally a quiet little place with hardly a soul to disturb the leafy peace. All buses arriving in Venice on a match day are diverted first to Tronchetto to disgorge their loads of fans before reaching Piazzale Roma.

Tickets are available at the *stadium* itself, from branches of the *Banca Antoniana Popolare Veneta* or *Vela* outlets. An average seat will cost around €18.05. The bank used as a ticket outlet can change from year to year, so you may want to ask at the tourist office or call *Venezia Calcio* (☎ *041 95 81 00)*. Because Venice is not one of Italy's more successful clubs, getting tickets on match day is rarely a problem. The only other Veneto team in Serie A is Verona.

Shopping

The main shopping area for clothing, shoes, accessories and jewellery is in the narrow streets between San Marco and the Rialto, particularly the Mercerie and around Campo San Luca. The more upmarket shops are west of St Mark's Square.

For arty stuff, ranging from Carnevale masks and costumes through ceramics and on to model gondolas, San Polo is the place to hunt. Another Venetian speciality is marbled paper – you'll find people doing this all over town.

Many places open on Sunday during the tourist season (which means at least Easter to October). Some shops close for the holidays for all or part of August. For more on opening hours, see Business Hours in the Facts for the Visitor chapter.

ANTIQUES

Laboratorio del Gerva (☎ *041 523 67 77, Campo Bandiera e Moro 3725, Castello)* **Map 8** In a higgledy-piggledy workshop, enough goods are stacked to whet the appetite of any antiques collector. If you are a serious purchaser, ask about the warehouse (which you can arrange to see by appointment, if genuinely interested). Michele Gervasuti is continuing the work of his father, Eugenio, a master craftsperson who opened the shop here in 1959. They concentrate on restoration and are involved in important projects across the city.

ART GALLERIES

Many shops (and artists in the city's numerous squares) sell simple watercolours of typical Venetian scenes. Several small art galleries are also dotted about the city.

The single biggest concentration of galleries, containing all kinds of stuff, is on the streets that lie between the Gallerie dell' Accademia and the Peggy Guggenheim Collection. A few stragglers line Calle del Bastion on the approach to the former Chiesa di San Gregorio (just east of the Guggenheim). Another area to look is Calle delle Carrozze, close to Palazzo Grassi. All of these places can be found on Map 6.

San Marco

Bugno Samueli Art Gallery (☎ *041 523 13 05, Campo San Fantin 1996/a)* **Map 5** This gallery has some works by contemporary artists on permanent display, although money is the object. While you might not be able to afford a Miró or De Chirico, there's plenty of other material for the modern art collector. Needless to say, this is not a hobby for impecunious backpackers (or anybody else short of Rockefeller status).

Studio Aoristico di Matteo lo Greco (☎ *041 521 25 82, Campo San Fantin 1998)* **Map 5** This is a one-man show with some interesting sculpture and paintings.

Galleria Traghetto (☎ *041 522 11 88, Calle delle Ostreghe 2457)* **Map 6** Here you will find a curious mix of sculpture and paintings.

ART PRINTS & POSTERS

One way to remember a visit to Venice is by taking home some images of the city. Several shops produce high-quality prints and etchings. As long as you don't bend them on the way home, they can be a good, lightweight souvenir or gift.

BAC Art Studio (☎ *041 522 81 71, Campo San Vio 862)* **Map 6** This studio has paintings, aquatints and engravings signed Cadore and Paolo Baruffaldi that can make fine gifts. You'll have seen cheaper depictions of Venice street and canal scenes at street stalls (and there is nothing wrong with a lot of them), but this stuff is a cut above those. Cadore concentrates his commercial efforts on Venetian scenes, while Baruffaldi depicts masked people. The store is a good place for quality postcards too. There is another branch *(Map 6; ☎ 041 523 11 08, Ruga Rialto 1069)* in San Polo.

Graffiti (☎ *041 522 88 43, Salizzada San Rocco 3045)* **Map 6** Graffiti has some fine depictions of Venice (though the best come

SHOPPING

attached with high prices), as well as some excellent postcards.

ART SUPPLIES
Dorsoduro
Cartoleria Accademia (☎ 042 520 70 86, Campo Santa Margherita 2928) **Map 6** This store has been selling artists' supplies since 1810, so they must have some idea!

San Polo
Artemisia (☎ 041 244 02 90, Campiello Zen 972) **Map 6** Here you can get just about anything imaginable for painting, restoration, sculpture and so on. Students get 20% off.

BOOKS
There are several good bookshops in Venice, but English-language titles can be pricey compared with the UK and USA.

San Marco
Libreria Cassini (☎ 041 523 18 15, Via XXII Marzo 2424) **Map 6** This bookshop has rare books and valuable prints, and will interest the discerning bibliophile with plenty of notes to burn.

Libreria Emiliana (☎ 041 522 07 93, Calle Goldoni 4484) **Map 5** You can find a broad range of books dealing with Venice in several languages here. Themes range from art to Pinocchio.

Libreria Goldoni (☎ 041 522 23 84, Calle dei Fabbri 4742) **Map 5** This is one of the city's establishment bookshops. It has an impressive range of material on Venice in Italian, English and French.

Libreria Il Fontego (☎ 041 520 04 70, San Marco 5361) **Map 5** This is a pleasingly topsy-turvy bookshop spread over a couple of floors.

Libreria al Ponte (☎ 041 522 40 30, Calle Cortesia 3717/d) **Map 5** In here they offer a solid range of guides and other books on Venice, as well as children's books, many in English.

San Marco Studium (☎ 041 522 23 82, Calle Canonica 337/a) **Map 5** For a good selection of English-language guides and books on Venice, try this shop handily placed just off St Mark's Square.

Dorsoduro
Peggy Guggenheim Museum Shop (☎ 04 240 54 24, Dorsoduro 701) **Map 6** This shop in the same building as the Peggy Guggenheim Collection (but with a different entrance), has a select choice of art books and souvenirs related to the gallery collections.

Cannaregio
Libreria Demetra (☎ 041 275 01 52, Campo San Geremia 282) **Map 3** Open 9am-10pm Sun, 9am-midnight Mon-Sat. A limited range of paperbacks and material on Venice is sold here.

Castello
Editore Filippi (☎ 041 523 56 35, Calle Casselleria 5763) **Map 5** This is a den of book on all kinds of subjects related to Venice many published and only on sale here. The Filippis have been in the book business for nearly a century. Scholars turn to them for their tomes and encyclopaedic knowledge.

Libraire Française (☎ 041 522 96 59 Barbaria delle Tole 6358) **Map 8** Voulez-vous vos livres en français? Here you will find everything from the latest novels to a plethora of tomes on Venice – all in French

CARNEVALE MASKS & COSTUMES
Carnevale masks make beautiful souvenirs Again, quality and price are uneven. You can find people selling masks on just about every canal corner, but for serious craftsmanship you have to look a little closer. The cheap touristy rubbish is manufactured industrially (in Padua, for instance) and worthless. The ceramic masks have absolutely nothing to do with the genuine articles, which are carefully crafted objects in *cartapesta* (papier-mache) or leather. The places listed here are all specialists and should give you a decent range of options.

Dorsoduro
Ca' Macana (☎ 041 520 32 29, Calle delle Botteghe 5176) **Map 6** This is one of several places where you can see how the masks are made. Leonardo di Caprio even popped by, as the autograph in the window clearly testifies!

San Polo

Atelier Pietro Longhi (☎ *041 71 44 78, Rio Terrà 2604/b*) **Map 6** This is the place to come if you've ever fancied buying a helmet and sword to go with your tailor-made Carnevale costume.

L'Arlecchino (☎ *041 71 65 91, Calle dei Cristi 1722–29*) **Map 3** L'Arlecchino claims that their masks are made only with papier-mache to their own designs. To prove it you can inspect their workshop. The quality of the masks is evident, but they aren't cheap. They have another place *(Map 5; ☎ 041 520 82 20, Ruga del Ravano 789)* close by.

Tragicomica (☎ *041 72 11 02, Calle Nomboli, San Polo 2800*) **Map 6** This is one of the city's bigger mask and costume merchants. They also organise costume parties during Carnevale. The place is quite overwhelming at first sight.

Castello

Ca' del Sole (☎ *041 528 55 49, Fondamenta dell'Osmarin 4964*) **Map 8** Costumes and masks that are aimed at both the public and the theatre are made and sold here.

CERAMICS

You'll see occasional shops selling pottery, tiles and various other ceramic items around town. Although this can't really be claimed to be a traditional Venetian art form (Gubbio in Umbria, and several towns in Sicily, are Italy's most renowned pottery producers), some pieces are particularly arresting.

Arca (☎ *041 71 04 27, Calle del Tintor 1811*) **Map 3** The designs here are powerful, and for some tastes the colours are possibly a little strong. Teresa della Valentina paints her tiles and other ceramic objects in bold, bright, rich colours – red here is deep blood red. You can organise to have your selections shipped directly home.

La Margherita Ceramiche (☎ *041 72 31 20, Sotoportego de Siora Bettina 2345*) **Map 3** The contrast between this place and Arca couldn't be greater. Margherita Rossetto's kitchen pots, clocks and other hand-painted items are all tranquil designs in soft blues and yellows – an altogether sunnier look.

CLOTHING, TEXTILES & FASHION

Central Venice, especially the streets leading away west from St Mark's Square towards the Teatro La Fenice, are flanked by all the fashion names you need. If you can't make it to Milan, you'll find a good selection right here. It has to be said, however, that Milan is cheaper. If you're into Benetton, make for the heartland – Treviso (see the Excursions chapter).

In Venice itself, one oddity is the *Fiorella Gallery* (☎ *041 520 92 28, Campo Santo Stefano 2806*) **Map 6**, where the window contains transsexual Doge mannequins that in themselves make this unusual clothing store stand out – and a little difficult to classify under Fashion. Make of it what you will.

There's no need to go into great detail here about the following list of fashion outlets – the label-collectors among you will know what all the following mean and what you want from them. You'll notice that quite a few are linked (they have the same phone number). They all appear on Map 5.

Agnona
  ☎ *041 520 57 33, Calle Vallaresso 1307*
Armani
  ☎ *041 523 78 08, Calle dei Fabbri 989*
Dolce & Gabbana
  ☎ *041 520 57 33, Calle Vallaresso 1313*
Fendi
  ☎ *041 520 57 33, Salizzada San Moisè 1474*
Gucci
  ☎ *041 520 74 84, Calle Vallaresso 1317*
Kenzo
  ☎ *041 520 57 33, Calle dei Fuseri 1814*
Laura Biagiotti
  ☎ *041 520 34 01, Calle Larga XXII Marzo 2400*
Missoni
  ☎ *041 520 57 33, Calle Vallaresso 1312/b*
Prada
  ☎ *041 528 39 66, Salizzada San Moisè 1464–9*
Roberto Cavalli
  ☎ *041 520 57 33, Calle Vallaresso 1316*
Valentino
  ☎ *041 520 57 33, Salizzada San Moisè 1473*
Versace
  ☎ *041 520 00 57, Campo San Moisè*

COSMETICS

Lush (☎ *041 241 11 20, Strada Nuova 3822, Cannaregio*) **Map 4** Handmade soaps and fragrances with a whiff of fresh fruit are the order of the day in this fine-smelling chain store.

CRAFTS
San Marco
Livio de Marchi (☎ *041 528 56 94, Salizzada San Samuele*) **Map 6** This place, with wooden sculptures of underpants, socks and shirts, is rather weird. It's quite endearing really but hard to know what you would do with such items in your lounge.

Dorsoduro
Legno e Dintorni (☎ *041 522 63 67, Fondamenta Gherardini 2840*) **Map 6** Wonderful little wooden models of various monuments and facades, akin to simple 3-D puzzles, are sold here. They make rather refined gifts for kids, but wouldn't go amiss with many an adult.

Loris Marazzi (☎ *041 523 90 01, Campo Santa Margherita 2903*) **Map 6** Like Livio de Marchi (see under San Marco above), Loris Marazzi offers sculptures on a weird wooden theme, but is perhaps better known.

San Polo
A Mano (☎ *041 71 57 42, Rio Terrà 2616*) **Map 6** All goods sold here are handmade. Quirky lampshades, mirrors and other odds and sods give this place a special attraction.

DEPARTMENT STORES
Le Barche (☎ *041 97 78 82, Piazza XXVII Ottobre I*) **Map 11** Open 9am-8.30pm Tues-Sat, 2pm-8.30pm Mon. There are no serious department stores in Venice itself. For this kind of thing you will need to head for Mestre to this shopping complex, just off Piazza XXII Marzo in the centre of town. It's home to several of the country's leading stores, including *Feltrinelli*, the bookshop chain, *Ricordi Mediastore*, for CDs and music, *Coin*, a leading budget department store and *PAM*, particularly noted for its value-for-money food department. For clothes you could try *Belfe & Belfe*, on the ground floor.

Coin (☎ *041 520 35 81, Salizzada San Giovanni Grisostomo 5790, Cannaregio*) **Map 4** A recently arrived tenant in central Venice, the shop brings a bit of department-store action to canalside shoppers, with this branch specialising in affordable men's and women's clothes and accessories.

FOOD & DRINK
Giacomo Rizzo (☎ *041 522 28 24, Salizzada S Giovanni Grisostomo 5778*) **Map 4** This place, just north of the post office, has been keeping the locals in pasta since 1905. Take a look if you want to buy handmade pastas – they produce quite a range, all made with natural products – or unusual pasta, for instance Curaçao blue tagliatelle. You'll find anything from *tagliolini con curry indiano* to *tagliolini con cacao amaro* (with bitter cocoa). They also sell imported specialities, such as olive oil from Modena and some pastas from Puglia.

Volpe Panetteria (☎ *041 71 51 78, Calle del Ghetto Vecchio 1142*) **Map 3** This bakery and delicatessen in the heart of the Ghetto sells kosher food and wine.

For details of shops where you can fill up your own containers with wine, see the boxed text 'Fill 'Er Up' in the Entertainment chapter.

FURNITURE
Segno di Lorenzo Usicco (☎ *041 71 09 75, Calle del Tintor 1809*) **Map 3** This place is worth a look, if only out of curiosity. The furniture is hand-painted and quite exquisite (for instance, a fine chest of drawers of hand-decorated cherry wood comes in at a cool €775) – and for those with lots of dough.

GLASS & CRYSTAL
When people shop in Venice, they tend to think of Murano glass and there is no shortage of workshops and showrooms full of the stuff, particularly between San Marco and Castello and on the island of Murano. Much of it is designed for tourists, so shop around. Quality and prices vary dramatically.

Always haggle, as the marked price is usually much higher than what the seller expects. If you decide to buy, the shop will quite often ship it home for you. Remember, though, that this can take a long time and you are likely to have to pay duty when it arrives.

You can see glass being blown in some of the glass shops on Murano. Look for the sign *fornace*, which means oven or furnace. You do not, however, need to go to Murano to buy glassware. Indeed, it is far more readily available in Venice itself and prices tend to be similar.

San Marco

***L'Isola** (☎ 041 523 19 73, Salizzada San Moisè 1468)* **Map 5** L'Isola has glass objects by Carlo Moretti that are much appreciated for their elegance and finesse. The prices aren't exactly low, however.

***Galleria Marina Barovier** (☎ 041 522 51 02, Calle delle Carrozze 3216)* **Map 6** Barovier is one of *the* names in glass and expensive, but wander down here to see the latest creations by some of the most outstanding artists in glass in Venice.

***La Gondola** (☎ 041 520 70 51, Fondamenta Orseolo, San Marco 1166)* **Map 5** While not as classy as Barovier, this place is remarkable for some of the flights of fantasy on display – astonishing as much for their sheer physical size as their inventiveness – and again for the price tags (not that we want to appear stingy or anything).

Murano

The bulk of the glass sellers are congregated, as they should be, along Fondamenta dei Vetrai. Ever since the *vetrai*, or glassmakers, were transferred to the island at the close of the 13th century, this is where they have practised their art. Quite a few occupy Fondamenta Manin, across the canal, and others can be found on Viale Garibaldi and Fondamenta Andrea Navagero – strategically placed by the vaporetto stops to intercept visitors to the island. See the Murano map in the Things to See & Do Chapter for the following shops.

***Barovier & Toso** (☎ 041 527 43 85, W www.barovier.com, Fondamenta dei Vetrai 28)* This is, as you may have already guessed from the San Marco entry, one of the leading names in quality artistic glassware. Your chequebook will tremble on entering.

***Venini** (☎ 041 73 99 55, W www.venini.it, Fondamenta dei Vetrai 47-50)* Venini is another place to browse the top-shelf stuff before wandering off to poke your nose into less exalted glass factories and shops. Again, independent wealth comes in handy. For a sneak preview, check out their Web site.

***Berengo** (☎ 041 527 63 64, W www.berengo.com, Fondamenta dei Vetrai 109/a)* At Berengo, they have abandoned almost completely any pretence at functionality. This is glass for art's sake. If you are into the idea of glass as sculpture, this is one of a couple of places that could interest you.

JEWELLERY
San Marco

***Codognato** (☎ 041 522 50 42, Calle Seconda dell'Ascensione 1295)* **Map 5** Possibly the city's best-known jewellers, Codognato sells classic pieces that attracted the likes of Jackie Onassis in their time.

JEWISH GOODS

In the Ghetto in Cannaregio you'll find a few interesting places. To the west of the Museo Ebraico is a nameless little *workshop* selling Jewish art (Map 3). Some of the porcelain is very attractive. Most of the stuff here is made to order and the place is not really designed for browsing.

On Calle del Ghetto Vecchio, you'll find a couple of shops purveying an odd mix of souvenirs and religious stuff.

***La Stamperia del Ghetto** (☎ 041 275 02 00, Calle del Ghetto Vecchio 1185/a)* **Map 3** Here you will encounter a pleasing collection of prints with general scenes of Venice, not only the Ghetto or Jewish themes.

LACE

The people on Isola di Burano traditionally lived off two activities – fishing and lacemaking. The former is rapidly losing importance and the latter has been converted into the main attraction for the tourist dollar.

You will find any number of shops along and near Via Galuppi on the island. Inspect the wares closely – although you can often see some of the island's more venerable ladies busily creating these products in quiet corners, the stuff on sale is sometimes of uneven quality and/or imported from Asia. The reason? It's a lot cheaper to import imitations than to make the real thing and most tourists aren't prepared to spend money on the genuine article. You don't need to get to Burano to buy lace – several stores sell it in Venice too.

San Marco

Jesurum *(☎ 041 520 60 85, Merceria del Capitello 4856)* **Map 5** Jesurum has been in business since 1860, when Michelangelo Jesurum opened a lace school on the Isola di Burano, then a deeply poor backwater. The quality and complexity of the women's work was such that Jesurum's laces won a prize at the Universal Exposition of 1878. Since then, it has been *the* name in lace – and the prices are commensurate.

LAMPSHADES
San Polo

Cenerentola *(☎ 041 527 44 55, Calle 2 dei Saoneri 2718)* A beautiful collection of lampshades is on display here, or you can have them custom-made.

MARBLED PAPER

Venice is noted for its marbled paper *(carta marmorizzata)*, often made to traditional and evocatively named designs. It has become something of a hit with visitors and is used for all sorts of things, from expensive giftwrap to book covers.

San Marco

Legatoria Piazzesi *(☎ 041 522 12 02, Campiello della Feltrina 2551/c)* **Map 6** This is the oldest shop purveying these materials; they employ time-honoured methods to turn out high-quality items.

   Il Papiro *(☎ 041 522 30 55, Calle del Piovan 2764)* **Map 6** This is another classic stop on the paper chase.

Dorsoduro

Il Pavone *(☎ 041 523 45 17, Fondamenta Venier dai Leoni 721)* **Map 6** This is also a quality store for marbled paper, veering away from the traditional and indulging in a little fantasy. They also have another branch *(San Marco 3287)*.

San Polo

Legatoria Polliero *(☎ 041 528 51 30, Campo dei Frari 2995)* **Map 6** Polliero is a traditional exponent of the art of Venetian book binding with (and without) marbled paper.

METALWORK

Valese *(☎ 041 522 72 82, Calle Fiubera 793)* **Map 5** Since 1918 the Valese family has cast figures in bronze, copper and other metals here. Their reputation is unequalled in the city. Although not all the items might suggest themselves as souvenirs as much as the horses that adorn the flanks of the city's gondolas, this is an interesting place.

MODELS

Gilberto Penzo *(☎ 041 71 93 72, Calle 2 dei Saoneri 2681)* **Map 6** Mr Penzo has long been passionate about gondolas. So much so that he began to build models and collect detailed plans of them and all other lagoon and Adriatic vessels. He founded an association aimed at keeping all this ancient knowledge fresh, and to finance it all he opened a shop. Here you can buy exquisite wooden models of various Venetian vessels hand built. He also takes in old ones for restoration. For the kids, you can fork out €23.25 on gondola model kits (or buy them ready-made and painted). Poster-size technical drawings of Venice's floating symbol sell for €10.35. And round the corner, you can have a peek at his workshop. This place is a gem.

MUSIC

Nalesso *(☎ 041 520 33 29, Calle de Spezier 2765/d)* **Map 6** In a small courtyard off the street, Nalesso specialises in CDs of music in some way connected with Venice concentrating on classical, Renaissance, Baroque and opera.

SHOES

Manuela Calzature *(☎ 041 522 66 52, Ruga Rialto 1046)* **Map 6** Here is a small family business with a nice range of shoes including more expensive footwear that they make under their own name. Don't judge it by the cheap junk outside.

Bruno Magli (☎ *041 522 72 10, Calle Vallaresso 1302)* **Map 5** This shop has fashionable footwear for men and women.

TEDDY BEARS

Il Baule Blu (☎ *041 71 94 48, Campo San Tomà 2916/a)* **Map 6** Want a luxury bear? The owners of this shop have turned cuddly teddies into a business for aficionados. If you can't live without yours and have brought it along to Venice, then you can feel at ease – the shop also operates a Teddy Hospital.

TOYS

The Disney Store (☎ *041 522 39 80, Campo San Bartolomeo 5257)* **Map 5** All right, perhaps you'll think it's as bad as mentioning McDonald's. Fact is, kids love Disney toys and this place may well save a failing parental relationship with loved little ones.

Excursions

The greater part of the Veneto, the region of which Venice is the capital, is plains country, stretching away from the mighty River Po. To the north, however, ranks of hills rise up gradually into the Dolomite mountains.

The entire area was long under the control of the Venetian Republic. Even today, the surrounding regions of Friuli-Venezia Giulia and Trentino (part of the joint region known as Trentino-Alto Adige), where the lion of St Mark long held sway, are often lumped in with the Veneto and called the Triveneto.

The destinations covered in this chapter are all do-able as day trips from Venice, with no need to spend even a night outside the lagoon city if you do not wish. The Dolomites, splendid skiing and hiking country, are not covered, as you really need to set aside several days for such a trip.

Highlights include the cities of Padua (Padova) and Verona, to the west, and the hilltop village of Asolo to the north-west. Architecture enthusiasts will want to consider touring the Riviera del Brenta and beyond. Palladio is an architectural theme unto himself – apart from villas along the Brenta and outside Vicenza, that city itself is a rich repository of his work.

For some local sun and sand you could try the beaches of Jesolo and beyond, on the coast curving away north-east of Venice.

RIVIERA DEL BRENTA

Dotted along the River Brenta, which passes through Padua and spills into the Venetian lagoon, are more than 100 villas built over the centuries by wealthy Venetian families as summer homes.

Many are closed to the public, but some of the more outstanding ones can be visited. Among them are Villa Foscari (1571), built by Palladio at Malcontenta, and Villa Pisani, also known as Villa Nazionale, at Strà. The latter, built for Doge Alvise Pisani, was later used by Napoleon and hosted Hitler's first meeting with Mussolini. Details of the principal villas open to the public follow.

Regular ACTV buses running between Padua and Venice (via Strà, Dolo, Mira, Oriago, Marghera and Mestre) stop at or near the villas. For the latest information on all the villas open to the public, ask at the Venice APT office. Bear in mind that their information may not always be accurate – since most of the villas are privately owned, opening times and prices can vary capriciously.

The luxurious *Burchiello* barge plied the River Brenta from Venice to Padua in the 17th and 18th centuries. Today's version, a rather drab and anything-but-luxurious old thing, lumbers up and down the river between Venice and Strà (from March to October) ferrying tourists for about €62 one way, including lunch and short tours. Shuttle buses connect with the docking point in Strà and Padua's main bus station. Call ☎ 049 877 47 12 (W www.ilburchiello.it) for information, or try travel agents in Venice. At least three other companies operate tours along the Brenta, including I Batelli del Brenta (☎ 049 876 02 33). Ask at the Venice or Padua tourist offices for more details on all four companies.

Apart from the villas mentioned in this section, several others occasionally open, in some cases only if you book ahead by phone – check with the Venice APT office.

See the Around Vicenza section later in this chapter for information on other Venetian villas.

Villa Foscari

No sooner do you roll out of the nightmare industry-scape of Marghera than you find yourself heading for Malcontenta (ACTV bus No 53; ask for the bus to Padua via Malcontenta). Here, the Foscari family commissioned Palladio to construct a pleasure dome on the River Brenta. The result was a Palladian trademark – the riverside facade, with its ionic columns and classical tympanum, echoes the ancients that inspired him. The villa **(Map 1)** (☎ 041 520 39 66; admission €6.20; open 9am-noon Tues & Sat; groups of

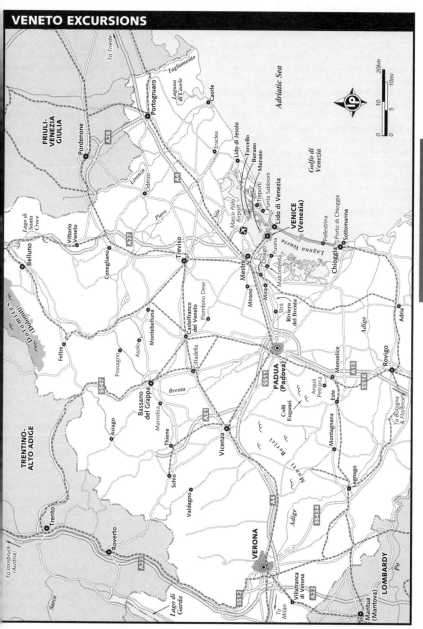

EXCURSIONS

10+ can book ahead for other times at €7.75 per person) is also known as La Malcontenta (The Malcontent), supposedly because a female family member was exiled here for fooling around with people other than hubby. Its interior is remarkable only for the frescoes with which it is covered. They mostly depict scenes from classical literature.

Villa Widmann Foscari
An 18th-century rococo caprice just west of Oriago, this villa *(☎ 041 42 41 56)* generally opens for groups that book ahead. At the time of writing, it was closed indefinitely for restoration.

Villa Barchessa Valmarana
Across the Brenta from Villa Widmann Foscari, this villa *(☎ 041 510 23 41; admission €5.15)*, noteworthy mainly for its frescoes, was built a century earlier. It opens only for prebooked groups (such as those on the *Burchiello* trips – see earlier in this chapter).

Villa Pisani
This is by far the most magnificent of the lot. The villa *(☎ 049 50 20 74; admission €5.15, grounds only €2.60; open 9am-6pm Apr-Sept)* is set in extensive gardens a few kilometres short of Strà and was completed in 1760. It is quite an exercise in family trumpet-blowing. From the outsize statues at the main entrance to Tiepolo's ceiling fresco (a pictorial eulogy to the Pisani clan), it is a flashy display of wealth. Outside, a close-cropped lawn and pond separate the main house from a lesser mansion. On either side, privacy is maintained by heavily wooded gardens.

Other Villas
Other villas worth keeping your eyes peeled for are: Villa Foscarini Rossi *(☎ 049 980 03 35)* in Strà; Villa Sagredo *(☎ 049 50 31 74)* in Vigonovo; Villa Gradenigo *(☎ 049 876 02 33)* in Oriago di Mira and Villa Barchessa Alessandri *(☎ 041 41 57 29)* in Mira. On Sundays and holidays in June, September and October, guided visits are sometimes organised to further villas in the area as part of the Ville Aperte (Open Villas) initiative.

TREVISO
postcode 31100 • pop 81,240
A small, pleasant city with historical importance as a Roman centre, Treviso is well worth a day trip from Venice, easily accomplished by train. You could also make a stopover if you are heading north for the Dolomites. People planning to stay overnight should note, however, that there is no decent cheap accommodation in the city.

Treviso claims Luciano Benetton, the clothing manufacturer, as its favourite son. You will find a huge Benetton shop in the centre of town, but factory outlets around the outskirts of town are the strict preserve of Benetton employees.

Orientation
From the train station, head north along Via Roma (over the canal), past the bus station and across the bridge (the nicely placed McDonald's on the river is an unmistakable landmark) and keep walking straight ahead along Corso del Popolo. At Piazza della Borsa, veer left down Via XX Settembre and you arrive in the heart of the city, Piazza dei Signori.

Information
The APT office *(☎ 0422 54 76 32)* is at Piazzetta Monte di Pietà 8, adjacent to Piazza dei Signori. It opens 9am to 12.30pm and 2.30pm to 6.30pm Monday to Friday. At the weekend the times are 9.30am to 12.30pm and 3.30pm to 6pm. From October to March, the afternoon hours shorten a little. The office sometimes organises free guided tours of the city.

Things to See & Do
The APT promotes Treviso as the *Città d' Acqua* (City of Water) and compares it to Venice. While the River Sile, which weaves through the centre, is quite beautiful in parts, the comparisons are more touching than realistic.

That said, the city is a delight to wander. Piazza dei Signori is dominated by the fine brick **Palazzo dei Trecento**, the one-time seat of city government beneath whose vaults you can now stop for coffee and a bite. The medieval main street is the porticoed Via Calmaggiore, which leads to the **cathedral** *(Piazza del Duomo; open 7.30am-noon & 3.30pm-7pm Mon-Fri, 7.30am-1pm & 3.30pm-8pm Sat & Sun)*, a massive structure whose main source of interest lies in the frescoes inside by Il Pordenone (1484–1539).

Backtrack to Piazza dei Signori and head east (around and behind the Palazzo dei Trecento) and you will soon find yourself in a little warren of lanes that leads to five delightful bridges across the Canal Cagnan, which runs roughly north-south and spills into the River Sile. Treviso is a comparatively leafy town and this is particularly the case at some points along the canal. You can also see the occasional mill wheel (the one by Vicolo Molinetto still turns). While on the right bank of the canal, you might pop into the deconsecrated **Chiesa di Santa Caterina** *(Via di Santa Caterina; admission €1.55; open 9am-noon & 3pm-7pm 1st Sun of month only)*, decorated with frescoes by Tommaso da Modena (1326–79). Tommaso also left frescoes in the imposing **Chiesa di San Nicolò** *(Via San Nicolò; open 7am-noon & 3.30pm-7pm)*, on the other side of town. Where the Canal Cagnan empties into the Sile is a particularly pleasant corner where part of the city walls remain intact. In summer, you can take a *boat cruise* (☎ 0422 78 86 63, 0422 78 86 71) on the *Silis* or *Altino* down the Sile to the Venetian lagoon and back. The tours are by reservation only – call or ask at the tourist office.

Places to Stay
Only one hotel favours central Treviso with its presence.

Albergo Campeol (☎ 0422 5 66 01, Piazza Ancilotto 4) Singles/doubles €46.50/77.50. This is a nicely maintained place in a restored building just off Piazza dei Signori, and it also boasts a good restaurant downstairs, the *Ristorante alle Beccherie*.

Otherwise a couple of more rundown establishments cluster close to the train station. The remaining 10 or so hotels are well out of the centre, some on the approach roads to town, and thus anything but handy (unless you are driving).

Places to Eat
Ristorante al Dante (☎ 0422 59 18 97, Piazza Garibaldi 6) Full meals around €15.50. Open Mon-Sat. This is an excellent budget option where you can sidle up to the bar for a host of *cicheti* (traditional bar snacks), or dine at one of the teeny tables. In summer you can sit outside and gaze across to the river. Typically people pop in for bar snacks and *prosecco* (sparkling white wine), or perhaps a crisp Friuli white.

Odeon (☎ 0422 54 48 04, Vicolo Rinaldi 3) Full meals around €21. Open 6.30pm-2am Tues-Sun. In the heart of the old centre, this is a recent addition to the small circuit of places that serve up good traditional Veneto *osteria* (traditional bar-restaurant) dishes and snacks. Here they do an admirable version of *sardine in saor* (sardines fried in an onion marinade) and in summer you can munch them outside.

Piola (☎ 0422 54 02 87, Via Carlo Alberto 11) Pizzas from around €6.20. Open Tues-Sun. This is a hip bar-cum-pizzeria, where you can sit outside on a little terrace or bury yourself in the dimly lit innards of the bar with Treviso's night crowd. The pizzas are good, with a wide choice of toppings.

Shopping
For many, the call of Benetton (☎ 0422 55 99 11), in the heart of town at Piazza dell' Indipendenza 5, will be hard to resist. The shop opens 3.30pm to 7.30pm Monday and 10am to 7.30pm Tuesday to Saturday.

Getting There & Away
The bus station is on Lungosile Mattei, near the train station in Piazzale Duca d'Aosta. ACTV buses connect Venice with Treviso, and La Marca buses link Treviso with other towns in the province. Buses travel to Conegliano (€2.25, 45 minutes) and Vittorio Veneto (€3.10, one hour five minutes).

It often makes better sense to get the train. Trains from Venice (€1.90) take 25 minutes. Other trains link the town with Belluno (via Conegliano and Vittorio Veneto), Oderzo, Padua and major cities to the south and west.

By car, take the SS53 from Treviso to Venice and Padua.

EXCURSIONS

AROUND TREVISO

With an early start from Venice and preferably your own transport, you could branch out a little from Treviso and explore some surrounding towns.

Oderzo, about 25km east of Treviso, is a microcosm of its grander neighbour. The central Piazza Grande is flanked by the 15th-century cathedral and a fine clock tower, and is frequently the scene of classical music recitals in summer. The town's handful of peaceful canals, crisscrossed by little bridges bearing pretty flower boxes is inevitably reminiscent of Treviso. In the Museo Civico Archeologico (☎ 0422 71 33 33, Via Garibaldi 65; admission €2.60; open 9am-noon & 3.30pm-6.30pm Wed-Sat, 3.30pm-8.30pm Sun) you can view an interesting collection of Roman-era artefacts. By far the most interesting are the 4th-century mosaics depicting hunting scenes. Trains (or substitute buses) run from Treviso (€1.90, 30 to 45 minutes).

North of Treviso, on the road to Belluno, you could call in at **Conegliano**, wine capital of the Veneto region and dominated by a castle (which you can reach on foot or by car). The centre of town, a few minutes' walk straight ahead down Via Carducci from the train station, is notable for the long Scuola dei Battuti on Via XX Settembre, decorated on the inside and out with frescoes. The cathedral, which you enter from the Scuola, is noteworthy for an altarpiece painted by local painter Cima da Conegliano in 1492–93.

The train from Venice (€3.20) takes 30 to 50 minutes. That same train goes a further 10km to the strange animal that is **Vittorio Veneto** (€3.90 from Venice). Actually a composite of two towns (Ceneda and Serravalle), Vittorio Veneto is most comfortably visited with your own transport. As you arrive from the south, do *not* follow signs for the centro (as you normally would). These take you to the modern part of the conglomerate, which lacks any real interest. Instead, follow signs for Ceneda, whose main attractions are the sweeping Piazza Giovanni Paolo I and Castello di San Martino, about a 1km hike up into the leafy hills. To reach the picturesque huddle of houses that is Serravalle, you need

to follow signs for Belluno. These apparently lead you out of Vittorio Veneto, and you may get that leaving feeling, but then you stumble on this northernmost, and prettiest, part of the sprawling municipality.

BELLUNO

postcode 32100 ● pop 35,230

Belluno is a beautiful little town at the foot of the Dolomites. If you start early enough, you could just about combine it with Treviso in a day trip from Venice, either by train or bus. Better still, hang around for a few days and use it as a base to explore the mountains.

Orientation

Buses arrive at Piazzale della Stazione, in front of the train station. From here take Via Dante (which becomes Via Loreto) and then turn left at the T-junction down Via Matteotti into the central Piazza dei Martiri.

Information

The IAT tourist office (☎ 0437 94 00 83), Piazza dei Martiri 8, produces a feast of information on walking, trekking, skiing and other sporting activities. It opens 9am to 12.30pm and 3pm to 6pm Monday to Saturday, 10am to 12.30pm and 3.30pm to 6.30pm Sunday (mornings only on Sunday in winter). You should pop in if you're planning to head into the Dolomites.

Things to See & Do

Although no greatly notable monuments await inspection in Belluno, a wander around the compact old town is a pleasant experience. The main square (really a broad pedestrian avenue), Piazza dei Martiri (Martyrs' Square), takes its name from four partisans hanged here in the dying stages of WWII.

The heart of the old town is formed by Piazza del Duomo, dominated on one side by the early-16th-century Renaissance Cattedrale di San Martino, the Palazzo Rosso, from about the same period, and the Palazzo dei Vescovi. The latter's tower is one of three that belonged to the original 12th-century structure, long gone.

For most, the reason for reaching Belluno is as a starting point for activities in the mountains, from summertime hiking to skiing in winter. Stretching away to the northwest of Belluno is the **Parco Nazionale Dolomiti Bellunesi**, a beautiful national park laden with opportunities for those who want some mountain air.

Six Alte Vie delle Dolomiti (high altitude walking trails through the Dolomites) pass through the territory surrounding Belluno and along them you will find *rifugi* (mountain huts), on route No 1 in particular, where you can stay at the end of a day's hiking. Route No 1 stretches between Belluno and Lago di Braies in the region of Trentino-Alto Adige. The refuges are generally open from late June to late September.

Places to Stay

Camping Park Nevegal (☎ *0437 90 81 43, fax 0437 90 81 44, Via Nevegal 347)* Sites per person/tent €6.70/€9.30. Open year round. This camping ground has room for about 250 people and lies about 10km from Belluno at Nevegal. Autolinee Dolomiti buses from Belluno run past (€1.80, 20 minutes).

Ostello Imperina (☎ *0437 6 24 51, Località Le Miniere, 32020 Rivamonte Agordino)* B&B €12.90. This, the nearest youth hostel, is 35km north-west at Rivamonte Agordino, and is open from April to September. You can get there on the Agordo bus (€2.60, 50 minutes) from Belluno.

Albergo Taverna (☎ *0437 2 51 92, Via Cipro 7)* Singles/doubles without bathroom €15.50/31. It also has a few nicer doubles with their own bathrooms for around €41.30. Equally important is the restaurant downstairs (see the Places to Eat chapter).

A handful of other hotels dot the town, as well as some B&Bs and *affittacamere* (rooms for rent). Both these categories basically amount to rooms in private houses, the difference being the breakfast in the B&Bs. Plenty more hotels and affittacamere are scattered about the surrounding towns and villages.

If you want to get into the countryside and mountains, there are many country properties and mountain refuges. The tourist office has all the details.

Places to Eat

La Taverna (☎ *0437 2 51 92, Via Cipro 7)* Full meals around €23. Open Mon-Sat. You can sit at the bar for snacks and prosecco or head on through to the restaurant area, where you will be treated to hearty cooking. Around Christmas they do a local speciality for experienced stomachs only – a snail and eel combo that won't be to everyone's liking!

Getting There & Away

Autolinee Dolomiti buses (☎ 0437 94 12 37) depart from in front of the train station, on the western edge of town, for Agordo, Cortina d'Ampezzo, Feltre and smaller towns in the mountains and south of town.

Trains from Venice (€5.25, one hour 50 minutes) run via Treviso.

By car you can take the A27 *autostrada* from Venice (Mestre) or follow the state roads via Treviso. The latter can be time-consuming because of heavy traffic.

BASSANO DEL GRAPPA
postcode 36061 • pop 39,000

Known above all for its firewater, grappa, and to a lesser degree for its production of ceramics, Bassano del Grappa sits astride the River Brenta just south of the first line of hills that are a prelude to the Dolomites. To art lovers, the name will ring another bell. The Da Ponte family of Renaissance painters, known to us now as the Bassano, came from here. The town's pretty centre and accessibility from Venice make it an enjoyable trip that takes you off the main tourist trails.

Orientation

From the train station it's about a five-minute walk west to the old centre and the APT tourist office. Buses halt a few minutes' walk south of the tourist office at Piazzale Trento. Another five-minute walk west and you are in the centre of the town. The River Brenta, crossed by the Ponte degli Alpini, flows to the west of the centre.

Information

The well stocked APT office (☎ 0424 52 43 51) is at Largo Corona d'Italia, close to the train and bus stations. It opens 9am to noon

EXCURSIONS

EXCURSIONS

and 2pm to 5pm Monday to Friday, 9am to 12.30pm on Saturday. The office sometimes organises free tours (generally in Italian) of the city.

Things to See

The centre of Bassano is composed of two sloping and interlinking squares, Piazza Garibaldi and Piazza Libertà. In the latter, the winged lion of St Mark stands guard on a pedestal to remind you of who was long in charge here.

In the **Museo Civico** (☎ 0424 52 22 35, Via del Museo 12; admission €2.60; open 9am-6pm Tues-Sat, 3.30pm-6.30pm Sun), attached to the Chiesa di San Francesco on Piazza Garibaldi, you can see an assortment of items, ranging from paintings by members of the Bassano clan through to archaeological finds (such as ancient Greek ceramics). Among the Bassano collection are 17 canvases by Jacopo. Also on display is a section devoted to the sculptor Canova, with his letters, books, drawings and plaster casts.

Follow Via Matteotti north off Piazza Libertà towards the remains of **Castello Ezzelini**, the stronghold that belonged to the medieval warlords of the same name.

Via Gamba slithers downhill from Via Matteotti to the River Brenta and the covered bridge known as the **Ponte degli Alpini**. It is named after the mountain troops who rebuilt it in 1948 after retreating German soldiers seriously damaged it at the tail end of WWII. Via Gamba and the bridge are lined with ceramics shops and a few grappa outlets. Throw in some bars and snack joints and it makes a pleasant stroll. The views across to old Bassano from the far riverbank alone make the walk from the centre worthwhile.

While down here, pop into the Poligrappa shop. Here they have created the **Poli Museo della Grappa** (☎ 0424 52 44 26, 🄴 museo@poligrappa.com, Ponte Vecchio; admission free; open 9am-1pm & 2.30pm-7.30pm daily), which briefly outlines the history of the production of the drink. You can of course also buy while you are here – it will be hard to resist the many variants and their elegant bottles.

Places to Stay & Eat

Victoria (☎ 0424 50 36 20, fax 0424 50 31 30, Viale Diaz 33) Single/doubles up to €41.30/62. The whitewashed and carpeted rooms are well kept and boast TV, minibar and all the usual bits and bobs. The location is nothing great but otherwise it's not a bad deal. Breakfast is extra.

Hotel Castello (☎/fax 0424 22 86 65, Via Bonamigo 19) Singles/doubles €41.30/72.30. This place, in the shadow of the old castle walls, is the only hotel within the old town. It's a fairly small and simple affair but is perfectly acceptable.

As far as eating is concerned, you can't go wrong at *Alla Riviera* (☎ 0424 50 37 00, Via San Giorgio 7), open Wednesday to Monday. Here you will be served hearty traditional Veneto cuisine, such as *pasta e fagioli* (pasta and beans) or rabbit in a tangy sauce. Main courses cost around €10.30.

Before dining, drop in at the *Nardini* bar right at the start of the Ponte degli Alpini on the old city centre side. You sit down among the grand old wine barrels and sip grappas. It closes by about 8pm.

Getting There & Away

The easiest way to reach Bassano from Venice is by train on the Venice-Trento line (€3.60, 1¼ hours). A train from Padua (€2.80, one hour) is another option. Buses also link Bassano with Padua and Vicenza.

AROUND BASSANO DEL GRAPPA

A half-dozen destinations are clustered around Bassano. Some are easily reached from Venice, while others could be considered in tandem with Bassano. Alternatively, you could make Bassano a base for a night or two. Except for Asolo, all of these places can be considered of secondary interest. Those with limited time may want to concentrate on more important destinations like Padua, Vicenza and Verona (see later in this chapter). If you have a vehicle, you can get around all these spots easily and quickly.

Asolo

Its position high in the hills, surrounded by fields, farms and woods, makes Asolo an

A Queen Cornered

In 1468, as 14-year-old Caterina Corner was escorted in pomp out of the family mansion in San Polo to the Palazzo Ducale, she must have wondered what was coming next. *Niente di buono* ('nothing good') would have been the response of wise onlookers. Betrothed to 28-year-old James, the usurper king of Cyprus, Caterina found herself four years later pregnant, widowed and surrounded by enemies in her new island home.

James' untimely (and suspicious) death convinced Venice that it must act to protect its growing interest in the island. Captain General Pietro Mocenigo was dispatched first to fortify Venetian forts and then later to reverse a coup against the queen. The Cypriots were none too enamoured of de facto Venetian rule in their island, but after the coup attempt, government was effectively in the hands of two Venetian *Consiglieri* (Councillors), ostensibly in the service of the queen.

After the death of her infant son in 1474, Caterina's problems only increased. Plots against her from Cypriot nobles came thick and fast, and her protectors, the Venetians, virtually held her prisoner. In 1488, Venice decided enough was enough. Cyprus was threatened by Turkish invasion and the latest plots against Caterina were proving insufferable. It was decided to absorb the island into the Venetian Empire. For this, Caterina had to be convinced to abdicate.

This she did with some reluctance but she had little choice. For her trouble she was compensated with a mainland fief centred on Asolo and a generous life pension. She only returned to her Venetian home in 1509, where she died the following year. She kept her title of queen until the end. Less than a century later Venice would lose Cyprus to the Turks anyway.

enchanting village. Caterina Corner, the ill-fated Venetian queen of Cyprus, was given the town and surrounding county towards the end of the 15th century in exchange for her abdication (see the boxed text 'A Queen Cornered' above). The writer Pietro Bembo attended Caterina's salons, and perhaps in search of a hint of that same atmosphere, Robert Browning also spent time in Asolo.

Things to See Piazza Garibaldi forms the centre of town, from where streets wind up in all directions between the tight ranks of golden-hued houses that lend this place so much of its charm. The **cathedral** lies below and just to the south of the square. It contains a few paintings by Jacopo Bassano and Lorenzo Lotto. Caterina Corner lived in the **castle**, now used as a theatre. An arduous climb up Via Collegio from Piazza Brugnoli will get you to the **rocca**, the town's medieval fortress. The walk north out of town to the **Cimitero di Sant'Anna** is rewarding for the views over the lush, green countryside. Eleonora Duse, a whirlwind actress romantically involved with poet Gabriele d'Annunzio, was buried here in 1924.

Places to Stay & Eat Staying here is unfortunately the preserve of the better off. You have three places to choose from.

Hotel Duse (☎ 0423 5 52 41, fax 0423 95 04 04, Via Browning 190) Doubles up to €129. The hotel has lovely rooms and they'd want to be at this price. Bear in mind that the Duse is the *cheapest* option in town.

If you don't stay, at least consider lunch at *Ca' Derton (☎ 0423 52 96 48, Piazza d' Annunzio 11)*, open Tuesday to Sunday. They do a tempting *capretto alle erbe aromatiche* (kid meat in herbs) and have a fine wine list and dessert menu.

Getting There & Away Buses (up to six per day) between Bassano and Montebelluna (€1.75, 25 minutes) stop below Asolo. You need to get the little orange shuttle bus to reach the centre, otherwise it's a long walk.

Villa Barbaro

About 7km east of Asolo, at Maser, this Palladian villa *(☎ 0423 92 30 04; admission €4.15; open 3pm-6pm Tues, Sat, Sun & holidays)* is one of the best of the genre. Palladio built it in the late 1550s for the

Barbari brothers – two eminent figures in Venetian public life – and it was decorated by Veronese, whose remarkable fresco cycle adorns the upper floor. In the grounds stands Palladio's **Tempietto**. Based on the Pantheon in Rome, it was his last project.

About five daily buses between Bassano and Montebelluna (€1.75, 35 minutes) stop here.

Possagno

Birth and resting place of Antonio Canova, Italy's master of neoclassical sculpture, Possagno is a good place to get an idea of how Canova worked. The **Gipsoteca** *(☎ 0423 54 43 23; admission €3.10; open 9am-noon & 3pm-6pm Tues-Sat, 9am-noon & 3pm-7pm Sun May-Sept; closing time 5pm Oct-Apr)* is home to a long series of clay models and other preparatory pieces for his finished work (you can see some statues and reliefs by Canova in Venice's Museo Correr).

Before you even reach the Gipsoteca, you'll have been astonished by the rather outsize **tempio** *(open 9am-noon & 3pm-6pm Mon-Sat, 9am-noon & 3pm-7pm Sun May-Sept; closing time 5pm Oct-Apr)*, to all intents and purposes the parish church, that Canova was considerate enough to leave to his town. Finished in 1832, it could be described as neo-mongrel-classical, as it is an amalgam of Greek and Roman models.

The best way to reach Possagno is by bus from Bassano (€2.25, one hour). There are about 10 departures per day.

Marostica

You know you have almost arrived here when you see the jagged line of battlements that climbs the hill from Marostica's town centre to the upper castle.

Pretty enough to warrant a brief stop in its own right, Marostica comes into its own every other year in September for the colourful **Partita a Scacchi** (Chess Match). Back in 1454, two knights challenged each other to a duel for the hand of the fair Lionora, elder daughter of the town's ruler, Taddeo Parisio. The latter, not wanting to lose either warrior, banned the duel and ordered them to 'fight' it out in a grand game of chess using real

people on a huge 'board' at the gates of the lower castle in the town centre. The two knights ordered the moves and the winner got Lionora. The loser didn't come off too badly, since he wed Parisio's younger daughter, apparently just as radiant.

The event today is as colourful as the original must have been, with an assembly of players and other characters in period costume. The game is choreographed in advance, using one of the classic matches between chess champions as the basis. If you can't be here for the second weekend of September in even years (2002, 2004, and so on), you can admire the costumes in the lower castle (Castello da Basso).

The tourist office (☎ 0424 7 21 27, fax 0424 47 09 95) is in the entrance to the castle at Piazza Castello 1. For information and tickets to the chess match, check out W www.marosticascacchi.it.

There are four hotels in Marostica, but finding a place to stay during the Partita a Scacchi is virtually impossible. The town is most easily reached by bus (€1.25, 15 to 20 minutes) from Bassano.

Cittadella

The main reason for getting to Cittadella, a 12km bus ride south of Bassano on the busy SS47 to Padua, is to inspect the towering red-brick walls and moat that still surround this one-time fortress town.

Padua raised the fort in the 13th century to face off the one built by Treviso at Castelfranco del Veneto (see the following section). In 1405 the small town that had grown up behind the 1.5km of walls came under Venice's control. There's not an awful lot to keep you busy here. Of the four gates, the northern Porta Bassano is the most elaborate.

A stream of buses stops here en route between Padua and Bassano. From Padua the trip takes about 50 minutes (€2.15). From Bassano (€1.45, 20 minutes) it's quicker.

Castelfranco del Veneto

Treviso built the 'Free Fort' (free because the rulers of Treviso exempted from all taxes anyone prepared to move in) at the end of the 12th century. From then until 1339, when it was absorbed into Venice's mainland empire, Castelfranco del Veneto remained a hotly contested site and frequently changed hands. Indeed, Padua laid siege to the town barely 10 years after its construction.

The square-based walls of the fort are less impressive than the circular version at Cittadella, but the town has an extra claim to fame as the birthplace of the mysterious painter Giorgione. Little is known about his life and only half-a-dozen works can be definitely attributed to him, one of them, the *Madonna col Bambino in Trono e Santi Francesco e Liberale* (Madonna and Child Enthroned with Saints Francis and Liberale), is in the **cathedral** *(admission free; open 8am-noon & 3.30pm-7pm)*.

In the unlikely event you want to stay, eight *hotels* offer doubles for around €51 to €93.

Alle Mura *(☎ 0423 49 80 98, Via Preti 69)* Meals around €41. Open Fri-Wed. This unassuming looking place is a fine dining option in Castelfranco but is a little rough on the wallet.

Castelfranco is on the train line that connects Venice (€2.80, 50 minutes) with Bassano del Grappa. A handful of buses runs to Padua and Treviso.

Piombino Dese

A little closer to Venice on the road from Bassano del Grappa, this nondescript town is home to the *Villa Cornaro* *(☎ 049 936 50 17; admission €4.15; open 3.30pm-6pm Sat May-Sept)*. The most impressive element of the mansion is its two-tiered portico, which you can see perfectly well from the street. The admission price is rather steep for what you get to see on the inside.

Piombino Dese is on the train line between Venice (€2.30, 40 minutes) and Bassano (€1.90, 30 minutes).

PADUA (PADOVA)

postcode 35100 • pop 211,985

Although famous as the city of St Anthony and for its university, one of the oldest in Europe, Padua is often seen merely as a convenient and cheap place to stay while visiting Venice. This is a shame, as the city offers a rich collection of art treasures (including Giotto's incredible frescoed chapel), and its many piazzas and arcaded streets are a pleasure to explore.

Padua's wealth grew during the 13th century, when it was controlled by the counts of Carrara who encouraged cultural and artistic pursuits (when they weren't busy warring with all and sundry) and established the Studium, the forerunner of the university.

Orientation

From the train station, it's a 10-minute walk across the square and up Corso del Popolo (later Corso Garibaldi) to the centre. Piazza della Frutta and the adjoining Piazza delle Erbe form the lively heart of the old city, bustling with market activity – take some time to drool over all the fine foods here. The Basilica del Santo and the vast Prato della Valle are a good 20-minute walk south from the train station.

Information

Tourist Offices The IAT office (☎ 049 875 20 77) at the train station opens 9.15am to 5.45pm Monday to Saturday, and 9am to noon on Sunday.

Another IAT office (☎ 049 876 79 27) operates in Vicolo Pedrocchi. Opening hours are 9am to 12.30pm and 3pm to 7pm Monday to Saturday. A third office (☎ 049 875 30 87) is located in a booth on Piazza del Santo. It opens only in peak season times with a variable timetable.

Post & Communications The post office, at Corso Garibaldi 33, opens 8.15am to 7pm Monday to Saturday and 8.30am to 6.30pm Sunday. Address poste restante mail to 35100 Padua. Mail Boxes Etc has a branch at Largo Europa 2. Here you can arrange to send parcels and have money wired to you through Western Union.

Telecom has an unstaffed phone office at Riviera Ponti Romani 33, open 7am to 10pm Monday to Saturday.

You can go online at Internet Point In Collegio (☎ 049 65 84 84), Via Petrarca 9. You pay a €1.55 membership fee, then €5.15 for the first hour. If you stay online

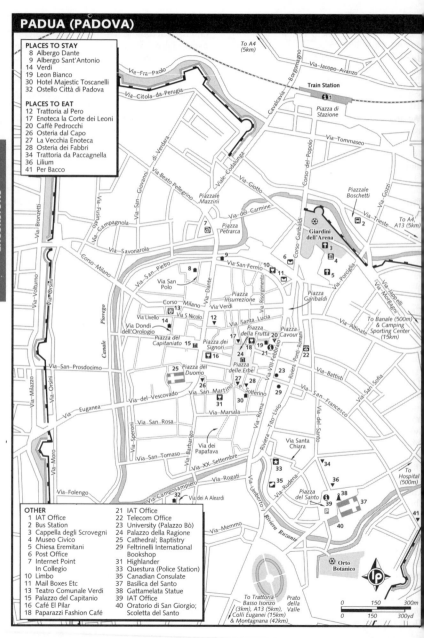

PADUA (PADOVA)

EXCURSIONS

To A4 (5km)
Via–Jacopo–Avanzo
Via–Fra–Paolo
Train Station
Via–Citola–da–Perugia
Piazza di Stazione
Via–Tommaseo
Cavalcavia–borgomagno
Corso–del–Popolo
Piazzale Boschetti
Via–Codalunga
To A4, A13 (5km)
Via–Trieste
Via–Gozzi
Via–Bronzetti
Via–Fusini–Feist
Via–Campagnola
Via–San–Giovanni
Via–di–Verdara
Via–Beato–Pellegrino
Viale–Codalunga
Via–Giotto
Piazzale Mazzini
Via–del–Carmine
Corso–Garibaldi
Via–San–Pietro
Via–Savonarola
Piazza Petrarca
Giardini dell'Arena
Via–Porciglia
Via–Morgagni
Via–Jappelli
Corso–Milano
Via–San–Fermo
Via San Polo
Via–Dante
Piazza Insurrezione
Via–Risorgimento
Piazza Garibaldi
To Banale (500m) & Camping Sporting Center (15km)
Via–Altinate
Corso–Milano
Via–Verdi
Via–Santa–Lucia
Via–Livello
Via S Nicolo
Via Dondi dell'Orologio
Piazza della Frutta
Piazza Cavour
Riviera–Ponti–Romani
Via–Battisti
Piazza del Capitaniato
Piazza dei Signori
Piazza delle Erbe
Via–VIII–Febbraio
Via–San–Prosdocimo
Piazza del Duomo
Via–San–Martino
Solferino
Riviera–Tito–Livio
Via–San–Francesco
Via San Sofia
Via del Santo
Via–del–Vescovado
Via–Marsala
Via–Roma
Via–Euganea
Via–San–Rosa
Via–Speroni
Via–Barbarigo
Via dei Papafava
Via Santa Chiara
To Hospital (500m)
Via–San–Tomaso
Via–XX–Settembre
Via–Rudena
Via–Rogati
Piazza del Santo
Via–Folengo
Via–Camposampiero
Via dei A Aleardi
Via–Umberto–I–Riviera Ruzante
Via–Memmo
Orto Botanico
Prato della Valle
To Trattoria Basso Isonzo (3km); A13 (5km); Colli Euganei (15km) & Montagnana (42km).

0   150   300m
0   150   300yd

onger, the fee for following hours drops to €2.60. It opens 9am to 2am.

Bookshops Padua is full of bookshops. For anything in languages other than Italian, try Feltrinelli International, at Via San Francesco 14.

Medical Services & Emergency Medical assistance is provided by the Complesso Clinico Ospedaliero (hospital; ☎ 049 821 11 11), Via Giustiniani 1. The *questura* (police station; ☎ 049 83 31 11) is at Riviera Ruzante 1, on the corner of Via Santa Chiara.

Things to See

A combined ticket, Padova Arte, costs €7.75 (€5.15 for students) and admits you to the main monuments. It's available from the IAT offices and ticket offices at the monuments concerned. (There's a similar ticket at the same price for sights in the surrounding province.)

Cappella degli Scrovegni Many art lovers visit Padua just to see this chapel *(bookings ☎ 049 820 45 50; admission €5.15 plus €1.05 booking fee or €1.55 booking fee only with Padova Arte ticket)* in the Giardini dell' Arena. Enrico Scrovegni commissioned it in 1303 as a resting place for his father, who was denied a Christian burial because of his money-lending practices. Giotto's remarkable fresco cycle, probably completed between 1304 and 1306, illustrates the lives of Mary and Christ and is arranged in three bands. You can pick up an adequate guide to the frescoes as you enter. Among the most famous scenes in the cycle is the *Bacio di Giuda* (Kiss of Judas). The series ends with the *Ultima Cena* (Last Supper) on the entrance wall and the Vices and Virtues are depicted around the lower parts of the walls. Keep in mind when the frescoes were painted – Giotto was moving well away from the two-dimensional figures of his medieval contemporaries and presaging greater things to come.

The flow of visitors has become such that you can no longer simply turn up and visit. Booking is obligatory. The admission ticket

is also valid for the adjacent **Museo Civico** *(open 9am-7pm Tues-Sun)*, whose collection of 14th- to 18th-century Veneto art and largely forgettable archaeological artefacts includes a remarkable crucifix by Giotto.

Chiesa Eremitani Completed in the early 14th century, this Augustinian church *(Giardini dell'Arena; open 8.30am-1pm & 4pm-7pm)* was painstakingly rebuilt after being almost totally destroyed by bombing in WWII. The remains of frescoes done by Andrea Mantegna during his 20s are displayed in a chapel to the left of the apse. Most were wiped out in the bombing, the greatest single loss to Italian art during the war. The *Martirio di San Jacopo* (Martyrdom of St James), on the left, was pieced together from fragments found in the rubble, while the *Martirio di San Cristoforo* (Martyrdom of St Christopher), opposite, was saved because it had been removed before the war.

Historic Centre Via VIII Febbraio leads to the city's **university** *(☎ 049 876 79 27; guided visits three times per day Mon-Sat)*, the main part of which is housed in the Palazzo Bò ('ox' in Veneto dialect – it's named after an inn that previously occupied the site). Established in 1222, the university is Italy's oldest after the one in Bologna. Europe's first anatomy theatre opened here in 1594 and Galileo Galilei taught at the university from 1592 to 1610. The main courtyard and its halls are plastered with coats of arms of the great and learned from across Europe. Ask at the IAT office in Vicolo Pedrocchi about joining a guided visit.

Continue along to Piazza delle Erbe and Piazza della Frutta, which are separated by the majestic **Palazzo della Ragione** *(admission €5.15 depending on exhibitions; open 9am-7pm Tues-Sun Mar-Oct, 9am-6pm Tues-Sun Nov-Feb)*, also known as the Salone for the grand hall on its upper floor. Built in the 13th and 14th centuries, the building features frescoes by Giusto de' Menabuoi and Nicolò Mireto depicting the astrological theories of Pietro d'Abano.

West from here is the Piazza dei Signori, dominated by the 14th-century **Palazzo del**

Capitanio, the former residence of the city's Venetian ruler. South is the **cathedral** *(open 7.30am-noon & 3.45pm-7pm Mon-Sat, 7.45am-1pm & 3.45pm-8.30pm Sun & holidays)*, built from a much-altered design by Michelangelo. The 13th-century Romanesque **baptistry** *(admission €2.05; open 10am-6pm)* features a series of frescoes of Old and New Testament scenes by Giusto de' Menabuoi, influenced by Giotto.

Piazza del Santo The city's most celebrated monument is the **Basilica del Santo** *(or di Sant'Antonio; open 6.30am-7.30pm)*, which houses the corpse of the town's patron saint and is an important place of pilgrimage. Construction of what is known to the people of Padua as Il Santo began in 1232. The saint's tomb, bedecked by requests for his intercession to cure illness or thanks for having done so, is in the Cappella del Santo, in the left transept. There was a time when the area surrounding the tomb was awash with crutches and other prosthetic devices of the grateful cured – these have been reduced to a symbolic few. Look out for the saint's relics in the apse. The sculptures and reliefs of the high altar are by Donatello, the master sculptor of the Florentine Renaissance.

Donatello remained in town long enough to carry out another assignment, the *Gattamelata* equestrian statue that dominates the square. This magnificent representation of the 15th-century Venetian *condottiero* (mercenary leader) Erasmos da Narni (whose nickname, Gattamelata, translates as 'Honeyed Cat'), done in 1453 is considered the first great bronze of the Italian Renaissance. Donatello made a lasting impression on Padua, leaving behind a whole school of sculptors that followed in his footsteps. They would come to specialise in *bronzetti* (bronze miniatures) coveted across Europe.

On the southern side of the piazza is the **Oratorio di San Giorgio** *(admission €1.55; open 9am-12.30pm & 2.30pm-6pm Mar-Oct, 9am-12.30pm & 2.30pm-5pm Nov-Feb)*, the burial chapel of the Lupi di Soranga family, with 14th-century frescoes. Next door is the **Scuola** (or **Scoletta**) **del Santo** *(admission €1.55; open 9am-12.30pm & 2.30pm-7pm*

From Portugal to Padua

St Anthony of Padua (1193–1232) was actually St Anthony of Portugal, where he was born (in Lisbon) and spent most of his life. At the age of 25, his wanderings began when he joined the Franciscans and headed for Morocco to preach among the Muslims. This could easily have proven little more than a suicide mission but before he had the chance to become a martyr, poor health brought him back to Europe, where he spent the ensuing years travelling and teaching in France and northern Italy. He earned great respect for his erudition and his capacity to preach to the learned as convincingly as to more simple folk. St Anthony died in Padua and the shrine built to him became a prime centre of pilgrimage. To this day countless miracles are attributed to him, as well as a knack for being the finder of lost articles.

Mar-Oct, 9am-12.30pm & 2.30pm-5pm Nov-Feb), which contains works believed to be by Titian.

Just south of Piazza del Santo, the **Orto Botanico** *(☎ 049 827 21 19; admission €2.60; open 9am-1pm & 3pm-6pm)* is purportedly the oldest botanical garden in Europe. It was first laid out in 1545.

Places to Stay

Padua has no shortage of budget hotels, but they fill up quickly in summer.

Camping Sporting Center (☎ 049 79 34 00, Via Roma 123) Sites per person/tent €6.70/12.50. This is the nearest camp site to Padua, about 15km out of town at Montegrotto Terme. It's big and boasts a swimming pool, shops and just about anything else your heart might desire. It can be reached by city bus M from the train station.

Ostello Città di Padova (☎ 049 875 22 19, fax 049 65 42 10, Via dei A Aleardi 30) B&B €12.40. To get to this place take bus No 3, 8 or 12 from the train station to Prato della Valle and then ask for directions. It's not bad as hostels go and has family rooms too.

The *Koko Nor Association (☎ 049 864 33 94, ⓔ kokonor@intercity.it, Via Selva 5)* can

elp you to find B&B-style accommodation
n family homes (they have about 10 on the
ooks) starting from around €31/57 for a
ingle/double.

*Verdi (☎ 049 875 57 44, Via Dondi dell'
Orologio 7)* Singles/doubles up to €22.50/
4.60. The rooms are simple but clean and
his is one of the cheapest deals in town.

*Albergo Sant'Antonio (☎ 049 875 13 93,
Via San Fermo 118)* Singles/doubles without
ath €33.60/48.55, singles/doubles with
ath €52.70/64.55. The comfortable rooms
ere are a good deal, all with TV and phone.

*Albergo Dante (☎ 049 876 04 08, Via
San Polo 5)* Singles/doubles €25.80/35.10.
This is a cheapie tucked away near the Sant'
Antonio. The bathroom is in the corridor
nd the rooms are a little bare but the prices
re tough to argue with. Parking is also
available.

*Leon Bianco (☎ 049 875 08 14; fax 049
875 61 84,* e *leonbianco@toscanelli.com,
Piazzetta Pedrocchi 12)* Singles/doubles
€73.85/95.55. This is an immaculately
maintained and charming hotel right in the
eart of the city. From your flower-box-
decorated balcony, you look right over the
elegant Caffè Pedrocchi (see Places to Eat).

*Hotel Majestic Toscanelli (☎ 049 66 32
44, fax 049 876 00 25,* e *majestic@tosca
nelli.com, Via dell'Arco 2)* Singles/doubles
up to €111/160. Hidden away in a leafy
corner of one of the lanes that twist away
from Piazza delle Erbe, the hotel boasts
classy, newly renovated rooms, all in various styles (ranging from Imperial to what
he owners call '19th-century English') and
complete with all the usual mod cons.

Places to Eat

Restaurants tend to open from around noon
to 2pm and about 7.30pm to 10pm. You will
find it hard to get served after this time in
the evening.

Cafes & Pastries Behind the blunt neoclassical facade of the newly refurbished
Caffè Pedrocchi, just off Via VIII Febbraio,
ay the meeting place for 19th-century lib-
erals and one of Stendhal's favourite haunts.
Today it's more posey than cosy.

*Lilium (☎ 049 875 11 07, Via del Santo
181)* Open 7.30am-8pm winter, 7.30am-
10pm summer Tues-Sun. This fine pastry
shop offers wonderful *gelato* (ice cream)
and delicious sweet things.

Restaurants *Trattoria al Pero (☎ 049 875
87 94, Via Santa Lucia 72)* Full meals around
€18. Open Mon-Sat. The 'Pear Tree' serves
tasty regional dishes in a straightforward dining area. You eat well for relatively little.

*Osteria dei Fabbri (☎ 049 65 03 36, Via
dei Fabbri 13)* Full meals around €20. Open
Mon-Sat. This lively spot is full of atmosphere, although more expensive than the
Pero. Try the *ravioloni di magro*, exquisite,
light ravioli done in a butter and sage sauce.

*Osteria dal Capo (☎ 049 66 31 05, Via
degli Obizzi 2, cnr Via Soncin)* Mains start at
around €10.30. Open Mon eve-Sat. A busy
little eatery, the 'Chief' offers home-style
Veneto cooking that is much appreciated by
locals.

*La Vecchia Enoteca (☎ 049 875 28 56,
Via San Martino e Solferino 32)* Mains from
€13.40. Open Mon eve-Sat. This is an altogether swankier joint where mouth-watering
meals can be had but with a greater impact
on the wallet. They do a divine *arrosto di
salmone* (lightly roasted salmon) with
rocket salad and a creamy sauce.

*Enoteca la Corte dei Leoni (☎ 049 875
00 83, Via Pietro d'Abano 1)* Full meals
€41.30. Open Tues-Sat. A modern temple of
wine (you can taste from a broad wine list
by the glass at the bar) in the heart of old
Padova is also the site of a fine dining experience. In summer especially, book a table
in the courtyard (where jazz concerts are
also occasionally staged). The food is very
good if a little nouvelle in terms of portions.
The wines are many and well selected.

*Trattoria da Paccagnella (☎ 049 875 05
49, Via del Santo 113)* Full meals around
€21. Open Mon-Sat. This trattoria is a comfortably elegant setting for fine Veneto cuisine – try their duck recipes as that is what
the restaurant is known for.

*Per Bacco (☎ 049 875 46 64 or 049 876
28 10,* e *per-bacco@libero.it, Piazzale Pon-
tecorvo 10)* Full meals around €26. Open

Tues-Sun. This is another of the city's better restaurants. Try their tagliatelle *alla norcina con tartufo nero* (with black truffles), a classic of Umbrian cuisine and a long-standing favourite here. The wine list is also strong.

Trattoria Basso Isonzo (☎ *049 68 08 13, Via Montepertica 1)* Full meals €15.50. Open Tues-Sun. A local favourite for simple, economically priced home cooking, the trattoria lies a way out of the town centre to the south-west. It's a pain to get to unless you opt for a cab from, say, Prato della Valle, but they do a mean creamy *baccalà* (cod). Bus No 22 from Prato della Valle also goes close.

Self-Catering Daily *markets* are held in the piazzas around the Palazzo della Ragione, with fresh produce sold in the Piazza delle Erbe and Piazza della Frutta, and bread, cheese and salami sold in the shops under the porticoes.

Entertainment

The city hosts the Notturni d'Arte festival from July to September each year, featuring concerts and outdoor events; many are free. The tourist office has details.

Some operatic and theatrical performances are held at the ***Teatro Comunale Verdi*** (☎ *049 877 70 11),* Via Livello 32.

There are several traditional spots around Piazza delle Erbe for taking the evening *spritz.* In summer especially, hundreds of people clutching their favourite tipples spread out across the square in the early evening. Much the same thing happens, on a reduced scale, on Piazza dei Signori.

Highlander (☎ *049 65 99 97, Via San Martino e Solferino 71)* Open 11am-3pm & 5pm-2am Mon-Sat. Beer lovers wanting a variation on the Irish theme could strike out for, you guessed it, a 'Scottish' pub. It's mostly full of locals and the beers are tasty. Try to ignore all the silly Scottish stuff on the walls.

Paparazzi Fashion Café (☎ *049 875 93 06, Via Marsilio da Padova 17)* Open 6pm-1am Tues-Sun. Far from the fake UK experience, this place attracts a young, cool crowd, all sunglasses at night and designer stubble, low red lights and dark drinking corners.

Café El Pilar (☎ *049 65 75 65, Piazza de Signori 8)* Open 11am-3pm & 6pm-midnight This is a classic example of a spot where a mix of beautiful souls and others converge for the evening spritz. Often by 10pm people have scarpered – off to the disco perhaps? Nearby on Piazza del Duomo, a crowd of pretty people, students and others hang about sipping cocktails later on in the evening.

For some tips on clubs and the like, start with the tourist office's *Dove Andiamo Sta sera* brochure. Many, as is the Italian custom in smaller cities, are located well outside town. About the only place in the town itself, which is OK but nothing spectacular, i ***Limbo*** (☎ *049 65 68 82, Via San Fermo 44)* open 9pm to 3am. More popular with a hip young student crowd is ***Banale*** (☎ *049 80; 18 48, Vicolo Ognissanti 1/c),* where live rock music is often on the cards.

Getting There & Away

Bus SITA buses (☎ 049 820 68 44) from Venice (€2.75) arrive at Piazzale Boschetti 200m south of the train station.

From Padua you can get buses to Monte grotto Terme, the Colli Euganei and as fa afield as Genoa. Often you are better off with the train. Details for surrounding destination appear in the course of this chapter.

Train The easiest way to Padua from Venice is by train. The standard regional trains (€2.30) take 40 minutes. If you want to go a little faster (30 minutes) you can pay almost double (€4.45) to travel on an InterCity train Regular trains proceed from Padua to Vi cenza, Verona, Bologna, Milan and beyond

Car & Motorcycle The A4 (Milan-Venice) passes to the north, while the A13, which connects Padua with Bologna, starts at the southern edge of town. The two motorways are connected by a ring road.

Getting Around

ACAP bus No 10 will get you to Piazza Ca vour from the train station, while No 12 wil take you to Prato della Valle. Buy ticket (€0.85 per ride) at tobacconists and stamp them in the machines on the bus.

If you need a taxi, you can try Radiotaxi (☎ 049 65 13 33).

AROUND PADUA
Colli Euganei

South-west of Padua, along the A13 or the SS16, the Colli Euganei (Euganean Hills) are dotted with vineyards and good walking trails – ask at the Padua IAT office for information about the trails and accommodation. As you move around, you will encounter numerous curious villages, along with the occasional castle and abbey scattered about the countryside.

If you are driving (which you pretty much have to, as public transport is abysmal in the area), follow the signposted Strada dei Vini dei Colli Euganei (Euganean Hills Wine Road), which will take you on a road tour of many vineyards. Pick up a map and itinerary from the IAT in Padua. Most of the vineyards are open to the public and some offer accommodation.

The area is also famous for its hot springs, or *terme*. The two main centres in this respect are Abano Terme and Montegrotto Terme. The tourist office (☎ 049 866 90 55) at the former is at Via Pietro d'Abano 18, while the one at Montegrotto (☎ 049 79 33 84) is at Viale Stazione 60.

Arquà Petrarca This quiet, hilly, medieval village in the southern Colli Euganei was where Italy's great poet Petrarch (Petrarca) chose to spend the last five years of his life. You can visit his **house** *(☎ 0429 71 82 94; admission €3.10; open 9am-noon & 3pm-7pm Tues-Sun Feb-Sept, 9am-12.30pm & 2.30pm-5pm Tues-Sun Oct-Jan)*, which is set in cheerful gardens and contains various bits and bobs that purportedly had something to do with the scribe. Buses run here from Este and Monselice, both a short distance to the south. A handful (around three per day) of buses from Padua run a route to Este that takes them through here.

Monselice

An easy train trip south from Padua, Monselice was once wrapped in no less than five protective layers of fortifications. The main point of interest here is the 11th-century **castle** *(☎ 049 7 29 31; admission €5.15; open 9am-11am & 3pm-5pm Apr-mid-Nov)*, which can only be visited by guided tour, lasting about an hour. If you decide to stay, you have the choice of two places. The train from Padua (€1.90) takes about 20 minutes.

Este

Heading west from Monselice, along the road to Mantua (Mantova), this town is yet another in the chain of fortified strongholds in the area. Padua's Carrara clan were assiduous fortress builders – it seems they had a good number of enemies to keep at bay. Although the walls of their castle are in reasonable shape, the inside is pretty much a ruin. On the bumpy lane that climbs northwards behind the castle is the **Villa Kunkler**, where Byron settled in for a year or so in 1817. Shelley also stayed here.

You'll find a couple of hotels here and the town is linked to Monselice by train (about 10 minutes). From Padua the train (€2.30) takes about 30 minutes. Buses also run here but they tend to take longer and are slightly more expensive.

Montagnana

The main attraction in this plains town is the remarkably well-preserved set of medieval defensive walls. Of all the Veneto's walled towns, this is the most impressive – from the outside. Once you get inside, there's not an awful lot to see.

Ostello Rocca degli Alberi (☎/fax 0429 8 10 76, Castello degli Alberi) €9.30 per person. Open Apr-mid-Oct. This unique HI youth hostel is in a former watchtower of the town's extraordinary walls, and is close to the town's train station.

The train from Padua (via Monselice and Este; €2.80) takes about 50 minutes.

VICENZA
postcode 36100 • pop 108,947

Vicenza is the centre for Italian textile manufacturing and a leader in the development and production of computer components, making it one of the country's wealthiest cities. Most tourists come to Vicenza to see the work of

---

Tickets Please

The city of Vicenza has come up with a series of cumulative tickets giving you entry to several monuments. This can be seen as good or bad, because it means that to get value from the ticket you need to visit everything. On the other hand, it's not so onerous so shouldn't be a big problem.

The Vicenza Musei card costs €6.70 and is valid for a month. It gives you entry to the Teatro Olimpico, Museo Civico, Basilica Palladiana and the Museo Naturalistico Archeologico. The Vicenza Musei Full ticket (€7.75) adds a couple of minor museums. The Vicenza Musei e Palazzi ticket (€10.30) includes all the above and the Palazzo Barbaran da Porto and the Gallerie di Palazzo Leoni Montanari. Finally, Vicenza e Le Ville ticket includes all this and the two main villas in the city, La Rotonda and the Villa Valmarana 'ai Nani'.

Palladio, who was particularly busy here. Vicenza flourished as the Roman Vicentia. In 1404 it became part of the Venetian Republic. Testimony to the close ties between the lagoon city and Vicenza are the many Venetian Gothic mansions here.

Orientation

From the train station, in the gardens of Campo Marzo, walk straight ahead along Via Roma into Piazzale de Gasperi. From here, the main street, Corso Andrea Palladio, leads to the cathedral and the centre of town.

Information

Tourist Office The APT office (☎ 0444 32 08 54) is at Piazza Matteotti 12. It opens 9am to 1pm and 2.30pm to 6pm Monday to Saturday, and 9am to 1pm Sunday.

The office organises free guided tours of the city – enquire for the latest details.

Post & Communications The main post office is at Contrà Garibaldi, near the cathedral. Address poste restante mail to 36100 Vicenza. The small, unstaffed Telecom office at Contrà Vescovado 2 opens 7am to 10pm.

Medical Services & Emergency For urgent medical assistance, go to the Ospedale Civile (hospital; ☎ 0444 99 31 11), Viale Ferdinando Rodolfi 37, north of the city centre from Piazza Matteotti. The *questura* (police station; ☎ 0444 54 33 33) is at Viale Giuseppe Mazzini 24.

Things to See

Piazza Castello contains several grand edifices, including the **Palazzo Porto-Breganze** on the southern side, designed by Palladio and built by Scamozzi, one of the city's leading 16th-century architects. Corso Andrea Palladio runs north-east from the square and is lined with fine buildings.

The nearby Piazza dei Signori is dominated by the immense **Basilica Palladiana** (☎ *0444 32 36 81; open 9am-5pm Tues-Sun*), which Palladio began in 1549 on top of an earlier Gothic building – the slender 12th-century bell tower is all that remains of the original structure. Palladio's **Loggia del Capitaniato**, at the north-western side of the piazza on the corner of Via del Monte, was left unfinished at his death. South-west from the basilica is the **cathedral**, a dull *duomo* destroyed during WWII and later rebuilt (some of its artworks were saved).

Contrà Porti, which runs north off Corso Andrea Palladio, is one of the city's most majestic streets. The **Palazzo Thiene** *(No 12)*, by Lorenzo da Bologna, was originally intended to occupy the entire block. Palladio's **Palazzo Barbaran da Porto** (☎ *0444 32 30 14, No 11; admission €5.15, or with cumulative ticket; open 10am-6pm Tues-Sun)* features a double row of columns. A World Heritage listed building, it is richly decorated and frequently hosts exhibitions. Palladio also built the **Palazzo Isoppo da Porto** *(No 21)*, which remains unfinished. His **Palazzo Valmarana** *(Corso Antonio Fogazzaro 18)* is considered one of his more eccentric creations. Across the River Bacchiglione is the **Parco Querini**, the city's largest park.

North along Corso Andrea Palladio and left into Contrà di Santa Corona is the **Chiesa di Santa Corona** *(open 8.30am-noon & 3pm-6pm Tues-Sun)*, established in 1261 by the Dominicans to house a relic from Christ's

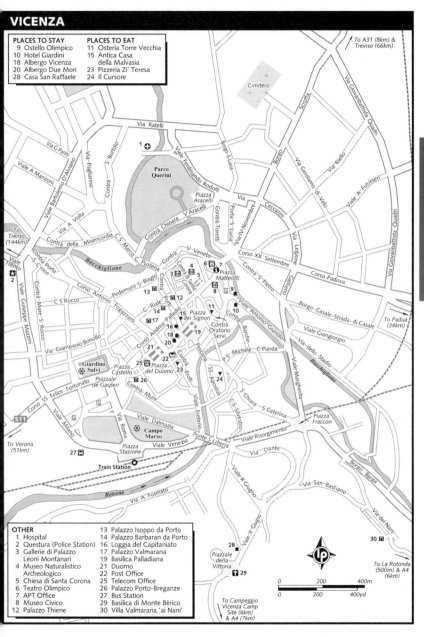

VICENZA

PLACES TO STAY
9 Ostello Olimpico
10 Hotel Giardini
18 Albergo Vicenza
20 Albergo Due Mori
28 Casa San Raffaele

PLACES TO EAT
11 Osteria Torre Vecchia
15 Antica Casa
   della Malvasia
23 Pizzeria Zi' Teresa
24 Il Cursore

OTHER
1 Hospital
2 Questura (Police Station)
3 Gallerie di Palazzo
   Leoni Montanari
4 Museo Naturalistico
   Archeologico
5 Chiesa di Santa Corona
6 Teatro Olimpico
7 APT Office
8 Museo Civico
12 Palazzo Thiene
13 Palazzo Isoppo da Porto
14 Palazzo Barbaran da Porto
16 Loggia del Capitaniato
17 Palazzo Valmarana
19 Basilica Palladiana
21 Duomo
22 Post Office
25 Telecom Office
26 Palazzo Porto-Breganze
27 Bus Station
29 Basilica di Monte Bèrico
30 Villa Valmarana 'ai Nani'

EXCURSIONS

crown of thorns. Inside are the *Battesimo di Gesù* (Baptism of Christ) by Giovanni Bellini and *Adorazione dei Magi* (Adoration of the Magi) by Veronese.

Corso Andrea Palladio ends at the **Teatro Olimpico** (☎ *0444 22 28 00; open 9am-5pm Tues-Sun Sept-June, 10am-7pm Tues-Sun July-Aug)*, started by Palladio in 1580 and completed by Scamozzi after the former's death. Considered one of the purest creations of Renaissance architecture, the theatre design was based on Palladio's studies of Roman structures. Scamozzi's remarkable street scene, stretching back from the main facade of the stage, is modelled on the ancient Greek city of Thebes. He created an impressive illusion of depth and perspective by slanting the streets up towards the rear of the set. The theatre was inaugurated in 1585 with a performance of *Oedipus Rex*, but soon fell into disuse – the ceiling caved in and it remained abandoned for centuries until 1934, when it was restored and reopened. Since then, the theatre has become a prized performance space for opera and drama – it is one of the few working theatres where the performers and audience are eyeball to eyeball.

The nearby **Museo Civico** (☎ *0444 32 13 48; open 9am-5pm Tues-Sun Sept-June, 10am-7pm Tues-Sun July-Aug)*, in the Palazzo Chiericati, contains works by local artists as well as by the Tiepolos and Veronese.

The **Gallerie di Palazzo Leoni Montanari** *(freephone ☎ 800 57 88 75, Contrà di Santa Corona 25; admission €3.10, or with cumulative ticket; open 10am-6pm Fri-Sun, but times and costs can change depending on temporary exhibitions)* is a new gallery in Vicenza. The sober Baroque facades belie a more extravagant interior. Long a private mansion and seat of a bank, it now contains a collection of 120 Russian icons (top floor) and mostly 18th-century Venetian paintings (1st floor). Among the outstanding works on show are some by Canaletto and Pietro Longhi.

South of the city, the **Basilica di Monte Bèrico** *(Piazzale della Vittoria; open from 6.15am-12.30pm & 2.30pm-7.30pm Mon-Sat, 6.15am-8pm Sun & holidays)*, set on top of a hill, presents magnificent views over the city. The basilica was built in the 18th century to replace a Gothic structure, itself raised on the supposed site of two appearances by the Virgin Mary in 1426. An impressive 18th-century colonnade runs most of the way up Viale X Giugno to the church – very handy when it's pouring with rain in autumn. Or catch city bus No 9.

A 20-minute walk, back down Viale X Giugno and then east along Via San Bastiano, will take you to the **Villa Valmarana 'ai Nani'** *(☎ 0444 54 39 76; admission €5.15, or with cumulative ticket; open 10am-noon Wed, Thur, Sat & Sun mid-Mar-early-Nov, also 2.30pm-5.30pm Tues-Sun Mar-Apr & Oct-Nov, & 3pm-6pm Tues-Sun May-Sept)*. The villa features brilliant frescoes by both Giambattista and Giandomenico Tiepolo. The 'ai Nani' (dwarves) refers to the statues perched on top of the gates surrounding the property.

A path leads on to Palladio's Villa Capra, better known as **La Rotonda** *(☎ 0444 32 17 93; admission to gardens €2.60, admission to villa €5.15, or with cumulative ticket; gardens open 10am-noon & 3pm-6pm Tues, Wed & Thur Mar-Nov, villa open 10am-noon & 3pm-6pm Wed Mar-Nov)*. It is one of the architect's most admired – and most copied – creations, having served as a model for buildings across Europe and the USA. Groups can book ahead to visit outside the normal opening hours – the price is hiked up to €10.30 per person in this case. Bus No 8 stops nearby.

Places to Stay

Many hotels close during the summer, particularly in August, so book ahead. At other times you should have no problems getting a room.

Campeggio Vicenza *(☎ 0444 58 23 11, fax 0444 58 24 34, Strada Pelosa 239)* Sites per person/tent up to €5.95/13.40. This is the closest camp site to Vicenza and is near the Vicenza Est exit from the A4.

Ostello Olimpico *(☎ 0444 54 02 22, fax 0444 54 77 62, Viale Antonio Giuriolo 7-9)* Beds €13.40. Open 7.30am-9.30am & 3.30pm-11.30pm. The HI youth hostel is in a fine building right by the Teatro Olimpico.

Albergo Vicenza (☎/fax 0444 32 15 12, Stradella dei Nodari 5-7) Singles/doubles without bath €36/49, singles/doubles with bath €41.30/56.80. Located near Piazza dei Signori, the hotel is one of only a few cheap-ish spots in central Vicenza. The rooms are basic but the place has a little character and it puts you in the thick of things.

Albergo Due Mori (☎ 0444 32 18 86, fax 0444 32 61 27, Contrà do Rode 26) Singles/doubles up to €38.75/67.15. Close by the Vicenza, it is a slight step up in quality but in much the same league.

Casa San Raffaele (☎ 0444 54 57 67, fax 0444 55 22 59, Viale X Giugno 10) Singles/doubles with bath €41.30/56.80. Located in a former convent behind the colonnade leading to Monte Bèrico, this is a charming spot to spend the night and the best choice in the lower budget range. The hotel has parking space. Prices include breakfast.

Hotel Giardini (☎/fax 0444 32 64 58, Via Antonio Giuriolo 10) Singles/doubles €83/114. A rather modern hotel (with decidedly little in the way of gardens), this is nevertheless a perfectly comfortable and handy choice for the heart of the town. They have parking too. Prices include breakfast.

Places to Eat

Pizzeria Zi' Teresa (☎ 0444 32 14 11, Contrà San Antonio 1) Pizzas €4.15-6.20. Open Tues-Sun. This is a handy place for a pizza. If you want a full meal, you are better off trying one of the following places.

Antica Casa della Malvasia (☎ 0444 54 37 04, Contrà delle Morette 5) Mains for €7.75. Open Tues-Sat. This den has been around since 1200. In those days, it was the local sales point for Malvasia wine imported from Greece by Venetian merchants, who usually gathered here in the evenings to sample the goods. Drinking is still a primary occupation in a locale that has changed little in all those centuries – on offer is an array of 80 types of wine (especially Malvasia varieties) and around a hundred types of grappa!

Il Cursore (☎ 0444 32 35 04, Stradella Pozzetto 10) Full meals around €18. Open Wed-Mon. They've been serving up food in here since the 19th century and although it's

been given a facelift, it's a great little spot for some local dishes, such as spaghetti *col baccalà mantecato* (with cod prepared in parsley and garlic).

Osteria Torre Vecchia (☎ 0444 32 00 50, Contrà Oratorio Servi 23) Full meals around €23. Open 7pm-2am Mon-Sat. This elegant old house with wooden ceilings offers fine eating at a high-ish price. The menu changes constantly and occasionally contains *sorprese* (surprises) – clearly for adventurous diners!

A large *produce market* takes place each Tuesday and Thursday in Piazza delle Erbe.

Entertainment

Concerts are held in summer at the Villa Valmarana ai Nani; check at the APT for details. For information about performances in the Teatro Olimpico (☎ 0444 22 21 11), contact the theatre or the APT. The APT can also give you some initial clues on bars and clubs, although there are few of the latter and they are well out of the centre. On summer afternoons and evenings, the central squares fill with people who gather for the *aperitivo*, that lingering evening tipple and chat.

Getting There & Away

Bus FTV buses (☎ 0444 22 31 15) leave from the bus station, just near the train station, for Thiene, Asiago (in the hilly north of the province), Bassano and towns throughout the nearby Monti Berici (Berici Hills).

Train Regular trains arrive from Venice (€3.60, 50 minutes) and Padua (€2.30, 30 minutes). You can speed things up by paying more for an InterCity. Other trains connect Vicenza with Milan, Verona, Treviso and smaller towns in the north.

Car & Motorbike By car, the city is on the A4 connecting Milan with Venice. The SS11 connects Vicenza with Verona and Padua, and this is the best route for hitchhikers. There is a large car park near Piazza Castello and the train station.

Getting Around

The city is best seen on foot, but bus Nos 1, 2, 3 and 7 link the train station and city centre.

AROUND VICENZA

As Venice's maritime power waned in the 16th century, the city's wealthy inhabitants turned their attention inland, acquiring land to build sumptuous villas (see also the Riviera del Brenta section earlier in this chapter). Forbidden from building castles by the Venetian senate, which feared a landscape dotted with well-defended forts, Vicenza's patricians were among those to join the villa construction spree. Many of the thousands that were built still remain, although most are inaccessible to the public and run down.

The APT in Vicenza can provide reams of information about the villas, including an illustrated map entitled *Ville dal 1400 al 1800*.

Drivers should have little trouble planning an itinerary. If you don't have a car, take the FTV bus north from Vicenza to Thiene, passing through Caldogno and Villaverla, and then continue on to Lugo. The Villa Godi-Valmarana, now known as the **Malinverni**, at Lonedo di Lugo, was Palladio's first villa.

A good driving itinerary is to take the SS11 south to Montecchio Maggiore and continue south to Lonigo and Pojana Maggiore before heading north for Longare and back to Vicenza. A round trip of 100km, the route takes in about a dozen villas.

Check with the APT in Vicenza for details of the Concerti in Villa Estate, a series of classical concerts held in villas around Vicenza each summer (usually July). You will need your own transport to get to the concerts and back. You can also ask about accommodation, which is available in some villas.

VERONA

postcode 37100 • pop 254,748

Wander the quiet streets of Verona on a winter's night and you might almost be forgiven for believing the tragic love story of Romeo and Juliet to be true. Get past the Shakespearean hyperbole, however, and you'll find plenty to keep you occupied in what is one of Italy's most beautiful cities. Known as *piccola Roma* (little Rome) for its importance in the days of the Roman Empire, its truly golden era came during the 13th and 14th centuries under the Della Scala family (also known as the Scaligeri). The period

was noted for the savage family feuding to which Shakespeare alluded in his play.

Orientation

Old Verona is small and easy to find your way around. There is a lot to see and it is a popular base for exploring surrounding towns. Buses leave for the centre from outside the train station; otherwise, walk to the right, past the bus station, cross the river and walk along Corso Porta Nuova to Piazza Brà, 15 minutes away. From the piazza, walk along Via Giuseppe Mazzini and turn left at Via Cappello to reach Piazza delle Erbe.

Information

Tourist Offices The main tourist office (☎ 045 806 86 80), at Via degli Alpini 9 (virtually on Piazza Brà), opens 1pm to 7pm on Monday, 9am to 7pm Tuesday to Saturday and 9am to 3pm on Sunday.

The other office (☎ 045 800 08 61), inside the train station (the eastern end) opens 9am to 6pm Monday to Saturday. Both have stacks of information on the city and surrounding province.

A third office (☎ 045 861 91 63) operates at the airport to meet flights. On the Web, check out ☒ www.tourism.verona.it.

Money Banks dot the town centre, including the Banca Popolare di Bergamo on Piazza Brà, one of several with a currency-exchange machine.

Post & Communications The main post office, on Piazza Viviani 7, opens 8am to 7pm Monday to Saturday. Address poste restante mail to 37100 Verona. You'll find telephones at the train station, as well as an unstaffed Telecom office on Via Leoncino just behind the Roman Arena.

You can get onto the Internet at a spot by platform 1 at the train station or at Diesis Via Sottoriva 15 (generally open 11am to between 10pm and midnight). You can also try Internet Train (☎ 045 801 33 94, ☒ www .internettrain.it), at Via Roma 19.

Laundry There is an Onda Blu laundrette at Via XX Settembre 62/a. It opens 8am to

0pm daily. It costs €5.15 to wash a 16kg oad, and the same to dry it.

Medical Services & Emergency The Ospedale Civile Maggiore (hospital; ☎ 045 807
1 11) is at Piazza A Stefani, north-west from
Ponte Vittoria. Also, the city's Guardia Med-
ca (☎ 045 807 56 27) offers medical services
from 8pm to 8am (they usually come to you).

The *questura* (police station; ☎ 045 809
04 11) is at Lungadige Porta Vittoria, near
Ponte Navi.

Things to See
Remember that just about everything is
closed on Monday – if you are only planning to spend a day here, make it any other
day of the week.

There is a joint ticket for getting into all the
main sights. Called the Verona Card, it is
great value at €11.35. With it you can enter
all the main monuments and churches and get
reduced admission on a few places of lesser
importance. The card also allows you to get
around town on the buses. It's valid for a year
at the time of writing from April 2001 to
March 2002).

On the first Sunday of the month, admission to the Tomba di Giulietta, the Museo
Lapidario Maffeiano, the Castelvecchio
museum and the Roman theatre is free. Admission to the Roman Arena on the same
day is reduced to €1.05.

Roman Arena This pink marble Roman
amphitheatre (☎ 045 800 32 04; admission
€3.10, joint ticket with Museo Lapidario
Maffeiano €3.60; open 9am-6.30pm Tues-
Sun, 8am-3.30pm during opera season), in
the bustling Piazza Brà, was built in the 1st
century AD and is now Verona's opera house.
The third-largest Roman amphitheatre in
existence, it could seat around 20,000 people.
It is remarkably well preserved, despite a
12th-century earthquake that destroyed most
of its outer wall. See the Entertainment section later in this chapter for information about
opera and plays at the arena.

Casa di Giulietta Just off Via Giuseppe
Mazzini, the main shopping street in Verona,

is Juliet's House (☎ 045 803 43 03, Via
Cappello 23; admission €3.10; open 9am-
6.30pm Tues-Sun). Romeo and Juliet may
have been fictional, but here you can swoon
beneath what popular myth says was her balcony or, if in need of a new lover, approach
a bronze statue of Juliet and rub her right
breast for good luck. Others have made their
eternal mark by adding to the slew of scribbled love graffiti on the house walls. It is, by
the way, doubtful there ever was a feud between the Cappello and Montecchi families,
on whom Shakespeare based the play.

If the theme excites you sufficiently, you
could also search out the **Tomba di Giulietta**
*(Juliet's Tomb; ☎ 045 800 03 61, Via del
Pontiere 5; admission €2.60; open 9am-
6.30pm Tues-Sun).* Also housed here is the
Museo degli Affreschi, with a collection of
frescoes of minor interest.

Piazza delle Erbe Originally the site of a
Roman forum, this piazza remains the
lively heart of the city today. Although the
permanent market stalls in its centre detract
from its beauty, the square is lined with
some of Verona's most sumptuous buildings, including the Baroque **Palazzo Maffei**,
at the northern end, with the adjoining 14th-
century **Torre del Gardello**. On the eastern
side is **Casa Mazzanti**, a former Della Scala
family residence. Its fresco-decorated facade stands out.

Separating Piazza delle Erbe from Piazza
dei Signori is the **Arco della Costa**, beneath
which is suspended a whale's rib. Legend
says it will fall on the first 'just' person to
walk beneath it. In several centuries, it has
never fallen, not even on the various popes
who have paraded beneath it. Ascend the
nearby 12th-century **Torre dei Lamberti** *(admission €2.05 by elevator, €1.55 on foot;
open 9am-6pm Tues-Sun)* for a great view of
the city. You can also get a joint ticket for the
tower and the Arche Scaligere (see later).

Piazza dei Signori The 15th-century **Loggia del Consiglio**, the former city council
building at the northern end of this square,
is regarded as Verona's finest Renaissance
structure. It is attached to the **Palazzo degli**

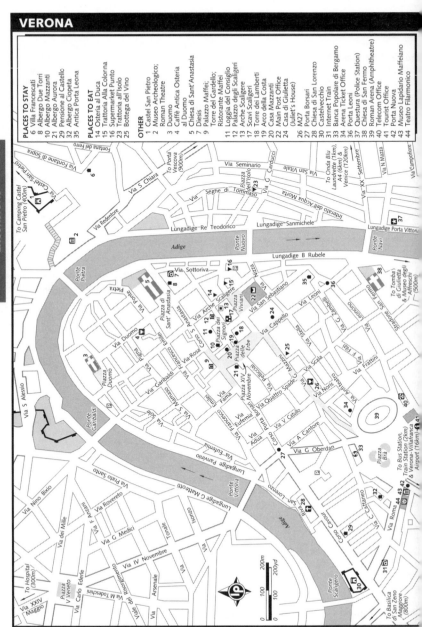

VERONA

PLACES TO STAY
6 Villa Francescati
8 Albergo Due Torri
10 Albergo Mazzanti
21 Albergo Aurora
29 Pensione al Castello
32 Albergo Ciopeta
35 Antica Porta Leona

PLACES TO EAT
14 Osteria al Duca
15 Trattoria Alla Colonna
16 Supermarket Punto
23 Trattoria all'Isolo
25 Bottega del Vino

OTHER
1 Castel San Pietro
2 Museo Archeologico;
   Roman Theatre
3 Duomo
4 Caffè Antica Osteria
   al Duomo
5 Chiesa di Sant'Anastasia
7 Diesis
9 Palazzo Maffei;
   Torre del Gardello;
   Ristorante Maffei
11 Loggia del Consiglio
12 Palazzo degli Scaligeri
13 Arche Scaligere
17 Scavi Scaligeri
18 Torre dei Lamberti
19 Arco della Costa
20 Casa Mazzanti
22 Main Post Office
24 Casa di Giulietta
   (Juliet's House)
26 M27
27 Porta Borsari
28 Chiesa di San Lorenzo
30 Castelvecchio
31 Internet Train
33 Banca Popolare di Bergamo
34 Arena Ticket Office
36 Porta Leoni
37 Questura (Police Station)
38 Chiesa di San Fermo
39 Roman Arena (Amphitheatre)
40 Telecom Office
41 Tourist Office
42 Porta Nuova
43 Museo Lapidario Maffeiano
44 Teatro Filarmonico

Scaligeri, once the main residence of the Della Scala family.

Through the archway at the far end of the piazza are the **Arche Scaligere** *(admission €2.60 with Torre dei Lamberti; open 9am-5pm Tues-Sun)*, the elaborate tombs of the Della Scala family. You can see them quite well from the outside, but the ticket for the Torre dei Lamberti allows you to wander in and have a closer inspection.

In the courtyard just behind the Arche you can now see some excavation work done on this part of Verona. You enter the **Scavi Scaligeri** *(Scaligeri Excavations; admission depends on the exhibition; open 10am-6pm Tues-Sun)*. The excavations are not so exciting as to warrant a big detour, so to make them more attractive the building is used to host international photographic exhibitions.

Churches A combined entrance ticket to all the following churches costs €4.15. Otherwise, admission to each costs €2.05.

North from the Arche Scaligere stands the Gothic **Chiesa di Sant'Anastasia** *(open 9am-6pm Mon-Sat, 1pm-6pm Sun)*, started in 1290 but not completed until the late-15th century. Inside are numerous works of art including, in the sacristy, a lovely fresco by Pisanello of *San Giorgio che Parte per Liberare la Donzella dal Drago* (St George Setting out to Free the Princess from the Dragon).

The 12th-century **cathedral** *(open 10am-5.30pm Mon-Sat, 1.30pm-5.30pm Sun)* combines Romanesque (lower section) and Gothic (upper section) styles and has some intriguing features. Look for the sculpture of Jonah and the Whale on the south porch and the statues of two of Charlemagne's paladins, Roland and Oliver, on the west porch. In the first chapel of the left aisle is an *Assumption* by Titian, in an altar frame by Jacopo Sansovino.

At the river end of Via Leoni, you'll find the **Chiesa di San Fermo** *(open 10am-6pm Mon-Sat, 1pm-6pm Sun)*, which is actually two churches. The Gothic church was built in the 13th century over the original 11th-century Romanesque structure. The **Chiesa di San Lorenzo** *(open 10am-6pm Mon-Sat, 1pm-6pm Sun)* is near the Castelvecchio

(see the following section) and the Basilica di San Zeno Maggiore (see that section after Castelvecchio) is farther to the west.

Castelvecchio South-west from Piazza delle Erbe, on the banks of the River Adige, is the 14th-century fortress of Cangrande II (of the Scaligeri family). The fortress was damaged by bombing during WWII and restored in the 1960s. It now houses a **museum** *(☎ 045 59 47 34; admission €3.10; open 9am-6.30pm Tues-Sun)* with a diverse collection of paintings, frescoes, jewellery and medieval artefacts. Among the paintings are works by Pisanello, Giovanni Bellini, Tiepolo, Carpaccio and Veronese. Also of note is a 14th-century equestrian statue of Cangrande I. The **Ponte Scaligero** spanning the Adige was rebuilt after being destroyed by WWII bombing.

Basilica di San Zeno Maggiore A masterpiece of Romanesque architecture, this church *(open 8.30am-6pm Mon-Sat, 1pm-6pm Sun)* in honour of the city's patron saint was built mainly in the 12th century, although its apse was rebuilt in the 14th century and its bell tower, a relic of an earlier structure on the site, was started in 1045. The basilica's magnificent rose window depicts the Wheel of Fortune. Before going inside, take a look at the sculptures on either side of the main doors. The doors themselves are decorated with bronze reliefs of biblical subjects. The highlight inside is Mantegna's triptych of the *Madonna col Bambino tra Angeli e Santi* (Madonna and Child with Angels and Saints), above the high altar.

Across the River Across Ponte Pietra, north of the city centre, is a **Roman theatre**, built in the 1st century AD and still used today for concerts and plays. Take the lift at the back of the theatre to the convent above, which houses an interesting collection of Greek and Roman pieces in the **Museo Archeologico** *(admission €2.60; open 9am-6.30pm Tues-Sun Apr-Oct, 9am-3.30pm Tues-Sun Nov-Mar)*. On a hill high behind the theatre and museum is the **Castel San Pietro**, built by the Austrians on the site of an earlier castle.

EXCURSIONS

City Gates Near the Casa di Giulietta, in Via Leoni, is the Porta Leoni, one of the gates to Roman Verona. The other is Porta Borsari, at the bottom end of Corso Porta Borsari.

Places to Stay

If you are having problems finding a hotel room, you could try calling the **Cooperativa Albergatori Veronesi** (☎ 045 800 98 44, fax 045 800 93 72). They start with two-star hotels and the service is free.

Camping Castel San Pietro (☎/fax 045 59 20 37, W www.campingcastelsanpietro.com, Via Castel San Pietro 2) Sites per person/large tent/car €4.90/6.20/3.10. This is not a bad camp site, away from the bustle of the town below. You can get here by bus No 41 or 95 from the train station. Ask the driver to let you off for the 'camping' or at the first stop along Via Marsala.

Villa Francescati (☎ 045 59 03 60, fax 045 800 91 27, Salita Fontana del Ferro 15) B&B €12.40. The beautifully restored HI youth hostel is housed in a 16th-century villa not far from the camp site and should be your first choice of budget lodging. The gardens are gorgeous and they have family rooms too. Meals cost €7.75.

Pensione al Castello (☎/fax 045 800 44 03, Vicolo Brusco 2/a) Singles/doubles without bathroom €49/72.30, singles/doubles with bathroom €62/88. This is a quiet and simple little hotel in a good spot near the river and castle. Rooms are clean and well maintained, without being spectacular.

Albergo Ciopeta (☎/fax 045 800 68 43, e ciopeta@iol.it, Vicolo Teatro Filarmonico 2) Singles/doubles €41.30/62. Just off Piazza Brà, this is a great little place with cosy welcoming rooms, but you'll need to book well in advance.

Albergo Aurora (☎ 045 59 47 17, fax 045 801 08 60, Piazza XIV Novembre 2) Singles/doubles with bathroom up to €98/108.50. The better rooms in this fairly sprawling hotel are spacious and comfortable, although time is beginning to take its toll. In the low season you may snag the odd single without a private bathroom for as little as €46.50. The position is about as central as possible.

Albergo Mazzanti (☎ 045 800 68 13, fax 045 801 12 62, Via Mazzanti 6) Singles/doubles up to €67/98. Just off Piazza dei Signori, this place is also well located and, if you can get one of the nicer rooms, is probably marginally better value. That said, some of the sleeping cubicles for singles are claustrophobic. In the low season, you might pay less than half the above prices for rooms without a private bathroom.

Antica Porta Leona (☎ 045 59 54 99, fax 045 59 52 14, Corticella Leoni 3) Singles/doubles up to €93/129. Located close to Juliet's supposed house, this is a reasonable three-star place whose rooms are full of character, if somewhat faded.

Albergo Due Torri (☎ 045 59 50 44, fax 045 800 41 30, e duetorri.verona@baglionihotels.com, Piazza di Sant'Anastasia 4) Singles/doubles up to €268/377. Verona's top address is a grand old mansion whose rooms take you back into a long-abandoned era of slightly stuffy, studied elegance. Antique wooden furniture dominates the rooms, which at their best are very generous. The place is often booked solid.

Places to Eat

Known for its fresh produce, its crisp Soave (a dry white wine) and boiled meats, Verona offers good eating at reasonable prices. Most places open about 11am to 3pm and 7.30pm to 10pm. You may be hard pressed to find somewhere still serving after these hours.

Osteria al Duca (☎ 045 59 44 74, Via Arche Scaligere 2) Set menu €13.40. Open 11am-3pm & 6.30pm-midnight Mon-Fri. Housed in the so-called Casa di Romeo (actually the former home of the Montecchis, one of the families on which Shakespeare's play is based), this place is a long-standing stalwart in central Verona, although its reputation has probably outrun the quality of the cooking. Still, the setting is attractive and the set meal not bad value.

Trattoria Alla Colonna (☎ 045 59 67 18, Via Pescheria Vecchia 4) Full meals around €23. Open Mon-Sat. For a more genuine traditional food experience than you are likely to get at the Duca, pop around the corner to this family-run place. The 'column' in the name is a red Verona marble job smack in the middle of the restaurant, around which huddle the tables. Several polenta dishes are on offer, and the wine list isn't bad.

Bottega del Vino (☎ *045 800 45 35, Vicolo Scudo di Francia 3/a)*. Full meals around €36. Open Wed-Mon. Of course, if wine is your thing then you want to come to this age-old wine cellar, which happens to serve up fine food. The wine list is endless and your choice will be served with all the ceremony you might expect at a high-flying wine-tasting. The cost of your meal can vary wildly depending on your choice of tipple. If nothing else, wander into this perennially busy dining hall – the frescoes, complemented by shelfloads of ancient bottles, are alone worth the effort.

Ristorante Maffei (☎ *045 801 00 15, Piazza delle Erbe 38)* Pasta from €7.75, mains from €18.60. The grand Palazzo Maffei makes an elegant setting for this restaurant. Dining in the central courtyard is especially pleasant.

Trattoria all'Isolo (☎ *045 59 42 91, Piazza dell'Isolo 5/a)* Full meals €18.10. Open Thur-Tues. If you scoot across the river, you find yourself in what feels like a more genuine, less touristy Verona. Much the same can be said of this tiny little eatery. Just about anything they do with *bigoli*, the Veneto version of a thick, rough spaghetti, is bound to please.

Entertainment

Throughout the year, the city hosts musical and cultural events, culminating in the season of opera and drama from July to September at the *Roman Arena*. Tickets cost from €16.50 to €155 and can be purchased at the Arena's ticket office (Ente Lirico Arena di Verona), at Via Dietro Anfiteatro 5/b; credit-card bookings can be made on ☎ 045 800 51 51. Otherwise you can buy tickets at nominated travel agents and banks in Verona and around the country. A list of these can be obtained from the theatre or the tourist office. For more information try the Web site at **W** www.arena.it.

A programme of ballet and opera is held during the winter at the 18th-century *Teatro Filarmonico* (☎ *045 800 28 80, Via dei Mutilati 4)*, just south of Piazza Brà, and Shakespeare is performed at the Roman theatre north of the river in summer. Information and tickets for these events are available at the Arena's ticket office.

Caffè Antica Osteria al Duomo (Via Duomo 7) Open noon-2pm & 7pm-10pm Mon-Sat. This is a cosy tavern with mandolins, balalaikas and other stringed instruments hanging on the wall. Pop in for a drop of *fragolino* (the local sweet strawberry wine).

M27 (☎ *045 803 42 42, Via Giuseppe Mazzini 27/a)* Open 10am-2am Tues-Sun. If you want something rather more up to date, get down to this angular, modern bar. Young, hip Veronese hang out here for morning coffee and evening cocktails, perched on improbable designer stools in a squeaky-clean, polished ambience.

The city boasts about half-a-dozen clubs/discos, all of which open from around 9pm to 4am. For a list (albeit incomplete) of these and other bars, ask for the *Verona di Notte* brochure from the tourist office.

Getting There & Away

Air The Verona-Villafranca airport (☎ 045 809 56 66) is 16km outside the town and accessible by regular bus from the train station (€4.15, 20 minutes). Flights arrive here from all over Italy and some European cities, including Amsterdam, Barcelona, Berlin, Brussels, Cologne, Frankfurt, Helsinki, London, Munich, Paris and Vienna.

Bus The main intercity bus station is in front of the train station, in an area known as Porta Nuova. Although buses travel to many big cities, they are generally only useful for those needing to reach provincial localities not served by train.

Train Verona has rail links with Milan, Venice, Padua, Mantua, Modena, Florence and Rome. There are also regular trains serving destinations in Austria, Switzerland and Germany (10 per day from Munich). The trip from Venice on a regional train (€5.75) takes one hour 35 minutes. It is faster and more expensive on InterCity services.

Car & Motorbike Verona is at the intersection of the Serenissima A4 (Milan-Venice) and Brennero A22 *autostrade*.

Getting Around
The AMT city transport company's bus Nos 11, 12, 13 and 72 (bus No 91 or 98 on Sunday and holidays) connect the train station with Piazza Brà, and bus No 70 goes to Piazza delle Erbe (tickets cost €0.85 and are valid for an hour). Otherwise, it's a 15-minute walk along Corso Porta Nuova. Day tickets for the buses cost €2.60. Buy tickets before you board the bus from newsagents and tobacconists.

Cars are banned from the city centre in the morning and early afternoon, but you will be allowed in if you are staying at a hotel. There are free car parks at Via Città di Nimes (near the train station) and Porta Vescovo, from where buses run to the city centre.

For a taxi, call ☎ 045 53 26 66.

EAST OF VENICE
The Adriatic coast, spreading east and gradually north away from Venice, is lined with popular local beach resorts. They tend to be pretty crowded on summer weekends but not quite so bad during the week. Quite a few foreigners flock to them too, using the resorts as the core of their summer holiday and chucking in the odd excursion to Venice as a diversion. These places are pleasant enough, but the northern Adriatic is not the place to plan a classic Mediterranean beach holiday.

Jesolo
Lido di Jesolo, the strand a couple of kilometres away from the main town, is far and away the Venetians' preferred beach. The sand is fine and clean, the water OK without being wonderfully crystal clear.

Jesolo marks the northern end of a long peninsula that becomes Litorale del Cavallino as you head south and culminates in Punta Sabbioni, which together with the northern end of the Lido forms the first of the three entrances into the Venetian lagoon from the Adriatic.

The beaches tend to be covered in umbrellas, recliners and the people using them,

but it makes for a pleasant change from all the sightseeing in summer. The area also has camp sites and plenty of hotels of all classes. The whole lot is predictably short on character.

ATVO buses run from Piazzale Roma in Venice (€3.35, one hour 10 minutes). Traffic can get horrendous, so try to make an early getaway. In summer, ferry services to Venice are sometimes available, but cannot be guaranteed from one year to the next. They cost €12.90 return and were operating once or twice daily in 2001.

Caorle
Nothing is left to remind you of the ancient roots of **Eraclea**, now a small agricultural town on the way from Jesolo to Caorle, itself around 30km east around the coast from Jesolo.

In the 1st century BC, Caorle was a Roman port and it remains a busy fishing centre even today. Small but proud, it only actually dropped resistance to Venetian pressure and passed under the paws of St Mark's lion in the 15th century.

The centre of the medieval town is watched over by the extraordinary cylindrical bell tower of the 11th-century **cathedral**. The cheerful streets present a pastel pageant. Although they haven't gone to quite the lengths of the people of Burano, the towns folk take a special pride in keeping their houses gleaming with a fresh coat of paint in an array of bright colours.

The beaches are busy but OK and the whole place has a nice restrained vibe. It is quite popular with Germans.

If you want to stay, the old town centre is blessed with a handful of places to lay down your weary head. The surrounding area and beachside waterfront are lined with phalanxes of hotels. There is no shortage of restaurants in which to enjoy the local seafood, although quality tends to be a little mediocre.

ATVO buses run from Piazzale Roma in Venice (€4.25, from 1½ to two hours). In summer, ferry services to Venice are sometimes available, but cannot be guaranteed from one year to the next.

Language

Italian is a Romance language related to French, Spanish, Portuguese and Romanian. The Romance languages belong to the Indo-European group of languages, which also includes English. Indeed, as many English and Italian words have common Latin roots, you will recognise many Italian words.

Modern literary Italian began to develop in the 13th and 14th centuries, predominantly through the works of Dante, Petrarch and Boccaccio, who wrote chiefly in the Florentine dialect. The language drew on its Latin heritage and many dialects to develop into the standard Italian of today. Although many dialects are still spoken in everyday conversation, standard Italian is the national language of schools, the media and literature, and is understood throughout the country.

Visitors to Italy who intend to try their hand at using more than just the basic phrases need to be aware that many Italians still expect to be addressed in the third person formal *(lei* instead of *tu)*. Also, it's not considered polite to use the greeting *ciao* when addressing strangers unless they use it first; it's better to say *buon giorno* (or *buona sera*, as the case may be) and *arrivederci* (or the more polite form, *arrivederla*). We have used the formal address for most of the phrases in this guide. Use of the informal address is indicated by 'inf' in brackets.

Italian also has both masculine and feminine forms (they usually end in 'o' and 'a' respectively). Where both forms are given in this guide, they are separated by a slash, the masculine form first.

If you'd like a more comprehensive guide to the language, get a copy of Lonely Planet's *Italian phrasebook*.

If you have a reasonable command of Italian and find you don't understand a great deal of what is being spoken around you in Venice, what you're hearing is probably Venessian (or Veneziano), the local dialect (see the boxed text 'Venice's Other Tongue' on the next page). Native Italian speakers have trouble with it too. At times you hear quite familiar words, then the flow seems to stream off into something that to the unaccustomed ear sounds like a strange mix of Portuguese and Spanish. Not only are the words different, the intonation is quite distinct as well.

Pronunciation

Italian pronunciation isn't difficult to master once you learn a few simple rules. Although some of the more clipped vowels, and stress on double letters, require careful practice for English speakers, it's easy enough to make yourself understood.

Vowels

Vowels are generally more clipped than in English:

a	as in 'art', eg, *caro* (dear); sometimes short, eg, *amico/a* (friend)
e	as in 'tell', eg, *mettere* (to put)
i	as in 'inn', eg, *inizio* (start)
o	as in 'dot', eg, *donna* (woman); as in 'port', eg, *dormire* (to sleep)
u	as the 'oo' in 'book', eg, *puro* (pure)

Consonants

The pronunciation of many Italian consonants is similar to that of their English counterparts. Pronunciation of some consonants depends on certain rules:

c	as the 'k' in 'kit' before **a, o** and **u**; as the 'ch' in 'choose' before **e** and **i**
ch	as the 'k' in 'kit'
g	as the 'g' in 'get' before **a, o, u** and **h**; as the 'j' in 'jet' before **e** and **i**
gli	as the 'lli' in 'million'
gn	as the 'ny' in 'canyon'
h	always silent
r	a rolled 'rr' sound
sc	as 'sk' before **a, o, u** and **h**; as the 'sh' in 'sheep' before **e** and **i**
z	as the 'ts' in 'lights', except at the beginning of a word, when it's as the 'ds' in 'suds'

Venice's Other Tongue

Some people do not take kindly to hearing their tongue referred to as a dialect. Such is the case with Venessian, the 'dialect' of Venice, which some linguists would instead identify as a variant of a regional language – Venet – that takes in the whole Veneto region (and even some way beyond).

Be that as it may, Venet and/or Venessian are generally, along with many other vestigial local languages spoken across Italy, dismissed as dialects of Italian. This can of worms is not worth opening here, but a couple of points should be considered.

Modern Italian has its roots in the medieval Tuscan Italian of Dante and has really developed as an amalgam ever since. Its primacy only came this century.

For 1000 years, the people of the Venetian Republic spoke Venessian, the local offshoot of Latin. Much influenced by Tuscan Italian over the centuries, Venessian nevertheless contains many Latin, Byzantine Greek and even Germanic words, and obeys different rules of pronunciation. Venetian linguists bristle at the suggestion that Venet/Venessian is merely a distortion of Italian. Given its 1000-year history, some place the local language on an equal footing with modern Italian, French and other Romance languages – all descendants, or dialects if you will, of Latin.

Evidence to support such claims can be found in Venessian vocabulary. From the Latin comes *pistor* (baker, which in Italian is *fornaio*) and from the Byzantine Greek *carega* (seat, in Italian *sedia*).

All this said, it is clear from Italian documents that Venessian was not the exclusive official language of the Venetian Republic, even though the use of certain spellings shows that it had a definite linguistic influence.

Since WWII, internal migration and the spread of the electronic media have to a great extent 'Italianised' Venetians and their linguistic habits. A series of provincial varieties of Venet (of which Venessian would be the main one) can be identified, but the language is not as robust as those in some of the minority language areas of other European countries. The vigorous promotion of Catalan and Basque in the north of Spain, for instance, has no real equivalent in Italy, if you except the small minorities that speak French or German in the country's north. To what extent locals are even interested in resuscitating the use of Venet is an open question. Curiously, one of the leading recognised experts on the Venet language is a Welshman!

Nevertheless, Venet/Venessian is still spoken to some degree by most natives of the Veneto. This is true not only in rural areas, where one would expect linguistic conservatism to be more prevalent, but also in the towns. Hearing is believing – wander around less touristy parts of Venice, such as Castello, and you'll soon be convinced. Venessian is also alive in the public eye – in Venice, at least, street signs and other public notices are increasingly appearing in Venessian, and you'll often see Venessian words on menus.

Forgetting Venessian, the Veneto accent itself is hard to miss, even when you hear many locals speaking Italian. Among its traits is the lack of double consonants and frequent dropping of consonants between vowels (*bela fia* for *bella figlia*, 'beautiful daughter'). Another is the frequent inversion of feminine and masculine: *il latte* (the milk) in Italian is *la latte* for many Venetians. The list of curiosities is immense – if you want to know more, you could pick up a pocket Venessian dictionary during your stay. We have abstained from providing phrases in Venessian in this book, as most locals will already be considerably surprised if you manage to do anything more than blurt out a few 'sì's and 'no's in standard Italian!

Note that when **ci**, **gi** and **sci** are followed by **a**, **o** or **u**, the 'i' is not pronounced unless the accent falls on the 'i'. Thus the name 'Giovanni' is pronounced 'joh-**vahn**-nee'.

Word Stress
A double consonant is pronounced as a longer, more forceful sound than a single consonant.

Stress generally falls on the second-last syllable, as in *spa-**ghet**-ti*. When a word has an accent, the stress falls on that syllable, as in *cit-**tà*** (city).

Greetings & Civilities
Hello.	*Buongiorno.*
	Ciao. (inf)
Goodbye.	*Arrivederci.*
	Ciao. (inf)
Yes.	*Sì.*
No.	*No.*
Please.	*Per favore/Per piacere.*
Thank you.	*Grazie.*
That's fine/	*Prego.*
You're welcome.	
Excuse me.	*Mi scusi.*
	Scusami. (inf)
Sorry (forgive me).	*Mi scusi/Mi perdoni.*

Small Talk
What's your name?	*Come si chiama?*
	Come ti chiami? (inf)
My name is ...	*Mi chiamo ...*
Where are you from?	*Di dov'è?*
	Di dove sei? (inf)

I'm from ...	*Sono ...*
Australia	*dall'Australia*
Belgium	*dal Belgio*
Canada	*dal Canada*
France	*dalla Francia*
Ireland	*dall'Irlanda*
Japan	*dal Giapone*
New Zealand	*dalla Nuova Zelanda*
Norway	*dalla Norvegia*
Scotland	*dalla Scozia*
Sweden	*dalla Svezia*
the UK	*dal Regno Unito*
the USA	*dagli Stati Uniti*

I (don't) like ...	*(Non) Mi piace ...*
Just a minute.	*Un momento.*

Language Difficulties
Do you speak English?	*Parla inglese?*
	Parli inglese? (inf)
Does anyone here speak English?	*C'è qualcuno che parla inglese?*
I understand.	*Capisco.*
I don't understand.	*Non capisco.*
How do you say ... in Italian?	*Come si dice ... in italiano?*
What does ... mean?	*Che vuole dire ...?*
Can you write it down, please?	*Può scriverlo, per favore?*
Can you show me (on the map)?	*Può mostrarmelo (sulla carta/pianta)?*

Paperwork
name	*nome*
nationality	*nazionalità*
date of birth	*data di nascita*
place of birth	*luogo di nascita*
sex (gender)	*sesso*
passport	*passaporto*
visa	*visto*

Getting Around
What time does ... leave/arrive?	*A che ora parte/ arriva ...?*
the aeroplane	*l'aereo*
the boat	*la barca*
the (city) bus	*l'autobus*
the (intercity) bus	*il pullman/ la corriera*
the train	*il treno*

I'd like a ... ticket.	*Vorrei un biglietto ...*
one-way	*di solo andata*
return	*di andata e ritorno*
1st-class	*di prima classe*
2nd-class	*di seconda classe*

I want to go to ...	*Voglio andare a ...*
The train has been cancelled/delayed.	*Il treno è soppresso/ in ritardo.*

the first	*il primo*
the last	*l'ultimo*
platform number	*binario numero*
ticket office	*biglietteria*
timetable	*orario*
train station	*stazione*

Signs

Ingresso/Entrata	Entrance
Uscita	Exit
Informazione	Information
Aperto	Open
Chiuso	Closed
Proibito/Vietato	Prohibited
Polizia/Carabinieri	Police
Questura	Police Station
Camere Libere	Rooms Available
Completo	Full/No Vacancies
Gabinetti/Bagni	Toilets
Uomini	Men
Donne	Women

I'd like to hire ... *Vorrei noleggiare ...*
  a bicycle   *una bicicletta*
  a car   *una macchina*
  a motorcycle   *una motocicletta*

Directions

Where is ...?	*Dov'è ...?*
Go straight ahead.	*Si va sempre diritto.*
	Vai sempre diritto. (inf)
Turn left.	*Giri a sinistra.*
Turn right.	*Giri a destra.*
at the next corner	*al prossimo angolo*
at the traffic lights	*al semaforo*
behind	*dietro*
in front of	*davanti*
far	*lontano*
near	*vicino*
opposite	*di fronte a*

Around Town

I'm looking for ...	*Cerco ...*
a bank	*un banco*
the church	*la chiesa*
the city centre	*il centro (città)*
the ... embassy	*l'ambasciata di ...*
my hotel	*il mio albergo*
the market	*il mercato*
the museum	*il museo*
the post office	*la posta*
a public toilet	*un gabinetto/ bagno pubblico*
the telephone centre	*il centro telefonico*
the tourist office	*l'ufficio di turismo/ d'informazione*

I want to change ... *Voglio cambiare ...*
  money   *del denaro*
  travellers cheques   *degli assegni per viaggiatori*

beach	*la spiaggia*
bridge	*il ponte*
castle	*il castello*
cathedral	*il duomo/la cattedrale*
church	*la chiesa*
island	*l'isola*
market	*il mercato*
mosque	*la moschea*
old city	*il centro storico*
palace	*il palazzo*
ruins	*le rovine*
sea	*il mare*
tower	*la torre*

Accommodation

I'm looking for ...	*Cerco ...*
a guesthouse	*una pensione*
a hotel	*un albergo*
a youth hostel	*un ostello per la gioventù*

Where is a cheap hotel?	*Dov'è un albergo che costa poco?*
What is the address?	*Cos'è l'indirizzo?*
Can you write the address, please?	*Può scrivere l'indirizzo, per favore?*
Do you have any rooms available?	*Ha camere libere/C'è una camera libera?*

I'd like ...	*Vorrei ...*
a bed	*un letto*
a single room	*una camera singola*
a double room	*una camera matrimoniale*
a room with two beds	*una camera doppia*
a room with a bathroom	*una camera con bagno*
to share a dorm	*un letto in dormitorio*

How much is it ...?	*Quanto costa ...?*
per night	*per la notte*
per person	*per ciascuno*

May I see it?	*Posso vederla?*
Where is the bathroom?	*Dov'è il bagno?*
I'm/We're leaving today.	*Parto/Partiamo oggi.*

Shopping

I'd like to buy ...	*Vorrei comprare ...*
How much is it?	*Quanto costa?*
I don't like it.	*Non mi piace.*
May I look at it?	*Posso dare un'occhiata?*
I'm just looking.	*Sto solo guardando.*
It's cheap.	*Non è caro/a.*
It's too expensive.	*È troppo caro/a.*
I'll take it.	*Lo/La compro.*
Do you accept ...?	*Accettate ...?*
credit cards	*carte di credito*
travellers cheques	*assegni per viaggiatori*
more	*più*
less	*meno*
smaller	*più piccolo/a*
bigger	*più grande*

Time, Date & Numbers

What time is it?	*Che ora è?/Che ore sono?*
It's (8 o'clock).	*Sono (le otto).*
in the morning	*di mattina*
in the afternoon	*di pomeriggio*
in the evening	*di sera*
today	*oggi*
tomorrow	*domani*
yesterday	*ieri*
Monday	*lunedì*
Tuesday	*martedì*
Wednesday	*mercoledì*
Thursday	*giovedì*
Friday	*venerdì*
Saturday	*sabato*
Sunday	*domenica*
January	*gennaio*
February	*febbraio*
March	*marzo*
April	*aprile*
May	*maggio*
June	*giugno*

July	*luglio*
August	*agosto*
September	*settembre*
October	*ottobre*
November	*novembre*
December	*dicembre*

0	*zero*
1	*uno*
2	*due*
3	*tre*
4	*quattro*
5	*cinque*
6	*sei*
7	*sette*
8	*otto*
9	*nove*
10	*dieci*
11	*undici*
12	*dodici*
13	*tredici*
14	*quattordici*
15	*quindici*
16	*sedici*
17	*diciassette*
18	*diciotto*
19	*diciannove*
20	*venti*
21	*ventuno*
22	*ventidue*
30	*trenta*
40	*quaranta*
50	*cinquanta*
60	*sessanta*
70	*settanta*
80	*ottanta*
90	*novanta*
100	*cento*
1000	*mille*
2000	*due mila*

one million	*un milione*

Health

I'm ill.	*Mi sento male.*
It hurts here.	*Mi fa male qui.*
I'm ...	*Sono ...*
asthmatic	*asmatico/a*
diabetic	*diabetico/a*
epileptic	*epilettico/a*

Emergencies

Help!	*Aiuto!*
There's been an accident!	*C'è stato un incidente!*
I'm lost.	*Mi sono perso/a.*
Go away!	*Lasciami in pace!*
	Vai via! (inf)
Call ...!	*Chiami ...!*
	Chiama ...! (inf)
a doctor	*un dottore/ un medico*
the police	*la polizia*

I'm allergic ...	*Sono allergico/a ...*
to antibiotics	*agli antibiotici*
to penicillin	*alla penicillina*

antiseptic	*antisettico*
aspirin	*aspirina*
condoms	*preservativi*
contraceptive	*anticoncezionale*
diarrhoea	*diarrea*
medicine	*medicina*
sunblock cream	*crema/latte solare (per protezione)*
tampons	*tamponi*

FOOD
Basics

breakfast	*prima colazione*
lunch	*pranzo*
dinner	*cena*
restaurant	*ristorante*
grocery store	*un alimentari*

I'd like the set lunch.	*Vorrei il menù turistico.*
Is service included in the bill?	*È compreso il servizio?*
I'm a vegetarian.	*Sono vegetariano/a.*
What is this?	*(Che) cos'è questo?*

bill/check	*conto*
menu	*menù*
waiter/waitress	*cameriere/a*
fork	*forchetta*
knife	*coltello*
plate	*piatto*
spoon	*cucchiaio*
teaspoon	*cucchiaino*

On the Menu
Cooking Methods

affumicato	smoked
al dente	firm (as all good pasta should be!)
alla brace	cooked over hot coals
alla griglia	grilled
arrosto	roasted
ben cotto	well done (cooked)
bollito	boiled
cotto	cooked
crudo	raw
fritto	fried

Staples & Condiments

aceto	vinegar
burro	butter
formaggio	cheese
marmellata	jam
miele	honey
olio	oil
olive	olives
pane	bread
pane integrale	wholemeal bread
panna	cream
pasta e fagioli	thick and hearty pasta and bean soup
pepe	pepper
peperoncino	chilli
polenta	cooked cornmeal
risi e bisi	risotto with green peas
riso	rice
risotto	rice cooked with wine and stock
sale	salt
uovo/uova	egg/eggs
zucchero	sugar

Meat & Fish

acciughe	anchovies
agnello	lamb
aragosta	lobster
baccalà	dried, salted cod with garlic and parsley
bistecca	steak
calamari	squid
coniglio	rabbit
cotoletta	cutlet or thin cut of meat, usually crumbed and fried

cozze	mussels
dentice	dentex (type of fish)
fegato	liver
gamberi	prawns
granchio	crab
manzo	beef
merluzzo	cod
ostriche	oysters
pesce spada	swordfish
pollo	chicken
polpo	octopus
salsiccia	sausage
sarde	sardines
sgombro	mackerel
sogliola	sole
tacchino	turkey
tonno	tuna
trippa	tripe
vitello	veal
vongole	clams

Vegetables

asparago	asparagus
carciofo (articioco in Venessian)	artichoke
carota	carrot
cavolo/verza	cabbage
cicoria	chicory
cipolla	onion
fagiolino	string bean
melanzana	aubergine/eggplant
patata	potato
peperone	pepper
piselli	peas
spinaci	spinach

Fruit

arancia	orange
banana	banana
ciliegie	cherries
fragola	strawberry
lampone	raspberry
limone	lemon
mela	apple
pera	pear
pesca	peach
uva	grapes

Soups & Antipasti

brodo – broth
carpaccio – very fine slices of raw meat
castraura – artichoke hearts
cotechino – pork sausage served with mustard
insalata caprese – sliced tomatoes with mozzarella and basil
insalata di mare – seafood, generally crustaceans
minestrina in brodo – pasta in broth
minestrone – vegetable and pasta soup
olive ascolane – stuffed, deep-fried olives
prosciutto e melone – cured ham with melon
ripieni – stuffed, oven-baked vegetables
stracciatella – egg in broth

Pasta Sauces

alla matriciana – tomato and bacon
al ragù – meat sauce (bolognese)
arrabbiata – tomato and chilli
carbonara – egg, bacon, cheese and black pepper
napoletana – tomato and basil
panna – cream, prosciutto and sometimes peas
pesto – basil, garlic and oil, often with pine nuts
vongole – clams, garlic, oil and sometimes tomato

Pizzas

All pizzas listed have a tomato (and sometimes mozzarella) base.

capricciosa – olives, prosciutto, mushrooms and artichokes
frutti di mare – seafood
funghi – mushrooms
margherita – oregano
napoletana – anchovies
pugliese – tomato, mozzarella and onions
quattro formaggi – four types of cheese
quattro stagioni – like a capricciosa, but sometimes with egg
verdura – mixed vegetables, eg, courgette/zucchini, aubergine/eggplant, carrot and spinach

Glossary

Listed below are useful Italian terms. Some appear in the Venetian dialect (V). In a few instances, Italian words used only in Venice and, at the most, elsewhere in the Veneto have been identified (Vz). A couple of entries in French (F) and English (E) also appear. They are specialised terms that may not be familiar to all readers.

abbonamento – transport pass valid for one month
ACI – Automobile Club Italiano; Italian Automobile Club
acqua alta (s), **acque alte** (pl) – high water (flooding that occurs in Venice during winter, when the sea level rises)
ACTV – bus and *vaporetti* company
aeroporto – airport
affittacamere – rooms for rent (sometimes cheaper than a *pensione* and not part of the classification system)
AIG – Associazione Italiana Alberghi per la Gioventù: Italian Youth Hostel Association
albergo – hotel (up to five stars)
alimentari – grocery shop
alloggio – general term for lodging of any kind; not part of the classification system
alto – high
ambulanza – ambulance
amuleto – lucky charm
andata e ritorno – round trip
anfiteatro – amphitheatre
antipasto (s), **antipasti** (pl) – starter (in a meal)
appartamento – apartment, flat
apse – (E) domed or arched area at the altar end of a church
APT – Azienda di Promozione Turistica; provincial tourist office
arco – arch
ASL – Azienda Sanitaria Locale; provincial health agency
autobus – bus
autostazione – bus station/terminal
autostop – hitchhiking
autostrada (s), **autostrade** (pl) – highway/motorway

bacaro – (V) traditional Venetian bar or eatery
bagno – bathroom; also toilet
bancomat – automated teller machine (ATM)
basilica – (E) style of church, with a hall flanked by two aisles
battistero – baptistry
benzina – petrol
bicicletta – bicycle
biglietteria – ticket office
biglietto (s), **biglietti** (pl) – ticket
bigoli – thick, rough Venetian pasta
binario – platform
blanco – white
bocca (s), **bocche** (pl) – mouth; also one of the three entrances to the Venice lagoon from the sea
bricola – (V) pylon marking navigable channel in Venetian lagoon
bucintoro – the doge's ceremonial barge

calle (s), **calli** (pl) – (Vz) street
camera – room
camera doppia – double room with twin beds
camera matrimoniale – double room with double bed
camera singola – single room
campanile – bell tower
campo – (Vz) square; equivalent to the piazza elsewhere in Italy
cappella – chapel
carabinieri – police with military and civil duties
carnet – book of tickets
carta marmorizzata – marbled paper
cartapesta – papier mache, used to make Carnevale masks
carta telefonica – phonecard
cartoleria – shop selling paper goods
cartolina (postale) – postcard
casa – house
castello – castle
cattedrale – cathedral
cena – evening meal
centro – centre

centro storico – (literally 'historical centre') old town

chiaroscuro – (literally 'light-dark') the use of strong light and dark contrasts in painting to put the main figures into stronger relief

chiesa – church

chiostro – cloister; covered walkway, usually enclosed by columns, around a quadrangle

cicheti – (Vz) traditional bar snacks eaten in bars and *osterie*

cimitero – cemetery

CIT – Compagnia Italiana di Turismo; Italian national travel agency

colazione – breakfast

colonna – column

comune – equivalent to a municipality or county; town or city council; historically, a commune (self-governing town or city)

condottiero – mercenary leader

consolato – consulate

contorni – side orders

convalida – validation

coperto – cover charge (in restaurant)

corte – (Vz) blind alley

CTS – Centro Turistico Studentesco e Giovanile; student/youth travel agency

cupola – dome

doge – (Vz) the dux, or leader, of the Venetian Republic

deposito bagagli – left luggage

digestivo – after-dinner liqueur

discoteca – nightclub

duomo – cathedral

ENIT – Ente Nazionale Italiano per il Turismo; Italian State Tourist Office

espresso – express mail; express train; short black coffee

farmacia – pharmacy, chemist's shop

farmacia di turno – late-night pharmacy

ferrovia – train station

festa – festival

fiume – river

fondaco (s), **fondachi** (pl) – merchant's house; (Vz) *fontego*

fondamenta – (Vz) street beside a canal

fontana – fountain

forcola – (V) wooden support for gondolier's oar

foresto – (V) stranger, foreigner (non-Venetian)

fornace – oven, furnace

forno – bakery

foro – forum

fragolino – non-commercial strawberry-flavoured red wine

francobollo (s), **francobolli** (pl) – postage stamp

fresco – (E) the painting method in which watercolour paint is applied to wet plaster

FS – Ferrovie dello Stato; Italian State Railway

funicolare – funicular railway

gabinetto – toilet, WC

gelateria (s), **gelaterie** (pl) – ice-cream shop

gelato (s), **gelati** (pl) – ice cream

gettoni – telephone tokens

giardino (s), **giardini** (pl) – garden, park

golfo – gulf

granita – drink made of crushed ice and fruit juice

intarsia – inlaid wood, marble or metal

lago – lake

largo – (small) square, boulevard

lavanderia (s) – laundrette

lavasecco – dry-cleaning

lettera – letter

lettera raccomandata – registered letter

lido – beach

locanda – inn, small hotel

loggia – covered area on the side of a building; porch; lodge

lungomare – seafront road, promenade

Maggior Consiglio – Grand Council; level of Venetian government (see History in the Facts about Venice chapter)

malvasia – tavern (named after the wine imported from former Venice-controlled Greek islands)

mare – sea

mercato – market

merceria – haberdashery shop

merletto – lace

monte – mountain
motonave – big, inter-island ferry on Venetian lagoon
motorino – moped
motoscafo – motorboat; in Venice a faster, fully enclosed ferry
municipio – town hall
museo (s), **musei** (pl) – museum

nave (s), **navi** (pl) – ship
necropoli – necropolis; (ancient) cemetery, burial site

oggetti smarriti – lost property
ombra – (Vz) small glass of wine
orario – timetable
orto botanico – botanical gardens
ospedale – hospital
ostello (per la gioventù) – (youth) hostel
osteria (s), **osterie** (pl) – traditional bar/restaurant

pacco – package, parcel
Pagine Gialle – Yellow Pages (telephone directory)
pala/pala d'altare – altarpiece; refers to a painting (often on wood) usually used as an ornament before the altar
palazzo (s), **palazzi** (pl) – palace, mansion; large building of any type, including an apartment block
panetteria – bakery
panino (s), **panini** (pl) – bread roll with filling
parco – park
passeggiata – traditional evening or Sunday stroll
passerelle (s), **passerelli** (pl) – raised walkway
pasta – cake; pasta; pastry or dough
pasticceria – shop selling cakes, pastries and biscuits
pensione (s), **pensioni** (pl) – guesthouse, small hotel
permesso di soggiorno – permit to stay for a period of time, residence permit
piazza (s), **piazze** (pl) – square
piazzale – (large) open square
pietà – (literally 'pity' or 'compassion') sculpture, drawing or painting of the dead Christ supported by the Madonna

pinacoteca – art gallery
pizzeria – pizza restaurant
polizia – police
poltrona – airline-type chair on a ferry
ponte – bridge
portico – portico; covered walkway, usually attached to the outside of buildings
porto – port
posta aerea – air mail
pozzo (s), **pozzi** (pl) – well
pronto soccorso – first aid, casualty ward
prosecco – lightly sparkling white wine
punto informativo – information booth

(La) Quarantia – (literally 'the 40') level of Venetian government (see History in the Facts about Venice chapter)
quartiere (s), **quartieri** (pl) – one of the 13 divisions of the Venice *comune*
questura – police station

ramo – (Vz) tiny side lane
rifugio (s), **rifugi** (pl) – shelter; mountain accommodation
rio (s), **rii** (pl) – (Vz) the name for most canals in Venice
rio terrà – (Vz) street following the course of a filled-in canal
riva – river bank
riva alta – high river bank
rivo – stream
rocca – fortress
rosso – red
ruga – (Vz) small street flanked by houses and shops

sala – room, hall
salizzada – (Vz) street, the first type in Venice to be paved
salumeria – delicatessen
santo, santa – saint (male/female)
santuario – sanctuary
scalinata – staircase
scavi – excavations
schola (s), **schole** (pl) – synagogue
scuola (s), **scuole** (pl) – school; former community and religious association
servizio – service charge (in restaurant)
sestiere (s), **sestieri** (pl) – (Vz) term for the six 12th-century municipal divisions of Venice

Signoria – top level of Venetian government (see History in the Facts about Venice chapter)
soccorso stradale – highway rescue
sotoportego (s), **sotoporteghi** (pl) – (Vz) in Italian *sottoportico*; street continuing under a building (like an extended archway)
spiaggia – beach
spiaggia libera – public beach
squero (s), **squeri** (pl) – gondola-building and repair yard
stazione (autobus) – (main bus) station
stazione di servizio – service station, petrol station
stazione marittima – ferry terminal
strada – street, road
strada provinciale – main road; sometimes just a country lane
strada statale – main road; often multi-lane and toll free
superstrada – toll-free highway

tabaccheria (s), **tabacchi** (pl) – tobacconist's shop
teatro – theatre
telegramma – telegram
tempio – temple
terme – thermal baths, hot springs
tesoro – treasury

torre – tower
traghetto – small ferry; in Venice, the commuter gondolas that crisscross the Grand Canal
tramezzino – sandwich
trattoria (s), **trattorie** (pl) – fairly cheap restaurant
treno – train
trompe l'oeil - (F) painting or other illustration which is designed to 'deceive the eye', creating the impression that the image is real
tympanum – (E) vertical (often triangular) space above a doorway between the lintel and arch

ufficio postale – post office
ufficio stranieri – foreigners' bureau (in police station)

vaporetto (s), **vaporetti** (pl) – ferry
vetrai – glass-makers
via – street, road
via aerea – air mail
vigili del fuoco – fire brigade
vigili urbani – traffic/local police
villa – town or country house; also the park surrounding the house
vinaio – wine merchant
vino – wine

LONELY PLANET

You already know that Lonely Planet produces more than this one guidebook, but you might not be aware of the other products we have on this region. Here is a selection of titles that you may want to check out as well:

Europe on a shoestring
ISBN 1 86450 150 2
US$24.99 • UK£14.99

Mediterrean Europe
ISBN 1 86450 154 5
US$27.99 • UK£15.99

Read This First: Europe
ISBN 1 86450 136 7
US$14.99 • UK£8.99

Italy
ISBN 1 86450 352 1
US$24.99 • UK£14.99

Milan, Turin & Genoa
ISBN 1 86450 362 9
US$14.99 • UK£8.99

Italian phrasebook
ISBN 0 86442 456 6
US$5.95 • UK£3.99

Rome
ISBN 1 86450 311 4
US$15.99 • UK£9.99

Tuscany
ISBN 1 86450 357 2
US$17.99 • UK£10.99

Florence
ISBN 1 74059 030 9
US$17.99 • UK£8.99

Walking in Italy
ISBN 0 86442 542 2
US$17.95 • UK£11.99

World Food Italy
ISBN 1 86450 022 0
US$12.95 • UK£7.99

Rome Condensed
ISBN 1 86450 360 2
US$11.99 • UK£5.99

Available wherever books are sold

LONELY PLANET

ON THE ROAD

Travel Guides explore cities, regions and countries, and supply information on transport, restaurants and accommodation, covering all budgets. They come with reliable, easy-to-use maps, practical advice, cultural and historical facts and a rundown on attractions both on and off the beaten track. There are over 200 titles in this classic series, covering nearly every country in the world.

 Lonely Planet Upgrades extend the shelf life of existing travel guides by detailing any changes that may affect travel in a region since a book has been published. Upgrades can be downloaded for free from **www.lonelyplanet.com/upgrades**

For travellers with more time than money, **Shoestring** guides offer dependable, first-hand information with hundreds of detailed maps, plus insider tips for stretching money as far as possible. Covering entire continents in most cases, the six-volume shoestring guides are known around the world as 'backpackers bibles'.

For the discerning short-term visitor, **Condensed** guides highlight the best a destination has to offer in a full-colour, pocket-sized format designed for quick access. They include everything from top sights and walking tours to opinionated reviews of where to eat, stay, shop and have fun.

CitySync lets travellers use their Palm™ or Visor™ hand-held computers to guide them through a city with handy tips on transport, history, cultural life, major sights, and shopping and entertainment options. It can also quickly search and sort hundreds of reviews of hotels, restaurants and attractions, and pinpoint their location on scrollable street maps. CitySync can be downloaded from **www.citysync.com**

MAPS & ATLASES

Lonely Planet's **City Maps** feature downtown and metropolitan maps, as well as transit routes and walking tours. The maps come complete with an index of streets, a listing of sights and a plastic coat for extra durability.

Road Atlases are an essential navigation tool for serious travellers. Cross-referenced with the guidebooks, they also feature distance and climate charts and a complete site index.

LONELY PLANET

ESSENTIALS

Read This First books help new travellers to hit the road with confidence. These invaluable predeparture guides give step-by-step advice on preparing for a trip, budgeting, arranging a visa, planning an itinerary and staying safe while still getting off the beaten track.

Healthy Travel pocket guides offer a regional rundown on disease hot spots and practical advice on predeparture health measures, staying well on the road and what to do in emergencies. The guides come with a user-friendly design and helpful diagrams and tables.

Lonely Planet's **Phrasebooks** cover the essential words and phrases travellers need when they're strangers in a strange land. They come in a pocket-sized format with colour tabs for quick reference, extensive vocabulary lists, easy-to-follow pronunciation keys and two-way dictionaries.

Miffed by blurry photos of the Taj Mahal? Tired of the classic 'top of the head cut off' shot? **Travel Photography: A Guide to Taking Better Pictures** will help you turn ordinary holiday snaps into striking images and give you the know-how to capture every scene, from frenetic festivals to peaceful beach sunrises.

Lonely Planet's **Travel Journal** is a lightweight but sturdy travel diary for jotting down all those on-the-road observations and significant travel moments. It comes with a handy time-zone wheel, a world map and useful travel information.

Lonely Planet's eKno is an all-in-one communication service developed especially for travellers. It offers low-cost international calls and free email and voicemail so that you can keep in touch while on the road. Check it out on **www.ekno.lonelyplanet.com**

FOOD & RESTAURANT GUIDES

Lonely Planet's **Out to Eat** guides recommend the brightest and best places to eat and drink in top international cities. These gourmet companions are arranged by neighbourhood, packed with dependable maps, garnished with scene-setting photos and served with quirky features.

For people who live to eat, drink and travel, **World Food** guides explore the culinary culture of each country. Entertaining and adventurous, each guide is packed with detail on staples and specialities, regional cuisine and local markets, as well as sumptuous recipes, comprehensive culinary dictionaries and lavish photos good enough to eat.

OUTDOOR GUIDES

For those who believe the best way to see the world is on foot, Lonely Planet's **Walking Guides** detail everything from family strolls to difficult treks, with 'when to go and how to do it' advice supplemented by reliable maps and essential travel information.

Cycling Guides map a destination's best bike tours, long and short, in day-by-day detail. They contain all the information a cyclist needs, including advice on bike maintenance, places to eat and stay, innovative maps with detailed cues to the rides, and elevation charts.

The **Watching Wildlife** series is perfect for travellers who want authoritative information but don't want to tote a heavy field guide. Packed with advice on where, when and how to view a region's wildlife, each title features photos of over 300 species and contains engaging comments on the local flora and fauna.

With underwater colour photos throughout, **Pisces Books** explore the world's best diving and snorkelling areas. Each book contains listings of diving services and dive resorts, detailed information on depth, visibility and difficulty of dives, and a roundup of the marine life you're likely to see through your mask.

LONELY PLANET

OFF THE ROAD

Journeys, the travel literature series written by renowned travel authors, capture the spirit of a place or illuminate a culture with a journalist's attention to detail and a novelist's flair for words. These are tales to soak up while you're actually on the road or dip into as an at-home armchair indulgence.

The range of lavishly illustrated **Pictorial** books is just the ticket for both travellers and dreamers. Off-beat tales and vivid photographs bring the adventure of travel to your doorstep long before the journey begins and long after it is over.

Lonely Planet **Videos** encourage the same independent, tough-minded approach as the guidebooks. Currently airing throughout the world, this award-winning series features innovative footage and an original soundtrack.

Yes, we know, work is tough, so do a little bit of deskside dreaming with the spiral-bound Lonely Planet **Diary** or a Lonely Planet **Wall Calendar**, filled with great photos from around the world.

TRAVELLERS NETWORK

Lonely Planet Online. Lonely Planet's award-winning Web site has insider information on hundreds of destinations, from Amsterdam to Zimbabwe, complete with interactive maps and relevant links. The site also offers the latest travel news, recent reports from travellers on the road, guidebook upgrades, a travel links site, an online book-buying option and a lively traveller's bulletin board. It can be viewed at **www.lonelyplanet.com** or AOL keyword: lp.

Planet Talk is a quarterly print newsletter, full of gossip, advice, anecdotes and author articles. It provides an antidote to the being-at-home blues and lets you plan and dream for the next trip. Contact the nearest Lonely Planet office for your free copy.

Comet, the free Lonely Planet newsletter, comes via email once a month. It's loaded with travel news, advice, dispatches from authors, travel competitions and letters from readers. To subscribe, click on the Comet subscription link on the front page of the Web site.

LONELY PLANET

Guides by Region

Lonely Planet is known worldwide for publishing practical, reliable and no-nonsense travel information in our guides and on our Web site. The Lonely Planet list covers just about every accessible part of the world. Currently there are 16 series: Travel guides, Shoestring guides, Condensed guides, Phrasebooks, Read This First, Healthy Travel, Walking guides, Cycling guides, Watching Wildlife guides, Pisces Diving & Snorkeling guides, City Maps, Road Atlases, Out to Eat, World Food, Journeys travel literature and Pictorials.

AFRICA Africa on a shoestring • Cairo • Cairo City Map • Cape Town • Cape Town City Map • East Africa • Egypt • Egyptian Arabic phrasebook • Ethiopia, Eritrea & Djibouti • Ethiopian Amharic phrasebook • The Gambia & Senegal • Healthy Travel Africa • Kenya • Malawi • Morocco • Moroccan Arabic phrasebook • Mozambique • Read This First: Africa • South Africa, Lesotho & Swaziland • Southern Africa • Southern Africa Road Atlas • Swahili phrasebook • Tanzania, Zanzibar & Pemba • Trekking in East Africa • Tunisia • Watching Wildlife East Africa • Watching Wildlife Southern Africa • West Africa • World Food Morocco • Zimbabwe, Botswana & Namibia
Travel Literature: Mali Blues: Traveling to an African Beat • The Rainbird: A Central African Journey • Songs to an African Sunset: A Zimbabwean Story

AUSTRALIA & THE PACIFIC Auckland • Australia • Australian phrasebook • Australia Road Atlas • Cycling Australia • Cycling New Zealand • Fiji • Fijian phrasebook • Healthy Travel Australia, NZ & the Pacific • Islands of Australia's Great Barrier Reef • Melbourne • Melbourne City Map • Micronesia • New Caledonia • New South Wales • New Zealand • Northern Territory • Outback Australia • Out to Eat – Melbourne • Out to Eat – Sydney • Papua New Guinea • Pidgin phrasebook • Queensland • Rarotonga & the Cook Islands • Samoa • Solomon Islands • South Australia • South Pacific • South Pacific phrasebook • Sydney • Sydney City Map • Sydney Condensed • Tahiti & French Polynesia • Tasmania • Tonga • Tramping in New Zealand • Vanuatu • Victoria • Walking in Australia • Watching Wildlife Australia • Western Australia
Travel Literature: Islands in the Clouds: Travels in the Highlands of New Guinea • Kiwi Tracks: A New Zealand Journey • Sean & David's Long Drive

CENTRAL AMERICA & THE CARIBBEAN Bahamas, Turks & Caicos • Baja California • Belize, Guatemala & Yucatán • Bermuda • Central America on a shoestring • Costa Rica • Costa Rica Spanish phrasebook • Cuba • Dominican Republic & Haiti • Eastern Caribbean • Guatemala • Havana • Healthy Travel Central & South America • Jamaica • Mexico • Mexico City • Panama • Puerto Rico • Read This First: Central & South America • World Food Mexico • Yucatán
Travel Literature: Green Dreams: Travels in Central America

EUROPE Amsterdam • Amsterdam City Map • Amsterdam Condensed • Andalucía • Austria • Baltic States phrasebook • Barcelona • Barcelona City Map • Belgium & Luxembourg • Berlin • Berlin City Map • Britain • British phrasebook • Brussels, Bruges & Antwerp • Brussels City Map • Budapest • Budapest City Map • Canary Islands • Central Europe • Central Europe phrasebook • Copenhagen • Corfu & the Ionians • Corsica • Crete • Crete Condensed • Croatia • Cycling Britain • Cycling France • Cyprus • Czech & Slovak Republics • Denmark • Dublin • Dublin City Map • Eastern Europe • Eastern Europe phrasebook • Edinburgh • England • Estonia, Latvia & Lithuania • Europe on a shoestring • Europe phrasebook • Finland • Florence • France • Frankfurt Condensed • French phrasebook • Georgia, Armenia & Azerbaijan • Germany • German phrasebook • Greece • Greek Islands • Greek phrasebook • Hungary • Iceland, Greenland & the Faroe Islands • Ireland • Italian phrasebook • Italy • Krakow • Lisbon • The Loire • London • London City Map • London Condensed • Madrid • Malta • Mediterranean Europe • Mediterranean Europe phrasebook • Moscow • Munich • Netherlands • Normandy • Norway • Out to Eat – London • Out to Eat – Paris • Paris • Paris City Map • Paris Condensed • Poland • Polish phrasebook • Portugal • Portuguese phrasebook • Prague • Prague City Map • Provence & the Côte d'Azur • Read This First: Europe • Rhodes & the Dodecanese • Romania & Moldova • Rome • Rome City Map • Russia, Ukraine & Belarus • Russian phrasebook • Scandinavian & Baltic Europe • Scandinavian phrasebook • Scotland • Sicily • Slovenia • South-West France • Spain • Spanish phrasebook • St Petersburg • St Petersburg City Map • Sweden • Switzerland • Tuscany • Ukrainian phrasebook • Venice • Vienna • Walking in Britain • Walking in France • Walking in Ireland • Walking in Italy • Walking in Spain • Walking in Switzerland • Western Europe • World Food France • World Food Ireland • World Food Italy • World Food Spain
Travel Literature: After Yugoslavia • Love and War in the Apennines • The Olive Grove: Travels in Greece • On the Shores of the Mediterranean • Round Ireland in Low Gear • A Small Place in Italy

LONELY PLANET

Mail Order

onely Planet products are distributed worldwide. They are also available by mail order from Lonely Planet, so if you have difficulty finding a title please write to us. North and South American residents should write to 150 Linden St, Oakland, CA 94607, USA; European and African residents should write to 10a Spring Place, London NW5 3BH, UK; and residents of other countries to Locked Bag 1, Footscray, Victoria 3011, Australia.

INDIAN SUBCONTINENT & THE INDIAN OCEAN Bangladesh • Bengali phrasebook • Bhutan • Delhi • Goa • Healthy Travel Asia & India • Hindi & Urdu phrasebook • India • Indian Himalaya • Karakoram Highway • Kerala • Madagascar • Maldives • Mauritius, Réunion & Seychelles • Mumbai (Bombay) • Nepal • Nepali phrasebook • Pakistan • Rajasthan • Read This First: Asia & India • South India • Sri Lanka • Sri Lanka phrasebook • Tibet • Tibetan phrasebook • Trekking in the Indian Himalaya • Trekking in the Karakoram & Hindukush • Trekking in the Nepal Himalaya
Travel Literature: The Age of Kali: Indian Travels and Encounters • Hello Goodnight: A Life of Goa • In Rajasthan • Maverick in Madagascar • A Season in Heaven: True Tales from the Road to Kathmandu • Shopping for Buddhas • A Short Walk in the Hindu Kush • Slowly Down the Ganges

MIDDLE EAST & CENTRAL ASIA Bahrain, Kuwait & Qatar • Central Asia • Central Asia phrasebook • Dubai • Farsi (Persian) phrasebook • Hebrew phrasebook • Iran • Israel & the Palestinian Territories • Istanbul • Istanbul City Map • Istanbul to Cairo • Istanbul to Kathmandu • Jerusalem • Jerusalem City Map • Jordan • Lebanon • Middle East • Oman & the United Arab Emirates • Syria • Turkey • Turkish phrasebook • World Food Turkey • Yemen
Travel Literature: Black on Black: Iran Revisited • The Gates of Damascus • Kingdom of the Film Stars: Journey into Jordan

NORTH AMERICA Alaska • Boston • Boston City Map • Boston Condensed • British Columbia • California & Nevada • California Condensed • Canada • Chicago • Chicago City Map • Florida • Great Lakes • Hawaii • Hiking in Alaska • Hiking in the USA • Las Vegas • Los Angeles • Los Angeles City Map • Louisiana & the Deep South • Miami • Miami City Map • Montreal • New England • New Orleans • New York City • New York City City Map • New York City Condensed • New York, New Jersey & Pennsylvania • Oahu • Out to Eat – San Francisco • Pacific Northwest • Rocky Mountains • San Francisco • San Francisco City Map • Seattle • Southwest • Texas • Toronto • USA • USA phrasebook • Vancouver • Virginia & the Capital Region • Washington, DC • Washington, DC City Map • World Food New Orleans
Travel Literature: Caught Inside: A Surfer's Year on the California Coast • Drive Thru America

NORTH-EAST ASIA Beijing • Beijing City Map • Cantonese phrasebook • China • Hiking in Japan • Hong Kong • Hong Kong City Map • Hong Kong Condensed • Hong Kong, Macau & Guangzhou • Japan • Japanese phrasebook • Korea • Korean phrasebook • Kyoto • Mandarin phrasebook • Mongolia • Mongolian phrasebook • Seoul • Shanghai • South-West China • Taiwan • Tokyo • World Food Hong Kong
Travel Literature: In Xanadu: A Quest • Lost Japan

SOUTH AMERICA Argentina, Uruguay & Paraguay • Bolivia • Brazil • Brazilian phrasebook • Buenos Aires • Chile & Easter Island • Colombia • Ecuador & the Galapagos Islands • Healthy Travel Central & South America • Latin American Spanish phrasebook • Peru • Quechua phrasebook • Read This First: Central & South America • Rio de Janeiro • Rio de Janeiro City Map • Santiago de Chile • South America on a shoestring • Trekking in the Patagonian Andes • Venezuela
Travel Literature: Full Circle: A South American Journey

SOUTH-EAST ASIA Bali & Lombok • Bangkok • Bangkok City Map • Burmese phrasebook • Cambodia • Hanoi • Healthy Travel Asia & India • Hill Tribes phrasebook • Ho Chi Minh City • Indonesia • Indonesian phrasebook • Indonesia's Eastern Islands • Java • Lao phrasebook • Laos • Malay phrasebook • Malaysia, Singapore & Brunei • Myanmar (Burma) • Philippines • Pilipino (Tagalog) phrasebook • Read This First: Asia & India • Singapore • Singapore City Map • South-East Asia on a shoestring • South-East Asia phrasebook • Thailand • Thailand's Islands & Beaches • Thailand, Vietnam, Laos & Cambodia Road Atlas • Thai phrasebook • Vietnam • Vietnamese phrasebook • World Food Thailand • World Food Vietnam

ALSO AVAILABLE: Antarctica • The Arctic • The Blue Man: Tales of Travel, Love and Coffee • Brief Encounters: Stories of Love, Sex & Travel • Chasing Rickshaws • The Last Grain Race • Lonely Planet ... On the Edge: Adventurous Escapades from Around the World • Lonely Planet Unpacked • Not the Only Planet: Science Fiction Travel Stories • Sacred India • Travel Photography: A Guide to Taking Better Pictures • Travel with Children

Index

Text

Bold indicates maps.

Bold indicates maps.

Boxed Text

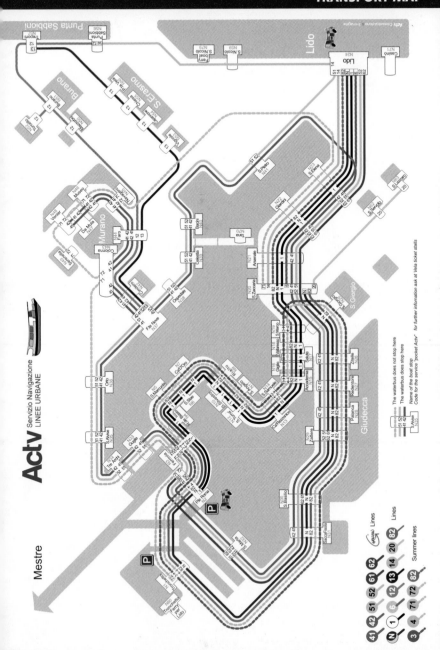

MAP 3

Canale Colombola

Fondamenta di San Giobbe

Corte Giustiniana

Calle del Forner

Calle Ferau

Calle del le Cooperative

Ponte Fondamenta Case
Moro

Fondamenta Carlo Coletti

Rio di San Girolamo

Fone

Fone

Calle Tintoria

Fondamenta del Batello

Rio del Batello

Tre Archi

Calle delle Beccarie

Calle del Scalzatto

Calle dei Colori

Calle del Tintori

Calle del Magazen

Calle delle Canne

Ponte
Saponello

Ponte di
Tre Archi

Fondamenta di Cannaregio

Calle della Madonna

Calle del Sotto Scuro

Calle Biscotella

Calle della Cerenia

Rio di San Giobbe

Campo
San
Giobbe

Canale di Cannaregio

Rio

Fon

Rio Terrà della Crea

Calle Busello

Fondamente Savorgnan

Calle Riello

CANNAREGIO

Rio della Crea

Rio della Crea

Parco
Savorgna

Ponte della Libertà

Calle Priuli detta dei Cavalletti

Calle Pesaro

60
59

Calle della Misericordia

58

Rio Te

Sabbioni

Rio

Rio della Crea

61

Rio Terrà Lista di Spagna

62

63

Fond Crotta

Grand Canal

67

Fondamenta dei Scalzi

64

Ponte dei
Scalzi

Calle Simeon

68

69

66 65

Ferrovia
Scalzi

Calle Lunga Chioverette

Calle

85

84

Bergami

Stazione di
Santa Lucia
(Ferrovia)

Ferrovia
Santa Lucia

83

Cllo di Comare

Ponte della Libertà

Fondamenta di Santa Lucia

82

Calle del Traghetto
di Santa Lucia

Calle Chioverette

Ramo
Chioverette

Piazzale Roma
Scomenzera

Piazzale Roma
Parisi

Stazione
Merci

Ferrovia
Traghetto
(Limited
Hours)

Fondamenta San Simeon Piccolo

Calle Bergamaschi

81

86

89

87

88

Corte

Fondamenta di Santa Chiara

Fondamenta di Santa Chiara

C. Volto di Santa Chiara

Piazzale Roma
Santa Chiara

78

80

Fondamenta dei Tolentini

Corte di Case Nuove

79

Campo della Lana

Calle de

Canale di Santa Chiara

70 71
72

73

Garage
Comunale

77

76

74

75

Piazzale
Roma

Campo di S Andrea

Fond del Croce

Rio Nuovo

Giardini
Papadopoli

Rio dei Tolentini

MAP 6

0   50   100m
0   50   100yd

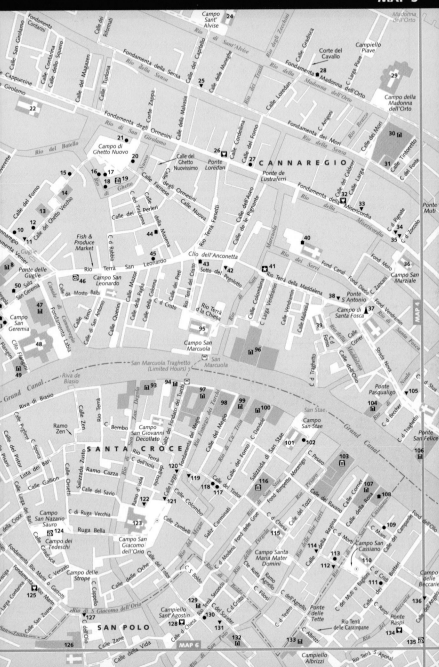

MAP 3

Madonna
dell'Orto

Campo
Sant'Alvise 24

Calle dei
Riformati

Fondamenta
Contarini

Calle San Girolamo

Calle Contarina

Calle dello Squero

Calle del Magazen

Calle Turlona

Rio di Sant'Alvise

Calle del Capitello

Rio degli Zecchini

Campiello
Piave

Calle Larga Piave

Corte del
Cavallo

Fondamenta della Sensa

Calle Gradisca

28 Madonna dell'Orto

Calle delle Muraegh

Rio della Sensa

Fondamenta dei

25

Madonna dell'Orto

29

Campo della
Madonna
dell'Orto

o Cappuccine

o Girolamo

22

Calle Lorredan

Fondamenta degli Ormesini

Corte Zappa

Calle della Malvasia

Rio di San
Girolamo

Rio del Batello

Calle del Ghetto Nuovissimo

Calle Cordellina

Ponte
Loredan

26

27

CANNAREGIO

Calle dei Calderer

Calle Larga

30

Calle Tintorelto

Campo di
Ghetto Nuovo

21

20

Rio della Sensa

Fondamenta dei Mori

Rio Brucco

31

C. del Fonte

15

16 17

18 19

Calle degli Ormesini

Ponte de
Lustraferri

Fondamenta della

Ponte
Muti

Calle del Forno

14

Calle del Ghetto Vecchio

Calle Farnese

Calle Nuova

Rio Terrà Farsetti

Calle de le Pignatte

32

Misericordia

33

34

35

C. di Locco

C. di Prigate

Ponte
Muti

13

10

12

11

Calle Terziana

Calle della Masena

44

43

Clio dell'Anconetta

42

41

Rio Terrà della Maddalena

40

Rio dei Servi

Fond Canal

Fond Dieco

Fond Moro

C. Zancani

Campo San
Marziale

36

Fish &
Produce
Market

45

Sotto del Pegolotto

Calle Colombina

Calle Larga Vendramin

Ponte
S Antonio

Fond S Antonio

Campo di
Santa Fosca

37

Fond Vendramin

MAP 4

8

Ponte delle
Guglie

Rio Terrà San Leonardo

46

Campo San
Leonardo

Calle da Mosto Balbi

Calle Vendramin

Calle Malvasia

38

39

Strada Nova

Calle Correr

C. d Traghetto

50

Saliz

San Geremia

47

Fondamenta Labia

Calle Querini

Rio Terrà
d la Chiesa

95

Campo San
Marcuola

San
Marcuola

96

Calle dell'Olio

Ponte
Pasqualigo

105

104

C. d Stua

3

Campo
San
Geremia

48

San Marcuola Traghetto
(Limited Hours)

Grand Canal

49

Riva de Biasio

93

94

97

98

99

100

San Stae

Grand Canal

C. Becher

Ponte
San Felice

106

Riva di Biasio

Ramo
Zen

Bembo

Campo
San Giovanni
Decollato

SANTA CROCE

Calle del Megio

Campo
San Stae

101

102

103

107

108

Ramo Cazza

119

118

117

116

115

109

Campo
San Nazario
Sauro

120

121

122

123

124

Campo dei
Tedeschi

Campo San
Giacomo
dell'Orio

Campo Santa
Maria Mater
Domini

114

113

112

110

111

136

125

Campo delle
Strope

126

127

128

129

130

131

132

133

134

135

SAN POLO

Campiello
Sant'Agostin

Ponte
Raspi

Campo
delle
Beccarie

MAP 6

Campiello
Albrizzi

MAP 3

PLACES TO STAY
3 Hotel Tre Archi
28 Grand Hotel Palazzo
    dei Dogi
40 Ostello Santa Fosca
43 Archies
44 Hotel Silva & Ariel
50 Hotel al Gobbo
51 Hotel San Geremia
52 Alloggi Calderan &
    Casa Gerotto
54 Hotel Minerva &
    Nettuno
55 Hotel Rossi
57 Hotel Adua
59 Hotel Santa Lucia
60 Hotel Villa Rosa
61 Hotel Abbazia
80 Hotel Canal
108 Hotel San Cassiano
    (Ca' Favretto)

PLACES TO EAT
4 Da Marisa
9 Alla Fontana
11 Gam Gam
25 Anice Stellato
33 Paradiso Perduto
34 Sahara
35 Iguana
38 Cantina Vecia
    Carbonera
42 La Colombina
62 Brek
89 Old Well Pub
105 Standa Supermarket
112 Al Nono Risorto
114 Vecio Fritolin
119 Osteria La Zucca
120 Trattoria al Ponte
121 Al Prosecco
122 Mini-Coop
127 Ganesh Ji
131 Da Fiore
136 Cantina do Spade

BARS
26 Osteria agli Ormesini
32 La Fondamenta
58 Casanova
125 Ai Postali
128 Taverna da Baffo
134 Pizzeria Jazz Club 900

SHOPPING
10 Wine Shop
12 Volpe Panetteria
15 La Stamperia del Ghetto
17 Jewish Art Workshop
27 Cantina del Baffo
45 Nave de Oro

53 Libreria Demetra
111 L'Arlecchino
113 La Margherita Ceramiche
117 Arca
118 Segno di Lorenzo Usicco

PALACES & MANSIONS
6 Palazzo Surian
7 Palazzo Savorgnan
8 Palazzo Venier
30 Palazzo Mastelli
47 Palazzo Labia
49 Palazzo Flangini
63 Palazzo Calbo-Crotta
81 Palazzo Emo-Diedo
85 Palazzo Foscari-Contarini
90 Palazzo Gradenigo
91 Palazzo Soranzo-Cappello
93 Palazzo Giovanelli
94 Casa Correr
96 Palazzo Vendramin-Calergi
    (Casinò Municipale di
    Venezia in Winter)
97 Fondaco dei Turchi
99 Palazzo Belloni Battaglia
100 Ca' Tron
104 Palazzo Gussoni-Grimani
    della Vida
106 Palazzo
    Fontana-Rezzonico
107 Palazzo Corner
    della Regina
129 Palazzo Soranzo-Pisani
132 Palazzo Bernardo
133 Palazzo Albrizzi

CHURCHES
2 Former Chiesa di
    Santa Maria delle
    Penitenti
5 Chiesa di San Giobbe
22 Chiesa di San Girolamo
23 Chiesa delle Cappuccine
24 Chiesa di Sant'Alvise
29 Chiesa della Madonna
    dell'Orto
36 Chiesa di San Marziale
39 Chiesa della Maddalena
48 Chiesa di San Geremia
67 Chiesa dei Scalzi
83 Chiesa di San
    Simeon Piccolo
92 Chiesa di San
    Simeon Grande
95 Chiesa di San Marcuola
101 Chiesa di San Stae
110 Chiesa di San Cassiano
115 Chiesa di Santa Maria
    Mater Domini
123 Chiesa di San Giacomo
    dell'Orio

OTHER
1 Macello Comunale
13 Schola Spagnola
14 Schola Levantina
16 Schola Italiana;
    Banco Verde
18 Schola Canton
19 Museo Ebraico;
    Schola Tedesca
20 Banco Rosso
21 Casa Israelitica
    di Riposo
31 Tintoretto's House
37 Paolo Sarpi Statue
41 Carabinieri
46 Planet Internet
56 Change
64 Scalzi Gondola Service
65 Water Taxis
66 Vela Ticket Point
    (ACTV)
68 APT Office;
    Associazione Veneziana
    Albergatori Hotel
    Booking Service
69 Vela Ticket Point
    (ACTV)
70 Hotel Booking Booth
71 Entrance to
    Garage Comunale
72 Expressway, Avis,
    Europcar & Hertz
    Car Rental Outlets
73 APT Office
74 ATVO & Other
    Bus Tickets;
    Agenzia Brusutti
75 Carabinieri
76 Main Bus Station
77 ACTV Tickets &
    Information
78 LineaBlù Boat Stop
79 Omniservice Internet Café
82 Ferrovia Gondola Service
84 Monte dei Paschi Bank
86 Bea Vita Lavanderia
87 Internet Café
88 Agenzia Arte e Storia
98 Deposito del Megio
102 Scuola dei Tiraoro
    e Battioro
103 Ca' Pesaro (Galleria
    d'Arte Moderna;
    Museo d'Arte Orientale)
109 Corte de Ca' Michiel
116 Palazzo Mocenigo
124 EasyContact
126 Scuola Grande di San
    Giovanni Evangelista
130 Site of Aldine Press
135 Internet Point

MAP 4

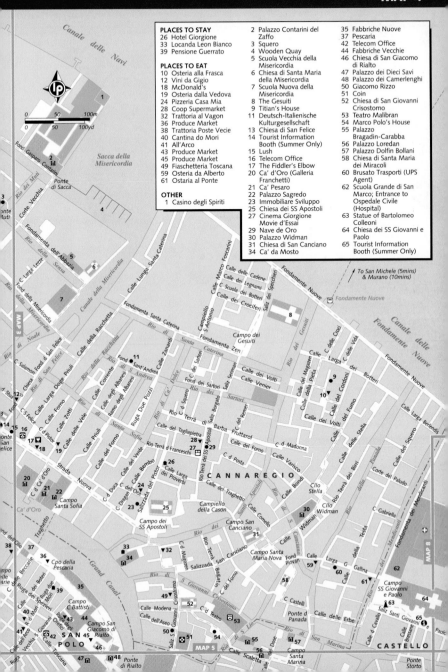

PLACES TO STAY
26 Hotel Giorgione
33 Locanda Leon Bianco
39 Pensione Guerrato

PLACES TO EAT
10 Osteria alla Frasca
12 Vini da Gigio
18 McDonald's
19 Osteria dalla Vedova
24 Pizzeria Casa Mia
28 Coop Supermarket
32 Trattoria al Vagon
36 Produce Market
38 Trattoria Poste Vecie
40 Cantina do Mori
41 All'Arco
43 Produce Market
45 Produce Market
49 Fiaschetteria Toscana
59 Osteria da Alberto
61 Ostaria al Ponte

OTHER
1 Casino degli Spiriti

2 Palazzo Contarini del Zaffo
3 Squero
4 Wooden Quay
5 Scuola Vecchia della Misericordia
6 Chiesa di Santa Maria della Misericordia
7 Scuola Nuova della Misericordia
8 The Gesuiti
9 Titian's House
11 Deutsch-Italienische Kulturgesellschaft
13 Chiesa di San Felice
14 Tourist Information Booth (Summer Only)
15 Lush
16 Telecom Office
17 The Fiddler's Elbow
20 Ca' d'Oro (Galleria Franchetti)
21 Ca' Pesaro
22 Palazzo Sagredo
23 Immobiliare Sviluppo
25 Chiesa dei SS Apostoli
27 Cinema Giorgione Movie d'Essai
29 Nave de Oro
30 Palazzo Widman
31 Chiesa di San Canciano
34 Ca' da Mosto

35 Fabbriche Nuove
37 Pescaria
42 Telecom Office
44 Fabbriche Vecchie
46 Chiesa di San Giacomo di Rialto
47 Palazzo dei Dieci Savi
48 Palazzo dei Camerlenghi
50 Giacomo Rizzo
51 Coin
52 Chiesa di San Giovanni Crisostomo
53 Teatro Malibran
54 Marco Polo's House
55 Palazzo Bragadin-Carabba
56 Palazzo Loredan
57 Palazzo Dolfin Bollani
58 Chiesa di Santa Maria dei Miracoli
60 Brusato Trasporti (UPS Agent)
62 Scuola Grande di San Marco; Entrance to Ospedale Civile (Hospital)
63 Statue of Bartolomeo Colleoni
64 Chiesa dei SS Giovanni e Paolo
65 Tourist Information Booth (Summer Only)

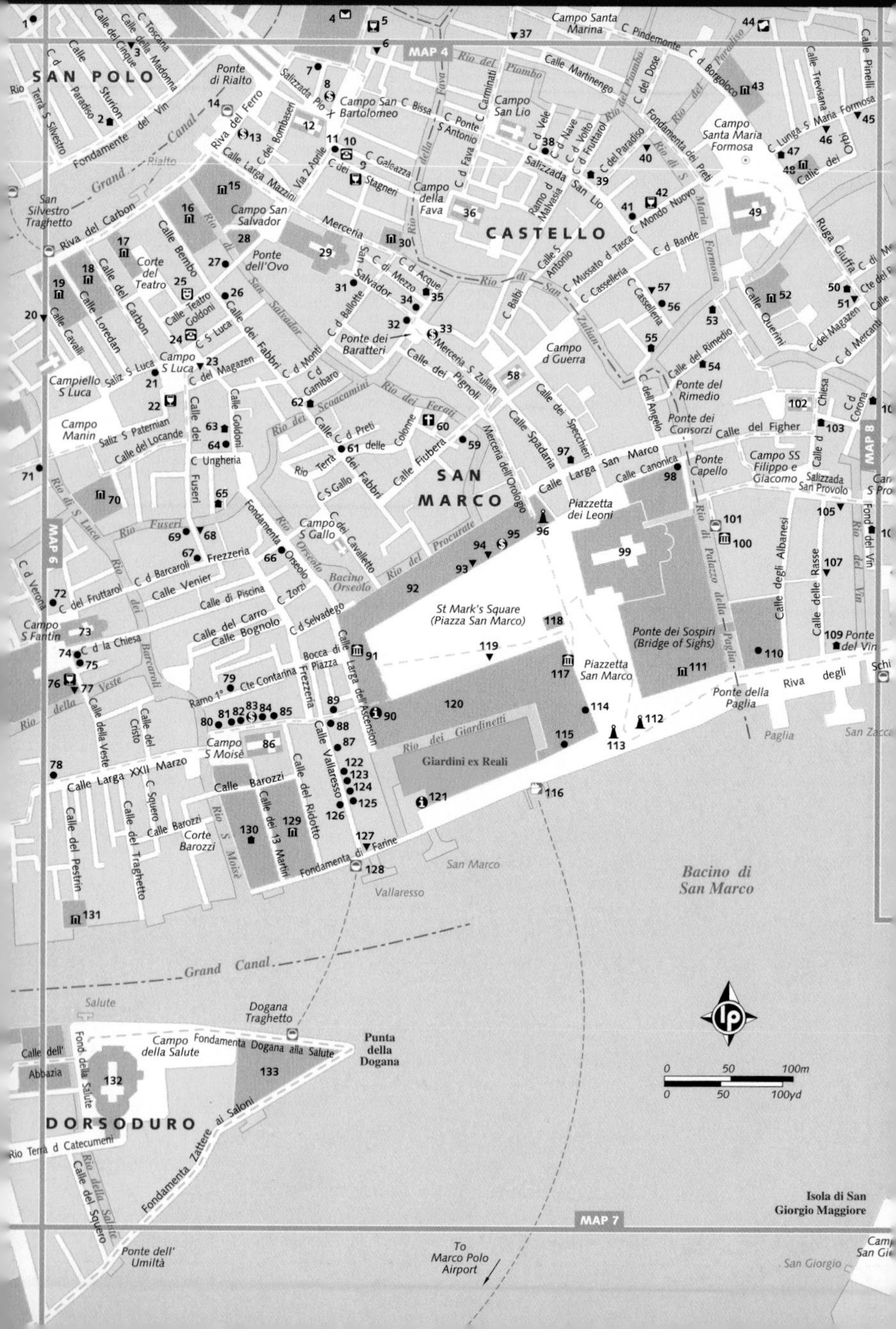

MAP 5

SAN POLO

Campo Santa Marina

C Pindemonte

C d Borgoloco

Calle Pinelli

Calle Trevisan

Campo Santa Maria Formosa

MAP 4

Rio del Piombo

Calle Martinengo

Calle del Paradiso

Fondamenta dei Preti

Ruga Giuffa

C Lunga S Maria Formosa

Ponte di Rialto

Saliterada Pio X

Campo San C Bissa
S Bartolomeo

C Ponte
S Antonio

Campo
San Lio

Ramo S Lio

Salizzada S Lio

C del Paradiso

Calle Toscana

Calle della Madonna

Calle del Cinque

Calle del Vin

Calle 2 Aprile

Calle Larga Mazzini

Riva del Ferro

Grand Canal

Rialto

Riva del Carbon

Corte del Teatro

Calle Teatro Goldoni

Campo San Salvador

Calle Galeazza

C Cuer

C Stagneri

Campo della Fava

CASTELLO

Campo Santa Maria Formosa

San Silvestro Traghetto

Corte del Carbon

Mercerie

Merceria del 2 Aprile

Merceria S Salvador

San Salvador

Ponte dei Baratteri

Merceria S Zulian

Calle dei Pignoli

Campo di Guerra

Campo San Luca

Campiello S Luca

Campo Manin

Saliz S Paternian

Calle del Locande

Rio Terra dei Preti

C S Gallo

Rio Terra dei Fabbri

SAN MARCO

Calle Larga San Marco

Ponte del Rimedio

Ponte dei Consorzi

Calle del Figher

Campo SS Filippo e Giacomo

Salizzada San Provolo

Procuratie

Bacino Orseolo

Campo San Gallo

Frezzeria

Calle Vallaresso

Piazzetta dei Leoni

Calle Canonica

Ponte Capello

St Mark's Square
(Piazza San Marco)

Piazzetta
San Marco

Ponte dei Sospiri
(Bridge of Sighs)

Ponte della Paglia

Riva degli

Campo S Fantin

Calle del Carro

Calle Bognolo

Bocca di Piazza

Calle Larga dell'Ascension

Giardini ex Reali

Calle degli Albanesi

Calle delle Rasse

Ponte del Vin

Calle Larga XXII Marzo

Campo S Moisè

Corte Barozzi

Calle dei 13 Martini

Fondamenta di Farine

San Marco

Vallaresso

Bacino di
San Marco

Grand Canal

Salute

Dogana Traghetto

Campo della Salute

Fondamenta Dogana alla Salute

Punta della Dogana

DORSODURO

Rio Terra di Catecumeni

Fondamenta Zattere ai Saloni

Ponte dell' Umiltà

To Marco Polo Airport

Isola di San
Giorgio Maggiore

San Giorgio

MAP 7

MAP 5

PLACES TO STAY
- 2 Locanda Sturion
- 35 Pensione al Gazzettino; Ristorante al Gazzettino
- 39 Hotel da Bruno
- 47 Hotel Scandinavia
- 50 Locanda al Piave
- 53 Locanda Silva
- 54 Locanda Remedio
- 55 Hotel Riva
- 62 Al Gambero; Le Bistrot de Venise
- 63 Serenissima
- 65 Locanda Casa Petrarca
- 97 Hotel ai do Mori
- 103 Hotel Bridge
- 104 Albergo Corona
- 106 Hotel Doni
- 109 Hotel Danieli
- 130 Bauer

PLACES TO EAT
- 3 Trattoria alla Madonna
- 6 Ai Rusteghi
- 20 Enoteca Il Volto
- 23 Spizzico; Burger King
- 37 Al Portego
- 40 Ristorante ai Barbacani
- 45 La Mascareta
- 46 Osteria al Mascaron
- 51 Trattoria agli Artisti
- 57 Tokyo Sushi Restaurant
- 68 Ristorante da Ivo
- 77 Vino Vino
- 93 Caffè Quadri
- 94 Lavena
- 105 Alla Rivetta
- 107 Al Vecchio Penasa
- 119 Caffè Florian
- 127 Harry's Bar

BARS
- 5 Bacaro Jazz
- 9 Devil's Forest
- 22 Black Jack Bar
- 42 Inishark
- 76 Martini Scala

SHOPPING
- 1 L'Arlecchino
- 7 Libreria Il Fontego
- 11 The Disney Store
- 26 Libreria Goldoni
- 31 Jesurum
- 41 Nave de Oro
- 56 Editore Filippi

- 59 Valese
- 61 Armani
- 64 Libreria Emiliana
- 66 La Gondola
- 67 Kenzo
- 71 Libreria al Ponte
- 74 Bugno Samueli Art Gallery
- 75 Studio Aoristico di Matteo Lo Greco
- 78 Laura Biagiotti
- 80 Versace
- 81 Prada
- 82 L'Isola
- 84 Valentino
- 85 Fendi
- 87 Agnona
- 88 Bruno Magli
- 89 Codognato
- 98 San Marco Studium
- 122 Missoni
- 123 Dolce & Gabbana
- 124 Roberto Cavalli
- 125 Gucci

PALACES & MANSIONS
- 15 Palazzo Dolfin-Manin
- 16 Palazzo Bembo
- 17 Palazzo Dandolo
- 18 Palazzo Loredan
- 19 Ca' Farsetti
- 30 Palazzo Giustinian-Faccanon
- 43 Palazzi Donà
- 48 Palazzo Vitturi
- 52 Palazzo Querini-Stampalia (Museo della Fondazione Querini-Stampalia)
- 70 Palazzo Contarini del Bovolo
- 111 Palazzo Ducale
- 129 Palazzo Giustinian
- 131 Palazzo Contarini-Fasan

CHURCHES
- 12 Chiesa di San Bartolomeo
- 29 Chiesa di San Salvador
- 36 Chiesa di Santa Maria della Fava
- 49 Chiesa di Santa Maria Formosa
- 58 Chiesa di San Zulian
- 60 Chiesa della Santa Croce degli Armeni
- 73 Chiesa di San Fantin
- 86 Chiesa di San Moisè
- 99 St Mark's Basilica
- 102 Former Chiesa di San Giovanni Novo

- 132 Chiesa di Santa Maria della Salute

OTHER
- 4 Main Post Office; Fondaco dei Tedeschi
- 8 Change
- 10 Telephones
- 13 Thomas Cook
- 14 Water Taxi Stand; Rialto Gondola Service
- 21 Cassa di Risparmio di Venezia (Tickets for La Fenice)
- 24 Telecom Office
- 25 Teatro Goldoni
- 27 Gran Canal Viaggi
- 28 Scuola Grande di San Teodoro
- 32 Agenzia Kele & Teo
- 33 Change
- 34 Alliance Française
- 38 Parole e Musica
- 44 French Consulate
- 69 ACTV Office; Vela Ticket Outlet
- 72 Ateneo Veneto
- 79 Assessorato alla Gioventù
- 83 American Express; City Sightseeing by Gondola & on Foot
- 90 Main APT Office
- 91 Museo Correr (Ala Napoleonica)
- 92 Procuratie Vecchie
- 95 Thomas Cook
- 96 Torre dell'Orologio
- 100 Museo Diocesano d'Arte Sacra
- 101 Gondola Service
- 108 Gondola Service
- 110 Prigioni Nuove (New Prisons)
- 112 Column with Lion of St Mark
- 113 Column with Statue of St Theodore
- 114 Libreria Nazionale Marciana
- 115 La Zecca (The Mint)
- 116 Alilaguna Hydrofoil to Airport
- 117 Museo Archeologico
- 118 Campanile
- 120 Procuratie Nuove
- 121 Venice Pavilion Infopoint Tourist Office (Vela Tickets)
- 126 Teatro al Ridotto
- 128 Gondola Service
- 133 Dogana da Mar

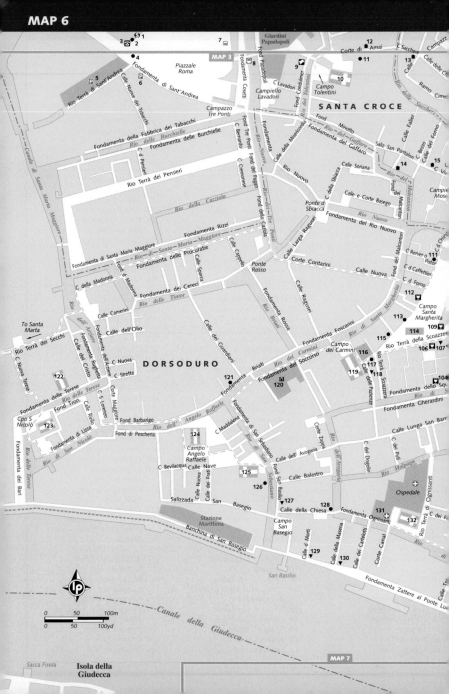

MAP 6

Giardini
Papadopoli

MAP 3

Corte di
Amai

E Sacchere

Campazz

E Faller

Calle delle Ch

Ramo Cime

Piazzale
Roma

Fondamenta di Sant'Andrea

Calle Nuove dei Tabacchi

Rio Terrà di Sant'Andrea

Fondamenta Cossetti

Fondamenta Papadopoli

Fond Contumer

C Lavadori

Campiello
Lavadori

Campazzo
Tre Ponti

Campo
Tolentini

SANTA CROCE

Ramo
delle
Sacchere

Calle del Forno

C Bezzo

Saliz San Pantalon

Fondamenta della Fabbrica dei Tabacchi

Rio delle Burchielle

Fondamenta delle Burchielle

C d Pensieri

C Bernardo

C Cremonese

Fond della Misericordia

Rio Nuovo

Fond Tre Ponti

Fond del Pagan

Fondamenta del Gaffaro

Fond Minotto

Rio del Gaffaro

C della Sbiacca

Calle Soriana

Rio del Malcanton

Calle Faller

C Vir

Fondamenta di Santa Maria Maggiore

Rio Terrà dei Pensieri

Rio della Cazziola

Fondamenta Rizzi

Rio di Santa Maria Maggiore

Fond di Santa Maria Maggiore

Fondamenta delle Procuratie

C della Madonna

Fond di Madonna

Fondamenta dei Cereci

Rio delle Tintor

Calle Cappella

Calle Sporca

Ponte
Rosso

Calle delle Tre Ponti

Rio di Santa Margherita

Ponte di
Sbiacca

Fondamenta del Rio Nuovo

Rio Nuovo

Campiello
Mose

Calle e Corte Basego

Fondamenta del Rio Nuovo

Rio del
Malcanton

Calle e Corte Basego

Calle Larga Ragusei

Corte Contarini

Calle Nuova

C Renier

C d Cheso

Pistor

C d Caffettier

C d Forno

Campo
Santa
Margherita

Fondamenta Rossa

Fondamenta Foscarini

Rio di Santa Margherita

Rio Terrà della Scoazzere

To Santa
Marta

Rio Terrà dei Secchi

Fondamenta dell'Arzere

Calle del Cristo

Calle Camerini

Calle dell'Olio

Calle dei Guardiani

Rio Briati

DORSODURO

C Nuova

C Stretta

Fondamenta Rughetta

Campo
dei Carmini

Fondamenta del Soccorso

Rio dei Carmini

Calle delle Pazienze

Fondamenta dello Squ

Rio di

Fondamenta Gherardini

C Nuova Terese

Fondamenta delle Terese

Rio delle Terese

Fond Tron

Calle Riello

Corte Maggiore

C S Lorenzo

Fond Barbarigo

Fondamenta di Lizza

Fond di Pescheria

Rio dell'Angelo Raffaele

Rio di San Sebastiano

Calle della Chiesa

Calle Lunga San Barr

C dei Puti

Rio Molpaga

Corte Zappa

C dei Dogolin

Cpo S
Nicolò

Fondamenta di San Nicolò

Rio di San Nicolò

Calle dell'Avogaria

Campo
Angelo
Raffaele

C Bevilacqua

Calle Nave

Calle Nuova

Calle dei Frati

C Maddalena

Calle San Basilio

Calle Balastro

Salizzada
San

Basegio

Stazione
Marittima

Campo
San
Basegio

Calle della Chiesa

Fondamenta Ognissanti

Ospedale

Rio Terrà di Ognissanti

C dei F

Fondamenta della Tana al Ponte Lu

Banchina di San Basegio

Calle d Morti

Calle della Masena

Calle dei Cartelotti

Corte Canal

San Basilio

Fondamenta Zattere al Ponte Lu

Calle Te

0   50   100m
0   50   100yd

Canale   della   Giudecca

Sacca Fisola

Isola della
Giudecca

MAP 7

MAP 6

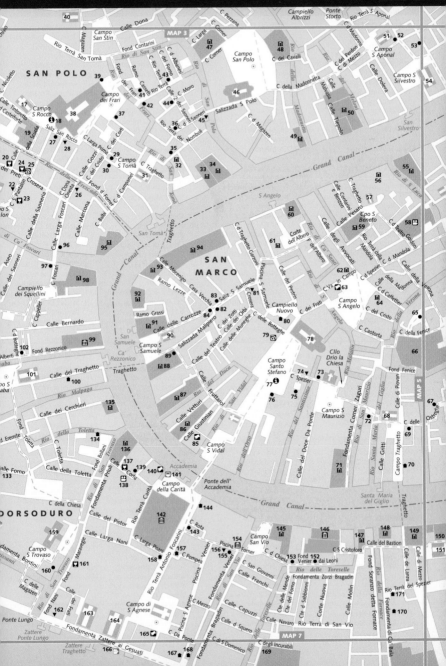

MAP 6

PLACES TO STAY
12 Hotel ai Tolentini
13 Domus Civica
14 Hotel dalla Mora
15 Albergo Casa Peron
70 Gritti Palace
80 Locanda Fiorita
100 Locanda San Barnaba
110 Albergo Antico Capon
133 Antica Locanda Montin
134 Albergo Accademia Villa Maravege
144 Hotel Galleria
157 Albergo agli Alboretti
158 Ca' Pisani Hotel
167 La Calcina
168 Pensione Seguso
170 Hotel alla Salute da Cici
171 Hotel Messner

PLACES TO EAT
22 Arca
26 Trattoria Dona Onesta
28 Gelateria Millefoglie da Tarcisio
45 Osteria alla Patatina
74 Pasticceria Marchini
81 Osteria al Bacareto
105 L'Incontro
107 Gelateria il Doge
118 Osteria ai Carmini
127 Osteria da Toni
129 Billa Supermarket
130 Riviera
156 Trattoria ai Cugnai
162 Gelateria Nico

BARS
20 Caffè Blue
23 Capo Horn
24 Café Noir
104 Round Midnight
106 Green Pub
109 Margaret Duchamp
112 Caffè
137 Piccolo Mondo
161 Cantina di Vini già Schiavi

SHOPPING
27 Graffiti
30 Il Baule Blu; Teddy Hospital
35 Tragicomica
36 Cenerentola
37 Legatoria Polliero
41 Artemisia
42 Atelier Pietro Longhi
43 A Mano
44 Gilberto Penzo
52 BAC Art Studio
53 Manuela Calzature
67 Libreria Cassini
69 Galleria Traghetto
72 Legatoria Piazzesi
73 Il Papiro
75 Nalesso
76 Fiorella Gallery
82 Livio de Marchi
84 Galleria Marina Barovier
102 Ca' Macana
103 Legno e Dintorni
111 Nave de Oro
113 Cartoleria Accademia
115 Loris Marazzi
117 Wine Shop
152 Peggy Guggenheim Museum Shop
153 Il Pavone
155 BAC Art Studio

PALACES & MANSIONS
32 Casa di Goldoni (Palazzo Centani)
33 Palazzo Tiepolo
34 Palazzo Pisani-Moretta
47 Palazzo Corner (on Campo San Polo)
48 Palazzi Soranzo
49 Palazzo Bernardo
50 Palazzo Papadopoli
55 Palazzo Grimani
56 Palazzo Tron
59 Palazzo Fortuny
60 Palazzo Corner-Spinelli
61 Casa Nardi
62 Palazzo Gritti
64 Palazzo Duodo
71 Palazzo Corner (Ca' Grande)
86 Palazzo Giustinian-Lolin
87 Ca' del Duca
88 Palazzo Malipiero
91 Palazzo Grassi
92 Palazzo Moro-Lin
93 Palazzo Contarini dalle Figure
94 Palazzi Mocenigo
95 Palazzo Balbi
98 Ca' Foscari (University)
120 Palazzo Zenobio
135 Palazzo Loredan dell'Ambasciatore
136 Palazzo Contarini degli Scrigni
145 Palazzo Barbarigo
147 Palazzo Dario
148 Palazzo Salviati
149 Palazzo Genovese

CHURCHES
10 Chiesa di San Nicolò da Tolentino
17 Chiesa di San Rocco
21 Chiesa di San Pantalon
31 Chiesa di San Tomà
38 Chiesa di Santa Maria Gloriosa dei Frari
40 Chiesa di San Giovanni Evangelista
46 Chiesa di San Polo
51 Former Chiesa di Sant'Aponal
54 Chiesa di San Silvestro
57 Chiesa di San Beneto
68 Chiesa di Santa Maria del Giglio (Chiesa di Santa Maria Zobenigo)
78 Chiesa di Santo Stefano
90 Former Chiesa di San Samuele
101 Chiesa di San Barnaba
119 Chiesa dei Carmini
122 Former Chiesa di Santa Teresa & Convent
123 Chiesa di San Nicolò dei Mendicoli
124 Angelo Raffaele (Chiesa di San Basilio)
125 Chiesa di San Sebastiano
132 Former Chiesa di Ognissanti
151 Former Chiesa di San Gregorio
159 Chiesa di San Trovaso
163 Chiesa di Santa Maria della Visitazione
164 Chiesa dei Gesuati (Chiesa di Santa Maria del Rosario)

OTHER
1 Bureau de Change
2 Left-Luggage Office (Deposito Bagagli)
3 Telecom Booth
4 Hotel Booking Office
5 Parking San Marco
6 Autopark Doge
7 ACTV Bus No 53 (To Padua via Malcontenta)
8 Gondola Service
9 Austrian Consulate
11 Istituto Universitario di Architettura di Venezia (IUAV)
16 Associazione Italiana Alberghi per la Gioventù (AIG)
18 Tourist Information Booth (Summer Only)
19 Scuola Grande di San Rocco
25 The Netgate
29 Scuola dei Calegh_ri
39 Archivio di Stato
58 Cinema Rossini
63 German Consulate
65 Campiello della Fenice
66 Teatro La Fenice
77 Tourist Information Booth (Summer Only)
79 Net House
83 House of Paolo Veronese
85 Netherlands Consulate
89 Birthplace of Giacomo Casanova
96 Università Ca' Foscari Notice Boards
97 CTS Travel Agency
99 Ca' Rezzonico (Museo del Settecento Veneziano)
108 Istituto Venezia
114 Scuola Varoteri
116 Scuola Grande dei Carmini
121 Dolcetti Renata "Alla Cerva d'Oro" Pharmacy
126 Università Ca' Foscari Notice Boards
128 Squero
131 Consultorio Familiare
138 Cinema Accademia d'Essai
139 Venezia Congressi
140 UK Consulate
141 Accademia Gondola Service
142 Gallerie dell'Accademia
143 Image Center Camera Shop
146 Peggy Guggenheim Collection (Palazzo Venier dei Leoni)
150 Abbazia di San Gregorio
154 Galleria di Palazzo Cini
160 Squero di San Trovaso
165 Swiss Consulate
166 Alilaguna Hydrofoil to Airport; LineaFusinaZattere Vaporetto to Fusina
169 Former Ospedale degli Incurabili

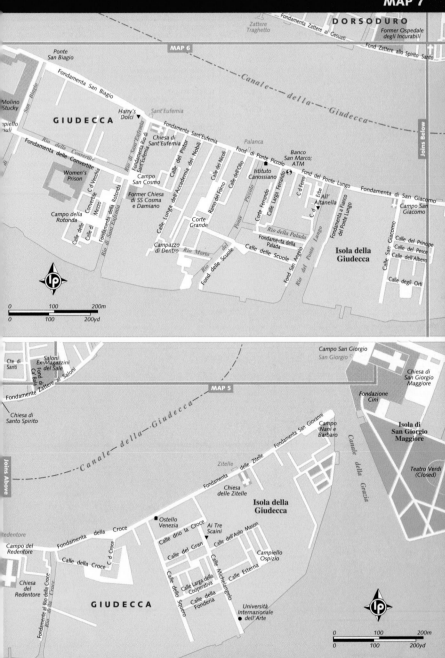

MAP 7

MAP 7

Zattere Traghetto

Fondamenta Zattere al Gesuati

DORSODURO

Former Ospedale degli Incurabili

Fond Zattere allo Spirito Santo

Ponte San Biagio

MAP 6

Canale---della---Giudecca

Fondamenta San Biagio

Molino Stucky

Sant'Eufemia

Harry's Dolci

GIUDECCA

Fondamenta Sant'Eufemia

Palanca

Joins Below

mpiello riuli

Fondamenta delle Convertite

Rio delle Convertite

Chiesa di Sant'Eufemia

Fondamenta Rio di Sant'Eufemia

Rio di Sant'Eufemia

Calle del Pistor

Calle Lunga dell'Accademia dei Nobili

Calle dei Nicoli

Fond di Ponte Piccolo

Banco San Marco; ATM

Fond del Ponte Lungo

Women's Prison

C d Vecchia

Campo San Cosmo

Calle dell'Olio

Istituto Canossiano

Calle Larga Ferrando

C d Ferro

Fondamenta di San Giacomo

Former Chiesa di SS Cosma e Damiano

Convertite

Fondamenta della Rotonda

Ramo del Forno

Corte Ferrando

Erbe

All' Altanella

Campo San Giacomo

Campo della Rotonda

Calle delle

C di

Rio della Rotonda

Corte Grande

Ponte Piccolo

Rio della Palada

Fondamenta a fianco del Ponte Lungo

Calle San Giacomo

Calle del Principe

Calle del Pesce

Calle dell'Albero

Campazzo di Dentro

Rio Marto

Fondamenta della Palada

Calle delle Scuole

Rio del Ponte Lungo

Calle San Angelo

Isola della Giudecca

Calle degli Orti

Fond delle Scuole

0   100   200m
0   100   200yd

Cte di Santi

Saloni Ex-Magazzini del Sale

Fond di Cà Bala

Fondamente Zattere ai Saloni

Campo San Giorgio

San Giorgio

Chiesa di San Giorgio Maggiore

MAP 5

Canale---della---Giudecca

Chiesa di Santo Spirito

Fondazione Cini

Isola di San Giorgio Maggiore

Fondamenta San Giovanni

Campo Nani e Barbaro

Canale della Grazia

Joins Above

Zitelle

Calle delle Zitelle

Fondamenta

Chiesa delle Zitelle

Isola della Giudecca

Teatro Verdi (Closed)

Ostello Venezia

Ai Tre Scaini

Calle drio la Croce

Fondamenta della Croce

Redentore

Campo del Redentore

Calle della Croce

C d Croce

Calle del Gran

Calle Michelangelo

Calle dell'Asilo Mason

Campiello Ospizio

Chiesa del Redentore

Calle dello

Calle Larga della Cooperativa

Calle Esterna

Calle della Fonderia

Fondamenta al Rio della Croce

Rio della Croce

GIUDECCA

Università Internazionale dell'Arte

0   100   200m
0   100   200yd

MAP 8

PLACES TO STAY
5 Foresteria Valdese
21 La Residenza
22 Casa Linger
29 Albergo Paganelli
30 Londra Palace
33 Albergo al Nuovo Teson
37 Pensione Bucintoro

PLACES TO EAT
18 Trattoria Corte Sconta
24 Trattoria da Remigio
32 Al Covo

OTHER
1 Ospedale Civile (Hospital)
2 Ospedaletto
3 Libraire Française
4 Nave de Oro
6 Società Dante Alighieri
7 Chiesa di San Francesco della Vigna
8 Chiesa di San Lorenzo
9 Questura (Main Police Station)
10 Scuola di San Giorgio degli Schiavoni
11 Casa Magno
12 Bucintoro Storage
13 Padiglione delle Navi
14 Sea Entrance to Arsenale
15 Land Entrance to Arsenale
16 Chiesa di San Martino
17 Palazzo Erizzo
19 Chiesa di San Giovanni in Bragora
20 Laboratorio del Gerva
23 Chiesa di San Giorgio dei Greci
25 Museo delle Icone
26 ENDAR (Veneto Congressi)
27 Ca' del Sole
28 Chiesa di San Zaccaria
31 La Pietà
34 Tourist Information Booth (Summer Only)
35 Museo Storico Navale
36 Palazzetto dello Sport

CASTELLO

Fondamente Nuove
Canale delle Fondamenta Nuove
Ospedale Civile
Canale delle
Celestia
Calle degli Orti
Fond Cese Nuove
Calle Sagredo
Calle dell'Oratorio
Moschette
Calle delle Cappucine
Calle Cavalli
Fondamenta di Santa Giustina
Calle del Caffettier
Calle del Tideum
Campo San Francesco della Vigna
Calle San Francesco
Barbaria delle Tole
Calle della Tetta
Rio di San Giovanni Laterno
Ramo Cappello
Calle Zen
Campo S Giustina
Campo della Confraternità
Calle del
Cimitero
Campo della Celestia
Rio di San Francesco
C d Fontego
Saliz Santa Giustina
C d Morion
Campo S Ternità
Rio della Celestia
Calle Larga San Lorenzo
Borgoloco San Lorenzo
Fondamenta di San Lorenzo
Campo San Lorenzo
Calle Zorzi
Calle Cappellera
C d Vida
Calle dell'Olio
Calle Dona
C Celsi
Fond di San Severo
Calle San Lorenzo
Corte Nuova
Calle Erizzo
Saliz di Gatte
Campo Ternità
Calle Drazzi
C d S Ternità
Calle Magno
C dell'Angelo
CASTELLO
Campo delle Gatte
Calle dei Furlani
Campo Do Pozzi
Calle del Forno
Calle del Lion
Calle dei Preti
C d Madonna
C d Magazen
Saliz dei Greci
Campo d'Gorne
Campo della Tana
Salizzada
Calle dell'Arco
S Antonin
Salizzada del Pignater
Calle di Piscina S Martin
C Venier
Campo Bandiera e Moro
Campiello della Pescaria
Salizzada del Pistrin
Calle del Pestrin
Calle Gritti
Calle Erizzo
Calle del Dose
Calle dietro la Pietà
Calle della Pietà
Calle Malvasia Vecchia
C Fiscaria
Fond di Fronte
Campo Arsenale
Fondamenta della Madonna
Rio dei Greci
Campo S Provolo
Corte Rotta
Fondamenta dell'Osmarin
Campo San Zaccaria
Corte Nuova
Calle del Vin
Riva degli Schiavoni
Ponte Selpolcro
Ponte della Pietà
Riva degli Schiavoni
San Zaccaria
Mon Vittorio Emanuele
Pietà
Calle del Forno
C Moresina
Campo Arsenale
Fond di Fronte
Fond Pegola
Calle del Dose
Calle del Forno
Calle della Vida
Rio Ca' di Dio
Riva Ca' di Dio
Fond dall'Arsenale
Campo della Tana
Canale di San Marco
Arsenale
Campo S Biagio
Riva S Biagio
C Fiscola la Chiesa di S Biagio

0   50   100m
0   50   100yd

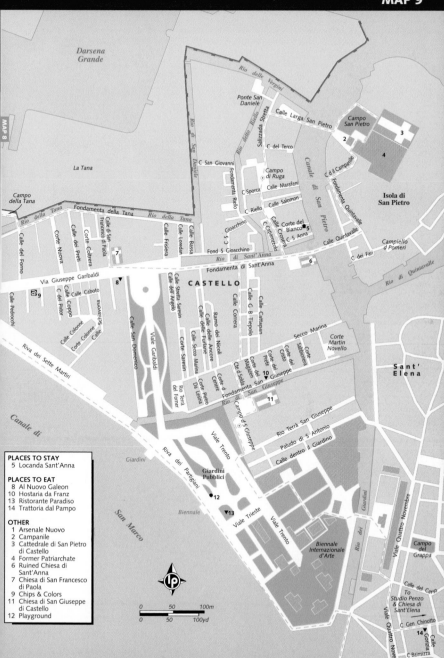

MAP 9

Darsena
Grande

MAP 8

Rio delle Vergini

Ponte San
Daniele

Calle Larga San Pietro

Campo
San Pietro

Stretta
Spezzieri

C del Terco

Canale di San Pietro

Isola di
San Pietro

C San Giovanni

Campo
di Ruga

C d il Campanile

Fondamenta Quintavalle

Fondamenta Rielo

C Sporca

Calle Marafani

La Tana

Calle Salomon

Campo
della Tana

Rio della Tana

Fondamenta della Tana

Rio della Tana

C Riello

Gioacchino

Calle Croseta

Corte del
Bianco

Calle S S Anna

C Caparozzolo

Campiello
d Pomeri

Rio di Quintavalle

Calle del Forno

Corte Nuova

Calle dei Preti

Corte Coltrera

Calle di San Francesco di Paola

Calle Loredan

Calle Bassa

Calle Frisiera

Fond S Gioacchino

Rio di Sant'Anna

Fondamenta di Sant'Anna

C dei Fani

Calle Quintavalle

Via Giuseppe Garibaldi

CASTELLO

Calle Pedrochi

Calle del Pistor

C del Coppo

Calle Caboto

Calle Colonne

Corte Colonne

Calle Schiavina

Corte Saresin

Calle San Domenico

Viale Garibaldi

Rio Terra del Forner

Calle Stretta Saresin

Calle dell'Angelo

Corte Secco Marina

Ramo dei Nicoli

Calle delle Furlane

Calle delle Ancore

Calle Correra

Calle G B Tiepolo

Calle Cattapan

Secco Marina

Corte
Martin
Novello

Cte d'Soldà

Fondamenta San Giuseppe

Corte dei Magazen

Corte del Cristo

Corte del Prete

Corte dei Salizzona

Corte
del

Riva dei Sette Martiri

Calle d Pietro Dà Lezna

Rio di San Giuseppe

Sant'
Elena

Rio Terrà San Giuseppe

Canale di

San Marco

Riva dei Partigiani

Rio Terà del Campo d'S Giuseppe

Paludo di S Antonio

Calle dentro il Giardino

Viale Trento

Viale Trieste

Viale Trento

Gidani

Giardini

Giardini
Pubblici

Biennale

Biennale
Internazionale
d'Arte

Parco delle
Rimembranze

Viale Quattro Novembre

Campo
del
Grappa

Rio Giardini

Calle del Cao

To
Studio Penzo
& Chiesa di
Sant'Elena

C Gen Chinotto

Calle Corazza

C Bainsizza

0   50   100m
0   50   100yd

LP

MAP 10 – LIDO DI VENEZIA

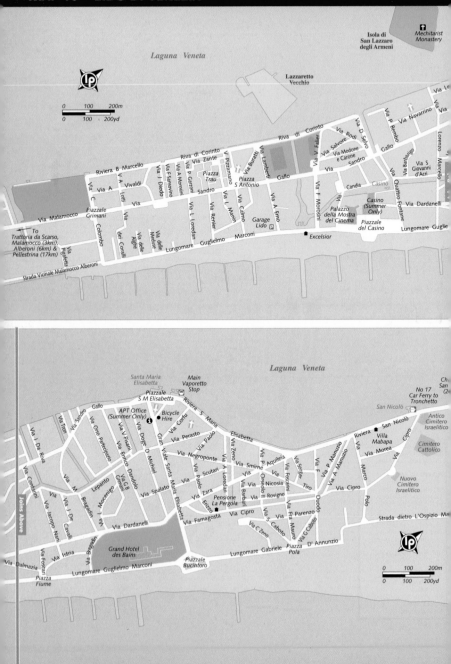

MAP 11 – MESTRE

PLACES TO STAY
6 Hotel Vivit
16 Hotel Monte Piana
17 Albergo Roberta
20 Hotel Giovannina
22 Tritone

PLACES TO EAT
8 Brek
13 Da Luca
15 Osteria La Pergola
18 Da Bepi Venesian

OTHER
1 Ospedale Umberto I
   (Hospital)
2 Metrò
3 Castello
4 Clipper Viaggi
   Travel Agency
5 Le Barche Shopping
   Complex
7 Chiesa di San Lorenzo
9 Post Office
10 ACTV Office
11 CTS Travel Agency
12 APT Office
14 Laundry
19 Cinema Dante d'Essai
21 Serenissima Parking
23 ATVO Bus Tickets;
   Marco Polo Airport Bus
24 ACTV Buses to Venice
   (No 2; Night Bus No N1)

MAP LEGEND

BOUNDARIES

—··—··—··—	International
—·—·—·	Provincial, State
—··—··—·	Regional, Suburb

HYDROGRAPHY

	Coastline
	River, Creek
	Lake
	Canal

ROUTES & TRANSPORT

	Freeway
	Highway
	Major Road
	Minor Road
	Unsealed Road
	City Freeway
	City Highway
	City Road
	City Street, Lane

	Pedestrian Mall
—)═══	Tunnel
—○—	Train Route & Station
—☐—	Ferry Route & Terminal
	San Marco Walk
	Dorsoduro Walk
	S Polo & S Croce Walk
	Cannaregio Walk
	Castello Walk

AREA FEATURES

	Building
	Urban Area
❀	Park, Gardens
	Cemetery
	Market
	Desert

MAP SYMBOLS

◉	**VENICE**	Large City	✣	Archaeological Site	
◉	**Treviso**	City	✪	Bank	
●	**Adria**	Town	⌐	Beach	
●	Pellestrina	Village	☐ ☐	Bus Stop, Station	
			⌂	Castle or Fort	
●		Point of Interest	⌂	Cave	
			✝	Church or Cathedral	
■		Place to Stay	⊞	Cinema	
⌂		Camp Site	▢	Embassy	
⌑		Caravan Park	⚱	Fountain	
▼		Place to Eat	✛	Hospital	
▣		Pub or Bar	◙	Internet Cafe	
			☼	Lighthouse	
✈		Airport	▲	Monument	
～		Ancient or City Wall	▲	Mountain or Hill	

🏛	Museum
🌲	National Park
P	Parking
✚	Questura (Police Sta)
✉	Post Office
✿	Shopping Centre
🏠	Stately Home
🏊	Swimming Pool
☎	Telephone
🎭	Theatre
⊙	Toilet
■	Tomb
❶	Tourist Information
⊙	Well
🦓	Zoo

Note: not all symbols displayed above appear in this book

LONELY PLANET OFFICES

Australia
Locked Bag 1, Footscray, Victoria 3011
☎ 03 8379 8000 fax 03 8379 8111
email: talk2us@lonelyplanet.com.au

USA
150 Linden St, Oakland, CA 94607
☎ 510 893 8555 TOLL FREE: 800 275 8555
fax 510 893 8572
email: info@lonelyplanet.com

UK
10a Spring Place, London NW5 3BH
☎ 020 7428 4800 fax 020 7428 4828
email: go@lonelyplanet.co.uk

France
1 rue du Dahomey, 75011 Paris
☎ 01 55 25 33 00 fax 01 55 25 33 01
email: bip@lonelyplanet.fr
www.lonelyplanet.fr

World Wide Web: www.lonelyplanet.com *or* AOL keyword: lp
Lonely Planet Images: lpi@lonelyplanet.com.au